RAMBLINGS OF A
MAD OUTLAW

RAMBLINGS OF A MAD OUTLAW

Batch G. Brennan

To order additional copies of this book, contact:
Xlibris
1-888-795-4274
www.Xlibris.com
Orders@Xlibris.com
704313

Important Preamble

The following work is a personal reflection about life and ideas. It is not a personal memoir; it is not autobiographical, nor is it a story. In fact, to have it driven by reflective ideas and thoughts, it is not even organised in a chapter format or structured chronologically. Instead, as the title would suggest, it is a 'stream of consciousness' that goes in many different directions and involves many different disciplines and takes many different stylistic forms.

This book is concerned with the thoughts, ideas, and personal insights of creative people who have shaped my personal experience and perceptions and who, throughout history, have known what it means to see life differently and to live outside social norms. Because this whole work is somewhat esoteric, the ideas, concepts, and uses of language may be difficult for some readers, especially in the initial stages of reading.

What you may experience is some confusion with various streams of discussion running simultaneously. You may get one idea but not the next; you may wonder what point is being made or where the writing is going. You may want to take the time to stop and reflect because there is too much stuff or you have too many questions. You may be discouraged.

If you are curious, enjoy the challenges of adventures into the unknown or even wonder what this is all about. It is important to be patient and to continue to read, maybe even make a note or two, because as you read, meanings will become clearer, and you will pick up the flow. Remember, this work is based on developing different perspectives. You may be going into the unknown, and part of the challenge is trying to figure out what is happening

Consider these examples of what you will find.

Be ready for the first few pages. They actually start with a distinction that may initially seem unimportant and maybe even confusing to some. I start with the following:

Is our physical existence a necessary condition for us to think? I am; therefore, I think. Or could we contend that our thinking defines how we define self (the human)? I think; therefore, I am. Or are both true?

Can you consider that it is possible to have a perception that two opposing political parties, with opposing platforms, are exactly the same?

If you are ready, read on and see where it takes you.

Contents

Part II: Becoming the Mad Outlaw

Part III: Approaching Oneness

Part IV: Reflections on Composing and Conducting

PART I: INITIAL RAMBLINGS

Initial Thoughts on the Experience of Being Different

This is the beginning. This is the end. It is the middle. Every moment is the same but different. In fact, there really is no beginning, no end, and no middle.

There is cogito. There is sum.[1] There is a relationship between the two, but which way it goes i am uncertain. However, in the realm of normal understanding and language, i would put 'sum' first since i would have to exist before i could think and, of course, before i could define *self*.

But enough of such thoughts.

The reason for this writing is to share a personal vision of understanding that works for me at this point and may have meaning for others who find themselves alone, different, not fitting, and not understood in a vast world of billions of people, great networks of communication, political movements, countries, environmentalists, armies, terrorists, churches, and religions.

Ezra Pound addresses those helpless few, those lovers of beauty as being thwarted, mistrusted.

The context of my vision and sense of beauty is based on a mixture of thoughts, emotions, visions, and structures from a myriad of sources that i have internalised and connected in different ways to find a place and meaning (which could be no meaning) in the whole scheme of things.

It is interesting that being different is usually misperceived. Often, the interpretation by regular folk of another who is seen as different is not

---

[1]   See glossary.

3

based on an understanding of what that person is like but on how that somewhat weird person is different. For instance, if my view is different from another's and doesn't fit into typical guidelines (may not even be formulated), it is typically considered as opposite to theirs. It is as if they needed to define my difference in concrete terms. Let's say that a person is highly supportive of right-wing or left-wing politics, and i offer some thoughts that question their beliefs. Even though my thoughts or questions may have no particular political bias, i have found that the person i am talking to may conclude that i must be of the other wing.

From my experience, it is clear that the clinical practitioner of modern medicine does not follow or even understand the tenets of good research science. They follow what they have learned or experienced. On numerous occasions, talking to a medical practitioner, who sees him/herself as understanding science (since they have had lots of training), about well-done new research may be difficult. A challenge to some of their assumptions can often trigger a defensive logic. First, they believe that they know and understand scientific facts and thinking. Second, they know that if something doesn't make sense to them or challenges their own standard of practice, it must not be based on good science. The result of their belief is that they cannot discriminate between bad science and well-designed research science. The common factor here is that they are both outside what they know and accept. Since it is important to me to think in a highly disciplined manner and even question some of their assumptions, what i might discuss with them may not be processed or seen as nonscientific.

Since i think differently, then i obviously have no ability to understand 'real life' or how to run things. It may seem strange, but i often get approached as if i am disabled or just don't understand.

However, by the same people and others, i get a high degree of sincere respect, but with this positive view comes an alienating distance. This respect can lead to a sense of awe, which in turn establishes a distance between me and others. This distance, though seen most often as positive, can also be negatively understood and seen as superiority, arrogance, and priggishness.

If i wanted to find a socially defined hook to hang my identity that would help me address the above, i would pick the term 'outlaw' as used by Tom Robbins. He defined 'the outlaw' as the person who is aware that there are whalers and whale protesters, loggers and logging protesters, good guys and bad guys, but the outlaw is one who lives outside these conditions. The outlaw is not the rebel; this person is outside the rebel and nonrebel. For me, his use of 'outlaw' has a number of appropriate connotations. First, it has a socially negative connotation and, therefore, does not give the connotation of 'above' or 'better than'. Second, it has the literal sense of being outside, not in the realm of social/human rules of good and bad or nonreflective thinking. Third, as mentioned, it does not suggest that the outlaw is against the law (rebel) but just outside the social yin/yang.

The event that triggered my need for a reevaluation of self

The recent requirement for me to clearly formulate my sense of self and relationship to others came from a good friend who, in her own exploratory questioning, triggered a vast and neglected sense of grounding in me. Over the last number of years, i had continuously read a lot of science, developed new ways of understanding given its limits, and tested these formulations by establishing my own (psychiatric) treatment program; but i had overlooked my need for personal connections, as well as connections with the impassioned creators and thinkers in all fields that had been the foundation of my own sense of being.

The triggering event clearly established the need to rebuild a schema that would help in answering some essential, fundamental questions that had been addressed in my past and still existed in the present but had not been continuously nurtured. It became highly evident to me that the respect of many, success in financial terms, and making a difference for others did nothing to decrease that separateness between me and others. I had no easy way to explain that what i had achieved and how i had helped others did not meet my inner needs. It also became evident that an anchoring or grounding in something outside the routine of day-to-day life was needed. For many years, this grounding had been an integral part of my daily life, but the fulfilment of using unique, creative thinking and the establishment of a miniculture that was consistent with this thinking had not offered the input necessary for sustaining myself. Even though scientific and intellectual input had been highly significant in developing aspects of my understanding and had been very rewarding, i realised that i had lost a certain joie de vivre. I had become too cognitive, too intellectual. I felt that my sense of self and life—which required an integration of being human, being spiritual and philosophical at the same time, being openly curious, being able to take the time to experience and not just observe, being able to take moments to absorb beauty—had been lost. In a moment of epiphany, i became aware that i needed to reestablish my life in a more connected manner (whatever *connected* means).

I also became vividly aware of my own frail human nature and its needs and my diminished desire and ability to achieve some state of compassionate distance from all sentient beings. For many years, i had assumed that the achievement of this state was the direction of my life experience.

My present sense is one of protest. I don't want that enlightened, compassionate state—at least not yet.

The profoundness of this quandary became immediately significant, and i knew that i would not be able to rest until i found a solution, which for me was finding a framework that would help unite conflicting stressors for someone who needed grounding in a nonsocial/human world but also needed human attachments with others of the same beyond the human sort.

My resolution came in a symbolic visual form at 4:30 a.m. I didn't need to read anything new or ask for guidance from others; i did, however, draw on some very personal support. This support came from my experience, more specifically from Carl Jung, William Butler Yeats, Ezra Pound, Thomas Stearns Eliot, and many years of commitment to the Buddhist thought. The intuitive relationship i had developed with the creative expressions of others was there when i needed them.

Please be patient with me and my pursuit as i digress for a moment to discuss style. Once we have addressed the language and structure of writing, we will move on to many pages of eclectic ramblings.

Some Important Notes on Style

It is important to remember or at least refer to these notes. You may find that these stylistic aspects may be forgotten. Please refer to them in the future.

Stylistically, i will use the pronoun 'you' to address 'you,' the reader, to be consistent with my explanation of me to you. It is important for you to be aware that this is not an attempt to imply that you are being included in my generalisations about others. If you are another who doesn't fit, then it is important to have you shift from you to me. When i am making a reference to myself, i will—from here until the end of the second part of these ramblings—use a lowercase *i*, except when grammatical rules require an uppercase one, such as at the beginning of a sentence. I will also use a lowercase letter at the beginning of many proper nouns in this first section. The purpose of the change in case—from *i* to *I*—will, i hope, make sense as you read through this work.

There is another stylistic shift i will make in this work that exemplifies bad grammar. At first, i thought this error has been committed by a few writers in letters and emails; but recently, i have reviewed some application forms for a government project in washington state (in the u.s.a.), and they have consistently made the same error. Before i mention what i will do stylistically, let me suggest that this error may have resulted from social/human influence. For many years, the singular pronoun 'he' can be used to refer to singular nouns, like *individual* and *person*. A number of years ago, academic stylistic manuals required that 'he/she' or 'she/he' (i guess) be used. So the stylistic dilemma became as follows:

The person (singular) enjoyed his (singular) dinner.

The person (singular) enjoyed his/her (singular) dinner (social/human correctness).

I think that, since this construction seems to lack a nice flow, the individual writer (singular) has resorted to using a plural pronoun because they (plural) feel more comfortable doing so.

At the busy restaurant, each individual enjoyed their dinner.

Watch because i will sometimes make this change. See if you pick it up.

Since i am uncertain about the different experiences that each one of you have had, i will review and recap with certain regularity. My point is not to pad out this work or to be unduly redundant but to reinforce some points with additional clarification. These are not about me but about the ideas, thinking, and creativity that has preceded me.

For most, me = BGB

you = reader

i = BGB

For others, me = you, reader

you = others

i/you = a personal reference that is not just about myself but includes also the person (you, the reader) who is sharing my perspective. Thus it may not apply to each one of you.

my/your = same as above

Some of you may see yourself as an 'other' and have lived a life of being different. You may not have had the same life as me, but probably, the underlying dynamics are the same. I have had an urge to write this in a somewhat academic manner and convey ideas and thoughts to others who also see themselves as different. I also have had the urge to write in a creative, more abstract manner, one that really does not consider you, the audience. I have realised that a third style, one that is the honest expression of how i feel, is not only the most honest but probably also the best way to say something that would be worthwhile and understandable to you.

This writing is a diary of ideas. I would like to think of it as sometimes 'poetic' and sometimes 'philosophical' in style. It is short on embellishment but tight in expression. I feel it will be coupled with some anomalies of style that will be somewhat like Laurence Sterne. As i write this, i remember, after i had read <u>The Life and Opinions of Tristram Shandy, Gentleman,</u> in paperback, i was exploring through our home library, where i grew up and found *Tristram Shandy* in seven volumes, published in 1796. I now have these in my own collection of books.

Since this work has many references and terms that you may or may not have run into in the past, i have included a comprehensive list of references, as well as a glossary of terms, in the appendix.

Reading these words for you who are interested may present some additional complications since these ramblings were not initially divided into readable chapters or sections. My reading support group felt breaks would be really helpful to the reader. As a consequence, i have made a number of breaks that i hope will be in line with your own comprehension and interest. Some of these breaks divide sections. Some of these breaks are changes in focused discussion. Usually, these will have a longish title and will start on a new page. Remember that these are breaks in a continuous composition. As you will see, these ramblings will have a significant musical theme to them, and so i have used symbols that operate like musical rests to let you know that it is time to take a short break. Sometimes i will want you not only to rest but also to reflect on something. This may seem unreasonable to you, lovers of music, since a rest should simply be a time of hearing no sound from a particular instrument or group of instruments. Please accept my apologies. These rests will be recorded by musical notations. Below are a couple of samples.

Though most breaks will be consistent with musical form, i will not ask you to count the number of beats but simply appreciate the length of rest in your own way.

Short pauses could be recorded as follows:

Long pauses could be recorded as follows:

These stylistic adjustments don't preclude the fact that the reader may find the need to go back a half page or so to pick up the flow before continuing to read. I hope you can find your own pace and enjoy the journey.

The Diagram

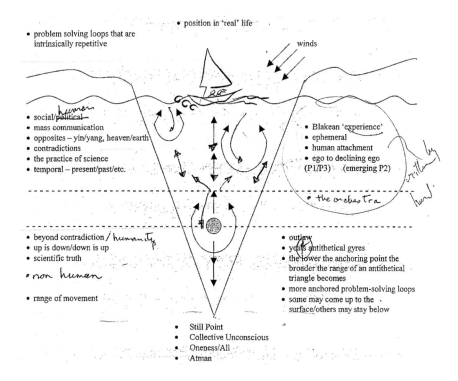

This diagram, like a mandala, offers me a supporting visual focus for putting myself and my life into some meaningful relationships. It is not an attempt to explain the nature of the universe, thought, or human condition; it is simply my shared human perception based on my experience. I am aware that i am someone who is different from others but looks the same, who has never fit but can play the role of fitting.

How does the diagram address sameness and difference?

First, i see the surface of the water as analogous to day-to-day life and how the person experiences it socially or from a human perspective.

Since i see differences in how i experience these phenomena, i will start by describing my generalised view of how you experience them. On the surface, waves are experienced personally. Something good or bad happens directly to you, and you react emotionally. I can see that there are no absolutes in what constitutes an experienced wave size. You may find yourselves more distressed by some trivial matter than some significant, life-changing event. For some of you, your course may become distressing because of the loss of a friend or relative or some other personal trauma. Sometimes something good or bad happens somewhere else, and you hear about it and react in an emotional way. However, this reaction could have the same intensity as a firsthand experience. Your favourite sports team wins an important game. Terrorists fly planes into icons of the united states because they want to make a political statement, but the 'you' who has nothing to do with the icons of the u.s.a. become fearful. So much for Marshall McLuhan and 'medium cool'.

Sometimes your life can be described as clear sailing, and at other times, there are stormy seas. Do you envy others or feel good about how your life has been? Some of you may have wished for a life of calm waters. Some of you may appreciate the storms, and some of you may have wished or wish for a different balance of the two.

These surface waters are the seas where wars are fought, where political and religious ideologies are propagated. I see civilisation as nothing more than the continuation of day-to-day life and not as a developing phenomenon.

W. D. Griffith (1916) produced the film <u>Intolerance</u>. It looked at how intolerance has existed throughout history.

You may say that things are much worse than they used to be: crime has increased, there is global warming, you can't do X or Y anymore, you need to be politically correct. On the surface of the water, throughout history, there seems to be this need to find security in a world that is beyond personal control. Do you build a better boat? Maybe you never leave shore. Do you find a political entity, a religion, an organisation? Do you tie yourself to family, or do you do all of the above? Surely, these connections are representative of something bigger, stronger, and more permanent, something fundamental in all societies throughout history.

From my point of view, you will be correct in wanting to feel a sense of security and in saying that the need for these connections has existed throughout history. However, what i see is that these needs, combined with other aspects of the human psyche, have resulted not in security but separate intolerances and human hostilities. Even at the time of Cicero, a lover of beauty, he looked back into history and felt that there had to have been a golden age in which there were no wars and all people lived in harmony. His view was unfortunately naively optimistic, but the reality of your world is that group unity, based on surface similarities, seems to need a negative concomitant to establish group identity.

There is an unfortunate, ironic relationship between surface water knowledge and respect for those who historically have been considered great writers, thinkers, artists, and creative persons. You may be able to list a large number of people who fit into this category, and you may even be able to name some of their works. If we assume that these people, who are frequently considered historically important individual thinkers, have offered some profound insights into understanding the nature of reality 'outside' the watery surface, then we might expect to see their influences of the surface movements of your social/human world. But they don't seem to exist.

If i dwell on this, i become very discouraged and feel a great sense of alienation because, from my own experience, i see no evidence of their influences. This leads me to the conclusion that you may recognise the uniqueness of a number of great thinkers but do not even know what they have expressed. More importantly, you may not be able to integrate what these highly respected people feel with yourself, even if you can verbalise their points of view.

By your articulated beliefs and opinions, you may accept that these creative thinkers are some of the most important people in the development of Western civilisation. However, what you probably don't see is that their influences have been profound on a select few who don't fit, and these different, creative outlaws have not been able to influence any of your fundamental qualities. I feel that it is only a small group of creative people who are *civilised* as we use the word culturally; your group, the rest, is unchanged. War, opposition, tolerance, intolerance, and 'us' and 'them' dominate. As a result, stating that mankind is now civilised is a joke. I see no change. To me, reading Aristotle's <u>Nicomachean Ethics</u> (written twenty-five hundred years ago) is a profound experience because of its insights. These insights are still not evident in your social/human world of today and read by me thirty-five years ago.

You may get a sense of my difficulty in dealing with the world on the surface, but this brings me to my conflicting human desires. If i didn't have a desire to live on this plane and enjoy many of its benefits, my sense of being different or alone would be less of a burden.

Participating in some sporting and leisure activities and the relationships defined within their context are enjoyable. There is enjoyment in sailing, sharing stories with fellow sailors, biking and skiing, and sharing stories with fellow bikers and skiers. Taking risks and improving skills offer important personal rewards. Even the pains from injury or challenges that can be frightening and difficult or may require ongoing practice before success is achieved are enjoyable to me. They are an essential part of my life.

I have been able to follow my own creative spirit and establish a real entity—a program that has helped many people, has hired staff, and has offered an environment that has helped fulfil many human needs. This entity has been hit by waves and challenges on the real-world plane. But this has certainly been rewarding. Human relationships in this environment have always been consistent in their dynamics.

Whether working therapeutically with people or directing, training, or inspiring staff, i have found fulfilment in these relationships. They are consistent with the 'outlaw,' connecting with others who are open and can integrate some of the tenets of creative thinking into their own lives. Though these relationships are wonderfully rewarding, they are limited by a teacher/student, therapist/patient-type dynamic. These connections are vulnerable to the aspect of respect i have mentioned earlier. My selfish enjoyment is based on the feedback i get from others' responsiveness. Though this feedback could be seen as personal and individual, i experience it more as nonpersonal in that others are responding to me as a vehicle of knowledge and understanding and not as a frail person who is alone. For me, human relationships, in a general social context, have been less fulfilling and are experienced in different ways.

Relationships with 'friends' have generally been polite and have included humour, respect, and a degree of caring. In recent years, i have spent less time in social gatherings since they are more of a chore than enjoyment. Since my areas of interest and what i focus on are different from others, i am unable to talk about—or at least not interested in talking about—the latest popular novel, movie, TV show, and news reports and about others' personal relationships, politics, sports, business, children, grandchildren, health, and getting older. However, i enjoy literature, music, wine, philosophy, science, mysticism and the history of ideas, riding my free-ride bike, and racing my car. But more importantly, i enjoy the fact that no area of understanding is separate from another and that all knowledge is connected.

An illustration of the social differences that exist between 'friends' and me is embodied in the fact that we dwell in different experiential worlds, and this difference can be found in our approach to drinking wine. For me, tasting wine is a multifaceted experience. It requires a glass that accentuates the characteristics of the varietal. I enjoy a Bordeaux-style wine the most (a mixture of cabernet sauvignon, merlot, and cabernet franc), and so i usually drink New World wines of that style or one of the first- to fifth-growth (est. 1855) Bordeaux wines. 'Life is too short to drink bad wine.' The actual tasting, which to me is almost ritualistic, requires the right environment, company, and time. The experience of the nose is, of course, a highly significant part of tasting. This is followed by its body and taste over the tongue and then its finish.

Since i only drink wine in this manner, i do not drink at dinner parties or social gatherings in general. If i try to explain to others who have no interest in understanding wine, though they may say they do, i have great difficulty. Most people i know have no interest in the glass, the nose, or the finish. They have no interest in the structure or notes; they simply like the taste or don't. I have known a number of people who are so used to drinking high-tannic wine that that is what they look for.

Just think of the responses i get from others. One friend told me that it was very selfish of me to only drink good wines because it made other people feel uncomfortable. Another person told me that they had tried a $150 bottle of wine (not really expensive) and was not impressed. When i asked about the name of the wine and its year, he didn't know. When i asked about the nose, nuances of taste, and finish, he had no idea what i was talking about. Some would ask me to taste a wine that they liked, and i have found over and over again that if i said, 'That's not bad' or 'Quite good,' they would hear my response. If i said anything else, they wouldn't listen. Others see me as a nice guy who is a wine snob. Others see me as someone who tries to be different. And others with me in social gatherings see me as someone who doesn't drink. In many ways, the 'not drinking' perception is the easiest.

This relationship with friends offers me no opportunity for an expression of my interests or passions, and so i have learned to focus social dialogue on what they enjoy. For you who are like these friends, i understand that you exist on the waters of life and discuss a myriad of topics that have nothing to do with the essence of life, some type of underlying truth, or culture. This is profoundly distressing to me because it establishes a vast gulf between me and others. But it also magnifies my loneliness.

To this point in my ramblings, i have talked about being alone; i have not touched on feelings of love and attachment. As a therapist, i might raise two questions of myself: Is your experience of being alone simply the result of not feeling loved or not being able to love? Having a different point of view and not being understood can certainly be distressing, but can't love and attachment to others be more important?

My immediate response to these questions is that i am uncertain about what love means, but i do strongly experience a sense of warm, empathic connection with others that is independent of individual differences. Though the most profound sense of connection in my adult life has been with my own children and grandchildren, this warm, empathic state is intense and can simply be indulged with wonder; and it can also create feelings of wanting to protect, care, and help. Strangely enough, i know they want to care for and protect their dad. This gives a wonderful emotional reciprocity. This reciprocity could be independent of thought and understanding, but because they have their unique ways of understanding the world and are individually different, they can mix surface- and outlaw-type traits.

I experience these as a profound, selfish, and positive part of my existence on the water's surface. I also see this warm, empathic state as a dominant influence in all my interactions with others. In a nonpersonal way, i experience a feeling for all others like the Buddhist use of compassion. I find that this feeling gives me a nonnegative view of all people. I do not understand revenge, nor can i have negative feelings about others, though i may not find any personal satisfaction in a friendship. The reciprocity on an emotional level here can be positive, especially for those who understand and are committed to the discussion of ideas and share a passion for our history of creative thinking. However, as mentioned earlier, this is more nonpersonal and, for me at this point, requires a different set of dynamics.

At this point in my writing, i have reached a very difficult time of expression. I know what i want to say, i have struggled with expression, and i have spent considerable time on writing and rewriting. As a result, the time i have been absorbed in thought and making expression attempts has and will far exceed the time it takes to read the end product. But it is important to me that my final expression does not minimise what i feel by the numbers of words on a page.

The richness of my life has only existed because of my openness to experience. I know it can result in elation or despair because openness exposes and makes one vulnerable. I know it can be wonderfully serendipitous or profoundly difficult. Many times during my life, i have wanted the challenging and difficult, knowing it will have a positive outcome; but in all cases, i have been ready for an 'it didn't work' outcome. When one is more humanly separate and something doesn't work as hoped, it is easy to problem-solve, find solutions, and carry on. With an emotional connection, it is far more difficult to deal with the 'it didn't work out' result. For you, these words may seem incredibly naïve; and for me, as i write them, i will agree. The difference between you and me is the starting point. For you who are living on the sea of relationship and feelings of love and hate, these heartfelt emotions are normal. For someone who doesn't fit in the same way as most and who has not experienced love and hate in a way that most of you have, a feeling of emotional connection to another person is new—somewhat wonderful but somewhat scary.

Recently, i have experienced another relationship that has made me more aware of my need for connections that not only embody a passion for creative thinking and an awareness of being different but also, more importantly, give me a profound feeling of connection with another. The only experience i can compare it to is the feeling i have with my own children and grandchildren. This experience has made me better understand that my needs require not just that i live alone but also that i be on different planes and make some personal connections. It is also interesting for me to reflect on the nature of the way each person i feel close to expresses feelings and how that influences my experience of emotional reciprocity.

For me, respecting another's rights and feelings is of paramount importance. For many years, i have frequently denied my own feelings in situations where i have been aware that they are at odds with another who will not be able to understand a different perspective. At one time in my life, i would have argued a point with someone who has held a position based on emotional necessity. For years now, i have accepted the futility of this exercise. However, i really enjoy conversations that are dialectical and thought-provoking, knowing that i and the person with whom i am discussing are open to reason. The side effect or perceived personal fault of my perspective could be that i avoid conflict, don't deal with anything stressful, or give in to others too easily. These perceptions are not only entirely correct but also entirely wrong. Ironically, they may be correct where you think they are wrong and wrong where you think they are correct (to be clarified later).

Another important point to discuss is based on my years of being a successful psychotherapist for these people who have been through many previous treatments without success. These successes have given me the socially articulated perception that i have great insight into the psyche of others. It is also something that, in a 'non-egotistic' way, i believe to be true. It isn't the 'i am the best' but simply that somehow i have talent to do this work and that it needs to be used. It can sometimes feel like a burden from which i cannot escape. This burden is especially evident when i move to personally experienced relationships. Can i assume that, because i have this great insight, i can read what is below the surface? In my therapist role, i have great confidence; but from a human point of view, i have a difficult time.

On a personal plane, i am close to one person who may be frequently nonexpressive and to another who may frequently engage in ongoing criticism. These styles may show a dislike or disdain, but they can also be individual adaptive styles that do not reflect actual feelings. If i consider my social ineptitude, i feel a sense of self-delusion if i assume that inner feelings of these two are not consistent with outer expression. Why would anyone want anything to do with you? If i consider life on a different plane and drop to a less wavy plane, i become wonderfully optimistic; and at this point, i oscillate between these two worlds.

I find that these short but profound reflections are difficult to write and have come to an expressive end. I return to being the philosopher. However, before returning, let's take some time to listen. In this way, you will get used to changing your perspective. Also, remember that no music has different sounds. There are, i suggest, many types of no music. Here are two of them. There is the music of no music, when you are out at sea and there is no wind, no motor, and no sails moving. There is also the no music not played by the orchestra.

Cage Interlude

John Cage is the first to express that rests are not just a part of music but also when the whole orchestra cannot play, and this is music. How much space does it take on a page to not read for four minutes and thirty-three seconds?

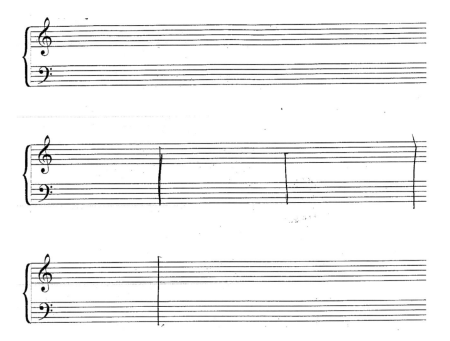

Reflections on Separateness

After a brief moment of reflection, i realised that even though there are many different aspects to the human psyche that give me a sense of connection, there can be other aspects of the same person that disappoint or establish separateness. You might comment that everybody feels a sense of separateness sometimes. It's part of life. Everybody will have profound loss at some time in life. You may contend that the loss of a child may be something that you may never get over. But this most profound loss is based on a set of beliefs and feelings that are part of the surface, the ephemerally understood nature of the world. I think most would agree that if you experienced a sense of being disconnected, abandoned, and alone because of some traumatic loss, remaining in this state would be the worst possible result, and getting support would be the best.

Let us consider your need for support using our metaphor of the waves on the surface of the water. If it were the waves of life that brought about your loss, then getting ashore as quickly as possible would be a necessary first step. Building a bigger boat or a safer boat that can take the waves would be a necessary next step for some. Possibly never venturing out onto the waters of life would be a safe alternative.

To fill this wavy void, you may find a religious ideology that gives a sense of bigger purpose and connection, but this too is still part of that surface plane. It satisfies your sense of self and need for meaning and purpose. It does not necessarily open you up into what it is like to be different, though it does give you a sense that you have enhanced your life experience in a meaningful way. However, i think life enhancement can only happen for people who have a readiness and the right guidance. Much of the process of understanding can be counterintuitive. My feeling is that there are no answers on the surface. You cannot find meaning or purpose because there isn't any. Cogito ergo sum.

At this point, i feel a need to, once again, speak directly to you, the reader, who has not experienced life outside this plane. Your question could be, 'Why do i even bother to be tolerant of this self-absorbed rhetoric?' For you who have experienced life outside this plane, you realise that this rhetoric is universal and, though expressed in personal terms, is really an expression of the human condition. If you have read this carefully, you will see that what i have just said contradicts what i have said before. This is simply the first of many important contradictions.

I mused on readiness. How do i know if someone is ready? I have realised that my needs for human connection with others who are ready to respond to guidance from an outlaw perspective are important. Could i possibly ask the following questions? What are your strong beliefs? What is your point of view? Does this point of view change? Do you have an intellectual curiosity that requires a wide range of experience? Do you find answers? Do you have a good grasp on this other reality? What are your passions? How do you express your emotions? Are your feelings of care for those you feel close to an important influence in what you do for them? Would you do the same for people you don't have any special connection with? Can you be open with your emotions in a self-reflective, sincere manner? Can you express an open physical expression of connection? Do you have a sense of personal identity? What are the defining characteristics of your identity? Can you integrate all of the above in a personal direction?

Though these questions don't have to be answered by anyone, they are ones that i thought would help me discriminate between people with a readiness to experience differently. In a sense, if others answer these questions in a certain way, they may meet my needs on many levels. However, after developing this list, i have realised it won't work, even though the answers are what i want to hear.[2] They can become simply judgemental if i consider my personal needs.

By this exercise in writing, i have also realised that there is a fine balance between meeting my personal needs and appreciating the qualities of others and that there are no clear formulae for making a connection. However, i have also realised that there are certain qualities that are essential for more meaningful connections. These connections may have something to do with my list of questions, but more importantly, they need to be manifestations of an essence that underlies, goes in opposite directions or in all directions, and constantly changes but always remains the same. It is this essence that holds the answer.

---

[2] Another interesting realisation for me was that there could be no 'right' or 'wrong' answers to any of these questions. The only outcome i could anticipate would be one based on patterns of responses, and the only conclusion i could probably make would be something like, 'That's interesting.'

Moving On

I feel the need to leave these self-reflections and move on. As i write this, i am aware that one of the limitations of human experience is an understanding of the status quo, which i will use in a somewhat metaphorical manner. I will have it refer to those basic beliefs that society holds about life on a social/human plane. It supports that old adage 'The more things change, the more they stay the same.' But as i see it, it is open to lateral movement and moving on, keeping up with the times, getting on with it, and asking questions about whether things are the same or different. Are they better or worse?

In a sense, consider the status quo as a thinking position that exists on the surface, that defines the way things are, is not open to change, and does not step outside itself (vertically) but probably does include some circular self-reflective thinking. But more of this later.

From my point of view, i see that trying to understand the status quo requires moving on, while in some ways moving on (laterally) could just be staying within the boundaries of the status quo and going nowhere. Once again, it is our perspective that is the determining factor.

Moving on takes us back to the beginning of this writing. The waves on the surface are constantly changing, and our boat moves on in one direction or another. I think we will all agree that, over time, the waves change but don't move on in any evolving sense. Our journey in our boat and the development of technology that helps us sail represent two types of moving on.

Our journey through life needs to move ahead, to go somewhere. Over the years, we have advanced; we can do things that have not even been thought about before because of advancements in science and technology.

I think you will also agree that we have advanced as a species and have become more civilised and cultured, though some of you might fear that the flip side of culture and being civilised is a tolerance for bad behaviour. As a result, you may see increased crime and that people are getting away with things. More waves on the surface.

To get away from this surface, i would like to look more specifically at moving on and status quo. Since life moves on and things change, one needs to keep up with the times. Whether it be new technology, fashions, exercises, leisure activities, dieting, what you watch on TV, your use of the Internet or your smartphone, what you read or drink, or what have you, they all help define the modern you. You may also hold on to the past and not want to change. 'Let's just keep things the same.' You may have liked the way things used to be.

To best explain one way of looking at the status quo and moving on, i am going to move momentarily from the metaphorical to the literal; and in doing this, i will consider technology. An example of moving technologically is having a new boat. So what we have today are new boats with GPS, satellite communications, air-conditioning, new hull design with new age materials, possibly even a wine cooler, and all the amenities you can think of. This is a long way from the ships of the early explorers.

But early sailing ships and a new 'state of the art' yacht are both *boats*. Both are vulnerable to the sea. In fact, there is no ship or yacht that is without risks at sea. If you travel at sea without an understanding of this relationship, you could see yourself as moving on in a lateral sense; you may be moving away from hardships and risk, going from A to B, or simply enjoying a cruise that just happens to be on water. The water is the medium you are dwelling on. What is important to most people who decide to travel is that they are going somewhere, and part of their overall goal may be to enjoy the process. But what you are missing is the essence. Historically, the basic ingredients for the explorer, professional seaman, or fisherman when at sea are 'man', 'boat', and 'sea'. This has not changed. This is the status quo to one who lives at sea.

Is going from A to B going somewhere? Possibly moving on is really just moving away from something, going in circles, or going back and forth.

These questions also consider the status quo. In these cases, the status quo could be seen as the reality that one would like some degree of personal happiness.

The behaviour of waves can be explained by certain principles and rules. Even though all waves are different, we can explain some of the characteristics of waves by looking at water depth, currents, temperature, wind strength, wind direction, previous wind current dynamics, fetch, and even wakes from other ships and boats.

There is an important distinction to be made here and about how we consider the status quo. Waves behave in a manner that we have tried to understand. Their functioning is based on natural phenomena, not on us. There is no social/human status quo; they just do their thing. However, to the sea captain, all these factors are important and always have been, and their experience has allowed them to develop great insight to how waves affect their boat or ship. It seems reasonable to assume that the seaman is grounded in a thought structure that could be considered as based on a status quo. 'This is how the sea behaves. I've seen it many times.'

So let's say that the 'status quo' thinking for most of you is based on a number of unquestioned assumptions that determine how you see and process experiences. The rationale for your view could be that your understanding is the same as everyone else.

Consider the following quote from *Hamlet* and who is saying what:

The 'all the world's a stage' speech of Shakespeare or, more specifically, his created character Hamlet has been quoted repeatedly over the years. What is often overlooked in this speech is the difference between Hamlet's point of view and the underlying perspective of the author.

From Hamlet's point of view, his life in the court/castle is one of himself and others playing roles, being emotionally dishonest, having selfish ambition, and doing anything to get ahead. In his speech, there is a strong sense of despair and expression of the meaninglessness of life. His sense of moving and getting ahead has fallen apart.

From the author's point of view, Hamlet's experience is limited to surface issues. He is not grounded in the natural human spirit that can be seen in characters who live in the woods and are outside the courts/castles. Macbeth, in the context of his own tragic play, has compared life to

> a walking shadow, a poor player
> That struts and frets his hour upon the stage
> And then is heard no more: it is a tale
> Told by an idiot, full of sound and fury,
> Signifying nothing.

Here is a more powerful statement on life and death and its meaninglessness. What is Shakespeare's point of view? We could say that Shakespeare's sense of life is that it is nothing more than a meaningless play. However, if we read his other works and understand his point of view, we would realise that he accepts that there is an underlying natural 'status quo' that anchors the human psyche, but this gets lost once someone tries to 'move on' within the social/human realm of the court. And more significantly, any sense of underlying meaning in life is lost, and social/human purpose dominates. If we want to experience some sense of essences, where do we go? If Shakespeare is correct, depth of life that underlies the status quo of social/human life isn't going to be found in our typical *court*-structured society. We know that Lear can see once he is blind and in the natural (outside-the-court) world. The other direction we can take—and move on—is through learning, developing, understanding, and immersing ourselves in the essence of some status quo.

To find an answer, could i take sailing lessons or move into the country? Move to my own Walden pond? Sign on a whaling ship with a captain who is obsessed with killing a white whale? Could i sail on an old ship like the *Judea* from England and, through hardships and the destruction of the ship, arrive at the still brown waters of the east? I could sit by the river at Tintern Abbey. Could i sit under the bodhi tree or become a boatman who takes people across the river?

Or are these moves only lateral?

All these experiences can help, whether real or imagined. As we know from writers like Thoreau, Melville, Conrad, Wordsworth, and Hesse (alluded to above) and their written work, they have taken social/human experiences and expressed something that has a more profound sense and something that has overlooked or gone beyond social/human purposes. They have integrated the intellectual exercise of not only writing about the world but also becoming a part of it in some deeper sense. They have, somewhat ironically, taken a personally created social/human world that is not factually real. (They created it; if not literally, they did so impressionistically.) But these works are expressively real. They are real expressions of their inner selves—selves that can see the status quo and the social/ human world from a different perspective. It is hoped that their writings work effectively (remember Kandinsky?) by giving the reader a personally profound experience. However, for those living with the angst of social/human goals, the influences of these works may result in rejection— the book was boring or not of any interest. If it is read and processed, it could result in an even bigger gulf between one's self-absorbed emotional social/human needs and anything that threatens their status quo. It could also result in developing one's curiosity and desire to find another path, even if that path leads nowhere.

For most of you, there isn't enough time or interest to become a sailor for many years to really experience man, boat, and sea. You aren't going to become a Henry David Thoreau or William Wordsworth. And you may not even have the time to read their works. You have too much to do.

I guess the operative question is, *Can i find meaning in life that gives me a greater sense of well-being without having to read a whole bunch of books or travel all over the place?*

Fortunately for you on the surface of the waters, there are some wonderful choices. Most are nicely packaged, don't take a lot of time, and are not unduly stressful.

Consider the following:

> Are you feeling lost, confused, uncertain?
> Life seems to have lost its meaning?
> Hate your job? Pay is low? Can't get ahead?
> In debt and can't seem to get out of it?
> Is everyone doing better than you are?
> THERE IS AN ANSWER!
> INSTANT SUCCESS—100% GUARANTEE
>
> YOU WILL FEEL GREAT FOREVER!
> NO COST*
> NO MEDICATION
> NO THERAPY
> NO COURSES**
> NO WORK
>
> NO NEW JOB OR CAREER
> OPEN TO EVERYONE—NO INTELLIGENCE, SKILL, OR TALENT REQUIRED
>
> All your questions will have answers!
> You are probably sceptical. Nothing can be this great, *but it is*!

---

*   Any cost is at your discretion.

**   You may become interested and learn a wealth of new 'facts'.

ACCEPT CHRIST INTO YOUR HEART!

Oops! Could there be some flaw here? Certainly, Christianity has been around for many years, though i believe it is predated on establishing a satisfying, delusionary personal state that has allowed people to be controlled by superiors (church leaders). A significant percentage of the Western world accepts its ideology. A significant percentage of the Western world accepts right and left political ideologies. A significant percentage of the Western world accepts that there are good guys and bad guys. A significant percentage of the Western world accepts that there are good sports teams (hopefully the ones they like) and bad sports teams. A significant percentage of the Western world accepts feelings of nationalism. A significant percentage of the Western world listens to the news. One hundred percent of people surveyed in six Western countries have agreed that the sun rises in the east and sets in the west.

If you believe in something and everyone else believes in it too, is it the truth? It is, of course, a sociological truth—everyone agrees.

There is another simple level of truth to consider here as well. If our hypothetical survey asked two questions—'in which direction does the sun rise?' and 'in which direction does the sun set?'—i would most likely get the same responses if i asked the questions 'in which direction do you look to see the sun rising?' and 'in which direction do you look to see the sun setting?' The obvious point here is that if we consider the sun and its relationship to the earth, it does not rise or set. The earth rotates. Where is Copernicus? You may say that i am making a big deal out of nothing—everyone knows the right answer. But as you will see, this distinction is *very* important to the person who is different and doesn't fit.

Let us return to the sea and . . .

The Loss of Perspective

I suggest that everyone will agree that there can be waves of different sizes and shapes on the surface of the water. I can also suggest that almost everyone will agree that there is something more in life than just these waves and life on the surface. These waves do not give us meaning. And you may not be very satisfied with currently understood scientific variables as your answer. A ship sinks, and hundreds are killed. If you lost a loved one, would you be consoled by a scientific explanation of the wave action that sank the ship? Or would this scientific 'status quo' that we have discussed do the job of giving you a sense of acceptance and comfort? Probably not.

If you are the Christian who has found Christ and contentment, you will have a supporting belief that makes this crisis more manageable. However, do you simply believe that you have found a boat that is more seaworthy? Or is your belief grounded in something else?

I think the best way to address these questions is to *not* answer them. But like the concerns in the scientific community about bias, we need to consider point of view and personal gain.

If i believe something and i feel better because of it, i will see that as personal gain. My ability to be somewhat objective is compromised. It can be a tragic day for the scientist who has spent years testing a hypothesis that he/she ultimately has to accept is wrong. This scientist could describe and believe that the hypothesis is true because he/she cannot humanly accept the alternative, or it could be because a drug company or some financially supporting organisation is supporting the hypothesis. Could that actually happen? Does personal gain outweigh the need for questioning some truth that my result in no answer?

Most religious beliefs are attractive because they have a number of personal benefits. These are tied to a sense of personal well-being, including a need for security, guidance, and the elimination of the unknown. Here, we have beliefs that result in long-term personal gain. In fact, these beliefs even have benefits after you die.

Think of how a religion can be promoted.

If you lack a sense of self-worth and feel you don't fit, you can become part of <u>our answer</u>—religious group. See yourself as superior to that nonreligious sinful mass that never accepted you. You don't have to do anything other than join and believe.

If you are fearful of dying, there is no need to worry because there is an afterlife—you'll live forever!

If you are anxious and feel insecure, you can adopt an all-loving father.

If you are poor at problem-solving and uncertain about moral decision making, you can adopt an infallible moral code.

When i reflect on some other aspects of these beliefs, i see some other interesting factors. Wouldn't someone have to feel a great sense of self-importance if this person felt 'i should live forever'?

It seems somewhat ironic that a religious group that believes in love and compassion can be the source of so many wars and extreme expressions of racism and intolerance. As we know, many wars have been fought in the name of religion. However, i do make a distinction between people who accept certain religious beliefs that exist on the surface and those who have religious beliefs that go far beyond this wavy plane.

However, here is another contradiction. If we consider religious thought and belief, we could arrive at the following conclusion: If you believe in god with no proofs, this will be okay. If you believe in god and you have proof, this leaves the door open to irrational thinking. If your approach to establishing proof is a default one and focuses on science not having an answer, then you are manipulating. If your proof is based on what the bible or a religious work says because you know it's the word of god or whatever, then you have a belief, not a truth, but it is clear you want to keep things simple. Unfortunately, it could be that the more you know that biblical proof to be true, the closer your thinking is to being delusional.

I would like to be part of the world and to have a human connection. I can not only feel alone but also feel this warm, empathic connection and realise that i need to live on different planes, but what i can't do is let my frail human needs influence my outlaw status. I cannot be funded by a drug company or a social entity that supports or creates its own proof. If i *believe* it impairs me, i cannot believe anything that offers some absolute form, or my freedom to think is gone. The person using a manipulative approach to support their 'proof' might suggest that there is a contradiction in my statement and ask, 'Is not accepting belief a belief?' The answer is 'No, it's an assumption based on logic.'

On this surface level, the need to believe in something beyond the human realm has existed throughout history. But if belief itself is a need, then it too can be seen as based on 'personal gain'.

This 'need to believe' can lead to some interesting thinking. I see another interesting contradiction in thought here, which to me is somewhat reminiscent of E. Fromm's <u>The Sane Society</u>. His premise is that most people in society meet the diagnostic criteria of psychopathology. Here is some fun logic to consider.

People who are very bright and psychotic are nuts. Persons like myself who are different, who have weird thoughts, and who don't seem to care about social and political issues are nuts. Therefore, since i am nuts, i must be psychotic. (In case you are unaware, this is not syllogistically logical.) The contradiction comes from the fact that this is not psychosis but may seem like it to you, the 'normal' person.

One of the hallmarks of psychosis is that the person *knows* that something is *true* and that no evidence can dispute this truth. This could be called a delusion. For instance, i have seen one person for therapy who knows that everyone in a community of over one hundred thousand people is gay. There is no evidence that anyone can offer him that might even have him question his knowledge. At this point, it is not belief. It is *true*! You may see that this belief is 'out-there', but you may overlook that your nonbelief of the 'out-there' is equally limiting. However, it could be that you, the normal person, believe that something is true, and you may even believe there is evidence.

From my point of view as the outlaw, if someone says, 'I have taken a leap of faith and believe everything is right in the world' or 'There is a god' and even if one is hopeful and believes that everyone will become enlightened (Hermann Hesse wished for this), but they also know they cannot prove what they feel, and they just have a sense, these beliefs give a feeling of comfort and optimism, and my connection with this type of belief is similar to how i feel about family friends. It is an honest expression of self and human need. It can be understood as an expression of self, and it is not going to be imposed on another or seen as a belief that must be right. There is no conflict between truth and personal gain since it is all personal gain.

Let me recap: if someone emphatically contends some of *this* is the truth, i can be somewhat concerned if i am the outlaw riding on the surface. Even if this 'truth' is shared by millions, it is of no consolation since, throughout history, common beliefs has been shown to be wrong, and not being open to other possible truths is consistent with the basic thought structure of the psychotic.

It seems to me that, historically, this 'psychosis' has manifested itself in religious, nationalistic, and moral ideologies. I think it has also somewhat interestingly developed. It could be considered as a way of rationalising most human needs and behaviour.

There seems to be a human need to find some truth, some certainty. However, there are those few, like myself, who experience life differently. Like Alan Watts, we understand that wisdom comes with insecurity, not certainty.

In our history of life on the surface, we can often explain social and political movements and changes in terms of causes and effects. But what really are the causes? What are the effects? Do conceptual entities like religion, politics, or beliefs cause anything? Or are these really an expression of a collection of individuals? Sum ergo cogito.

You may ask, 'Are all these really just conceptual?' You may correctly state that a country is real. It has laws, borders, police, armies, economies, taxes; it has power over you. It can control many aspects of your life. How could it simply be an expression of human thought and need?

From my experience, i have to remind myself that, for these entities to exist, you need to accept that there are nations with boundaries that give the illusion of separateness, differences, individual national beliefs, and ultimately delusions. I often ask, 'How come people don't see that these nations, religions, etc., are all surface noise and have nothing to do with an inherent or given reality? How can they believe in themselves?' Let me explain how i arrive at this perception.

I see icarus flying to the sun; his wings melt, and he ends up falling into the sea. He attempts to fly to the heavens but ends up on the earth (water). He attempts to dwell in the world of ideals/ideas/mind (the nonorganic) but ends up immersed in the organic. He attempts to free himself from the biological/primitive nature of the human species but ends up immersed in the sea, the species' basic elements.

It seems to me that, since the earliest recorded history, the species has attempted the same trip to find enlightenment/truth but with an interesting contradictory result. The species hasn't recognised that they have fallen into their basic biological essence as icarus did (really never left). Consider the sea as representative of fundamental human drives that result from subcortical regions of the brain. They produce drives like fear, fight, flight, anger, and need for security. So what's actually happening?

He (the species) believes that he is still flying in the heavens, and any social behaviour is a result of this. He is behaving in accordance with god's word, and he is expressing the accepted tenets of belief without hesitation. Onward, Christian soldiers! What is really happening, however, is that expressions of biological need and want are disguised and rationalised as idealistic/religious thought. Ironically, the same social behaviours expressed by a non-Christian people may be judged by our Christian soldier as being violent and the expression of uncivilised barbarians.

What i have read and observed leads me to the conclusion (really a hypothesis) that there are basic physical and emotional needs, probably some primary processes (things that are natural drives and specific to the species). Since this is not a scientific treatise, i am not going to try to analyse, classify, or rework all the science that has been done in these areas. But i will accept that humans tend to have needs, drives, or whatever that—from a socially perceived point of view—seem to go in two almost contradictory directions. There is the need for some answer, truth, ideals, and identity, both personally and collectively. These are often idealised in religions, constitutions, human rights legislation, social/human theories, and other such thought-out belief structures. For these to work (assist in regulating the behaviour of many people), they need to be sellable to large groups of people so the masses *believe*.

In essence, starting a religious group, one needs to consider some of the factors we discussed previously. One needs to give preestablished answers and truths to eliminate mental anxiety, but also, somewhat ironically, one needs to define a community uniqueness and with it a clearly understood separateness from others—as you may recall, i think that the human species needs some kind of group identity that requires a sense of difference from others. As we have also discussed, this works laterally on a social/ human level; but from my experience, i can see that it works vertically as well. The only difference is that those lovers of beauty and others who perceive an underlying sameness are not a group and have no group identity (other than the group of all and none). One area of consideration in starting a religious group is to have the group define themselves as not only different but also better than others, and it is also important to have the human and their identity as 'above' the other species—acting like an animal is bad!

To keep this belief, it is important to deny the impact of subcortical (animal-like) drives and processes in humans, which have become much distorted over the years. Ironically, human behaviour may be driven by a fear (subcortical) of people in another group whom they don't know and who are different and, let's say, have a different ideology. If a war or expressions of intolerance occur, which we know happens frequently, the human rationale is not that humans are driven by a basic primitive fear but that there is a need to eradicate certain types of thinking, ideologies, and the people who support them.

This, of course, leads us to another direction, to one of basic subcortical (primitive) drives. One textbook i have read years ago describes the four functions of the hypothalamus as the four f's: fear, fight, flight, and sexual intercourse. A vast range of lower species respond the same way. In fact, recent biological research shows that even cells (which don't have a hypothalamus) can display some similar behaviour.

Of course, humans—because of their wonderfully evolved state even centuries ago—have gone beyond these drives that are typical of lower forms of life. I feel the need to say this in a sarcastic manner (hopefully you picked this up) because, as the outsider, this belief is very distressing to me, though i do not feel any personal negative feeling towards others who believe they are evolved, much like i will never feel anything negative about a schizophrenic with delusions. But if i am so involved with others who have this deluded sense of an evolved state, it increases my sense of being alone. I have difficulty being in a gathering where all the personal expression by others has no meaning to me. I either don't talk or go along with whatever is being talked about.

The essence of beauty is hidden by a social/human malaise.

As i write this, i feel a newfound sense of not only being alone but also connection with another. This person knows she understands. She has a rare intuitive sense of this beauty but has no idea how to deal with this 'pressure expectation'. She has had experiences in life—though interesting, challenging, and individual—and had not enhanced her ability to really appreciate her insight and be able to let go of some 'surface' beliefs. She is not yet free from the shackles of impairing personal experience and social/human views. The potential is there! The difficulty for me is that, from my selfish point of view, this relationship offers so much for me on all levels—from subcortical to belief. For you, the reader, this may sound great. Is there a difficulty? The difficulty to me is obvious: i cannot impose myself—even though i may do it anyway—on someone else, especially if there is personal gain. Though i do agree that the personal gain i get as the therapist from a positive outcome is acceptable, the outcome needs to be considered from the patient's point of view, not mine.

Here, we have had a short digression. For you, the reader, it is only seconds in duration. But like the poet, i have spent time crafting my words and expressing my spirit. As you can see, the logic of this rambling isn't driven by some idea or cognitive process. It combines all aspects of my experience of being different with an individualised perception of how i see the world.

Back to the point at hand

What are these traits that people have supposedly gone beyond? It seems to me that, even if we look at the simple textbook functions of the hypothalamus, we haven't changed. In fact, i feel an honest acceptance of the expression of these functions as part of human nature. Maybe being human results in a better balance and control of these functions. I am not tempted to fly to the sun and fall short.

For instance, let us consider the lot of many priests who have accepted that being celibate is an essential part of the priesthood. Here are some contextual points to consider.

To propagate the species, some type of sexual drive is essential, though i suggest that the object (person) of attraction can vary. Even though the female is the essential object of procreation, we can see from history that, even as far back as Athenian city-state times, the object of sexual interest for the high-functioning male can be another male. However, priests have been so strongly committed to a set of religious beliefs that they have dedicated their lives to this commitment and celibacy. But even with this level of commitment, some priests have not been able to deny the existence of a sexual drive.

To me, this conflict between natural biological human drives and needs to believe in some ideal or god has been understood in many different ways throughout the history of Western civilisation. But rarely have these forces been considered realistically. By realistically, i am not considering social/human aspects but more the nature of the beast.

To explore some of the dynamics in the priest's dilemma and, on a grander scale, the way civilisation has been over time, i would like to use some simple neurological descriptions. These are so simple in their dynamics that they can be considered more as structured metaphors. But whatever, here we go.

I will use a number of chemistry-type equations to explain these dynamics and will base our equations on two components.

I will use SC to refer to subcortical drives. These include those hypothalamic functions mentioned previously, plus limbic system functions like emotional feelings, such as empathy, love, hate, and anger. Stephen Porges calls all these polyvagal. Whatever their basic functions are can be seen in nature.I will use PFC to refer to the cognitive, the idea, the knowledge of what one should do. These are all partially a function of the prefrontal cortex.

If our hypothetical priest had an SC and no PFC, then his sexual gratification would be easily attained. An object of sexual gratification would elicit a sexual response. There would be no thought or rule that said, 'Be celibate.' If our hypothetical priest had no SC, there would be no sexual drive. In this case, the ideal that said he must be celibate at all times could be followed without hesitation.

$$SC + (no\ PFC) \longrightarrow sexual\ behaviour$$

$$(no\ SC) + PFC \longrightarrow celibate\ behaviour$$

But neither of these conditions represents the way a human works. What should happen is that the PFC inhibits the SC drive. In normal functioning, the drive is there, but the cortex reduces (inhibits) the SC drive and offers a social script that says something like, 'This is not right', which typically results in thought or urge but no politically incorrect behaviour.

$$[SC + (-PFC)] \longrightarrow behaviour\ that\ is\ celibate$$
drive/urge inhibition

If the SC is higher than the inhibitory impact of PFC, then the sexual urge dominates. If the PFC inhibitory impact is higher than the SC urge, then celibacy dominates.

What can unfortunately happen is that if a person feels significant pressure to conform or repress an urge, the repression itself can reduce the urge but can actually increase the basic urge that is being repressed. For instance, one can experience fear or anxiety that actually increases the urge. Let us expand the application of these simple dynamics to a more generalised expression of human behaviour as seen throughout history.

To me, one of the most baffling aspects of human behaviour, if we take it at face value, is the coexistence of religious belief and violent/aggressive behaviour. Here, we have beliefs that extol the virtues of loving one's fellow man no matter who they are, forgiving another's sins, and in Christianity establishing very specific commandments based on loving and selfless virtues.

However, humans have killed/tortured and abused others in the name of religion. My suggestion for resolving my baffling state goes back to our equations concerning the priest.

Suppose you know that you are a Christian and accept its tenets. However, you also know that not everyone believes the way 'they should'. There are idolaters, heretics, barbarians, sinners, and people who do evil things. Let us assume that knowing this influences you neurologically so that your thoughts about these evil people are very stimulating, and they put you into a fear/fight mode subcortically. However, you are not self-aware or reflective, and so what you experience is a stronger personal belief that you are right and not a sense of being conflicted. With this, you experience an equally strong belief that these others are evil/bad and possibly even a threat to Christianity.

In this case, you have made a transformation of the SC + (PFC) $\longrightarrow$ equation. SC is the dominant driver, but since you don't see it, you only see PFC thinking that supports the SC drive at a heightened level. The result is as follows:

Step 1 SC + ($\downarrow$PFC) $\longrightarrow$ a transformation from the usual inhibitory PFC that might say it is wrong to kill to a PFC that rationalises the killing of those who are threats to your religious beliefs.

Step 2 SC + ($\uparrow$PFC) $\longrightarrow$ Kill the evil guys!

What we have is an animal-type killing behaviour (ironically, the behaviour can be considered as worse than animal-like) in the guise of civilised behaviour. Here is a highly delusionary belief.

You are not killing for food or survival; you are killing because of belief and ideology! What comes first? The individual, the groups, the state, the church, the nature, the earth? My simple reflection is that people have needs that include some inherent physiological characteristics that include acceptance by others, security, some sense of order, and some kind of meaning. These people, by nature, are grouped in families and communities, which in turn include more people, and with these groupings come the creation of social/human values and religious entities. Once these social/human and religious entities are established, their collective identity returns to ruling the people.

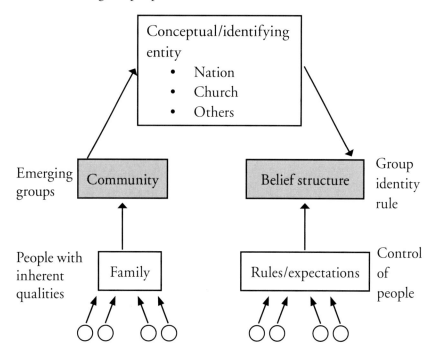

Here, we have another contradiction. For many Western cultures, the rights and freedoms of the person are seen as of paramount importance. But is this what really happens? It seems to me that one can look at a nation that believes in the freedom of the person within a democratic society and conclude that the nation exists to serve each person.

What we see instead is the requirement that each person not only follow the expectations of the state but also, in highly nationalistic nations, put the state before self. 'You have freedom! But do not break the law!'

I thought it was interesting that many people in the United States a few years ago were convinced that speaking negatively about the government was un-American. I thought there was something in their history about freedom of speech?

What we have then on this surface is the person serving the state, church, or other entity of belief often without question.

From an outlaw point of view, i see these as conceptualisations. They are not real, except in the minds of the people who believe in them. We could say they are sociologically real in the sense that people have created them and believe them, but if we look at them from a physiological, scientific point of view, they don't exist. I have become aware many years ago that, as a person of different perspective who uses a different frame of reference for understanding, discussions with others about politics and religion are pointless because they have no way of stepping outside their common knowledge. All conversations become no more than meaningless loops.

As i write this, i am reminded of an old movie dialogue that went something like this:

> PERSON 1. What's life?
> PERSON 2. A magazine.
> PERSON 1. How much?
> PERSON 2. Ten cents.
> PERSON 1. That's too much.
> PERSON 2. Well, that's life.
> PERSON 1. What's life?
> PERSON 2. A magazine.
> PERSON 1. How much?

Well, okay, where do we go?

The Building of Other Structures and the Nature of Dualities

Heaven-earth, male-female, spiritual-biological, yin-yang, prajna-upaya—there are a myriad of literal and symbolic descriptors of dualities in the world. These dualities are descriptors that can be considered as building blocks of our vision of the world/reality. They are not just social/human and are not simply the focus of belief. They are cognitively generated and descriptive. But these descriptors can be understood on different planes.

The impact of my need to discuss the different ways in which these descriptors were used was part of the triggering event i mentioned at the beginning of this work. As we were discussing life, ideas, and relationships to others, my friend made a reference to her martial arts experiences and the fact that we had two interactive energies: 'push' or 'pull'. My internal reaction to this was profound. I knew she understood and could experience the life of the outlaw, but i also knew she could get drawn to the surface at times. I considered myself and my reaction. Would normal people react so strongly to push and pull?

It is clearly a yin/yang duality that is accepted. These are only words, someone's momentary expression. It's not that big a deal! But for a moment, my frail human need for a connection has been lost, and here is why. (I apologise to you, the reader, who may be distressed by a copula verb with an adverbal 'why', but the expression felt right).

First, she used push/pull in a 'it's either this or that' manner. The context of questioning herself made it a kind of 'You're either left wing or right wing.' In a sense, she used it in such a way that a duality became more akin to how you may describe something as right or wrong. I felt it as she was being too social/human and limited by surface perception. Though she didn't mean it in that manner, it was really an expression of insecurity. It was this insecurity i felt.

Second, i have experienced feelings of connection to her on many levels, and that felt good to me. But i also knew that my experience was not necessarily hers, and that had given me not only a sense of cautious optimism but also vulnerability. The momentary loss of connection made me aware of not only my own need for connection but also my need to reestablish my own grounding. However, this need for grounding could not be reconsidered as a defence with secondary gain, or i would simply be finding a convenient truth to make me feel better.

Third, if i wasn't emotionally open in this way, my response to push/pull could have taken many different directions. I could have become the teacher. I could have been the social 'what's life' guy. I could have been rejecting and argumentative. Or i could have realised that these symbolic duality descriptors could be understood in different ways and that my task is to rethink how i see myself, my sense of grounding, and how all the pieces of all life connect in many different ways. What may seem separate at one level is connecting at another, and what seems connected may be a disconnection.

Fourth, i was reminded that the use of this terminology may have nothing to do with the understanding of something outside the realm of social thinking.

But whatever.

I think we need to explore a little about how these yin/yang, push/pull, mind/body, heaven/earth terms can be understood and how they can help us develop a different perspective.

Before considering any spiritual or other type of perspective, let us consider these in terms of mathematics and science.

A fundamental counting system that does not consider our digits (toes and fingers) is base 2. We have 0 and 1. This system applies nicely to simple electrical connections in computers and electrical neurological assumptions for how neurons fire or don't fire in the brain. However, this base 2 system can also be considered as a limiting factor in our capacity to understand. If our brain functions in a base 2 manner, are we limited by our own system to think and understand differently? Douglas Hofstadter has written extensively on the limitations of computer thinking. How complex can multiple combinations of base 2 get? Computers are limited not just in what they can calculate but also in what questions they can ask or answer. Humans can go beyond the computer, but unless there is some different perspective or belief, humans can be seen as pretty limited.

Where could we go with our 0-1 system? Buddhist philosophies, from early on, realised the challenge of trying to describe 0. Sunyata, the voidlike nature of the universe, when talked about and defined became not void because it was a term, a defined concept. In essence, nothing became something. J. P. Sartre describes the same difficulty in <u>Being and Nothingness</u>. If i think i have twenty francs in my pocket and i look and there is nothing there, it is my mental state that has defined 'nothing'; it is not an absolute.

The same difficulty can be seen with trying to define a 'meaning' to life. If i say there is no meaning, is that being nihilistic, atheistic, antireligious? Or is my 'no meaning' statement one of truth from some point of view? The meaning is that there isn't any. Cogito ergo sum? Sum ergo cogito?

So where does zero exist? If we have a simple electrical circuit, we can say it is 'on' or 'off'. There is a current or no current. In a no-current state (zero), can we say that there is no electrical energy? No. What we can say is that the amount, location, and direction of currents that we are interested in are not sufficient or lined up enough to complete the circuit. Therefore, if we measure electrical activity with reference to the circuit, we can apply zero; if we look at it from a more dynamic perspective, we will say the electrical is 'other than zero'.

Zero is also a point in a number line. It can tell you how much money you have in your bank account. At face value 0, money can be seen as nothing. However, if you live in an overdraft, having $0 might be a good position.

What is important to me is that, for most of you, zero is pretty simple to understand. It is nothing, zilch, nada. It's what it is. Any discussion of all its nuances or other interpretations may seem frivolous and a waste of time. There is no practical purpose. But as i hope you will discover, experiencing life without some type of open-ended thinking keeps you stuck in a delusion built on unquestioned truths.

What about one? Is it as difficult to nail down? We have one universe. We have one earth. We can say there is one country, and here is another. We can show you one person. We have one centimetre. We have one brain. We have one neuron. We have one cell. We have one atom. We have one electron. Do i need to say any more?

So maybe we need to consider zero and one as practical operational terms in day-to-day life. But understand that they can also be considered in almost symbolic terms if we regard them in a broader sense. It is in this way we need to consider other dualities.

Probably the most popular dualities are mind/body, heaven/earth, and yin/yang. On the surface, these dualities may be seen as different areas of discussion; yet from another point of view, they are all the same.

Let us start with mind and body. Mind is often represented by the greek letter ψ (psyche) and is, of course, nonmaterial. It has an identity that is separate from the physiological, organic body. Mind may be seen by many of you as the feature that makes humans superior to all other species. It is akin to the soul, the spirit. It can also be seen as being deluded, pathological, evil. Yet what is its relationship to body?

K. Pribram saw mind like a hologram, while thousands of years earlier Aristotle saw it as beyond a structure/substance threshold.

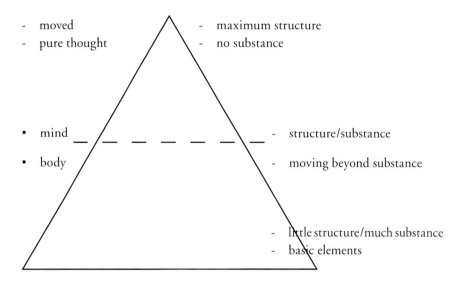

He used terms like *substance, quantity, quality, relation, place, time, position, possession, action,* and *passion* to describe how a purpose and structure could explain how nature and human life worked.

The development of psychodynamic theories in the twentieth century created a whole nomenclature for mind. We would probably have to blame Freud for really getting this trend started. His terms like *id, ego, superego, unconscious,* and *preconscious* are a few of those 'mind' terms. C. Jung used the concept of collective unconsciousness to describe a way in which minds could connect. The whole basis of psychopathology started with mind, and as we would discuss later, these previous views didn't adequately deal with mind/brain distinctions.

I feel somewhat apologetic to you, the reader, at this point because thinkers throughout history have written many books, researched, hypothesised, and philosophised on the distinction between mind and brain and its importance in the history of thought. And here, i have reviewed it in a few short paragraphs. Since this is an expression of rambling thoughts, i feel we must move on.

The first limitation i see with our understanding of concepts like mind/brain, which isn't a very exciting one, is our use of language. I have commented earlier about how these terms can be considered as social/human entities and thus limited in their scope.

A number of years ago, a not well-known philosopher named Flew addressed the 'paradigm case argument'. However, before i carry on with this discussion, i need to digress for a moment to address the definition and practice of philosophy. Philosophers love to argue, or is it really debate? We could probably all agree with this. However, for you who have not read and done philosophy in an academic manner, i feel the need to give an explanation of philosophy since it is so widely misunderstood.

If i said, 'Here is my philosophy,' you may say, 'Okay, tell me what it is, and i'll listen.' In this case, i would proceed to tell you about what i believe or my views of life. I could use many clichés to describe my views. 'Life is a bowl of cherries,' 'Man is by nature good,' or a myriad of other type of phrases. My personal philosophy may be formed on platitudes or describe a view of my raison d'être. I could say that i follow a Hebrew/Christian or Buddhist philosophy.

If someone says any of the above, he/she could be expressing a feeling, but *it is not doing philosophy*! It is probably a statement of belief, of delusion. The real world of philosophy requires a rigour of thought and expression that is as tight and disciplined as any mathematics. Every word, expression, and logical connection that is made must be done with ultimate precision. Assumptions and hypotheses need to be articulated.

The development of philosophical thinking, like mathematics and science, comes from seeing deficiencies in previous thinking and then developing new ways to address these deficiencies. One of the interesting limitations in doing philosophy, science, or mathematics is that, even though we may solve the problem of some deficiency, we may never be any closer to the truth. If we accept our numerical system on a very simple level, we may reach a state that is an inverse absolute, let's say numerically equals zero. Consider this fun analogy:

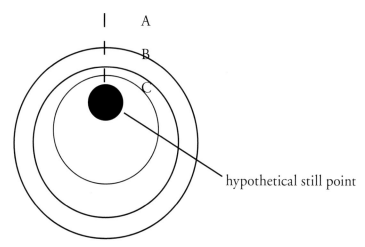

hypothetical still point

In one revolution of this wheel, point A moves 1.0 m. In one revolution, point B moves 0.5 m. In one revolution, point C moves 0.2 m. As we move closer and closer to the hypothetical centre, our point moves progressively smaller distances. It can be 1 mm, 1/1000 mm, 1/10,000 mm, $1/10^{10}$ mm, but it still has not stopped moving. It has not reached the state of no movement—the still point.

If we follow this simple progression, we could conclude that we will never reach zero and that, following the same progression of numbers, we will never reach some absolute end to a numbering system.

In doing these disciplines, one has to be prepared to accept that we will never find an absolute truth, truth, ultimate answer, or philosophy of life that meets some type of absolute statement of truth. But for some of us, not doing this is like falling into an abyss (there's a contradictory simile for you), staying in the world of avidia, or remaining in a social/human/religious delusion.

Meanwhile, back to Flew and the 'paradigm case argument', let us assume somewhat simplistically that, in every language, nouns (person, place, thing) refer to some tangible object or at least a concept where some referent exists. Sometimes these are objects. I am now looking out a window and see two squirrels, three chairs, a tree, a house, and a sky. I am in a house (that's pretty specific) in the city of Toronto, Canada (this city stuff is a little more difficult). The house is a box with boundaries, and i can see it's a single something. The squirrels, chairs, tree, and sky have the same concrete specificity. We don't have to have a definition or even a word. It's one of those things. A city or country has boundaries, but their limits are more like arbitrary 'lines in the sand'. We know where the bird ends and the sky begins. They are different entities. We can see the difference. We can have one house in the city and one house outside the city. We can see the separation between one house and another, but can we see a difference in the same way if we look at a city or noncity or sometimes one city and another adjoining city? If we don't know there is some line that separates city and noncity, we have no way of seeing this distinction.

What separates our understanding of words like *house* and *city*? Let us say that the word house refers to a specific, tangible object.

house =

(Reader aside) If you feel this style to be a little too pedantic, i will ask you to stay with me. This is a very simple, user-friendly 'doing philosophy'.

To make sense of cityness, we need more information. We can say that the word 'city' has two parts to it. First, there is a 'conceptualisation' that includes a number of required defining criteria. For instance, its definition includes some specific features. It represents a group of buildings or houses in a collective manner. It probably needs to have a certain number of people. It will have some type of governing body. It may have a cathedral as it was in the United Kingdom. As we can see, this first part of understanding *city* can be somewhat variable. And we cannot draw a picture of it in the same way we have drawn a picture of our house.

Second, if we look on a map, we can see clearly defined limits to the city, just like the house, but that is only on a map. Consider Google Maps and Google Earth or walking down a street or road. There may not be any obvious boundary between city and noncity.

$$\text{city} = \begin{cases} \text{defined features that have} \\ \text{more open specificity} \\ \text{(concept of city)} \end{cases} = \begin{cases} \boxed{\text{Toronto}} \\ \text{Lake Ontario} \end{cases}$$

As i write these words and diagrams, i feel a sense of humbleness and apology. Partially, it is the result of being different and wanting to communicate with you (the reader). I don't know what is familiar and what is not known. I'm not sure how to discuss something you probably don't really care about since it doesn't seem that important. In itself, it is not that important to me either, but it is a necessary step in seeing the world differently. So i ask you to please stay with me. I also feel stuck in the middle of things. I want to make this reader friendly. As a result, i feel that i need to apologise not only to you but also to the philosophers i know. Here i am making some simple distinctions in our use of concepts. They do not begin to address the work of a philosopher like Wittgenstein and his <u>Philosophical Investigations</u>. Hopefully, you, the reader, are following along and experiencing some new ways of thinking.

You might ask at this point, 'Where did Flew go?' All i can say is that he'll be back (just like that Austrian bodybuilder). Let us consider another type of concept. What is love? It has features, it can describe a feeling and experience, and it doesn't have a concrete, specific referent. It's not like a house or city. Of course, it can be seen as no points in a game of tennis. But if we're not talking about tennis, we can't nail it down. Or maybe love is simply a poorly pronounced l'oeuf. That is easier. If love is too difficult, we can ask a more fundamental question that we have addressed before, 'What is life?' Of course, it was a magazine (or at least was).

We have two choices here: we either have to struggle with what these words mean or transform them into simple definable entities. Certainly, transforming them is easier.

Love = 0

Life =

If we want to struggle, we can start defining *love* in terms of personal experience. Love is blind (not rational); it's emotional (oops, another unclear concept). In fact, when we think about how we define *love*, we use many other nontangible concepts to do so. But of course, we all know what it is. We can experience love even if we can't accurately define it.

So let's say that we have some words that are easy to understand because they name objects like house, bird, and so on. It is almost like they exist and we give them a name. Some words have been created by man, like 'city', that combine some nontangible defining characteristics with a tangible end result; some other words, like 'love', are not tangible, are experienced, and don't have clearly defined characteristics.

We have many words that we use daily that cannot be easily or adequately defined. Flew has taken this one step further and considered the concept 'free will'. First, it is important to note that many academic philosophers have held that there is no such thing as 'free will'. I will ask you to leave your belief aside for a minute, if you don't agree with this, and follow Flew's contention.

Flew's argument considers language and paradigm as its basis. It is not about free will. He points out that our use of concepts can be such that we can use words that are not based on a real, concrete, or experienced paradigm. He has used free will as an example of this. What he is saying then is that we have words that describe something that doesn't exist. Even though Flew's conclusion seems somewhat self-evident, some of you may have gone beyond 'free will'. You may have said to yourself, 'Of course, there is free will,' and that may have ended your ability to follow any discussion beyond that belief. Of course, there is free will! If you have made this shift, that tells us something about your ability to follow a structured discussion. This brings me to the 'belief' problem i have encountered years ago.

I had a friend whom i wanted to explain an idea to. To do this, he had to make a false assumption. I asked him, 'Pretend for a moment that there are dragons.'

He responded, 'There aren't any.'

'Just suppose,' i asked.

'But there aren't any.'

'Just pretend!' i repeated, somewhat frustrated.

'I can't because there aren't any.'

I eventually gave up. The highly significant point i was going to make was lost, though i couldn't remember what it was. However, i have experienced the same type of situation repeatedly throughout my life.

Let me repeat. What Flew has shared is that we have concepts that have meaning, even when no paradigm or situation exists. In simple terms, he is saying that we can have concepts, which are the name of something, but no one can show you an example of the concept. You may say, 'Yeah, that makes sense, but what's the big deal?'

What is important here is that we have many concepts that are transformed into a sense of being real because we use them in that way. God is real because we have a word. Sunyata is real because we have a word. God is real because i have a good feeling. We talk about mind as if it were real. 'It's my mind; i have one.'

Words—we need to keep them in perspective. For most of you, words are concrete. If they are not concrete, you transform them into something concrete and literal. At the beginning of this section, i have listed a number of dualities and talked about the difficulties i have had when they are understood on a social/human level. From my point of view, one important aspect for you, the reader, to appreciate is that the structure of one's thought shapes one's understanding of words; however, i am uncertain whether the understanding of words can shape one's structure of thought (but i hope they can).

Another important concern of mine is mutual understanding. I now realise how important a shared understanding of words is to me and know that it influences my ability to feel close to another person. I think about the profound sense of this experience frequently. Savouring words, like experiencing the nuances of wine, is important to me. I have felt the separation that words can create but have been unsure how to bridge it, especially with others who don't have the same sensitivity.

For me, this separation from others is not related to language that is critical or negative. 'You're fat, ugly, and dumb!' In fact, this language in the right context can be meaningful and show respect for language. For the writer to express self and have another share the experience can be seen as the essence of expression. It is Wassily Kandinsky who has felt that same ideal. To him, the goal of the visual arts is to have the observer share the artist's experience.

Before we return to considering symbolic dualities, i would like to talk about how concepts are used, often transformed, and in essence abused.

A Real Interlude

What is real? To one friend, the response is simple. Budgets and doing business in a manner that shows an understanding of markets and political realities, social perception, and the politically defined needs of a city, province, state, or country are real. He knows that people who agree with him are in touch with reality and that those who aren't need to change. He also has solutions to most of the world's problems. He has let me know that my concerns are removed from real life. He has no interest in exploring the possibility that his 'real world' is the creation of mankind and that reality can exist somewhere else. Even though i am describing one person, he really is representative of a vast number.

There are those who know that doing one's job and paying bills is reality, and there are others who know that the control of the world is in the hands of large multinational corporations.

'Get Real' is the name of a vegetarian restaurant. Being real can be seen as expressing yourself in a manner consistent with 'some view' of what constitutes honest self-expression.

War is real.

Death is real.

I don't know if real is used in referring to heaven, but i think real is applied to hell.

I think it is interesting that *real* is a word that has a strong tangible, concrete connotation. But it is often used to describe conceptualisations like <u>life</u>. Is it a magazine that was, or is it a word that refers to a wide range of meanings? *Real* and *life* are probably both used more metaphorically or symbolically in that they transform a nontangible referent concept into something concrete. But most who use them are not aware of this. A delusion?

If you are a person who holds that reality requires following the rules and regulations of our society, you have a common perception of reality. If you believe that you could have an influence on others but have not been given the opportunity, life/reality may be somewhat depressing; but if you are in a position where you do direct others and have an influence on their lives and what happens in the world, your view of life may be broad and consider what might be 'best' or may be highly self-absorbed.

Thomas Hardy saw the profound influence of any large collection of people who all believed in a set of social/human values that they knew were 'real'. In his pessimistic view, he felt that this belief by many was like an inert force that impaired the freedom of those who were different. However, this adverse influence of behaviour of the mass was seen differently in the film King of Hearts (by Philippe de Broca).

In this film, which takes place in a small town in France during WWII, we see the life of a number of institutionalised mental patients and their lives. We also see a battle between British and German soldiers that results in their killing each other. As a result, the mental patients are freed and enjoy their 'crazy' lives in the town.

As i write, i feel the need to apologise to you, the reader, again. People want to show off. I've read this and know this. Am i not bright! I find myself using references and acknowledging those who have influenced my thought. It is important to realise that this is me. Like my love for the world of wine, music, literature, philosophy, science, mathematics, and strangely enough religion, it is with humbleness that I apologise for being different, that is, my experience. Wow, that is a lot! Can someone really expect to know or appreciate all these? As you will see, these are all parts of the same thing.

So what *is* real?

Can real be changed? A new reality?

The area of 'real' life that is of most concern to me on a practical, helping-people, get-better level is how words are used in medicine, psychiatry, and some clinical psychology. In these areas, we have a problem with limited definitions of reality because we have a requirement to define a real cause, a real pathology, and a real treatment. To further complicate the situation, we assume that there is a cause/effect relationship that needs to be clearly defined. For some mechanistic conditions, this relationship can be evident. The person fell and broke a leg. For many other conditions, the relationship is unclear. As new research is finding out, many conditions are developmentally based, like cancer, and their aetiologies can be the result of dynamic cellular interactions. There is frequently confusion in the general practice of medicine and in psychiatry between conditional and biconditional logic. Please keep this in mind since i will explain this further down this page. As we will see, the lack of understanding language and how it is conceptualised can adversely affect the validity of any new scientific insights.

In medicine, we generally assume that pathology is 'something' that's broken. Just like your car, it isn't running properly because some 'mechanism' (the real) is not doing what it should do. When it is adjusted or replaced, it works. Let us say that

problem X is caused by broken part Y.

We also know with our car (here is a biconditional factor) that, in some circumstances, problem X will only exist when part Y is broken. This relationship can be rewritten in the following manner:

If and only if there is a broken part Y ⟷ problem X

So when the mechanic talks about problem X, he associates it immediately with broken part Y. You might ask, 'Why even diagram this? It is obvious!' However, when people talk about many conditions in medicine and psychiatry, they do so as if this biconditional connection existed, but it often doesn't. In fact, in psychiatry, it *doesn't* exist in the above-mentioned way. This doesn't mean that disorders don't exist; they do! But their dynamics and causes are unclear. And part of the problem is language based. For example, most of you have probably heard of

Tourette's. Its symptoms seem pretty straightforward. Can we say the following?

Tourette's is caused by neurological dysfunction Y, and there is a biconditional relationship between T and Y.

Here is a case where we can say that something like Tourette's is a real phenomenon and that neurological dysfunction Y is also real, but we cannot say that Tourette's is the real expression of dysfunction Y. Is Tourette's then real?

Just think of how important it is for the advancement of understanding of science to realise that we have a name for something, we may even have a definition, and we may even give treatment for it that works a lot of the time. But we don't know what it is. Here, we have dualities that are considered real but used inconsistently—pathology or no pathology, cause or effect, broken or not broken, symptom or not a symptom, conceptual or mechanistic, and conditional or biconditional.

Maybe we can conclude that *real* also includes all those human expressions that give some indication of how humans think and how their thought is structured.

Well, we have gone a long way from our discussion of dualities—or have we?

What i hope you can appreciate is that our use of words and dualities—like mind/body, yin/yang, heaven/earth—are not just simple terms and, like all concepts, can be considered from many points of view. These can be considered real because they give an indication of the human thought structure that underlies the 'real'.

I will use the metaphor of 'below the surface' to suggest a more timeless, less clearly defined sense of how these terms are used and what they mean. As we will consider, these dualities have many below-the-surface qualities that, if addressed, will give you an understanding and vision that is far beyond a simple face value acceptance.

Mixing Dualities and the Expressed Reality of Literature and Physiology

Some of these dualities mentioned earlier can be seen as tangible and 'houselike', such as male and female, while some others may have one term with a concrete referent, like brain and earth, while the opposite terms are built upon conceptual referents, like mind and heaven. Some dualities are both conceptual, such as good/evil, and others may describe a class of similar concepts, like yin/yang.

From a sexist point of view, it is fun (if you are a male) listing these dualities:

> heaven-earth
>
> mind-brain
>
> spiritual-organic/physical
>
> father-mother
>
> prajna-upaya
>
> good-evil
>
> male-female
>
> yin-yang

We could probably conclude that the 'objective scientific' support for the 'reality' of how these dualities line up comes from the Christian Bible. Adam is just hanging out, doing nothing wrong (typical good-guy male), and then Eve comes along (not so good) and tempts him. As a result, female and evil are on the same side. The rest is history.

Just in case you question this reality, i will try another approach.

What is important with this list of dualities is that they are a starting point. Since they are mutually defining, they are sometimes referred to as 'negative concomitants'. From this perspective, we can see that these opposites are really two polarised expressions of the same thing. However, as we have noted, their conceptualisations can be mixed.

But there is another way of looking at these, and that is symbolically. In this way, the terms can be used in a far more expansive manner. These symbolic energies can be seen as underlying the surface of life. The symbolic use of these negative concomitants has been extensively evident in both Western and Eastern literature.

To start with, i will pick one of my favourite writers, James Joyce.

Stephen Dedalus is a nerdy kid in a Christian brothers boarding school who has had bad experiences with water. Kids have pushed him in the ditch, and he has wet his bed. This has led to embarrassment, being teased, and alienation by peers. At the story level, there is a kind of literal cause and effect that is fairly evident. However, with Joyce, we can see that this experience has no significance in itself. What is important is that the symbolic nature of water ties into a whole set of 'organic' symbols used in <u>The Portrait of the Artist as a Young Man</u> and <u>Ulysses</u>, which are somewhat consistent with our list.

To Joyce, in these novels, water is organic, biological, and earthy and is expressive of physical drives and experiences that include sexual drive, bathing, toileting, his motherland, and the creation of bad art. For instance, Stephen has his first feeling of sexual attraction to a girl who is wading in water at the beach. At this point, Stephen has a conflicting 'organic' experience. Sexual attraction is experienced as positive, but there is a conflict for him because water has been experienced as negative. However, this momentary symbolic experience needs to be considered within the context of a dominant symbolic theme. But because of Stephen's nerdy intellectual abilities and acceptance of the Christian brothers dogma, which is coupled with this avoidance of the organic, he has developed a desire to be intellectual/spiritual and avoid water and human urges.

I ask you, Joyce scholars, to be tolerant since i suggest that the dynamics are correct, but in trying to make this simple, the chronological manifestation of these dynamics in *The Portrait* are not correct. Once again, i feel a sense of distress because i find it difficult to not meet the standard of the most astute critic. But i do appreciate that most of you have not even read James Joyce. Not unlike Stephen, i can experience a certain amount of loneliness in having my self-imposed standards that can only be appreciated by so few. Most of you may not understand or care. It may be seen as unrealistic—'maybe one cannot be expected to meet all those expectations'—but i say why not?

Joyce in <u>Ulysses</u> offers a symbolic way out for Stephen and partially for myself. At the beginning of the novel, Stephen avoids water and bathing. He lives in a small tower. Leopold Bloom, who can be seen as a symbolic 'opposite' of Stephen, is first seen in the bath. Bloom is seen as a father without a son, while Stephen is seen as a son without a father (as his father died). Both of these characters are symbolically incomplete. What Joyce does is bring these two characters together, but more importantly, he addresses the need for having an integration or union of the intellectual and organic. Father and son, organic and intellectual are combined with the meeting of the two characters.

Though Joyce was not thinking about neurophysiology nor were the thinkers who have used these dualities, i could use the same chemistry-type equations to explain these practical dynamics.

- SC is the organic and can be seen as a driver of emotional experience that he wants to avoid.
- PFC is the intellectual and cognitive safety of ideas.

At the end of *The Portrait,*

Stephen: (SC + (PFC)) ———————▶ intellectual/alone/avoidance of
            inhibition   water/earth/female
            of SC

At the beginning of *Ulysses*:

      (SC + (PFC)) ———————▶ intellectual/alone/avoidance of
                           water/earth/female

Leopold Bloom: (SC + (not expressed PFC)) ———▶ the symbolic
                                       expression of father
                                       combined with the
                                       organic

As you read novels like <u>Ulysses</u>, you may find the story somewhat hidden not just because of complexities in Joyce's writing style but also because the story is simply a structure for establishing an important symbolic transformation. In a sense, it is also an expression of emphasis. Within the microcosm of one day is the macrocosm of the epic. Specifically, it's a story about one day in Dublin, June 16, 1904. The two main characters spend some time together and end up at 7 Eccles Street, Leopold Bloom's home. But it is also an epic. Each part of Stephen's day in Dublin parallels a part of the adventures of Ulysses. On another level, it is the bringing together of symbolic opposites. It is a study of creative thinking and art.

If what i have expressed is somewhat clear to you, then we can begin to see that there is a way of understanding a story and life that is below the surface. We need to be cautiously aware because sometimes the excitement of the story may distract us from other dynamics but probably not in Joyce. Excitement in Joyce comes from the discovery of following symbolic connections.

For instance, we can have an exciting sea story and relate the tale. Let us say that the protagonist goes out to sea against another's advice and achieves some personal goal, such as catching a fish (Hemingway), sailing from A to B (Conrad), saving someone, or achieving some other important goal. The challenges are described in detail, and you, the reader, are uncertain about whether the protagonist will achieve his goal or return to his home port.

The reader's experience may focus on how exciting the story is, whether the story is predictable or has some unexpected elements, whether characters are believable, and other such elements. If one is studying this in school, the instructor may begin by looking at plot, theme, and types of conflict. All of the above are certainly part of the reading experience, but they are at a social/human level. They may not address the essence of a work, though it could be, of course, that the story has been written to entertain and does not attempt to go beyond this.

As a child, i liked reading novels on sea battles that were fiction or historical fiction. They entertained me, and i learned something.

The work of Joseph Conrad and Hemingway's <u>The Old Man and the Sea</u> can be experienced on different levels. Conrad's descriptions of adversity at sea can be exciting, and Santiago's voyage can be considered more trying, but both are user-friendly stories.

There's a self-evident conclusion here. So let's state the obvious. Some writing that is easy to read on the surface may have depth, and some other writing that also has depth may be less user-friendly.

So what is this depth?

The surface story of Ulysses is an epic. Telemachus has many sailing adventures, his voyage takes years, and his journey influences the world. The Joycean story of Ulysses takes place in one day. But no day can be epic. Or can it? It is a story of two people. His characters are not leaders or able to influence the world. So where's the epic? What is epic isn't what is seen by just reading the story; it is its universal significance. In the case of Joyce, it is universal importance of the creative process that is of significance.

A metaphor using two anchored ships may help.

The Epic Ship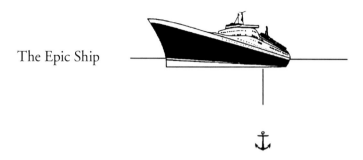

The huge ship, of epic proportions, is anchored in shallow water with a small anchor. Its importance is what we see on the surface. Both its timeless significance and its vulnerability can only be evident by looking below the surface and what and how it is anchored.

The Joycean Epic Ship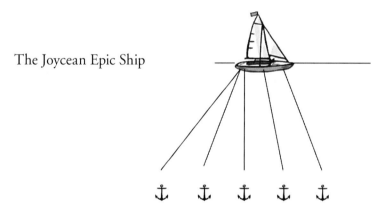

The epic ship is small and unassuming on the surface, but underneath, it is anchored into a depth of universal significance.

From a literary criticism point of view, this depth is expressed by underlying structures and dynamics. And some of these structures and dynamics can be described in terms of dualities, like the organic and intellect (physical/mental). Thematically then, the novel isn't just about a developing relationship or about Stephen Dedalus showing the readiness to be the artist. It is about the need to combine the organic and intellect in artistic expression. It is creative expression that requires the integration of mind and body with a grounding in the universal. The epicness is this combination. It is universal and timeless.

T. S. Eliot, in 'The Wasteland', describes Cleopatra in a world of opulence and grandeur, and this image is juxtaposed with the image of a labouring woman who is home from work and is alone in her tiny room in London. What is important here is that both images express the despairing loneliness of these two people.

We may have wars based on ideologies, like freedom/democracy, religion, human rights, or other such social/human concerns. These seem like 'real' important issues. But what we may structurally have can be something quite different. All these can be seen as expressions of the species, an underlying order (structure).

If this underlying structure is actually reality, we might conclude that it is in the arts that reality is often spoken. Let's see the social/human reality first.

Let us assume that country A is attacking country B because B is a threat to A. The leaders of country A hold the following views: 'We in country A know that we have the right set of values, and we do not behave in a manner inconsistent with our values. Our values are based on religious teachings that are unquestionably correct. People who don't accept our values are bad, wrong, and possibly evil.'

Guess what? Country B probably holds the exact same set of beliefs.

If country A is big and country B is small, B may use terrorist tactics to counter the perceived imperialism of A (the IRA, al-Qaeda). A then comes back with armies to defeat B—more imperialism. What we have are two structurally identical entities battling. The universal here can be considered as the myriad of human qualities. I often say that it is the nature of the beast that is expressed. It continuously manifests itself in the social/human world. But more about this later.

If these battles were considered in the same underlying manner as we have discussed, we would see the surface conflict entirely differently.

Consider the following species factors:

- surface management of the world and attempts to obtain international agreements
- extreme expressions of the species from intolerance to racism, imperialism, wars, and terrorism
- species expressions that are ephemerally and selectively evident
- ethnocentrism of the species

Consider some symbolic factors that might explain country B's rationale:

- good against evil
- spiritual against physical
- father against mother
- yin against yang

What we could say using our symbolic dualities from a single country's perspective:

From country A's point of view, it is good vs. evil.

From country B's point of view, it is good vs. evil.

What might we see using our symbolic dualities from a more global perspective?

Country B may be seen as overaggressive, terrorist, or guilty of violating human rights from a global perspective. For some but not all, B could be seen as evil, and B could hold on to an ideology that makes them good and others evil.

So how does this happen? Are these the result of surface conditions?

Throughout history, the arts have often presented another perspective of this world of 'experience' as William Blake called it. They have often considered similarities, not differences, or offered a self-reflective picture of the human condition. In a different manner, medical and psychological sciences have approached an understanding of the human condition and expressed behaviours.

So what lies beneath all these human behaviours from a physiological point of view? Surely, this is the basis of what is real.

Let's return to our discussions for the basic elements of human drive and our chemistry-type equations used on pages 30 and 31. By using a combined social science/neuroscience perspective and the descriptors used before, we have the following:

There is a basic (SC) driven emotion with, let's say, a highly ethnocentric, deluded thought, which gains strength by having bimodal, negatively concomitant drives that are both very strongly held. The people have strongly held beliefs that derive part of their intensity from an antagonistic view and even fear of other beliefs. This drive can be defined in terms of a basic, (SC) subcortical fear/fight and emotion coupled with deluded thought.

Though not scientifically correct, i will define *deluded thought* in these cases as thought that has unsupported ethnocentric beliefs that don't inhibit basic drives (fear, fight) but transforms (rationalises) these beliefs into a life-and-death struggle. Consider the following:

SC + (PFC deluded) $\longrightarrow$ (conflict with) $\longleftarrow$ SC + (PFC deluded)

Here is a simple proof:

SC (fear/fight) + (deluded PFC) $\longrightarrow$ I'll kill you or be killed.

(no SC) + (ideological belief) $\longrightarrow$ no SC drive of fear/fight; openness or lack of openness would be a function of cognitive ability.

$\uparrow$

- increased (SC) $\longrightarrow$ transformation of PFC (into i am right/good, and you are bad/evil)
  (PFC doesn't inhibit but integrates SC and PFC in a rationalised manner.)

$\uparrow$

- increased (SC) + (no PFC influence) $\longrightarrow$ I'll fight you because you are a threat; no inhibition occurs.

SC sensitivity and driving influence is increased. As a result, at least with humans, a threat to safety and fear can be generated not just by physical safety but also by ideology.

So if both sides are in the same state, we have these opposing conditions of the same thinking. At the surface, they seem different; but if we just go slightly under, we can see they are the same.

We have <u>i am right</u> battling <u>i am right</u>.

If we review the above statement, we can reask an earlier question.

What is real?

Is reality the things that happen in the story of life? Or is reality the underlying dynamics that help explain this story?

Let us reconsider our dualities as symbols of underlying energies that help explain how things work. The irony of Icarus's attempt to find spiritual truth and fly to the sun is that he ends up immersed in the organic.

We might say that his dilemma is real. It is what the church has done to priests. It is what our two battling countries actually achieve. They want to see themselves as controlled by PFC, but in reality, their SC sexual needs have not diminished.

My own balance can be seen in the same manner. To not be connected is one side of a 'connection/no connection' duality. But of course, a connection can be on different levels.

I can say that i don't connect with living people, but i do connect with people i don't know are dead. Now that will be weird! By the way, i don't disagree with this, but let me explain.

Years ago, while being trained in group therapy, we did an exercise that was used to give participants a sense of the variable nature of their qualitative human relationship experience. Concentric circles were drawn on a sheet of paper, and each person's task was to place friends and family

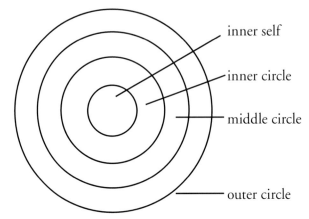

inner self

inner circle

middle circle

outer circle

(people you know) at different distances from self. Typically, inner-circle people included spouses, parents, children, lifelong friends. As you would expect, most participants would be able to clearly decide the position of ten to twelve people in these different circles.

Given that i was young with no children and absorbed in writing, i responded a little differently. I placed authors (all of whom had died, but that was coincidental, not by design) in my inner circles. Real people, i moved further out.

When responses were reviewed, i was told, 'You can't do that.' Of course, i asked why. I explained that reading all the works of a person was like meeting them many times. I knew them intimately and, in many ways, much better than most other human relationships. At the end of this particular training session, which was a several-day retreat, all participants put their arms around one another, got into a circle, and verbally expressed how they felt. Others used words like 'caring' and 'sharing'. I said nothing but felt like saying 'distressed' and 'vomit'. It was not that i didn't appreciate the positive nature of expressed feelings but realised that these positive feelings were based on little real connection that could be easily transformed into negative, if not at one another, at some socially defined 'bad guy'. It was this vulnerability of the human spirit that concerned me.

Here is another reality.

So what about connections for me?

Reflections on Relationships
for Nonducks

I realise that i cannot live, as i mentioned earlier, only grounded in those realities below the surface. I need a human relationship that embodies a number of levels. This relationship doesn't have to be exclusive, but the personal satisfaction of having someone as part of my life is profound.

It would be interesting to note that, from a language point of view, i could have used 'it' to replace the antecedent 'relationship' but couldn't do it. The word 'it' didn't work. Using the word 'it' significantly weakened the importance of 'relationship'.

My survival (wow, that's a strange word) had been predicated on, except for family, moving on. This moving on has had several connotations to me. In my late teens and twenties, i lived in many different places. I travelled, worked at odd jobs, coached skiing, and studied at a number of universities. During these years, i spent considerable time with people, but i would move on and never see them again. During my years of working for someone else (not many), i met and spent time with people whom i never saw again once i moved on. I also found that my life was enriched while practising psychotherapy. It was interesting because it required the depth of what i found in literature, but it also had the element of dealing with a real person; these people got better and moved on.

As i have discussed, social friendships have been there for a long time, but the level of personal satisfaction has generally been very limited. But they are 'nice' people. Bertrand Russell has written a chapter in his book <u>Why I Am Not a Christian</u> called '<u>Nice People</u>'. I assume the content, given that our thinking is similar (mine is to his), is self-evident.

Putting all this aside for a moment, i can simplify my experience by expressing my feelings; i have a desire to connect that sounds healthy and normal. I have someone who satisfies this desire for me. That sounds positive. I think i can even say that my friend feels positively about me. However, the nature, degree, and interactive dynamics of this positiveness are important. Is this 'two guys hanging out together', or are the positives experienced by both people reciprocal, or are there differences (duality of reciprocal/not reciprocal)?

If we look at this at face value, the 'two people hanging out together' sounds male/male but can be female/female or male/male. And of course, the romantic relationship can have the same gender dualities. Some other dualities come to play here also.

As you, i hope, will appreciate, my experience isn't simply one of self-indulgence but is a representation of the dynamics of one human's surface frailty. The little sailboat in our epic picture experiences life on many integrated levels. This little boat cannot sail away until all factors at all levels work together.

The whole sense of hetero/homosexual (another duality) or sexual/platonic (yet another duality) relationship is also considerations in explaining desire. If i apply these dualities to me, i can say that the real expression of my desire is heterosexual in one of its dynamics; but strangely enough, it is neither sexual nor platonic. But to say that it is both is not correct. As an expression of my needs, using dualities in their typical form doesn't work.

If i am going to have any relationship with another (a highly selfish motivation) in which i see the potential for many levels of connection, i need to never become a victim of delusion. We have discussed this. You can say, 'This is how i feel. This is great. You should feel the same way.' You can also say, 'I am a christian. Christianity is the answer for everyone. You must feel the same way!'

If you practised psychotherapy, you could say, 'I have been a very successful psychotherapist. I have great insight into the human psyche. Therefore, i know what you want.' It is amazing when i think of how these attitudes can be used in promoting a sense of arrogance, especially with those people who have had social/human success.

If i were to dwell on me, i would not be leading you or me anywhere. What about my friend (self/other duality, or to me, it is really self/self)? What is her experience? How does she see herself? How does she see me?

Before considering my understanding, i would like to talk a little more about the range of experiences that the creative (outlaw) person can have. Some people, while growing up, have less than positive experiences because of their own nature, their needs, and their fit with others. Stephen Dedalus, our nerdy Joycean kid, is a good example of this. Fortunately for people like Stephen, experience can be very negative on one level but can be very enriching on other levels, though people may or may not appreciate that distressing experiences are positive. Here is another duality of a different sort—positive/negative becomes negative = positive.

From a social/human point of view, what might be someone's experience if they were not to follow their own natural insights and talents? Their behaviour could seemingly be transformed into social/human directed behaviour. Thus working, being responsible, understanding the value of money, and doing well in school are all learned as important since we could consider that there is also a peer influence that sees that it is important to be part of the group and that belonging in some manner is also important. If we assume that there is a need for all people to have some fairly significant identifying entity to reinforce that you are okay, then the need to be connected may override those unique qualities and needs that are inherent. Some adolescents may become overcompliant and focus on being good and doing good schoolwork. Others may become obsessed with computers, playing the role of the artist, while others may play the role of the social rebel and be part of the party group and just have fun. These roles may be more extreme for some than others. If i consider these roles from a social/human point of view and from a long-term expression of self, i see them all very differently.

Socially, most people will probably agree that being the good student is the most desirable and that being the party kid is the least desirable.

However, consider the reverse order. Even though there may be some risk in being the party adolescent, this usually doesn't last; and at least it is an expression of the person's adolescent individuality, of letting go, and of having fun. Conversely, being overcompliant to adult norms may destroy the development of individual creative thought and experience. So we could have *good* social behaviour that is *bad* for the person. We could also speculate that thought and behaviour that could be seen as socially bad may be observed while creative thinking is developing, which in turn could have a *good* social outcome (e.g., this bad person develops some new technology that has a good effect on society).

Here are some more contradictory dualities.

If we consider connections using our concentric circles, we could see several possibilities in the relationship dynamics for a unique person. But before we go any further in looking at connections, i will break the self down into two further circles:

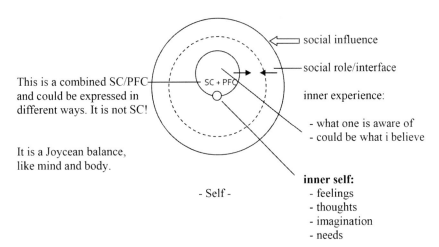

In essence, i am considering that each of us has some characteristics that are unique to us and somewhat define who we are in some hypothetical sense. For example, some children have a great imagination and enjoy their own thinking and fantasy, while others are more outgoing and are not so reflective. Some children are sensitive, and others aren't; some are into everything, and others aren't. Some children are outgoing, and others aren't. We can list many of these types of characteristics.

Let's call the driver of these traits the 'inner self'. The next level, the broken line, is used to define the area of experience and awareness. Younger children may not be aware of their own characters; they just do what is enjoyable. Once the awareness of experience kicks in, it may offer enjoyment, but it may also offer conflict. Let me consider the next circle, the one of social role. Because we live on this social/human plane, we learn that there are certain things you are supposed to do and not do. There will be times when my inner self wishes to express itself, but one may learn that what i would like to do is not socially correct. You might enjoy thinking about an enjoyable experience, but social expectations require that you listen to a lecture on molluscs. A child may enjoy playing and doesn't want to come to dinner. To function in society, we learn and adapt to social influences/expectations, but are we defined by these influences?

If your ways of thinking and feeling are somewhat consistent with the ways society thinks, the fit is easy; if your makeup is different, making connections could be difficult or even very difficult.

It is important to note that my conceptualisation of this inner self is not necessarily an SC as we have referred to it previously since one important function of the midbrain is a need for safety. For most of us who have a different way of experiencing thought, this inner self is probably more PF in character. SC may underlie this thinking when one becomes aware that he/she is different and not understood, which could include a lack of feeling safe. It may even be experienced as depressive or anxious in character or even seen as psychotic.

If we take this information and reconsider our concentric circles that describe connections, we can see childhood and adolescent connections more dynamically.

If our unique person who has not fit because his/her inner self has never had the kind of connection that validates self, life could be one of isolation, even with family love and support. These certainly, for the child, would be experienced emotionally in their inner circle (core), but this experience of being loved would not necessarily undo a sense of not being understood. In fact, it could most likely magnify it. We could make a distinction here between being loved and being understood by placing this 'not understood' piece in an outer circle just outside the 'being loved' (inner) one.

A simple metaphor for expressing this is Hans Christian Andersen's 'The Ugly Duckling'. The baby swan, a.k.a. the ugly duck, is loved by the mother duck but is still ugly and not accepted by other ducks. Unfortunately, our social/human life does not offer a large number of swans for our unique person to identify with. Is the swan not only an ugly duck but also a bad duck?

Here is yet another tangent. Anthony Burgess in A Clockwork Orange and Stanley Kubrick, in the film, address an important social/human dilemma. To me, the fundamental questions of these works relate to the freedom of creative expression. The artist in his/her expression of inner self may violate social/human comfort. Beethoven in the movie is coupled with sexual assault. Both potentially violate social norms. Since most people are now ambivalently comfortable with Beethoven, possibly a better composer who offered a creative 'threat', but still in the last century, is Stravinsky. However, the important point here is that the expression of the inner self of some of us can be seen as the source of beauty. Please note that i will use beauty in a somewhat generic manner. Consider 'beauty' as expressive of any profoundly moving artistic work, and to this i will add that these forms of creative expression may be the only driving force that gives this social/human plane any meaning, any hope.

'Beauty is so rare a thing / So few drink of its fountain.'

So let's ignore the social/human plain for a second; therefore, good and bad have those opposite connotations. If you are the good student and want to please all the adult ducks, teachers, and parents and you are really the swan, you have sacrificed who you are. Connections here are being accepted (emotionally) and could override who i am. This is bad!

On the opposite side, if you spent time being the party, rebel duck, you may not have given up your sense (though it could be quite buried) of being different (the swan). Your social connection may really have nothing to do with your uniqueness, but your social expression may say, 'I'm part of the group, but i am different.' This may be good as long as you don't get lost on the expressive social/human surface. This sense of being lost could actually be the conflict between social expression and a sense of self that doesn't fit. Think of all the jazz/rock musicians that may lose their way often with drugs or alcohol and may even die at twenty-seven. But at least they create!

The middle ground here may be that of the 'nerd'; one realises that they are not a duck and don't care to be a duck and maybe haven't really even cared that much about it. This could be okay. But you could be labelled as autistic, and you may not have the social/human drive to deal with that social/human plane. Your view could be 'Society can do whatever. I'll just live in my head.' Here, human connections don't really matter; you have realised that you don't get them, so why dwell on them? This is not so good because there is no attempt to express, but maybe that's not so bad.

My Friend and Others:
The Nonduck Realities[3]

To return to my friend, i see her as having an inner self that is wonderfully gifted. She has an intuitive ability to sense, feel, experience, and articulate (if other factors don't dampen) an underlying beauty that is beyond what i have ever experienced before, without considering any selfish motivation because at one point i had none. This person lives a life that, from a social/human point of view, is very distant from me. There is no similarity, but i have come to realise we are totally different in almost every way but totally the same (another contradictory duality).

As i write this, i feel the need to explain that my writing must be understood, knowing that i use poetic licence. As she reads this, i am worried that she will feel some pressure of expectation; but for the moment, consider this only as poetic. For you who are not familiar with the concept of poetic licence, it refers to those expressions that meet the structures of writing and emphasis but may not reflect reality.

We need to remember that for the regular kid, typical social/human expectations are congruent with their human needs.

From a simplistic point of view, someone grows up as a swan in a world of ducks, but there are no swans to be found, at least in the early years. For these people, life is somewhat similar to Stephen Dedalus, but there isn't an intellectual/creative mode to hang on to. What there is, is confusion, ambivalence, isolation, dulled senses. Here is another example where our symbolic dualities can be accounted for but are unable to explain the dynamics of human experience. It's not one or the other.

---

[3]   A consideration from a number of conceptual points of view.

What is the relationship between self and others, self and the world? How has this influenced your life experience? One socially perceived duality for the creative, inner-focused person is 'strong/weak'. Please note that these are taken from physics and, as you will see, are used in this manner. These forces that can emerge with different balances throughout life can influence what i call integration. In essence, what can happen is that the 'working together' of the 'inner self' and the social role interface can become disconnected. Interestingly enough, i can see this happening in two ways. One way i diagram this separation is with concentric circles. I draw a heavy line between the inner self and the social self.

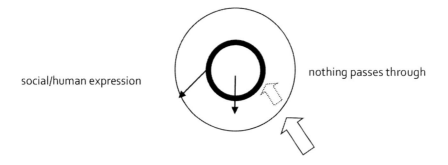

The other way i diagram this is in a vertical manner, with a vertical barrier that is moveable (laterally).

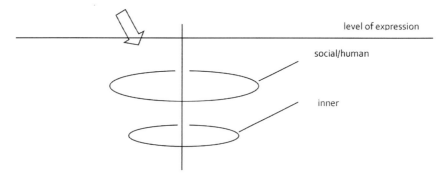

Let me explain these two.

The first one is fairly simple in its dynamics. It can describe the person who gives up on his/her inner self. (It becomes atrophied.) This person could become politically correct and see all life on that level. It can describe the person who has no unique aspects of inner self.

Years ago, i had many discussions with a Canadian writer by the name of George Ryga about the creative potential of all people. He felt that all people have the potential for unique creative thought, and my sense was they didn't. I think i still hold that view. Some people are ducks all the way through.

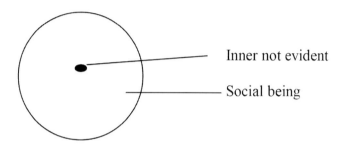

Inner not evident

Social being

It can describe the rebel who may have lost a sense of inner self, but the energy possibly driven by the frustration of being different is transformed into social/human protest.

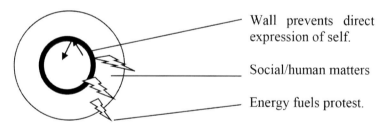

Wall prevents direct expression of self.

Social/human matters

Energy fuels protest.

It can also describe the depressed, social-anxious person who still thinks and feels differently and has no understanding of how to be accepted in society.

All these tie nicely into our dualities but don't explain the more complex person.

The other way i describe this interaction is more dynamic and allows for all the above expressions but many more, all from the same person.

To better understand and appreciate my friend and her life, i needed to develop something new—something more fluid, changeable, and dynamic that didn't minimise her importance. Of course, in doing this, i was developing a better understanding of the human psyche. (Nonorganic?)

It is almost as if the following could be the underlying structure for a novel. This is not a deep, symbolic structure but is the skeleton upon which a story could be built. In a sense, it could be considered that the interpretation exists before the novel. It could also be seen as a very personal account that helps us expand our understanding of the dynamics that lie beneath the surface. To some of you, describing human dynamics in mathematical and analytical terms may seem unfeeling. But as i will attempt to explain, they inspire the dynamics that can result in giving one a good feeling. What i feel is that we have yet another contradiction. It is possible that this nonfeeling structure may be necessary for giving one's ability to feel. What i will describe is very personal but not personal at all. Here we go.

I will consider my friend in a very personal/nonpersonal manner. Let us start with considering a Blakean inner innocence, coupled with a sensitivity that picks up different energies and has different ways of experiencing. My sense, in looking back from the present through her life as i feel it, is that this inner self is at one with the magical, the exciting, and the fantastic.

In many ways, her sensitivity to people was the object of these. We could speculate that if we could connect the inner with the inner, this would be wonderful.

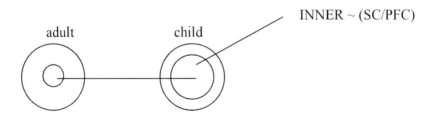

But before exploring her spirit, we need to consider some contextual aspects. If we consider little children from an adult perspective, we would see them as more honest, probably more inner self with PFC naivety. I think my friend had a different balance of inner dynamics than the usual child. SC was probably more empathy, and PFC was probably fulfilled with curiosity and a stream of conscious thinking at an enhanced level. I think she would have felt and experienced her own inner life in a much enriched manner, but we could also see that she expressed herself socially in a very cautious manner, especially in her early years. We could assume that her family environment was loving and typical in its acceptance of social norms. The mother was caring and supportive, though probably a bit confused about her somewhat different daughter. She probably worried. The dad (notice the difference in noun), who had strength in his convictions, knew that you need to work hard and understand the value of money, and he could appreciate the need for entrepreneurial drive (though could see their strengths and weaknesses). But he was not their type, though he had tried some ventures. He had never felt successful in a social/human way, but it would seem that he also realised that some people who saw themselves as successful were 'less' successful than he was. To be somewhat cliché, he—in many ways—represented the work ethic that has been a fundamental principle in North American social/human culture.

What i find interesting here is the 'strong/weak'. Here is a duality that can be seen from several points of view. In physics, let's say that the strong force keeps the components of the atom together, and the weak force (which isn't weak in the typical sense of the word) is involved with transformations. From our symbolic perspective, we could consider the strong force as holding the inner self together and the weak force as a social transformation force. In the same way, we could consider that the artist needs a strong inner self force but also requires a weak force to have this inner voice transformed and socially expressed. Somewhat ironically, from a purely social/human perspective, what may be commonly seen as strength may be nothing more than social vibrato that is without any inner strength.

From our consideration of these forces, another important characteristic of my friend emerges. It ties nicely into our dualities at one level, but unfortunately for some readers, i feel that any explanation of influential factors requires a further explanation of dynamics. Let us assume that someone could say, 'I could be seen as relatively unassertive in my expression of self in a social context, but i do have strength in character!' This statement makes complete sense once we look at it but may not make sense at face value.

If we take the influences in my friend's life in symbolic terms, we have a number of factors.

- We have an inner self that is unique and could be considered as enriched.
- We have maternal influences that are composed of emotional/social/value qualities. For our discussions, we could consider the mother as symbolically maternal with some integration of forces.
- We have dad influences that are more social/human in focus. The dad has to deal with the world and may even overlook his personal well-being. He has a strongly articulated sense of social/human values. He could be considered symbolically paternal.
- We have strong/weak dualities, which can be defined from different points of view and, therefore, can have symbolically contradictory meanings.
- We also have the influence of reading, fantasy, or others who, like my connection with writers, in that inner circle, offer an important connection.

If we take these dynamics, put on a quasi-mathematical hat, we can see a number of possible outcomes.

Let us consider the strong/weak duality from three points of view. Let's start with a social/human point of view. We will consider the 'self' of the developing child as weak, to represent a beginning state with the potential to develop, and the 'paternal' dealing with the world as strong.

<u>self</u>	<u>mother</u>	/<u>dad</u>	<u>ideal/fantasy</u>
weak	weak	strong	weak

If we accept those at a simple symbolic level, we are saying that dealing with the social/human world is what one has to do. That's reality! It is 'strong'!

Before exploring the symbolic, there is another use of the socially defined 'strong' and 'weak' i need to express. In physics, these terms are more akin to describing balancing forces in the universe, like up and down, + and -. There is no value judgement. So as i describe the symbol and my friend, i see strong/weak duality in many different ways simultaneously. Ibsen has addressed the fallacy of this socially defined 'strong/weak' in <u>A Doll's House</u> (first produced in 1899). In this play, the audience slowly learns that Nora, who is called 'my little songbird' by her husband, has actually supported her husband both financially and emotionally through some bad times. She has the strength, not him. In fact, present humour will often see the male as weak and wimpy and women as strong, especially in the face of human stressed adversity.

So we could have another assumed structure:

<u>self</u>	<u>mother</u>	<u>dad</u>	<u>ideal/fantasy</u>
weak	strong	weak	weak

But this is still social in nature. What comes with this strong/weak duality is a belief/value concomitant. You would probably accept that strength of character is based on such qualities as 'living up to your convictions', doing what needs to be done even if you don't like doing it, and being responsible and accountable. Typically, at a social/human level, these strengths are defined by appropriate social behaviour.

So you could say that you have strength of character if you meet some of the above criteria, but if you don't do anything, it would be pretty hard to convince yourself or another of your strength. However, i would suggest, just to complicate the picture, that it is possible to separate the strong + social qualities union. What i am suggesting is that one could have the experience of strength and identify with it, but it could manifest itself in different ways. One could be a rebel, avoidant, passive-resistant, stubborn, strongly opinionated, persistent, aggressive, or argumentative or show a bunch of other such qualities and behaviours.

An interesting irony is evident here. If we consider the above examples of strength, we could consider them as frequently inappropriate socially. Rebels are anti. Avoidant, resistant, and stubborn are not qualities that are seen as socially desirable. And for people like rebels, their social/human strength is seen as their nonacceptance of social norms. But as we have discussed earlier in looking at the outlaw, the rebel is simply the other side of the 'for or against' coin. The rebel accepts the reality of the social/human world. The use of the word *cathexis* may help explain this acceptance. Cathecting an object or person means that you are giving it a special significance. This significance could be considered literally or symbolically. Let's say that someone is rebelling against the society's need to chase the almighty dollar/pound/euro. This person contends that he/she doesn't need money and so makes a point of having just enough to get by and rejects any opportunity to make more. What we see is that this person cathects money in the same way a person who wants it does. In essence, money is very important, but his/her belief is the opposite. This belief blocks one's ability to be self-reflective and understand the dynamics of their own feelings. Is this position weak or strong?

From a social perspective, the person lacking inner strength but socially resilient can be seen as 'strong' based on social expression. Here is our big ship poorly anchored. However, there is a third more insightful way of considering this duality.

Let's consider 'strong' not from a social perspective but from a sense/experience of self and its connection with 'universal significance', the 'beyond self' and the 'within self'. Let's say that this person has freedom of thoughts and imagination that are not compromised by 'social have-tos. The self could be seen as the embodiment of a free spirit. Here is the strong force.

But in this case, the social/human label of 'weak' could be applied because this free spirit is *not* becoming engulfed in social/human surface pressures and dealing with reality; and from this perspective, the socially 'strong' could be seen as 'weak', and the weak could be seen as 'strong'. 'Jesus loves us, this we know, for the Bible tells us so.' Is it because he is weak and we are strong or the opposite? Cogito ergo sum.

Symbolically, this perspective gives us a balance of weak and strong.

self	mother	dad	ideal/functioning
strong/weak	strong/weak	weak/strong	strong

So what does all this say about my friend? Is she weak or strong? Is she tied to the social/human plane or not? Is she the rebel or not? Is she a combination of both?

I would say yes. My sense is that her experience as a child did have an aspect of dissociation, but she did develop an identification with her dad and his 'strong' symbolic qualities. Though her identification, i think, could be seen as somewhat conflicted because she sensed an inner strength in her dad that was his sense of self, that was not expressed in the social realm. She also experienced his social/human 'strength', which sometimes made her feel anxious and question her own socially expressive behaviour.

However, i would say that the development of her natural inner self, which could be seen as weak from a social/human point of view and strong inner perspective, would probably have benefitted from a philosopher father, but who knows? It would seem that a parent who had a strong inner being would have enhanced her development and helped in the emergence of her own unique identity, though her inner strengths did come from reading and her own stream of conscious thinking. But from a family perspective, they were seen as being in the realm of fantasy, not reality. Her experience was also influenced by an unconscious acceptance of a social/human definition of 'strong' and 'weak'. As a result, she saw herself as socially different, internally strong but wanting socially meaningful attachments. My sense of her is that when she was in school, she tried to be a regular kid, but it didn't really work.

It wouldn't be a big jump in logic to equate socially different and somewhat inept to the weak.

What she has picked up from her dad is a sense of 'strength with integrity'. What i feel resulted from these dynamics goes in a number of different directions. First, i don't feel that a good sense of self could be established. Let us return to our equation.

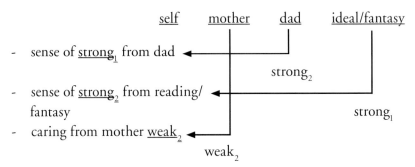

$$\underline{self} \qquad \underline{mother} \qquad \underline{dad} \qquad \underline{ideal/fantasy}$$

- sense of $\underline{strong}_1$ from dad

$$strong_2$$

- sense of $\underline{strong}_2$ from reading/ fantasy

$$strong_1$$

- caring from mother $\underline{weak}_2$

$$weak_2$$

This diagram makes things even more confusing. Our sub_1 represents inner states and our sub_2 represents socially defined states. But the result is that we have a dynamic mess.

I feel that her challenge of this strong/weak duality is complicated by the fact that the strong is typically seen as a package deal. One is either strong or weak; that's reality. My friend certainly has a sense of her own 'strength', but with it comes the social/human perception because that is the way it is manifested in her experience, thus her confusion and sometimes defensiveness.

We know that writers like Henry Miller would never be seen as symbolically 'weak', but reading fantasy on life about a family and children growing up on the prairies could be seen as 'weak'. That's someone else's fictional life!

In essence, what needed to happen was for her to take her dad's 'strength', drop the social/human, and replace it with the fantasy/novel. In this case, the 'weak' force would represent the transformation of her fantasy into social expression, which we know may still be seen as weak by the driven type A personality.

What she did was both.

However, doing both presents some problems, especially since she does not have an external real person, swan, or adult to identify with and to draw out her 'inner self'. Ideally, this kind of child will benefit from an adult who dwells on the surface but is anchored below or a child friend with whom there is a shared spirit.

As just mentioned, her emerging sense of strong/weak duality became very confusing and conflicting in some contexts until she could be understood.

If we keep our social/human definition of 'strong', we can see the following:

- She identified with her dad, his strength, his integrity, and many of his social/human values in a cathected manner. On the surface, she wouldn't necessarily agree (strong/weak).
- She could have identified with the rebel and make her point of being different by not complying or caring about certain social norms (strong).
- She could hold on to her passions (strong) that could also be seen as symbolically strong and included keeping a sense of inner self. She held on to her curiosity and had a rare openness to learning. But she also wanted to be more like others (strong/weak).
- She could always integrate what she learned with her own experience so that it became part of her psyche. Sometimes her learning matched her inner self, but sometimes it could be seen as conflicting with her spirit (strong/weak).

However, on the surface, she would often be seen as 'weak' since she didn't seem to be happy on her own, but this perception would be incorrect. From her own perspective, i would see that her enjoyment was often being on her own. It would seem that, in her childhood, she could experience life in a Blakean-type, innocent fashion, and this state has not really been shared.

7

As i struggle through his section, i am experiencing considerable uncertainty. How will this be read? Are my words adequate? I can make this a flight of fantasy and write anything that comes to mind and not be concerned about being in touch with her truth and then expressing what i feel in a way that works. In my ramblings, i need to respect not only my friend but also the whole history of literature, philosophy, science, and spiritual thinking. I also feel a sense of my human limits and what i can express. In an academic work, the rigours of doing the job determine the whole structure of what is written. In these ramblings, i have a loose direction and some sense of where i want to go, but i have no idea whether that will take five more words or ten thousand. What i do know is i need to return to the subject at hand.

After my short digression, i realise that one of the problems in writing this section is that when i describe one condition from one point of view, i am not addressing another condition that exists simultaneously from another point of view.

For instance, i would see that her lack of opportunity to share her inner passions was okay but not okay. 'What?' you may ask.

Before we go any further, i think i need to offer some further examples of weak/strong duality and its relative nature since i will need to consider it in a future discussion. For you readers who understand, please be patient and consider some more discussion.

For most of you, the use of weak/strong duality in physics or some type of artistic/metaphorical context doesn't mean anything. Dealing with the social/human reality would seem to really define it. It's obvious!

Let's try a different spin. Without debating the truth or limitations of Charles Darwin and his 'survival of the fittest', let us accept that he has a point of view that describes the underlying dynamics that influence which species survive and which ones don't. Let us also assume that he is using survival in terms of life on the earth. From a more contemporary point of view, maybe we could say that organisms that can adapt to different environmental changes would continue to exist and organisms that don't would become extinct. If we consider the strong/weak duality, it may look like 'strong' from a social/human point of view is the same as Darwin's. The strong will survive, and the weak will perish. But no!

Consider the following. There are many British and American movies that show a brave soldier who dies in battle fighting their 'just cause'. Remember he's dead, but he's seen as 'strong'. In Louis-Ferdinand Céline's novel <u>Journey to the End of Night</u>, a french soldier is confronted with a german soldier. He doesn't know the german. He could be a good guy, have a family, and so on. He asks the question 'Why would i want to kill him?' This frenchman also realises that the german's point of view may not be the same as his. He may want to kill a frenchman. The frenchman actually wants to live, so he goes and hides in the basement of a farmhouse and lives. From a survival-of-the-fittest point of view, his position is 'strong'. His behaviour from a British/American-hero point of view is that he is a coward and 'weak'!

So it could be that the social/human position, from an evolutionary perspective, is 'weak' and that—oops, there could be more.

Consider the driven, strong type A executive who dies of a heart attack.

Consider another factor—religious delusion, whether it be Western Christian fundamentalism or a number of Middle Eastern religions that consider that survival of the fittest needs to be defined in terms of fighting for the ideological truth, a.k.a. 'the truth' and going to heaven. Of course, for the nonbeliever, the belief that you don't really die could be a bit of a stretch. And heaven would be pretty crowded.

Well, if we don't accept this religious position, we are left with the fact that 'strong' functional adaptability may have nothing to do with social/human values, even if we are looking at literal, real-world survival. As i will discuss later, i will take this to another level. Be patient.

Meanwhile, back to my friend and some of the dynamics of her development.

So her weak points could be strong and her strong weak? I would see her dynamics more like the following:

Level of experience / Point of view	creative/different/other	social/human
As seen social/human	weak	strong
As seen from an intellectual/creative/ historical perspective	strong	weak
My friend's experience		strong/weak

To some of you, the above diagram will probably make sense. You may even know the yin/yang figure on one side of the page. But how does it fit? I have selected this figure because it clearly shows how the dualities we have discussed are not simply one or the other but have qualities of one in the other as well. The small white and black circles within the figure help emphasise the integration of the composite dualities.

At the beginning of my ramblings and its triggering event, i described my reaction to her use of push/pull. If i used a social/human perspective, i would suggest that both exist:

Don't do that! (push)

Do this! (pull)

In a martial arts sense:

Go against another's energy/motion. (push)

Go with another's energy/motion. (pull)

Even though the martial arts person may accept these tenets, we can be literal in our thinking and suggest that since pull isn't really pull, he/she is not 'pulling' anyone but is letting the other's energy/motion complete its expression without resistance. I see this at a social/human level. It is an interface strategy. It is not spiritual but can be seen as a useful, nonassertive social/human communication approach.

My friend's spirit is far beyond those platitudes! But since she has focused on these at one point, let's add these push/pull factors to our diagram to see how they may express her vision/experience.

Level of experience / Point of view	creative/different/other	social/human
As seen social/human	weak pull	strong push/pull
As seen from an intellectual/creative/ historical perspective	strong neither/both	weak push/pull
My friend's experience	push/pull weak/strong - experiences the separation between these two like opposing forces with no resolution	strong/antistrong push with some social/human pull

If you question these dynamics, you are right but wrong. In essence, she has experienced too much strong/weak, push/pull dualities with a myriad of other factors. Without going into more variables and more confusion, it is very important to look at where we are and where she is. For you on the social/human plane, you may be making the judgement that this person doesn't easily fit into how things should be or the way things are. She is confused. There is a problem. And i agree at one level. *However*, what is far more important is that our simple descriptions don't work. They are inadequate! They are inadequate because they cannot describe the unique dynamics of each person. Do we have to go further and find a different schema? Is she the only one?

Yes! But no. There are others who don't fit but also make a difference in the world.

So let us carry on.

A caveat

I see that my explanation of her experience and the multisymbolic qualities used to describe her state are a function of our simplistic view of these dualities, and an approach is used to explain them. If my ramblings are working, i hope that you find these expressions interesting but also somewhat confusing.

That Didn't Work, so Let's Try Again, but Should We?

Let's go back and start at the beginning. Like anyone, we can describe my friend's life from many points of view. I, of course, don't mean to use point of view from a personal, mum/dad, peer, teacher manner but from a theoretical/academic perspective and, more importantly, from a 'nonself/very self-based' perspective. From this perspective, we can use a completely different framework. But before doing this, let me review some of the dualities we have used.

- self-others
- inner self–social self
- SC-PFC
- swan (different)–duck (same)
- mother-dad
- weak-strong
- adult-child
- fantasy–real life
- yin-yang
- creative-social/human
- push-pull

But hold it. This whole work has been about being different, creative, artistic, compassionate, open, egoless, connected, perspectiveless, insecure, philosophical, and scientific with intellectual integrity, being beyond dualities, and here is a list of dualities!

Interestingly enough, my friend, as i have mentioned before, is very different in life experience from me but has many of the same 'self' qualities we have discussed.

'Beauty is so rare a thing / So few drink of its fountain.'

As you, the reader, might also be asking, would it not be a lot better for her to have everything in symbolic order? If her experience had been simpler with yin/yang, push/pull, strong/weak factors in all the right places, wouldn't her life have been better?

Yes. Let's move on. But first . . .

Here is a time to do a little self-check.

- If you thought of how my friend was raised but hadn't thought about other ways of structuring the nature of the person given your social/human perspective, then you haven't begun on your voyage of discovery. Ironically, you could be at the end of this voyage and see the truth, which is simple and complete. You may know all the answers. To paraphrase a statement attributed to Braque, 'If you are completely aware of self and know all, you're either dead or a liar.'
- If you thought of the previous dynamics, you have probably been intellectually open and curious.
- If you thought about my friend's experiences and added, 'She needs to use the weak force' (in metaphorical terms), you're beginning to move.
- If you were reflective enough to see that these applied dualities are a way of describing her experience and their underlying dynamics from a symbolic point of view and that this perspective could be accurate, you are getting the point.
- If you also appreciate that bringing about symbolic order in her life that could have been achieved by creative expression or by using

analyses that underlie some approaches to psychotherapy, you're getting the picture. In this writing and in introspective approaches to psychotherapy, there is often a need to resolve conflict at a multifactorial, interpretive level that can also be structured in many different ways. If you understand this, you are right with me.

I feel the need to apologise to you, the reader, at this point because i think that most people just read along and don't stop to reflect and internalise; however, i feel that some reflectivity is essential in any reading of content that questions the essence of life, thought, or existence.

Taking Some Different Points of View and Seeing Where We End Up

Let me start by asking, 'Where am i?'

It is interesting to me that as i consider a different point of view, i am not discounting, in any way, the dualities we have discussed. I am simply saying that if we can take a different point of view, we may arrive at completely different answers.

What is our point of view from academic study? What this question should really ask is, what are our points of view if we put diverse academic points of view together? At face value, it would seem that these are very distant from each one of us because they can be broad in scope and often impersonal in language. There are the points of view established by the ethnologists and work on species-specific behaviour. There are genetics. There are those who look at physiology, biochemistry, cell biology, neurophysiology, internal medicine, biomechanics. You may ask, 'Do these have any relevance to you, your friend, or ourselves if none of us have any problems in any of these areas?'

Of course, these are all essential, they all are important, and they could all work in a manner that we feel is a healthy expression of the human; however, 'healthy' expressions can also result in war, racism, politics, religion, terrorism, and love. Conversely, we could have someone who is highly disabled, and all they know is love.

We can consider cognitive development and intelligence. These are concepts, like mind, that have no physical referent. Here, we have the structure of thought influencing words and words influencing the structure of thought.

One person who was interested in the structure of thought was Jean Piaget, a swiss biologist who was first interested in the adaptive behaviours of cells. Once he moved to humans, he moved into some interesting work. He approached cognition from a developmental point of view and assumed that the dynamics of thought structure changed qualitatively over time. He described four states, the last two being most representative of the adult type of thinking. Though many years ago a fellow doctoral student and i found that many people, even at a graduate-university level, did not meet the thinking criteria that Piaget defined as his final stage of development, we also felt that we could describe some stages that went beyond Piaget's final stage.

An interesting irony has become evident to me after many years of being an outlaw, reflecting on the nature of the human and experiencing the limitations in social/human thinking. In recent years, 'the theory of mind' has become a popular way of describing one's ability to understand another's feelings and thoughts, which from my experience is very rare. My somewhat critical description of the theory is a circular one. Those who accept the theory as a typical human capacity do not have the ability to think in a manner that their theory describes. Thus proponents of the theory of mind do not meet its criteria.

For the purposes of my rambling, my sense of being different, and considering my friend, there are some qualities of thought structures that we need to consider. From a very human point of view, we have asked people about how they see 'same' and 'different' (another duality). In this case, we are not asking about others, just about self. Consider this: could a mechanic tell you that he/she knows how your car works but knows little about his/her own?

Are you the same person you used to be?

This simple question has elicited a wide range of responses, and as you can imagine, a clear yes or no with some explanation better shows a simpler, less developed way of thinking. Responses that question how i am defining a person or what i mean by *same* and *different* are of a higher order. The first thing the more comprehensive thinking does is transform

101

what looks like a simple, straightforward question into a multifactorial one since the question triggers a complex set of thoughts and questions that make it impossible to respond and what might be considered as an expected marker.

So are more complex thinkers more uncertain in how to respond?

We assumed so. We expected that they may have more questions about what we were asking and would also have less straightforward answers with lots of contributing variables and some uncertainty about the mix, and this was what we found.

But this is not a very concrete example for you to get an understanding of what this high level of thinking is all about. The problem we often have in understanding more complex thinking is that we have different ways of 'assessing' someone's thought structure because all measures are limited. For instance, we can ask some probability or combinatorial questions (these are tasks believed to be indicative of higher-order cognitive thinking), but the person who is uncertain about math can fail. We can ask ethical questions, but a person who has not developed any ethical schema and thought about rules, principles, and higher-order principles may not respond in a manner reflective of a highly developed thought. We may attempt to assess whether someone can appreciate someone else's point of view, but we may not be able to measure the quality of thinking of the person with social anxiety. What i have found is that the people i have met who think differently, in a very comprehensive manner, are able to clearly understand that, often, contradictions may not be contradictions; that the social/human plane is not real; that reality is the creation of the human psyche, which could really be a delusion or real; and that even our need to find order in the universe and have things line up and be predictable may meet our human needs but could also be a circular trap and limiting.

It is interesting because i think my friend would have had some difficulty in responding to some of our measures of her thinking in a consistent 'high level' manner, though i know she completely understands what i feel is that highest level of thought. It is almost as if the structure were all in place, but there needs to be some exposure to certain information and some experience that gives content that will fit into the structure. Once that is done, it remains intact.

What i like about cognitive structure, as described in this developmental way, is that it is open-ended. It has no clear practical limits, though some hypothetical limits will make sense. What i find difficult with intelligence and the way it is understood and measured is that it is limited by the person(s) who devises the measure and the range of social responses to the test.

There are, of course, many ways to test intelligence. There are psychometric instruments that are administered in a one-to-one setting, and there are written tests. All these measure intelligence by the number of correct responses, and in some cases, the responses are measured within certain time elements. The premise is that if i can operationally define *intelligence* (remember, a conceptual referent only), then i can create a test of intelligence. I can have a limited number of questions for which there are 'correct' or better answers. I can decide what types of questions to ask based on my definition. I give it to thousands of people and find that some people do very poorly, some do really well, and magically, most fall in the middle. To really assess my test, i then compare the results on my test with a long-established one and find a significant relationship between my full-scale IQ and others; and if they are very similar in outcome scores, i could conclude that my test is a reasonable measure of intelligence. Of course, my outcome still doesn't answer the conceptual questions about what intelligence is. What we could conclude, however, is that there is a close similarity in the skills required to do well in my test as there are in others and that results may be predictive of how one is doing at school.

Some interesting relationships arise for me when i consider cognitive functioning, measured intelligence, and creative thinking. Because measured intelligence is limited, as i have mentioned, i see it as a measure at a social/human level. Intelligence itself, like Flew's argument, has no paradigm case, referent, or even an absolute because it can't test beyond the capacities of the people who created it. We can see that certain people are bright, do really well at school, and therefore, must be smart, but some people are considered bright but have no common sense; they could be book smart or whatever. If we look at the types of questions used to 'measure' intelligence, we see that they do not require the open-ended, multivariable, 'seeing something from a unique point of view' type of thinking. In fact, i suggest that the creative, high-cognitive-functioning person may be confused by questions that seem simple and straightforward to others because they see so many other variables to consider.

As a twelve-year-old, i was completing an interest inventory and not getting past the question—which certainly seemed like a stupid one, but it was on the test—'Would you like to run a ski tow (lift)?' I stopped answering all the remaining questions because i got lost in the following (please note that i loved skiing):

- Are they asking about skiing?
- Are they asking about running some machinery?
- If i ran a ski lift some of the time and could ski, that would be great.
- If i ran the ski lift a lot of the time and could not ski, that wouldn't be so great.
- Our local lift broke down frequently; are they asking about not just running machinery but also having to repair it?
- Are they asking about just working in a resort and doing something to live there?
- How does this question tie into the style of other questions?

I looked around and found another question that asked, 'Would you like to drive a bulldozer?' At age twelve, i realised this test was completely confusing and too difficult for me!

Of course, confusion is usually considered as dumbness, not brightness.

From my point of view, we have lower-level 'not understanding' and higher-level 'not understanding', and social/human intelligence, i guess, is somewhere in the middle. The problem could be some people who could be recognised as brilliant. Yet this is not being measured. And in a similar manner, many who are measured as extremely intelligent have no creative genius or brilliance. I would see my friend as testing at a statistically high level, but this would not have been an indication of her insight and overall cognitive abilities.

What do these cognitive qualities do to life experience? Unfortunately, they help confuse. And for my friend, like myself, it can be difficult to have a single enjoyable experience as defined within social/human limits. Experiences need to meet a range of her inner needs because awareness of different factors at different levels of experience can ebb and flow (another duality). In a sense, these ebbs and flows clearly have an up-and-down and back-and-forth motion and are composed of multiple variables. Only one or two may be obvious on the surface at any one time. I see these dynamics as 'emerging to the surface' in different, complex forms, and these may influence how she presents herself at a social/human level. Sometimes these can be seen as expressions of insight by others, and sometimes they can be seen as 'what!' by others. 'Be careful of those logging trucks if you are driving into the mountains.' This is good maternal advice.

Sometimes cognitive complexity can be experienced as the enemy because even if i am not aware of a myriad of thoughts that cover a wide range of points of view, they are always there. However, this cognition is also an essential ingredient in going beyond/below (another duality) the limitation of normal thinking.

Before going any further in our discussion of cognition and its influence, we need to consider the whole area of psychodynamics. On the social/human level, this considers mind, emotions, social interactions, and life experiences. The psychotherapist/counsellor is the essence of the person.

At the social/human level, there are many different ways to approach analysis and treatment. At this point, i am not interested in reviewing treatment methodologies but in looking at the assumptions that bring about understanding. My experience with group training that considers the qualitative nature of human relationships has very definite nonstated assumptions. All people need connections to real people. Some people are going to be closer than others. Inner-circle relationships should be family or *very* close friends. Conversely, if one doesn't have these relationships, there is something wrong, or one is defensive or dishonest.

In fact, it was from this experience that i became aware of another quality i had that was similar to others throughout history who thought differently. This awareness influenced my sense of not fitting, even with those who considered themselves as thinking outside the box and interested in mind. For those offering the group therapy training, which i discussed on pages 71-72, it was their socially/humanly defined motherhood position and their assumption that all people need close relationships. However, it was very clear to me that their definition of 'close' was a very superficial one and not anchored in any depth.

So what was their view? What made it so superficial?

I have more recently referred to their type of connection as the psychopathology of social skills. And remember that many of these people accept the theory of mind. Anyway, everyone has to have friends! And for those children who don't have friends, the answer is to teach them social skills. Their goal, in metaphorical terms, is to teach a swan how to act like a duck, and in doing this, the swan will have friends and live happily ever after. Of course, it is not that one shouldn't have friends, but it is probably more important to be friendly or polite with others, but meaningful friendships, depending on their depth, are very selective and established in a way that works for each one of us. To some of us, having none or even one is better than having a number of unfulfilling ones. As it seems, from the social/human point of view, having friends is important.

Here enters what is called the 'naturalistic fallacy'. Logically, we cannot contend that because the human species are social, all people should have friends. To learn more, turn to pages 347-350. So everyone should have them, even if there is no meaningful connection. From my point of view, as i have discussed before, i can be friendly with many people (i think), but being friends is another story. And of course, it is a cliché.

My discussion of symbols and use of circles in describing *social role* (weak?) and *inner self* (strong) is my own way of describing some aspects of psychodynamics, but of course, there are many ways that have given meaning to the human psyche. Freud and his description of *id, ego, superego, conscious,* and *unconscious* have become part of popular language. His views of psychosexual stages of development and descriptions of some specific psychopathologies have been lost to general perception. His views have also been lost to many psychologists who realise that his work is, in my own terms, more like literary criticism, not science. This is true. However, the irony, from my point of view, is twofold. The present understanding of clinical practice is not any more scientific than Freud's (it's social science) and that the understanding of the human psyche (though it could be limited as we have already considered) is probably far more profoundly dynamic and interesting than anything published in clinical psychology.

In the '60s, gestalt psychology (not to be confused with the actual meaning of *gestalt* in the studies of perception) was popularised by psychotherapists like Fritz Perls. His ability to work with people, shape their perceptions, and get them to have heuristic moments of self-reflection was well-known. Mind/body focus, meditation, the study of mysticism, and holistic understanding were all seen as approaches for developing and even freeing the human psyche. All these approaches were based on idealised values and mental structures. It was not that these were bad or poorly founded because they weren't. But let's consider the 'outlaw' perspective. Can we assume without question that good, bad, or indifferent; the values of mutual love and respect; being able to relax; getting rid of defensiveness; becoming self-aware; and having one's symbolic structure line up are clinically necessary? If not necessary, certainly desirable? Why?

Yet another irony is unfortunately evident here. Some of these attributes, as you will see in a future discussion, are consistent with what i will consider as part of a deeper sense of experience, but the problem is this.

If your experience is defined by social/human descriptors and you do not have a cognitive structure or sense of how things are experienced in a nonephemeral manner, then what i see happening is that those values related to love, self-awareness, and the meaning of life can be understood in terms of popular perceptions. If you are uncertain, you can look it up on the Internet. In fact, the reward for finding no satisfactory answer may lead to self-exploration and a vertical direction of exploration. Immerse yourself in what has gone before and what is expressed at present by those lovers of beauty—the artist, the mystic, the philosopher, the poet, the composer, the musician. An amazing outcome can emerge here. With an understanding and immersion in this other, noncommonplace social/human level, you can actually gain an almost intuitive sense of how to transform these more profound perceptions (weak force) into ethically well-thought-out social/ human judgements. As i write this, i am reminded of the word 'karma' since it is essentially not a social/human concept, though i think that if i asked almost anyone about the meaning of *karma*, i would get a Hebrew/ Christian-influenced (even for you who are not religious) response. In fact, it can be shown that someone who spends time and efforts in caring for others (certainly a wonderful thing to do) could actually be described as displaying bad karma.

Here is the contradiction.

Considering others before yourself is *bad* karma.

Considering others before yourself is *good* karma.

If you don't understand this, that's okay. (There's a karma judgement for you.) Karma is an outlaw phenomenon.

I know that my friend understands this but is more vulnerable to the ebb and flow of that social/human reality. I say it is more in relationship to me, though i still have that vulnerability, and as i have described, my need for meaningful connection is important. What she has not had is years of nonsocial/human grounding in a social/human environment. An environment that, from her experience, seems to be dominated by social/ human expectations can overwhelm her, and she can lose her perspective. As you, the reader, need to appreciate, the world in which you dwell seems to allow for different opinions and different points of view. It gives the illusion of free thinking, but it is limited:

• Ants live in their colony—nothing else exists.

- People live under a world of religion, nations, or ideology—nothing else exists.
- Earth is a small planet in one galaxy—you may contend that you are cognitively aware that there is more to the universe than our earth, but you don't even think of that daily or weekly and certainly never experience its vastness.
- Our vision tells us that people are separate—i end, there is space, and you begin.
- I die, yet do all the molecules, atoms, quarks, mesons, and so on stop moving and my spirit continue (though i could be part of a whole existent energy)?
- Is the big bang theory and expansion of the universe a function of human limitation?

On one level, i see us living in a 'string theory' type perceived universe. Our being is a function of making some kind of structural meaning of our understanding. We have small particles and big ones that seem to behave differently. But we can't have two opposing theories to describe matter, unless we can find a unifying theory that explains both.

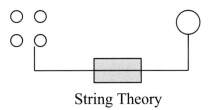

String Theory

Our being and scientific understanding needs rational explanations. But our beings are significantly limited.

For most of you, thinking about these ideas may seem irrelevant to life. Except for a small few, one can't pay bills thinking about string theory! We are back to 'what is life?' However, i don't think we could have a magazine, economics, nations, or religions without subatomic particles.

Even though the creative people throughout history may not have always been concerned about the scientific limitations of human thought, what i suggest is that they have been aware of the unexplained 'otherness', which is beyond definition, description, and comprehension and which is the driving force.

Are these the expressions of mind? Physiology? Or something else? In some ways, it doesn't really matter.

For you who don't have a more social/human focus for thought, imagine—if you can—what it would be like to be cognizant of all these variables all the time. With an academic framework, it helps, but it is still difficult, maybe impossible. With my friend, she has the same thought structure but has only recently found (from my point of view) some framework for organising with her wonderfully complex, sensitive spirit.

We have started off talking about psychodynamics and seemed to have digressed into the discussion of those characteristics that differentiate the creative person from those of you experiencing life on a more social/human level. What we do need to do, though, is to consider psychodynamics from a 'does it work for the person?' point of view. Can developing a better understanding of self using a psychodynamic point of view assist someone in organising thoughts and feelings in such a way that it enhances that person's own evolution/development?

Let me return to some individual analyses, which are psychodynamic in nature, and consider thought structure and content. The Necker cube may be a simple 'gestalt' example of structure/content. The works of Escher, the German printmaker, has also explored this structure/content relationship.

I will consider these somewhat simplistically to start. I will use structure to represent the number of ways one's cognitive schema can perceive something. It is somewhat like noticing that something is missing, or there is another way. It is like a black hole or directions that need filling. What does that mean? Hold on, i will explain.

I will use content as the socially accepted definition of 'what it is'.

From a content, 'what is it?' point of view, it is a box, a cube.

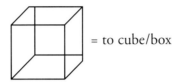

If, however, you say that there is more than meets the eye (cliché) and ask the question 'which side is the front?' it could be

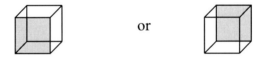

This is called the Necker cube because a person named Necker has articulated the obvious ambivalent nature of the cube. For those who know the work of Escher, you will be aware of how he plays with perspective on a two-dimensional plain.

Of course, these are based on our consideration that this is a representation of a three-dimensional figure. We have an understanding based on experience and thought structures. This example may remind you of many of the creative-thinking-type tests used in popular literature or psychology texts. Supposedly, people who see things differently are creative thinkers.

These figures could also be seen as two-dimensional in a number of ways.

We could organise our perception in a geometric manner and see this figure as two squares and four parallelograms.

We could also see it as one small square, two triangles, and four quadrilaterals.

My reference to this simple cube is an example of how different perceptions and questions raised are based on people's perceptions. Each of us may consciously or unconsciously make assumptions about what we see. *This is an example of awareness; it is not a measure!* I stress this because these types of examples are often used with a judgement about those who see in some desired way. Probably *no creative* person would ever be concerned with such a perception unless it is someone like Escher, who is having fun with visual perception. Just think, like intelligence tests, people may make up clever trick questions and then test others to see if they have an answer that they want. Then they use it as some type of measure.

Probably one of my more fun, tempting thoughts, where i end up feeling like the rebel instead of the 'outlaw', is in response to measures of creative thinking. With my rebel hat on, i often have fun with the thought of offering a seminar on creative thinking (unlike de Bono, who would actually give them something tangible) and let the group there know that their act of going to a seminar to learn to think creatively means they will never be a creative thinker. Thanks for coming.

My friend grew up in an environment, like almost all of you, that was pretty completely well-defined in social/human terms. No weird, weird, only weird normal people. Even though her family details, as described earlier, may be different from yours, they are probably structurally the same. Families may have many very different details, conditions, points of view, languages, social classes, jobs, and so on, but they all dwell on a social/human level.

What she did sense was that something was missing; there were holes to be filled. I feel that she didn't know what it was, but she did (another contradiction). Even though she kind of knew, she was still the ugly duckling.

Some Approaches to Experiencing and Accepting New Points of View

I find this next section challenging to write because i see a number of conditions influencing one another in a dynamic manner. And any discussion of one significant condition doesn't allow for a discussion of another or others. You need to bear with me, knowing that i will be discussing only parts of a picture, but in doing so, no one part, in itself, is correct. Let me try by considering some of these conditions generally. In these next few sections, i will sometimes use 'one' to represent my generalised 'personal representation' of other people; it could be you, but if these are not, then consider them as representative of my own experience being projected.

Movement away

If one sees things differently, where does one go? One could look for a place where there is an absence of difference (all swans). Or one could find an environment that doesn't remind oneself of being different.

Social/human attachment and mixed influences

If one has strong human attachments to certain people, one may have respect and care for them; but with this attachment, one may accept their values, at least on a human level. This may naturally happen over time, even though one might realise that these accepted values are actually different from one's own. In a very simple way, one may feel that good people hold good values and beliefs. However, if one is different and sees the world through slightly different eyes, one may have developed some ideas, as well as feelings, about how the social/human world works that are not understood or accepted by those with whom one's attachment is strong. Consider my friend and her father. This dichotomy could leave one somewhat anxious, distressed, or even detached. It may even lead to others feeling detached from oneself.

I think my observations about attachment and values may not make sense to some of you at face value. Let me add some other pieces. Let's assume that holding a point of view and having human support for it can give a sense of comfort and help in strengthening that point of view. Conversely, if one holds a point of view that has no supporting person, then one could be left alone. If this is the case, then it would seem likely that it would be far more difficult to have a sense of confidence or strength in that personally held view.

The important question arises here: what happens if the people whom one feels most attached to have values/beliefs that are in conflict with one's own views?

Lateral movement

One may feel the need to 'move on' to another phase in one's life. One who feels trapped may feel like they are going nowhere or lost in one environment and may feel that it is essential to move on. However, this move can have many different faces. Take the following examples:

- A new job or job opportunity may require relocation.
- The student does his/her international trip. To the North American, it is often the 'trip to Europe' or the Far East.
- The small town doesn't have opportunities.
- One may have gone on a trip, met someone, found a new opportunity, and stayed there.
- What one knows is that there is a need for some type of movement away, but to where is not known. It could be just going anywhere.

Does 'lateral movement' offer a new freedom?

Let's assume that one's lateral movement (one of many choices) is not only to free oneself from one environment but also to connect with another; it is not just to see the world or get a new job but also to obtain a freedom. It could be a freedom from what Thomas Hardy sees as the imprisoning limits of a social/human rigidity/inertia, which manifests itself in beliefs and social connection. These dominate how society operates and limit the freedom of the person. We see this as one thematic component in <u>Jude the Obscure</u>, <u>Tess of the d'Urbervilles</u>, <u>Mayor of Casterbridge</u>, <u>Return of the Native,</u> just to mention a few. His work paints a somewhat pessimistic view of the universality of this force.

I consider this force as somewhat similar but different to the way Hardy sees it. One is restricted by the limits of their being and their acceptance of the reality of the social/human environment. Can one find, given one's own sense of self, a deeper inner level of connection?

Ezra Pound wrote, 'I have weathered the storm, I have beaten out my exile.'

In a sense, we may have the possibility of transforming lateral into vertical.

A twenty-five-year-old woman wanted to be free. Should she get married and be tied down or be free, spend her life travelling, and never settle down? She didn't realise that her desire to free was actually not freedom at all. She was tied down to her belief.

Vertical movement

In my metaphor of the water and levels of life back on pages 8 and 9, i have considered one's understanding of life as a level of depth. In my ongoing discussion, i have considered the symbolic structure that underlies Joyce's <u>A Portrait of the Artist as a Young Man</u> and <u>Ulysses</u>. I have also considered some simple neurophysiological systems and structures that underlie behaviour. I have considered the challenge of looking at concepts and what they mean. In all these situations, my consideration has been to make a distinction between what we see on the surface (social/human) and what is really going on underneath. In my consideration of our use of dualities, our measurement of intelligence, and even our definition of creative thinking, the limitations are evident. This is especially the case if these are defined at a social/human level. But as i will demonstrate, we can look at these in another way.

Vertical movement could partially be considered in terms of point of view, based on one's level of perception. If i am engaged in a discussion about good guys or bad guys, good karma and bad karma, which one is the front of the Necker cube, Stephen Dedalus's story, or what people should and shouldn't do, <u>i am dwelling on the surface</u>.

If my point of view sees good and bad guys and good and bad karma as the same and i actually see life at its symbolic, underlying dynamic level, then i would see those perceptions as a below the surface, a lower level. Of course, as i have mentioned before, i see this as getting closer to the *real*, some kind of truth. For almost all others, the *real* exists on the surface where death and taxes are synonymous. This lower *unreal* level, on a human basis, may be experienced as a sense of being detached. What is important to me is probably seen as naïve, unrealistic, irresponsible, or whatever. If i don't like that sense of being detached because of my point of view, i may find it comforting to move into the social/human realm because i feel connected, but i may not.

Thus vertical movement, because we all have to at least function in a social/human world, could be seen as dynamic. In a simplistic way, for the purposes of example, i could offer the following duality: one's experience at any moment in time is either creative/deeper/different or social/human.

This vertical movement could be influenced by my desire to keep my creative/deeper/different perspective intact at any given moment. Let's assume that ideally, for me, i would like to feel that it is what cognitively suits me that determines the level i dwell on. However, if i am feeling distracted and stressed, i may move vertically and become part of the social/human realm or, like Ezra, withdraw to life at a deeper level. As a result, i may be present at a social/human level but may not be there cognitively, though in this situation i may participate and emotionally have a sense of belonging. Of course, at another time, i could move to my more cognitively appropriate state, and i may feel somewhat detached. What do i do? I'd like to have both.

What we can have here is an interesting interplay between lateral and vertical dimensions. (Once again, we have dualities, in this case, interacting.)

In the following diagram, i consider which state is the one being expressed/experienced. Here is the basic structure i see when considering lateral and vertical changes:

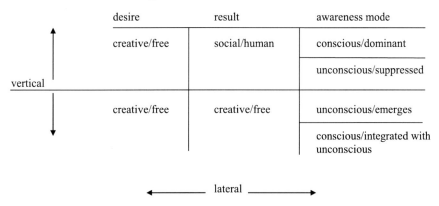

	desire	result	awareness mode
vertical ↑	creative/free	social/human	conscious/dominant
			unconscious/suppressed
↓	creative/free	creative/free	unconscious/emerges
			conscious/integrated with unconscious

← lateral →

Oops, as you can see, i have put in another duality—unconscious/conscious—into the mix.

In this diagram, i have used general psychodynamic concepts that most of you will have some conceptual sense of, including how they are used. I will be lazy in my conceptual rigour here because, probably, your general understanding will work for our discussion, though if you have read critically up to this point you will know that these are conceptually referenced like mind.

Since i feel lazy at this point, i will use some simple metaphors to describe some essential features of the conscious/unconscious. As you may be able to appreciate, the task of even attempting to describe many terms in some detail can be overwhelming.

Let's say that the unconscious is like a closet, attic, or basement. You have put something there and, at one level, have forgotten about it but not really. It is as if it were always there. It can even influence how one behaves. It can influence how one moves laterally and vertically. You may avoid part of the attic, even if there are lots of neat things in it, because something there reminds you of something negative. Typically, in how unconsciousness is conceptualised, one may have no 'conscious' awareness of why one avoids or what is avoided.

As you will see, consciousness/unconsciousness may be experienced at a social/human level, and this experience may possibly result in a defence for those who are different. Once one can integrate all these states, unconsciousness and consciousness become one. But we're not there yet.

Let us see consciousness as simply what we are aware of and how we understand it.

If you're reflecting about our discussion of different vertical levels of cognition, you may be saying to yourself, 'Consciousness isn't that simple.'

Here's another test of your own level of self-awareness and about your own conscious/unconscious awareness.

If you have stopped and asked any questions of yourself, possibly about such things as your conscious or unconscious experiences and their influences or the differences between lateral and vertical directions, that's great. *Or* even if you have asked yourself, 'Do i get what he is talking about?' you're close to being with me.

You are probably right on board. That's great. As you can see, if you look ahead, we have a long way to go.

If all the concepts and details are clear but you are aware of some deficiencies, which could be couched in metaphorical language, then i would assume that you are either

- a good academically trained philosopher, scientist, or thinker, and to you i apologise because you need more detail, *or*
- a highly defended social/human thinker, and i hope you will benefit from carrying on; thoughts and thinking in new ways can't hurt you and may actually be like an adventure.

Please read on and be open.

As the scripture reader may say, here ends my reading of conscious/unconscious.

Transformations: The Essence of Change?

Now for something completely different, before we discuss how all these pieces come together, we need to consider two more variables.

One is transformation/nontransformation (duality).

The other is salience.

I have discussed these in neurological terms previously. This time, i will address them from a psychodynamic point of view. For the moment, please overlook our previous discussions; we will bring them together later.

Okay, let's bring in the following: social/human and creative/free and unconscious/conscious. Also, let's consider movement variables, vertical and lateral. And now we will add transformation/nontransformation, as well as salience. I have warned you this may get a bit complicated. Be patient.

Let us start with transformation.

What my friend experienced, after being exposed to different academic experiences, was that they helped fill some of holes, in essence questions she had about a wide range of topics, with content. In a short written fictional piece, she addressed not only her need to deal with her personal creative self but also her need to deal with her relationship with her dad. She wanted to study philosophy as a graduate student and ignore any career path for the moment. But this, of course, would overlook the need to be practical, get a job, and get on with life.

Her respect for his strength of character, his integrity, and his point of view (even though very limited) comes through clearly in the piece. We experience a daughter/dad tension as she discusses her personal need for impractical (vertically lower) academic pursuits. It is wonderfully balanced and shows how a surface conflict can exist but at the same time be resolved at a lower level. In this case, both daughter and father can experience her need to be herself and follow her own path.

Initially, this father/daughter discussion reminds me of David French in his play, Leaving Home; but in this play, the essence of emotional respect goes in a totally different direction. In French's play, there is an emotional 'leaving'. In this situation, all members of the family leave a father who only sees the negative and is recalcitrant. Though lateral movement by the family is evident at the end of the play, it also shows the tragic nature of a man who is a prisoner of rigid surface thinking and belief and also shows the need of others to move vertically and find a different plane of existence.

What these written pieces have done is address the possibility that vertical movement, as we have described it, can have cognitively different perspectives that can separate people or can still be different but retain acceptance and attachment.

Given these situations, i can see three possibilities. A transformation could exist vertically if we changed our point of view to a more common one so that we didn't feel detached. Conversely, if we felt a warm affection for someone and we didn't agree with his/her point of view, we could transform that feeling into dislike/hate (some more implied dualities). In my friend's written piece, there was an emerging third possibility. In her case, neither person changed their cognitive point of view, nor was the relationship transformed. A resolution was achieved without transformation. She understood and respected the nature of her dad's feelings and was able to respond to his emotional needs as a dad but still retained her own path. In a sense, she was making a vertical move to address underlying dynamics of his being. In this case, as the outcome, possible disagreement was transformed, but neither cognitive nor emotional/attachment factors were changed.

So let's look again at this outcome transformation. For illustrative purposes, i will use cognition and emotional/attachment and how each one of them may change (be transformed). As illustrated above, if we feel a strong emotional connection to another person, but we cannot accept their values/ point of view, we can, as my friend did in her writing, keep our emotional connection intact but not compromise our own values. However, to achieve this type of transformation, another factor needs to be considered.

And since we don't have enough terms to juggle, i will throw in another—ego strength. We will use this term in a somewhat academic manner since ego can often be used in a rather self-absorbed, negative manner.

From my point of view, the acceptance of another person and the respect afforded them, even if their values and point of view are different, requires a certain amount of ego strength. In essence, my sense of self remains intact even when i accept and respect another who sees life very differently. As we will discuss later, this is a composite part of compassion.

What we have is a good sense of self and good sense of another but different values.

However, we do have the other transformations.

Emotional transformation. This could show less ego strength if indeed it is values that help define who we are. Consider the following:

You can keep your values intact, and you can 'transform' your 'love' into 'hate'. As we will see, this transformation is not a sign of ego strength and holding on to values; it is an emotional transformation and can weaken ego strength that is weak in nature but looks strong on the surface.

Cognitive transformation. If we accept these specific relationships between ego strength and our example of transformation, we have a number of possibilities.

1. You hold both <u>positive feelings</u> and <u>different points of view</u>.

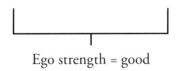

Ego strength = good

2. You transform feeling to a negative and hold different points of view.

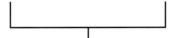

Ego strength could be experienced as stronger by establishing feelings of detachment and rigidly holding on to your point of view. This could suggest some ego strength; however, it could be a fine balance between two factors. Ego could also be fragile or weak. This transformation could be indicative of the person who has very poor ego strength and has found some social/human/religious belief that makes them feel good. As a result, transformation of attachment to others with different views would need to take place when beliefs are questioned.

3. You hold feelings and transform point of view.

Ego strength could be influenced by fear of detachment. If you change important aspects of your beliefs and point of view, you will be accepted. However, you may be clearly compromising yourself, and this could suggest poor ego strength. If your point of view was not held with any great conviction, it doesn't matter, and change could suggest a stronger ego.

So which one does my friend use in her own life?

All of them.

Wouldn't it be easier if she just used one? Then we could define her ego strength based on where she uses transformations.

That certainly is true. She simply is not cooperative.

Unfortunately for you who don't like to juggle all sorts of variables, there is yet another duality to include in our discussion, salient and nonsalient. We can see some interesting dynamics if we consider salience. We will use salient as descriptive of those factors, features, events, and situations that we consider relevant. But to see the dynamics of salience, i will use our two freudian concepts, conscious and unconscious.

So let's review.

As you can imagine, we can now have a whole bunch of states just using these variables. Let's go back a bit and consider salience factors with reference to creative/free vs. social/human and attachment vs. dejected. Just to make things interesting, let's use some of our terminology and apply them to a simple transformation.

In this example, let's consider the creative child who makes a conscious/unconscious shift and goes from not fitting to fitting in the social/human world.

State 1: This child lives in a world of creative thought and imagination and is happy. Even though this child is the swan, he/she is not aware of the 'nonduck' status.

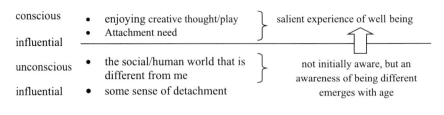

Beginning transformation

State 2

conscious
influential

- enjoying creative thought/play
- sense of being different from others } salient
- attachment need

- doesn't fit in social/human world,   more developed individual thought
  not consciously salient but these   that is emerging into consciousness,
  unconscious aspects   may tend to avoid and dislike the
  consider structure of thought   social/human world without any
  that fits (curious) needing content   specific knowledge about why

unconscious
influential

===

<u>State 3:</u> As our examples have addressed, this next state can have different dynamics. Let's assume that this person is conscious of the environmental context and what is required to fit. Oh no, not another variable!

conscious
influential

- Attachment requires living in a social/human
  world.   } conflict evident, but a
- Sense of detachment and need to fit are both   balance is understood
  experienced.

- Creative thought/imagination is needed
- Attachment is needed without having to   unconsciously salient but
  accept the limitations of a social/human   there; leading is conscious
  existence. One is just visiting.   impact
  Enjoyment is in being alone.

influential

===

With transformation, over a long period, our creative child has become unhappy but is living in the *real* world, and creative thought has been suppressed. Reversing this process may seem almost impossible. Dylan Thomas in 'Fern Hill' considered time and becoming conscious like original sin, the fall of man. I can hear his voice reading the following:

And then to awake, and the farm, like a wanderer white

With the dew, come back, the cock on his shoulder: it was all

    Shining, it was Adam and maiden,

        The sky gathered again

    And the sun grew round that very day.

So it must have been after the birth of the simple light

In the first, spinning place, the spellbound horses walking warm

    Out of the whinnying green stable

        On to the fields of praise.

Here, we have a loss of innocence. It is like Blake's innocence to experience. Is it also a loss of the free and creative inner self?

Is this process reversible? Could lateral movement offer a solution? Could lateral movement to an environment that is not typical in its social/human attachment nature allow for a reemergence of the creative? Could this environment allow one to feel better? Could it allow for a return of important aspects of self (i.e., the creative)?

Let's look at one way in which this move may have a positive influence. Assume that lateral movement has given one the opportunity for attachments or for an attachment that feels good because the environment is different enough from previously experienced environments, where one either felt detached or connected on a duck-type social/human level. But for this lateral movement to work, they unfortunately need to be open to vertical influences.

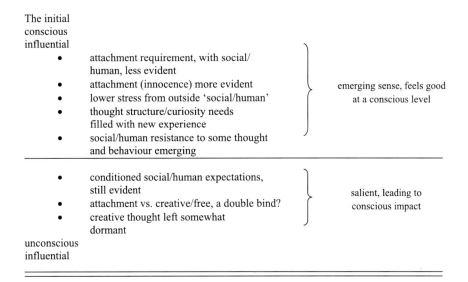

The initial
conscious
influential
- attachment requirement, with social/
  human, less evident
- attachment (innocence) more evident
- lower stress from outside 'social/human'
- thought structure/curiosity needs
  filled with new experience
- social/human resistance to some thought
  and behaviour emerging

emerging sense, feels good
at a conscious level

- conditioned social/human expectations,
  still evident
- attachment vs. creative/free, a double bind?
- creative thought left somewhat
  dormant

salient, leading to
conscious impact

unconscious
influential

What we can see here is that a strong human attachment may be evident, but in these cases, it would be with person(s) who seem somewhat free of 'duck' expectations. People in this state would not necessarily respond unreflectively to conditioned social/human expectations or accept any one-sided view, for instance, that life is great or is terrible (worse than ever). As we will discuss, this social/human life is ephemeral, but it is also an ongoing phenomena. There is and always has been an ephemeral present.

What we may want lateral movement to do is give a better balance of conscious and unconscious influences. What it doesn't do, in itself, is give freedom from the unconscious acceptance of the presence of the social/human influence. It may, however, give relief. It may allow for the emergence of creative expression, but it is also possible that an attachment experience or other self-absorbing experience may override the emergence of a creative self. The risk factor with lateral movement is that some core social/human essentials of the person may manifest themselves. The place may be different, but the structure of the social/human world may be the same.

In Hermann Hesse's <u>Siddhartha,</u> the different experiences of Gautama could be seen as lateral movement. However, there was lateral awareness in his experience because he found no answers.

In a somewhat ironic way, i consider ego, in how it is generally used, as a quality that limits or controls the psyche, but i have grown to understand that it is transitionally needed. From a psychodynamic point of view, ego is needed to initially integrate conscious and unconscious thought. (This is my spin, not Freud's). But more of this later.

What we can see is a possible transitional relief for the creative, different person in a lateral move. It could be seen as a partial transformation in some conscious/unconscious dynamics. Yet i would sense that there would be no movement ahead (whatever that means in vertical terms) and the possibility of increased vulnerability to other situations. My conscious experience gives a sense of experienced comfort, innocence, and attachment but nothing else. This would probably be coupled with low inner-self ego strength, especially if attachment to people, life, and beliefs results in stress reduction and if it is felt that creative thinking has emerged. But actually, i would assume that it is still buried. In considering this, two factors are relevant here:

1. A new laterally found environment could simply be a different social/human environment that is the same, same but different. It could be that i'm not engaging it on a self-reflective level or on a creative level. So it does not require a conscious/unconscious change (vertical movement).
2. It could be that i have simply moved attachment/social/human views into the unconscious. (They're not relevant at the moment.) They are still there and influential. One still has skeletons in the closet.

The middle diagram on page 83 can be applied to these dynamics. However, it offers another lateral qualitative feature of lateral movement.

ENVIRONMENT A (any environment with dominant social/human pressures)

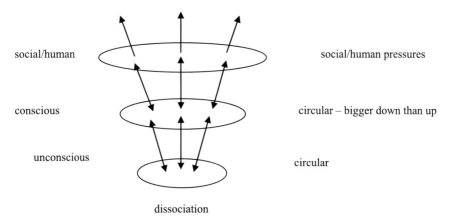

ENVIRONMENT B (an environment without social/human pressures)

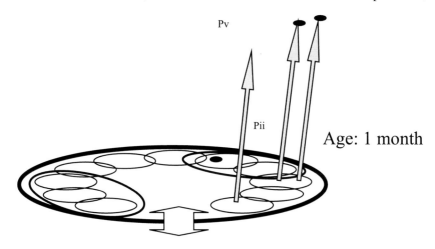

However

Before leaving this discussion of transformation behind us, i would like to take this one step further.

Let's consider some possible dynamics that influence the expression of vertically integrated and 'dissociated' (oops, another term) conscious and unconscious states in different (lateral) environments. In simple terms, we will think of dissociation as a disconnect; no vertical connection is made.

Environment A: A dominant social/human environment, like my friend at home or someone who has a strong conscious sense of self that doesn't fit in a particular social/human environment, is often dissociated. It is sometimes attached. But it also has a variable, integrated dissociated relationship with unconscious influences.

So here are some possibilities to consider:

In environment A, one's expression may be dominated by expected social/human behaviours (attached) but conflict (dissociation) with consciousness, and unconscious influences (dissociation) develop because these expressions do not feel right.

A second set of expressions may also be evident because, at a conscious level, they feel good (integrated), and they feel good because they are contrary (dissociated) with social/human expectation. Here is the expression of rebel and antiestablishment expression.

A third set of expressions is integrated at the unconscious and conscious level and may be expressed in some type of form in self-expression or shared expression. One may write, draw, paint, or compose and keep it in a drawer at home or share it with others.

Thus we have all these different expressions, with the most important being the least expressed.

Environment B: If the attached social/human pressures are reduced and they are not influenced by one's own conditioned ways of expression, the creative/free could emerge. There could still be some social/human day-to-day responsiveness, and the need to be the rebel could disappear.

I would like the reader to appreciate that, even if all these details are a bit too much, human expression, particularly creative expression, has complex structures and influences, if it can take many forms.

I will pause here for a moment because i think i may be getting too detailed and lost in the complexity of possible structures. What we are seeing, as i have just mentioned, is a wonderful interplay of factors—like the orchestra, we can have a constant and changing score in which the instrumental voices may sound cacophonous or dissonant at one moment, if we don't follow some of the social/human values that offer comfort. It could be that the music structure follows a different set of rules or plays with existing structures in innovative ways, but we could also have some sections of our score or even a score itself that are very listener friendly and beautifully melodic to the social/human and creative ear.

Like our laterally moving listener, their own musical expression of day-to-day life in environment A may, with its perceived inconsistencies, certainly express the social/human self. They could be the rebel or a self who seems uncertain and maybe even lost. It is important to note that these expressions of self could be true and honest. But we could ask, 'Are they an expression of unconscious/repressed creative self?' Not necessarily.

The difficulty with our metaphorical use of musical expression, as with the expression of self in our examples, isn't that of social perception and judgement but of inner discourse. The repression of creative energies and the unconscious cathecting of some social/human need can impair optimal expression and freedom. If these dynamics are in place, ego strength, by itself, may reduce openness to self-reflection, but it may also give strength to explore the 'weak' forces that are necessary for integrated expressions of self (the unconscious aspects of self).

I don't know if my use of 'weak' in the last sentence helps make my point. You may appreciate my one-sided use of the word and the fun one can have with contradictions, or this whole exercise may simply confuse you; i use it because it feels good/poetic and even scientific.

Some other interesting dynamics also emerge (with time) in environment A as well. The first point that may not be initially experienced consciously after a lateral move is that, in all environments, people exist on a social/human level. Their points of view may be interesting, refreshing, and different, but they may all be the same structurally and really be based on the same tired social/human values. We can learn, and need to remember, that there are a 'hapless few' who are 'lovers of beauty' (Ezra Pound). But we may find that these rare few are probably only found serendipitously. I think Ezra would agree that these people do not seem to exist exclusively in any location (geographical) or community (artistic, writing, etc.).

Another factor that can ultimately affect the expressions of self with lateral movement is that the dynamics of self may end up being no different from the A that was left. The new A is equally trapping/limiting—that is, of course, unless lateral and vertical movement are completely interactive.

Let's look at a nonintegrated example of lateral movement with the dynamics listed in our lateral movement diagram on page 83. So just to recap, one has reduced social/human stress that exists in one environment. The new experience is different and interesting. It may fill some thought structure holes (new ideas), it may meet one's need for attachment, and without adverse social/human influences, it may allow an innocence to emerge. This use of lateral movement for freeing the spirit sounds somewhat convincing.

After reading this paragraph, you may think that finding another environment could be the answer. In a sense, another environment A could make life enjoyable, satisfying, and rewarding for the creative, different person. However, looking at this lateral move from a disciplined philosophical point of view, we could consider that a lateral move could be a necessary condition for some to achieve vertical development, but it would not be considered certainly as sufficient.

So what happens vertically?

If one is in an environment A for a while, one would most likely start to sense, at an unconscious level, that this environment is 'same, same but different' (a reference used by people in Vietnam to describe my daughter and her friend who were travelling there) from the environment one has moved from. Here is one of the positive negatives of being the different/ creative person. Others may see differences but rarely experience similarities. You who are open vertically may find that underlying (repressed) social/ human values that have been accepted or rejected can emerge and may find out, as just discussed, that functioning in a new environment has reestablished the same old social/human values. It is just that they look different; they could be disguised. It may not take long before one becomes aware that what one is doing is inimical to one's intent. One wants to be free of nationalistic beliefs and becomes a rebel.

My friend had an interesting experience, though 'interesting' understates the personal significance of her experience. In fact, this experience was challenging and ended up being very different from what she expected. What is important from our structural perspective is that her experience gives a good example of how lateral movement and meeting attachment needs can, with time, be affected by vertical conscious and unconscious levels of thought. She grew up with a set of social/human values from her dad that stressed (please appreciate my double entendre) being responsible and appreciating the value of the dollar, franc (now euro), pound, yen, whatever.

She also grew up with a self-fulfilling imagination, a feeling of being different, and a passion for 'caring for others'. Others saw her often as 'caring for others before self'. Her passion was considered by others to be overcaring and somewhat unrealistic and impractical. There was another factor here as well. Her lifetime experience of feeling different and wanting some freedom from her family's social/human expectations led her to the conclusion that making a lateral move would bring about contentment and the opportunity to make a meaningful relationship with another like person. Though she didn't think of it in these terms, she felt it would give her a lateral/vertical sense of completeness. So what happens is a lateral move to an environment where the needs of relationship and attachment to others in a vertical manner are overridden by the social/human/value drives of her dad, his personal qualities, and family culture.

In her new chosen environment, she met a young local who took an interest in her and gave her a wonderful sense of attachment. He wanted to be a rock promoter and liked playing the role but had no real drive, work ethic, or organisational skills. He was not artistic or creative and existed totally on a day-to-day social level. He needed help.

What she did was respond in a manner that was like the social/human parent. She became responsible. She did all those things she had felt were not her. Though she could not be criticised on a human (social/human) level, she could be seen on that same social/human level as someone with a great heart. At a conscious level, she felt accepted and contented, but there was no vertical integration. The irony here could be described in terms of her momentary belief and the underlying structural reality.

She felt the new environment (i.e., environment B) would give her a vertical integration and acceptance for who she was. What actually happened was a social/human acceptance based on her being, not a free creative spirit but a social/human parent to a young man whom she met. What she was doing in this situation was actually replicating the social/human factors of environment A that she felt separate from. From an environment B perspective, we would wonder what she was doing.

From my point of view, what she did cannot be criticised from a human point of view. In fact, we have what might be seen as another contradiction. Throughout this work, i have equated the social/human level to a delusion, as being a creation of socially dominated mankind, as being somewhat negative. So here is an example of the social/human influences bringing someone to the surface. My friend overlooked her own underlying sense of self to address a need for attachment and a desire to be free from a social/human-dominated world. But at the same time, she overlooked that important need for vertical integration and creative self-presence. What is important to note is that she experienced her own ironic trap. Vertical awareness allowed her to see that she ended up, like Icarus, in a negative concomitant state, from which she was able to escape. But one might ask, 'What's next?'

So is the social/human good or bad? And of course, the answer is yes.

Looking at all the possible combinations of those states could be academically interesting but wouldn't serve any constructive purpose in this work.

In all our discussions up to this point, i have described lots of phenomena; however, my analyses have always fallen short of being able to explain the essence of a situation without ending up with contradictions or clear limits in understanding. We have referred to a myriad of dualities that can shift— weak can be strong, and strong can be weak. We can also see that a simple application of symbolic structure to a novel or poem describes only one set of dynamics where there may be many. And even if we see many variables, we often have to think about them individually. Though we may be able to find more and more in written work, it itself is fixed, and it can't change over time. We have considered some simple aspects of several neurological functions; we have also considered psychodynamics. We have looked at myself, my friend, poets, painters, philosophers, novelists, filmmakers, composers, scientists, mathematicians, and religious thinkers/believers. But i have not offered any way of addressing the complex dynamics of human expression. I will assume that all that we have discussed so far is the utterance of the individual or group of individuals. Back to Descartes, cogito ergo sum.

Mixed States and On to the Music

There is a way in which we can describe these dynamics. Instead of having multiple dualities applied in a single 'this or that' manner, we can have mixed states. A mixed state considers the fact (hypothesis) that all the terms we have used to this point are defined in such a way that we would assume that their presence is evident in some form all the time. And just to complicate this, they can be defined from different points of view and in different settings (lateral movements). So we can't even have the comfort of knowing that any one term will always have the same meaning. Our mixed state, i will contend, describes all human states since any human moment, whether consciously experienced or not, can be understood by looking at the descriptors we have used so far.

As you most likely are aware, i find that my appreciation of the world can, strangely enough, be described most comfortably by referring to diverse fields of interest. I enjoy both pure science and metaphors and symbols, physics and aesthetics and can even appreciate formalistic goods and bads. To address the challenge of describing mixed and dynamic states, i will use a musical metaphor. What i want to do is tie all these variables and human experience and expression together.

A little while ago, i paused and referred to the orchestra (in this case as a simile). I referred to musical scores and instrumental voices as (producing) an overall sound. To me, this is the best metaphor i can find since the structure of this music and its expressed tonal quality can vary dramatically and are dynamic.

The musical expression of the human beyond dualities

As an introduction, i need to give a little background concerning musical expressive styles, structure, and the relationships among rules, composer, and expression. Some composers have rebelled against the standard of established rules of key and key modulation.

Stravinsky uses polytonality; Schoenberg uses atonality and serialism. Both are very musically structured but are often experienced as uncomfortable to the unappreciative ear. 'This is noise! Not melodic!'

Charles Ives integrated a number of different elements in his music. He reflected on the experience of being in a church tower and listening to what has happened in the world below—hearing sounds and maybe music coming from different places and integrating these into his experience. Some of his music portrayed the experience. In one of his symphonies, he used two orchestras in part to represent the possible diversity of musical expression.

An Eastern Canadian composer, i think, used a visual score that left it open to a musician to play his/her interpretation of a pictured line on a specific instrument with visual association.

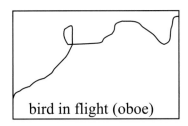

bird in flight (oboe)

The duration of this section was open to the player with direction from the conductor since the piece, which included a number of instruments, needed some kind of coordination. As we can imagine, the coordination of a number of different players, following their own interpretive sense at a given moment in time, may vary dramatically every time it is played (even by the same musicians).

Scriabin was interested in the relationship between colour and music. James Baldwin (an american writer) described listening to a free-form jazz trumpet solo as being led out into the water and then brought back in again.

Back in the early seventies, we looked at the physiological effect of meditation and the use of aum (om). What we found was a reduction in EMG (muscular tension) in the lower back. At the same time, we listened to and felt the power of electronically produced music not only on the eardrum but also on the body. Large fifteen-inch speakers with a large horn above, as produced by JBL (the voice of the theatre speakers), pushed enough air that they could be physically felt more than ten feet (three metres) away.

We can also consider mathematics of music; certainly, Bach and counterpoint are prime examples of this. But we can go beyond. We can consider different tonal qualities of instruments as another variable that influences the sound, which is often one of the factors that are paramount in the composer's mind. But this would not be evident to the untrained ear, just by looking at the score.

Let's consider some other musical variables. We can consider a twelve-tone scale (the number of semitones in an entire scale). Remember also that we have clearly defined wavelengths that are more a function of the human ear than science. In fact, just to confuse the situation, there are times when some musicians may tune a little flat or sharp (related to 440 cps) for expressive purposes. So 440 cps is not 440 cps. From there, notes have relative consistency; therefore, none of them are 'correct'.

Even with all these variables, you might ask a simple probability question. Music has been around forever (now my iPod can play different music forever), but it seems it must repeat. There can't be that much variability.

Before going further, we need to consider a few mathematical points.

Are 220 cps and 440 cps the same? Obviously not. But to most people listening to music, they sound the same. They are both C. As we progress through the scale, it also sounds the same as long as the intervals are the same.

C   E   G

A simple C-major chord can start at 220 cps or at 440 cps; they are different but the same.

To make the math simple, we will keep our universe of notes to 12 tones and will also bring into the sequence a number of instruments but won't consider 'time' or rhythm structure. So if we have an instrument playing a sequence of 3 notes within the 12-tone scale, we have 1,728 possibilities. If we add on 2 instruments, we have 2,985,984. However, many possible combinations can be eliminated (somewhat unfairly) because they are not friendly to the human ear.

If we have a string quartet . . .

If we have a whole symphony orchestra, wow!

My point here is simply to consider the nature of musical expression and the fact that it is an adequate metaphor for considering the vast variability of human expression. This variability of musical articulation, especially in the symphony orchestra (if we consider all possible permutations and combinations of expression), is beyond the known number of people who have ever existed. But i don't think we listen to it for that. It also involves the expression of a number of voice qualities (timbre), which to the human ear make a difference. If we consider the number of different instruments that typically play in an orchestra throughout most pieces, i come up with fifteen as an approximation. This excludes any percussion or solo instruments like piano, organ, and vocal. A question i have at this point, whose answer requires a consideration of levels of understanding, is the range of what is comfortable to the human ear. It could be that all mathematical probabilities are ultimately acceptable from a musical expressive point of view, but who knows?

The orchestra

Let me create a metaphorical symphony orchestra that reflects the integration of all our dualities, individual differences, and lateral and vertical movements. What is important for me is that my chosen metaphor allows for the free expression of a complex set of a myriad of dynamic factors, and we can't judge the expression based on set criteria. In its expressive forms, we can say that different types of music may follow a tradition and harmonic rules, while other parts may break away; all are part of the expression. For instance, i have shown how my friend's response to a situation in a social/human manner may have been hard on her; but from all levels, it can be seen as the right thing to do at the time.

The resulting difficulty in this exercise is that any judgement is limited by its point of view. Hypothetically, it would be ideal to have no point of view; and since that isn't possible, the other side is to have as many points of view as possible.

It is important to remember that the view of the outlaw is not for or against anything; it is independent. It may seem that since i have considered the social/human level as delusion, created by mankind, it doesn't mean that there is no value to its perspective. We simply need to understand its limitations; it can certainly be part of expression.

So here is my symphonic metaphor. It is composed of the following elements:

- a score similar to our bird in flight, which allows for creative expression. In this way, there is an open-ended structure that gives form to voices over time but is not limited by social/human or even conscious influence.
- a wide range of instruments that can be divided in the following manner (to keep the math simple, i will keep with musical consistency and consider two parts for each instrument, principal and secondary (a duality)):

principal	secondary
violin 1	violin 2

viola 1	viola 2
cello 1	cello 2
string bass 1	string bass 2
trumpet 1	trumpet 2
baritone horn 1	baritone horn 2
tuba 1	tuba 2
french horn 1	french horn 2
flute 1	flute 2
piccolo 1	piccolo 2
cor anglais 1	cor anglais 2
bassoon 1	bassoon 2
oboe 1	oboe 2
clarinet 1	clarinet 2
bass clarinet 1	bass clarinet 2

We will leave percussion, piano, organ, and other solo instruments out of our ongoing playing example since we have enough variables already. I have also omitted the guitar, which many of you may be familiar with.

To develop my metaphor, i will begin with a somewhat vertical interchange. It could be considered where the principal represents conscious and the secondary represents unconscious states. If we had only two instruments, we might expect that the principal would play the melody and that the secondary would play the harmony. But of course, we could have two parts playing counterpoint with two melody lines and have an interplay where melody is expressed, in turn, by each instrument. We could also have both instruments playing the same notes or one playing while the other rests (nothing). If there are many other instruments, the principal may play a harmony while other instruments play the melody, and then the secondary could offer an ancillary 'other' harmony part. It is also important to not forget John Cage and the fact that a 'rest' or no music (another duality) is still music—the sound of silence, which could allow the listener's conscious or unconsciousness to emerge.

So for two instruments, we could have the following:

conscious	unconscious
melody	melody
harmony to others	harmony to others
melody	0
0	melody
0	0 (others playing)
0	0 (no other playing)
melody	harmony
harmony	melody

In our parallel unconscious, we could have the following:

conscious	unconscious
strong	weak
strong	strong
weak	weak
strong	0
0	strong
weak	0
0	weak

This strong/weak duality could be substituted with an endless number of dualities. So if we assume that we could have a number of sets of two instruments, then we have a vast number of possibilities. Thus the expression of the orchestra (the expression of individual) at any one moment in time is the result of all these voices.

To add to these dynamics, we can consider all the other terms that we have used and metaphorically apply them to different instruments—the expressive mode of a specific sound could change. It could be that violins, using different tonal qualities, were expressing an organic, earthy sense at one moment, followed by a spiritual, ethereal expression. This same duality could then be picked up by the flute, or the flute could play the 'organic' and the 'violin' the spiritual.

This leads us into another complicating dynamic. Do you see the wonderful complexity that underlies?

There are a number of instruments whose timbre may be considered as better at expressing the spiritual, while others may be better at expressing the organic. As a result, our spiritual/organic duality could be expressed by the principal flute and the principal baritone horn.

Since we are getting into many other variables here, i would like to stop for a moment and reflect.

Let's just consider for a moment what you may hear when listening to popular music. If you are like many people i have been with, you don't listen to music without doing something else. It may be the background at a party or club. It may be something you dance to. (My apologies to anyone doing creative dance, ballet, etc. I'm not including you.) It may be that you love the lyrics. Like many people who drink wine, you may not have developed the sensitivity to all the nuances and their integration. It's a single experience, not a multifaceted experience that has come together as one. You listen to others, you hear their point of view and their 'musical' expression, you observe what they do and make judgements about their expressiveness. But before you and i make judgements, we need to make sure we are sensitive to the many variables that constitute their expression.

If your only point of view is a social/human perspective and you have had no experience 'below the surface', then your judgement will be limited, and you will not be able to explore the vast universe of possibilities and dynamics. You just don't know what to listen for.

The myriad becomes a selected 'one', and you either like it or don't— end of story. You may think, 'Don't upset my universe. I don't care' or 'I don't understand and so don't hear.' These, of course, are indicative of your own dynamics.

These thoughts bring me back to George Ryga, a friend, and Hermann Hesse, just to mention a couple. The question is, can all people potentially understand and be at one with a more abstract multivariate formulation of the universe? Is it just that they don't know it, *or* is it that the potential isn't there? At one point in their lives, they both thought the potential was there.

Somewhat ironically, my response is that for you who are highly successful socially and for those of you who are not concerned but whose vision is limited to this social/human plane, an emerging understanding with experience is unlikely. You may see that listening to music is a leisure activity, but work is needed to make a living. Yet innovation, according to Jeffrey H. Dyer et al., includes the ability to associate—to successfully connect the seemingly unrelated to different fields and to seeing different variables. It's not logical on a superficial level but experiential (vertically).

Our mental patients in the film King of Hearts didn't experience real social/human life. The soldiers who killed one another did. But the mental patients ended up with control over the real world by default. They were saved by their own delusions.

However, if i am correct, the potential may not be there for all. But there are certainly many who have the potential to see, hear, and experience an ever-deepening universe.

Could it be that the creative with 'innovations' and the mental patients with delusions often hear and see what others don't? They may hear parts of a musical piece and, as a result, hear different sounds. An interesting question emerges here. If we assume that the mental patients who have delusions (as defined socially) don't have the delusions that reality is real, the question arises. What happens if we have a delusion of a delusion? Is music that is creatively expressed 'real' or a 'delusion'? With that question, let me return to the music.

We left our discussion about instruments and their role in expression. But these expressions are influenced by other factors. Musical pieces are typically arranged. Who arranges them? If we go back to the score produced by a composer and directed by a conductor, we have two organising entities. We also have, at our simplest level, let's say, thirty musicians all wanting to play and express.

In my metaphor of human expression, i will go further and consider that there are some patterns of functioning that may limit the range and consistency of expression, but these are so highly variable that the structure is unknown.

The Composer

So who is the composer?

My first response to my own question about the composer is i don't know. The first problem, which is the one that exists with the creation of god, is that the metaphor implies a person. This, of course, leads us in the wrong direction.

A somewhat momentary response to my question, which i will address later, is to use a term from the Upanishads, Atman.[4] For those of you who are unfamiliar with the term 'Atman', it will be somewhat confusing. I think its meaning will become clear as you read through this work. Let me give you some of the basics. It has two forms, one with uppercase A (Atman) and one with a lowercase a (atman). The lowercase atman refers to a single-god-type figure, let's say like the Christian God. This form of atman meets the needs of those who have faith but are not spiritually complex. There is atman, one believes in him, he is all powerful—end of story. The uppercase Atman is an entirely different concept. This use refers to an abstract whole universe beyond knowledge and beyond structure but structured. Atman is not really definable—Flew's problem with the paradigm case argument.

Let's consider some relationships. Our first atman is easy:

atman = composer = father = creator

Our second Atman may look easy at first when we consider it in terms of some relationship. So let's redefine composer with an uppercase C.

Let me define some qualitative features of Atman = Composer.

---

4   See glossary.

As i write this, i am reminded of looking at a music contract for my son who was living in the United Kingdom at the time and was writing music. One clause referred to the geographical area covered by the contract; it wasn't just the United Kingdom but also Europe and North America. It was the 'known universe'. The difference between the record company and the Hindu concept of Atman is that, to the enlightened Hindu, Atman is not restricted to the known universe; Atman is all present and all past. In this case,

Atman = Composer = Universe/All Time = Composer = Atman.

There is no individual, no composer, no expression of an individual. The individual doesn't exist as a separate entity; it is an expression of the universe and all time.

I feel i may be either losing you or reinforcing the view that the potential for all composers, writers of music, or in fact many of you is the capacity to be at one with Atman in them; within the microcosm of self is the macrocosm of all space and time.

Strangely enough, i feel a certain vertical state defensiveness at this point since i have a need to be attached on a human level, at least some of the time. If others whom i feel connected with feel differently about human expression or even feel a degree of discomfort with me, i have a need to resolve this. I know that i often feel the need to explain or give up and momentarily walk away. I can feel overwhelmed. There is too much to explain. There are too many factors, thus the need for these ramblings.

However, my need to explain my point of view and how it influences perception has been written about for thousands of years. Whether you are reading the Mahabharata, studying Buddhism, talking to Jesuits, reading Thomas Merton, reading poetry, or recently reading a book on the history of ideas by Watson, all have come to the same point. Becoming one with the universe will require karma/samsara, rebirth (both metaphorical and literal), an evolution from something to nothing—those lovers of beauty, Siddhartha Gautama, those rare people who do really exist on an enlightened plane. However, these states don't exist for everyone at all stages, though it is potentially there. For instance, in some Buddhist writings, enlightenment is considered as nirvana and pali nirvana. The view is that no one person can become enlightened (pali nirvana) until all sentient beings have become enlightened.

So we could say that on a practical day-to-day level of existence, the hypothetical composer in my metaphor doesn't exist, at least as being one with Atman, yet i feel that this conceptualisation is too abstract. What we could say is that the composer could be deeply rooted in the *all* (as considered in all known dimensions) but in a less removed manner; the composer could be considered as somewhat 'beyond' human consciousness structure or at one with some Jungian-type collective unconscious. I also assume that this connection has nothing to do with human individuality as we know it, at least on the social/human level.

I felt that my discussion of Atman being the Composer needed to be introduced here, even though i would not expect that you are going to understand and experience the essence of an entity that is not an entity, especially at this point. So i will return to my question 'who is the composer?' and reconsider my answer and will do this in a slightly different manner.

To keep our metaphors within some kind of limits, i am going to move Charles Ives from the church tower to the top of the ship's mast. Let's have our ship anchored just offshore so we can hear and see others' boats, land, human activities on land, sea life, and the sea.

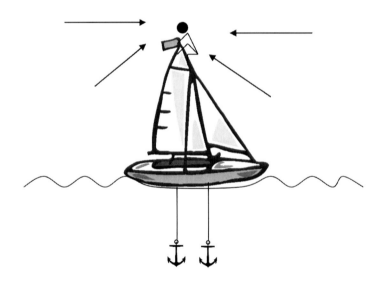

Let's assume Charles, the composer, is an embodiment of different energies, structures, and talents and that these qualities are anchored in some type of universal, underlying structure, an inner self, a strong force and are like our description of the Joycean epic ship that seems insignificant on the surface but grounded in universal significance.

We may not know the nature or depth of his grounding, but we know it is clearly reflective of other levels of experience.

Here, we have a bottom-up, vertical connection to an inner self. We could also consider that his work is an expression of his inner self and that, as a composer, it is structured in a musical fashion. He has a full range of instruments, both principal and secondary. He has timbre, tempo, key, melody, and harmonies. We can assume that his inner self has been nurtured by a wide range of musical experiences and is open to many different modes of expression. So what he hears and sees has a wide, multifaceted salience. He may find the loud noise from the pub, which might be considered typically strong, less interesting at some point than listening to the waves lapping against the shore, which could be considered typically weak in volume. There could be birds, people talking on the street; there could be a marching band, a choir practising at a church. He may have mixed visual/auditory impressions, and because of the musical essence of his expression, these components of his experience are transformed into a musical composition (the weak force).

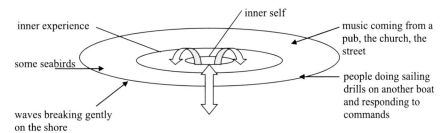

bottom-up connection

I hope that this hypothetical example of Charles and the possible vastness of his experience are not limited by time or point of view; in a sense, it is going towards the nature of Atman. Conversely, if he did not have this inner experience but held on to a clearly defined set of social/

human rules or had experience limited by living on the surface, he would probably only experience those things that fit into established musical forms. In a creative experience, there are no good and bad, there are expressions that work and ones that don't, there are those things that can be expressed by music and those that can't, and maybe 'can't' is simply a limitation of the noncreative and not in any way an absolute. There are rules of harmony, key modulation, and other structures that require a rigid adherence. These, of course, can be selectively used or not used. Both express. There is simply experience and expression. There doesn't have to be a consistent key signature.

In fact, just to confuse you more, i could conceptualise the Composer as those qualities of the universe, Atman-like, that are connected with the unlimited that are evident in the composer.

In simple terms, the Composer could be considered as those underlying universal qualities that compose the composer. We finish this section with this nice tautology.

The Conductor

So what about the conductor? Once again, my initial response is i don't know.

Typically, the conductor selects pieces that he/she wants to play. I think that the conductor—right, wrong, or indifferent—needs to be more selective of music and needs to consider its audience and its social/human appeal, though we know that the audience at the first performance of Stravinsky's <u>Rite of Spring</u> were outraged. Obviously, this was a poor selection.

Please note that this is good, not bad; but it could be bad, not good. Up until recently, many of you might get the sense that i am anti (a nonoutlaw term) religion, anti-anything-social/human; and others know i'm not, even though i used my friend and her consideration of a social/human perspective as the right thing to do, even though it may not have been what she felt was best for her own being. I also discussed the fact that this social/human perspective is a delusion that has dominated society's point of view forever; this is a description of the plane of existence. It is part of the overall essence of reality. People live and die (their energies carry on); popular music has a verse, chorus, verse, chorus, structure (and tonal frequencies carry on). The conductor needs to conduct the orchestra in this social/human world.

If we use the above editorial on the conductor, we could consider our internal (metaphorical) conductor as that aspect of self that bridges the inner self with the world outside. The conductor needs to understand the expression of the composer (maybe at many levels) but would also typically consider the readiness of the audience. And of course, there are many times, like our Stravinsky example, where the audience may not ready; but the conductor, weighing the importance of the music, plays the piece. The act of conducting can also be seen as an expression of self, somewhat akin to how we have considered the positive influences of ego. It is like balancing different energies. It could be balancing psychodynamic forces, like the id and superego, within oneself or expressing some inner experience insight in a social/human context. The ego strength gives confidence to express but does not become a shallow arrogance. This internal conductor is an important figure in adaptive functioning in a social/human world. Of course, some of the same dynamics play out here as they did with the composer. Hypothetically, the conductor could be entirely internally focused without a socially influenced ego and play a piece without an audience and without a sense of defensiveness because no one listened.

Gulley Jimson in Joyce Cary's <u>The Horse's Mouth</u> is a good example of this type of artist without a need to be the conductor. He wanted to express his work and paint a leviathan on a brick wall. He completed the work, and the wall was demolished. However, he was fulfilled because he completed his dream opus.

For other artists as well, it is the act of creation; the production is all important. Jean Cocteau wrote,

Mon oeuvre encoche et là

et là

et là

et

là

dort

la profonde poésie.

From a different perspective, the conductor could select a piece to play that may not appeal to an audience as written. So rather than playing it as intended by the Composer, he/she could arrange and play the piece in a manner that has transformed the Composer's work into one that would meet audience acceptance. In my metaphorical sense, the conductor aspect of self is structuring 'whatever' that underlies expressive behaviour.

It might be interesting, at this point, to consider some of my previous discussions of human dynamics and how the conductor (somewhat like an ego) may orchestrate the aspects of self. For instance, from a neurological point of view, i could say that our conductor, to achieve a balance between the creative and the social/human, would need to integrate or at least regulate the influences of PFC (cognitive thought structure) and SC (basic drives). To this i might ask, 'What would that look like?'

Taking this or any one duality is limiting because it only considers two aspects of neurological influence. Let's go back to our orchestra. At a neurological level, all parts of the brain work all the time. Our discussion of PFC and SC doesn't say but implies that all other neurological systems and structures are not doing anything or are irrelevant. Untrue? However, to control variables in neurological research, the researcher needs to focus on a limited number of variables to draw any conclusions. Of interest are the functions of specific entities, systems, and structures. As you can appreciate, the control of variables is a requirement in research design; even with the best design, successful research may not reflect how things actually work.

With our metaphor, we need to consider the whole orchestra, which includes multiple instruments and players. It could be that some are playing while others are silent. But we know that from the Composer's design that the playing and not playing of certain instruments is all part of the expression. As a result, all instruments, whether playing or not, are relevant. And as we have discussed before, if we know that there are instruments that could play, their silence, their actual denial of play, is part of the music.

As i write this, i wonder if my expression of 'thought structure with holes' is somewhat like having an intuitive sense of musical instrumentation possibilities without the experience or ability to hear a vast range of musical expressive possibilities. It is like sensing a possibility but not knowing how to articulate it. *Or* it could be that one has an intuitive sense of some overall dynamic conceptualisation, but they may also have the personal realisation that their own ability to express is limited or at least has not been discovered.

The solely social/human conductor who is not anchored simply responds to the fact that the pub has Bud Light. Boy, that seems like a non sequitur. A moment ago, i have looked at the conductor as the one who bridges the inner and outer. I have also considered the conductor's possible desire to appeal to the audience. Is it possible that a conductor could select music created for mass social/human appeal? Yes. In this case, we could consider that there is no 'bottom-up connection', no inner to outer; it could be lateral at best. 'This is what people like, and it is understood as the reality. Therefore, this is what i will conduct. This is music that is akin to Bud Light.' Is it because it is not anchored? Would Anchor Steam beer be better? It has an anchor. I think most beer drinkers would agree that Anchor Steam is a more enjoyable and probably a more bottom-up-connected drink. And of course, it is not that there is anything wrong with Bud Light; it is the singleness of its mass appeal focus that is limiting.

This leaves me a bit anxious as i have paused to reflect and realised that using an example or taking a particular point of view can unintentionally alienate an audience. And this can be the dilemma of the conductor. If i feel that my desire, as the conductor, is to offer a developing mind-expanding experience without the use of Timothy Leary and acid—drop in and drop out or drop out and drop in—then i need to be sensitive to your perspective and that you may assume that i am connecting 'pub' and 'Bud Light' with social perceptions that lack depth and are indicative of life on the social/human plane. And from a limited perspective, that would be correct, but please note the presence of the pun, some humour, and more importantly the appreciation that even simple, popular music has a context that is expressive of underlying structures. Being present on one plane does not necessarily preclude living on other levels.

From my personal value (social/human) point of view, pubs are great. I can be anywhere, and as long as i can meet people and have good conversations, my experience is fulfilling. These people could be philosophers, artists, or scientists or could be people i haven't met before and have lives that they see as meaningful in their own unique way. Their personal interests and understanding of life could be like Bach or the blues, but in either situation, my curiosity and enjoyment is generated by those who are open conversationalists and have a passion for what they experience.

I met some locals in a pub in St. Louis. I can't say i enjoy Bud Light, so i didn't have any, but the experience would always remain with me. Ironically, they had lives that—from a middle-class, social/human perspective—would seem like a struggle. They lived down by the river in poorly built homes with no heat, had many children, and worked sporadically. But they saw their lives as rewarding and really okay. They were americans, could go to the pub every day if they had money, had kids who were okay (they all went to school), and had wives who were nags (but that was okay). And they both felt a sense of freedom. In fact, one of these guys confessed that his biggest stress in life was that the St. Louis Cardinals won over one hundred league games but didn't make the playoffs. What became very clear in our conversation, if one considered how they lived from politically motivated, social/human perspective, was that they should be highly discontented, especially living in america, and should rebel. But they had no awareness that there is anything wrong.

I facilitated encounter groups years ago, and a constant parallel given by many who attended was that the group experience was like being in the pub. Some would contend that they could have a great anchoring human experience and Bud beer, but we could have great beer and a less inspiring experience. We could have had beer and bad company as an artistic statement, which can make a profound statement. Robert Zimmerman expressed his down-and-out poetry with a matching voice. It works. Conversely, i once heard an internationally renounced tenor singing nursery rhymes. For me, it didn't work. But for some, it may introduce a good beer in a comfortable context.

These factors are the 'conductor' challenges. If my desire is to offer some kind of 'mind expansion' or simply broaden social/human experience, i have to offer something that does not immediately result in 'closing the door' because it is beyond another's comfort levels.

In discussing those challenges as the conductor, i have digressed from the generic point of view to a personal one. Instead of considering how the metaphorical conductor orchestrates the function of each one of you, i have considered, at least for a moment, my role as the conductor.

Just to increase the conceptual variability, i will introduce a new term—vehicle. This is a mystical frequently translated term referring to a symbolically defined method/symbol of communicating spiritual truths. At the same time, we will leave Bud Light, and so back to the orchestra. But don't forget: same, same but different.

So let's consider some of the possible dynamics of our thirty-piece orchestra. I may express myself using selected instruments because these are all i know, or i may express in a selected manner because that's what feels right—given my experience with all instruments. If we assume that all instruments typically come in pairs (principal and secondary, melody and harmony) and, as a result, could be seen as consistent with our other dualities, we could have a within-instrument duality. We could have a between-section duality by considering the parts played by two sections. But as we know, there are unlimited variations of the structure and resultant expression that can't be described in terms of dualities.

To continue our discussion of emerging possibilities and resultant complexity, let's start by making a suitable harmonic change in what the principal and secondary oboe play (within) while the orchestra is playing a familiar melody. This will be different structurally (the score will be slightly changed), but their new harmonic part may not be evident to most of the audience. We could also have a change in instruments. What has been played by the oboes is now played by the flute (between). In this 'between' situation, the concept of duality does not apply because we could have french horns, violins, and so on all playing the same melody or a wide range of harmonic parts. For the people who hear the melody line, the harmonies may not even be consciously heard.

We could also have changes in the 'loudness' or 'quietness' of each instrument. Crescendo and diminuendo—a duality of terms by their definitions, but they are continuous, not a duality. Rhythms and decisions about instrument salience and relative volume are other significant variables that are continuous and not dualities.

For the conductor who wishes to take some licence, there are unlimited possibilities in how a score can be integrated or changed to meet the conductor's expressive modes.

We also have an ethical question here about what we have discussed. Is it acceptable that a work be transformed from a more deeply anchored, non-user-friendly one into a 'Bud Light'? Or does the conductor need to keep the essence of a work knowing it may only be appreciated by a select few? Let's assume that, in both cases, the conductor has the capacity to draw from a creative/free expressive depth and that the conductor has the choice to select the expressive outcome.

If i consider myself as a conductor, i can see that my score is based on the essential structure of the universe and that my mode of expression, not defined by dualities, is limited by the instruments used and the total range of their expression. In writing this, i am limited by words and their sounds, shapes, meanings, and collective meanings.

Let's take a moment to look at my discussions of my friend where i considered her using symbolic language. There were the weak/strong influences and the creative social/human realms she experienced. The number of dualities i used seemed to define her existence!

If i were the conductor, i could see that the orchestrated expression of her life could be seen quite differently. As a rare, more deeply connected person, we could see her as an expression of that 'beyond' human consciousness and structures. Her life could be orchestrated as a musical composition. It could include a myriad of sounds and phrases sometimes played together and sometimes separately. It could integrate different points of view, it could develop different emphases, and symbolically defined dualities could be seen as limitations in the conductor's expressive genre. As a result, the range of expression could be less contained, less limited.

In my previous discussion, all aspects of her psyche have to fit into either/or dualities. What we are saying now is that these perceptions are extremely limited because they acknowledge that the trumpets are playing a popular melody and that the strings are playing harmonically (social/human). This is the strong and weak (social/human). Our question now considers what all the other instruments are doing. What's the musical context? We can also realise that there could be musical dissonance and listener-friendly harmony at the same time or one after the other. But the musical question might be whether that works (whatever that means). Whether it works for the person and whether it works for the listener are two separate questions.

Back to the music

We have the potential of having all things happening simultaneously. For instance, the principal violin plays a series of notes that represent yin; the second plays something representing yang (a duality), but we could have the cello play a yang line (mixed duality) instead of the second violin. At the same time, we could have a push/pull dialogue between another set of instruments, and we also could have an instrument playing a popular melody while another is playing a newly created musical phrase.

And to give this yet another layer, one could use a popular melody and place it within the context of a newly formed piece. Ives has marching bands; Dvorak and Vaughan Williams use folk melodies. In the visual arts, Andy Warhol uses commercial images. They all integrate the creative and social/human.

We have considered level of experience and point of view, as well as social/creative influences. As i hope you can appreciate, there are an unlimited number of variables in an orchestrated expression, and the sounds they produce can be an expression of all our discussed dualities at the same time or can be an expression by a single note or no note at all. It can be creative and social/human at the same moment. The impasse that seems evident with my friend doesn't exist. Is she influenced by the creative or the social/human? Is there a conflict between the two? Is one better than the other? Are they either/or in nature. In the orchestra, we can have one or the other and, of course, both. It would seem that she has pushes and pulls and conflicts in forces. Or are these 'forces' nothing more than the degree of presence of instrumental expressions in a context of a whole orchestra of many voices? In fact, maybe.

> force (some kind of qualitative feature of the composer or
> conductor) = voice presence (knowing that every voice has
> a created instrumental context)

The expression of self is not an either/or or even something that can be represented by a 2×2 matrix. It is the expression of our thirty-piece orchestra to make it simple.

If we accept our orchestra metaphor and it's structure, we could consider that all expressions are played by a thirty-piece orchestra and that the duality of creative/different vs. social/human doesn't exist in a simple either/or manner but that what does exist is a combined expression of instrument, notes, timbre, et cetera, within a context at any given moment in time. Of course, the overall orchestrated impression could be described in terms of dominant dualities. It is a creative piece, and these are the elements that make it such. The piece could be described by its combination of push/pull collection of instruments playing off one another. But what we know is that the order/structure is a function of 'bottom-up connections' mixed with experiences on the surface.

Though i am comfortable with my above explanation, i am concerned and overwhelmed at the same time. Since i have historically produced 'glassy-eyed' responses from others to my enthusiastic expression of ideas (i have a tendency to go on and on), i am hesitant to even entertain a number of wonderful (to me) ways of diagramming orchestrated combinations of some possible expressions because we have such a vast number of possibilities. Here, we can have music based on a simple rule or set of rules or a loose set of rules that help structure desired expressions that can have unlimited possibilities.

My thoughts about the unlimited possibilities in musical expression remind me of a book written by Stephen Wolfram, A New Kind of Science. He looks at the patterns generated by computers (base 2) who—interesting faux pas (the use of who)—are programmed to follow one or two very simple rules. The program will generate visual patterns of squares (using a graph-paper-type layout) that are coloured either black or white. What is really interesting is that we would expect that if a computer were given one or two very simple rules about how black and white cells should be combined, they would produce a recognisable pattern and that we could find the rules that generated the pattern by analysing patterns even after thousands of trials. What we see are patterns that change in a way that we would never predict. *They have no observable pattern! And they don't repeat!*

To me, this is crazy! We could actually have a conductor establish a starting point—the oboe played an A—and then have a simple structural rule about what should happen next and next and next. Maybe we could have an orchestra play forever (though this would certainly be tiring for the musicians) and never repeat themselves in any predictable manner. So this just covers 'playing' and 'not playing' if we consider Wolfram's discovery.

But in our discussion of music, we have twelve tones, a thirty-piece (symbolic) orchestra, our expressive dualities, arrangements of melodies and harmonies, voices, and forces. Wow.

Even with all these things being said, actually, the composer composes, the conductor conducts, and the players play. That's what music is all about. It is the composer/conductor (duality of influences) that directs what is played or not played and how it is played or not played.

The conductor's influence may say that we have to play duck/social/human music. In this case, let us assume that the music meets popular appeal; it is in 4/4 time in C major, follows popular musical structure, and uses instrument tuning that may even be a bit sharp. The conductor may decide to use 'non-orchestra' instruments because of their duck-friendly nature. In this case, the following are used: lead, rhythm, and bass guitars (all electric); a typical rock drum kit; and a vocal that carries the melody. The conductor's arrangement includes some lead guitar expression of the melody line, a rhythm guitar playing a simple progression of bar chords, a bass playing a repeated four-note bass line, and a drummer establishing and sustaining the tempo. The production of the music is safe. Of course, the composition could use the same instruments, the same key, and the same time signature but be highly innovative or have a beautifully crafted melody. But what we could say is that our duck music is safe; it doesn't articulate the beauty of the swan or innovative expression. Its defining quality is that it is like the marching band without a musical depth or context, like Ives. It offers a pleasurable sensory experience at a social/human level with mass appeal.

You may rightly question my expression here. Though not stated, my comments seem to imply that a music that offers a pleasing sensory experience is in some way lacking. Isn't the essence of any musical experience sensory? And of course, it is.

'Beauty is so rare at thing.' Sensory beauty can, of course, be simple and profound and can be overwhelming.

For me, Vaughan Williams's <u>The Lark Ascending</u> is a good example. Here, we have a simple dominant melody line that expresses the beauty of an ethereal freeness of spirit. For me, the experience of listening to this piece with all elements working together is profound (like a great wine).

As i reflect on my experiences as a participant listener, i can understand the absolute importance of composer, conductor, and musician.

The composer experiences a sense of liberated, ethereal freedom and transposes it into a musical score. The conductor orchestrates the piece in a manner that feels right, and this includes selecting the right musician. In this case, it needs to be someone who can play the piece in a manner that will best express the composer-conductor experience.

Here is the simple progression: Vaughan Williams selected the violin as the best solo instrument to express his experience. The conductor would need to appreciate his selection since many instruments could play it. From my listening perspective and having heard the piece many times, i feel that making it magical requires the right conductor, the violin, and the right musician. Here is a vertical harmony from the creative depth of the composer's creation to its expression on a social/human plane. It is a vertically influenced expression that is a function of the unique expressive qualities of the conductor, orchestra, instrument, and musician.

Does the lark have the same beauty as the swan? The lark, like the swan, is not a duck, and besides that, what's wrong with ducks anyway? But i guess Hans Christian Andersen isn't really that interested in ducks or swans anyway. Maybe he is just concerned about the acceptance of individual beauty, even when it's different.

So if we accept all this orchestra, composer, and conductor stuff and that human expression is a combination of an unlimited set of variables and that it cannot be explained by simple dualities or even combinations of them, we are left with some confusion. You may question much of what i have said now because it may seem to conflict with what i have said before. It would seem that i have made many negative comments about religion, the social/human plane, ducks, and just general human functioning.

Let's take a moment to reflect.

Have i described one thing as good and another as bad? Or have i considered the differences between more limited perceptions and unlimited perceptions with the concomitant irony that the 'unlimited perception' is one that incorporates an awareness of limits where the limited perceptions (the delusion) knows that what is seen is the truth? Have i said that this or that is the truth in some absolute sense, or have i written previously from the humble point of view of someone who doesn't fit, which, of course, could be seen as a statement of 'truth'? I have described my friend from a very human and personal point of view. I have done this at such a personal level that she felt very uncomfortable and even felt somewhat imposed on unfairly by my writings.

My desire to include her is twofold. First, there is my respect for her; and second, there is my desire to illustrate on a personal level the inadequacies of using established schema to describe her state. However, in reading my manuscript, she was not able to see that what i have written is taking a limited perspective and establishing a schema. I want her to see that my writings are founded on a humble attempt to show others the complexity of and the expressive challenges in describing her uniqueness and of others like her. It is not, in any way, meant to be critical of her or even to focus attention on her and create a pressure in being the focus.

As i reread this section on the orchestra, i feel it is important to write a specific statement about where we are at this point. To me, it is stating the obvious, but i feel it is necessary for you who may get lost in the details.

As i have developed so far, you can see that the best analogy that i can think of to adequately describe the dynamic nature of the person and how he or she integrates these dynamics and fits into a diverse universe is the symphony orchestra.

As noted earlier, an old Buddhist saying makes this kind of point: within the microcosm of self is the macrocosm of the universe.

Many of you, as a function of my style or your own background, have perceptions that influence how you have responded to what i have written so far. Since it is very important to me that this work be viewed as a compilation of the work of many others and that their work at least be appreciated, i think it is a good idea to review where we are.

Another Review

To do this, i will start at the beginning and will do this quickly. Please check to see if this makes sense to you.

I have written about the following, which all sound very self-indulgent on one level but are actually expressions of all those 'hapless few'. I guess i could say, 'My, my.'

- my experience of being different
- my sense of being the outlaw
- my need to articulate who i am and where i fit
- my personal needs to connect
- my visual, symbolic resolution
- my personal feelings about a friend
- my views of the social/human (as i call it) and its limits
- my views of easy answers
- my departure from self, a move to ideas, science, philosophy—the human need to find some type of truth
- neurophysiology and mankind (a rather interesting word considering a feministic point of view and the species' propensity for intolerance and war)
- dualities as a way of understanding human dynamics
- the limitations of our conceptualisation and organisation of thought and understanding
- how literature considers underlying structures in a symbolic manner
- dualities and how they can be used to explain the nature of being but, in doing so, limit our perspective because of their either/or nature

- my friend as an application of how these dualities work but are inadequate
- going beyond measurement since measurement is no better than those measuring
- our limits of thinking
- changes in state with an expanded view of dualities; we could have a 3×2 matrix or an $n \times n \times n$ figure
- transformations developmentally in terms of lateral and vertical movement
- the orchestra that, for the moment, is limited to thirty pieces

Can Things Fit Together?

Is there some kind of definitive truth? Is it human or nonhuman? Where do we go next?

Let's return to the diagram on page 11. But in a moment, we will consider it with an antithetical orientation. As we drop into our water/gyre/lake/sea on page 11, we can see loops and arrows going in different directions. We have arrows coming down from the surface, mixing with those coming from below. Here is the mix of influences on the composer and the expression of the conductor. At the bottom, we have the 'still point'—the integration of time, space, and movement, where the microcosm and the macrocosm unite.

However, we can consider my orchestra analogy and the fact that a single moment-to-moment expression in music is a unitary expression of an unlimited number of variables, and complexity might trigger the question about the gyre on page 11. Why is it getting smaller, not larger? It seems like more and more variables, dualities, and multidualities exist underneath the surface. Let's explore this 'getting larger' direction. That is certainly what we have been talking about.

Person on the surface

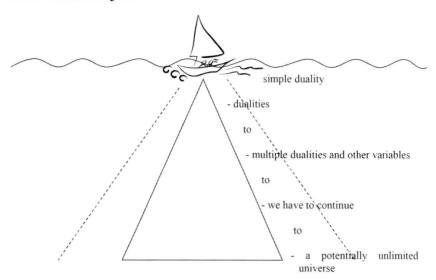

On the surface, this diagram makes sense. We could start with the perception of one person (one small boat). But this person could be described in many ways. We have good guys and bad guys, we have right wing and left wing, we have big boats and small boats, we have strong people and weak people, we have creative people and noncreative people. If we understand the nature of the person, we can see that even those straightforward perceptions can be considered as a combination of a myriad of elements, like our simple popular tune. It can still be understood by using an unlimited number of variables; it is just that all these influences may be seen as more or less responsive to social/human life. Some kind of deeper nonhuman connection may not be seen.

However, if we think about it and accept that everything that is expressed are just sounds, tonal qualities, symbols, and expressed dualities with unlimited combinations and if we assume that this is symbolically correct, then we can consider that the person is composed of many separated parts (instruments and musicians) whose expression is unified, structured, and orchestrated by our metaphorical composer and conductor.

the human = the orchestra?

For the moment, think of people as personified, undefined, structured entities. In doing this, we can expand our view of the human using our orchestra analogy. However, we will have to consider the possibility that the human is composed of a large number of building blocks (musicians playing instruments) that when put together in a structural manner establish an orchestrated expression (the person/the human being), and it could be that the qualities we think of as human are a function of the composer/conductor. My position is that what we think of as human doesn't exist. At best, humanity is reflective of the musical structure of the composer/conductor, not the musicians. Musicians may not really be human! In fact, humans may not be human.

This is a description that may be difficult to follow for some of you, but it is very important. Without an understanding of this, it will be very difficult to move on. For you who clearly understand, please bear with me. For you who are uncertain, let me develop this understanding in some detail.

From human to nonhuman, or is it nonhuman to human?

Over the history of mankind, there have been billions of people; i will not bother to find an estimated number. We will assume that each person has been different/unique (like the range of unique musical expressions) and that their composition has been, and is, expressed only once. All these people were made of the same stuff (musicians with instruments). There are also some forces, laws of nature, laws of physics, and even beliefs in gods or what have you that have been shown to influence human physiology, development, thinking, emotions, and behaviour. In essence, these influences represent the composer and conductor of each one of us.

Let's assume that the behaviour, thoughts, and feelings of each one of us have the consistency of musical expression in that certain structure and rules (like our natural ones) are adhered to and that any expression is arranged by a conductor. Yet there are two caveats here. Sometimes the laws and forces of nature, that we assume we know, have unexpected outcomes that produce 'different' people. From a musical perspective, we know that even the same musical composition can never be played by a group of musicians in exactly the same way a second or third time or in any ongoing manner.

Could we contend that all people are unique and clearly individual no matter what level they live on but they are all simply an orchestrated expression of scientifically based phenomena?

My point here is that the 'myth', 'delusion', or maybe just 'belief' of what defines humanity can't be supported from a social/human perspective. This view, i suggest, is based on the tautology that humans are very special because they are human. However, it could be that the human is really a combination of 'nonhuman' elements that, to use our musical metaphor, may sound impressive when played by an orchestra.

For some of you, the position that humans are nonhuman may be difficult. It should be clearly distinguished from inhumane. One can be humane and not human or inhumane and be human. In fact, some may argue that inhumane behaviour is the result of there being inhumane humans. 'Man's inhumanity to man?'

I feel a sense of apology at this point. If you are still reading this, which, of course, you are, you may find that my making of this elaborate distinction between human/nonhuman and humane/inhumane is somewhat intellectually trivial, but i do not know. Oops, there is a self-contradictory clause at the beginning of the last sentence. This may have slipped by you if you are reading quickly or skimming over some of the material. My use of 'if' is certainly ludicrous at face value. In fact, i have written this in my first 'stream of consciousness' draft without even being aware of what i have done. But when i have considered my obvious mistake, i can see that it is inherent in my feeling a need to apologise and be humble.

Anyway, to me, making clear conceptual distinctions is important. If we reflect on it, we can see that language influences perception and that perception influences language.

So back to the task at hand

Let's just say that inhumane could be seen as 'mean and nasty' and may be used to describe humans that are not respectful or caring of other humans or even domesticated animals. I will consider 'not human' as referring to that class of entities that do not meet the defining characteristics of human either literally (not of human composition) or metaphorically (not having human qualitative features), though our metaphorical use of human could imply a negative or worse value. Being human could imply that you can kill others of your species because you don't accept their ideology. This is not a trait of the not human.

I will use 'nonhuman' as meeting the same literal class requirements as 'not human', but metaphorically, i see it as outside the value-laden human/not-human duality. Like my use of 'outlaw', it is outside social judgements. Nonhuman refers to all those things that do not fall into the conceptual category of human. (Think of our earlier conceptual discussions.) It is important to note, as we have discussed, that this category includes the building blocks of the human (e.g., cells and organs). And for the moment, this will be the focus of our discussion.

For you who are philosophers, there is always the problem of a threshold of sufficiency. The question is, as we build the human, when does the sum of nonhuman parts become human? The classic example in philosophy of the thresholds of sufficiency is used in defining 'chariot'. How many parts are needed for a chariot to be a chariot? Which parts and how many of them are necessary for us to consider a certain combination of parts of a chariot? Is a wheel a chariot? Are two wheels a chariot? Is the body without any other parts a chariot? Without belabouring this discussion, we can see that there may be many difficulties in defining what parts are necessary and sufficient to be human. Usually, being alive, having mind/

soul, or having consciousness or some other quality would probably be seen as a necessary condition for this existence.

As i write this, i am reminded of a time when talking to a female friend who is adamantly opposed to being put in a coffin after death, even if cremated, because she has always been claustrophobic. She knows that her human experience will exist before and after death. I guess that is life after death.

In philosophy, the terms 'necessary' and 'sufficient' are often used in tackling this kind of conceptual challenge. These terms consider the questions 'what do you have to have?' and 'how many of other attributes do you need to meet defined criteria?' To be human, 'You've gotta have heart. All you need is heart.' These are then necessary and sufficient. However, philosophers may have a problem with this. In some popularised alternative health approaches, a holistic consideration of the human is assumed. Holism understands that the whole is greater than the sum of its parts.

To address the questions above, i think we need to consider two factors: First, what do we consider as human, and what is nonhuman? Second, what are the necessary and sufficient components (either human or nonhuman) that we have to have for us to accept that we have formed a complete individual human?

It is really interesting that music, in its simplest form, may have the answer to human existence. Consider the piano piece's heart and soul. The metaphorical heart and literal heart combined with the literal soul (can soul be literal?) and the metaphorical soul come together in a simple repetitive piece that everyone can play.

So let's leave this more esoteric discussion and return to our duality of human/nonhuman. What are the qualities that you feel are necessary to define a human? I know we will never find an answer that we would all agree with, but we would probably have agreement in classifying some things as human and some things as nonhuman. For instance, neither chariots' wheels nor chariots are human. That is easy. Are the cells that form the human body human? I think most of you would probably agree that they have genetic qualities that are expressive of a human; they are programmed in such a way as to produce a human, but they are not human per se. In the same manner, the skin cells of a human are human cells but are not human as individual entities. Some cells, like bacteria, though essential for functioning, may be seen as visitors and not part of human building blocks.

One way of considering the generally perceived nonhuman status of a cell is from a social/human perspective. We do not have groups that champion the rights of specific human cells. The rights of cells are only considered in a functional manner. Do we really care about one white blood cell named George, or are we only concerned about him as one of many white blood cells in rick that keep him healthy? However, some people living on the social/human plane know that any stem cells are human in themselves. With these people, the part equals the whole.

Unwanted cells

We also have some cells that we may respond to with a somewhat or very intolerant attitude. These are alien cells (though they may not see themselves as aliens) that are able to overpower the host cells and, in a sense, move in.

I am going to use an analogy here. Several hundred years ago, the british and french (b/f) moved into an area; killed many of the native population, who were unable to effectively defend themselves; and lived on their land. In the same way, some (strong, dominate) alien-type cells can move into parts of the body, kill the local cells that are unable to defend themselves, and take over their territory. We don't like those cells, not just because they can kill other human cells per se but also because they can kill a specific person in which they reside. But from their point of view, they are just trying to exist and find a place to live. I guess we could call these cells b/f's.

If we went one step further, we might conclude that it is not those terrible b/f's but this desire to 'take over' that has happened almost everywhere by almost everyone. It seems to be part of human nature. But if we accept the above point of view, at least as an interesting one, we could consider that the human perspective limits itself in how it views human and nonhuman. I could be Christian, b/f, civilised, democratic, or whatever and believe that these points of view are human. But it is also the ideology of the cancer cell. I feel a sense of apology not to humans but to the cell that is labelled as cancerous and, therefore, assumed bad. It could also be considered an insult to be compared to being human.

Even though new neuroscience can identify how new neurons fit with existing neurons, i think that popular opinion would not think of individual cells in that manner; besides, we have far more neurons in one brain than there are people on the earth. So let's agree that, even though we haven't defined what 'human' really means, it would make sense to say that we don't consider individual cells in the same ways as individual humans.

As an interesting aside, cells have been shown to respond to conditioning in the same way animals and humans have. They have no brain but respond in a manner that suggests they have one. For instance, they can be conditioned in a Pavlovian manner and learn to respond to a neutral stimulus (conditioned stimulus), like water, in the same way they do to a noxious stimuli (unconditioned stimulus), like a mild acidic solution.

Step 1: Water is dropped on a cell—no adverse response.

Step 2: Acidic solution is dropped on a cell—adverse reaction.

Step 3: Water and acidic solution is dropped on cell numerous times—adverse reaction.

Step 4: Acidic solution is withdrawn, and only water is dropped—adverse reaction.

The new neurons that i have mentioned a couple of paragraphs ago need to fit in. They need social skills training; otherwise, they may not survive. If it looks like a duck and walks like a duck, it must be a duck. I guess humans don't look like cells or neurons, even though that's what we are collectively. My sense is that this whole area of insight is complicated by human insecurities, fears, and conditioning over centuries, and some of this we have discussed before. However, in saying that, we still haven't considered what makes the human into human and nonhuman.

You might ask at this point, 'Does this distinction really matter?' This could require a whole book on its own. However, i feel that this distinction is an important one to cover before we move on.

Let's move from the cells for a moment and consider our discussion of symbolic dualities in this human/nonhuman light. And of course, because of their symbolic nature, even terms that have human referents represent qualities that are nonhuman in scope. For example, mother/father—or should it be father/mother? Well, whatever. We have mother earth. We have 'our father', who could be an old guy with a long white beard up in heaven for the literal thinking person or could represent something else to the less literal person. However, the person who thinks symbolically may consider symbolic dualities as a way of describing the nature of things. But as we have discussed, this symbolic approach is also limiting. If you would like, refer to the dualities listed on page 62.

In a sense, these symbols tie human qualities and nonhuman (or beyond human) energies together. Even though these are created by man, they represent something much bigger. Sum ergo cogito.

Could we consider that the existence of human cells is somehow beyond the human or at least not dependent on a specific human for their existence? I could say that i need my cells and they are uniquely mine. Of course, we know that isn't the case. If blood cells have type compatibility with others, they can live in different humans. Organs, as we have found out, can do the same thing. Cells can live in a lab without any human body. So unless we accept some belief of an individual soul or spirit, we are left with the fact that our nonhuman building blocks can live without us. We know the following to be true about our need for some of these building blocks:

Without some, we can't live.

Without some others, we can't live normally.

Without some less essential ones, we live normally.

Cogito ergo sum? Is this not complicated by insecurities?

Some of you may feel confused about our whole discussion of what is human, especially at the social/human level. You might say to yourself, 'I am often confused about the consistency of these views.' You may be a person who strongly supports the sacrosanct essence of each human life and accepts that abortion is sinful. You may be strongly opposed to the act of killing any human life and believe that human life begins in utero.

Okay, let's accept this point of view. However, for some of you, there may be some inconsistencies since this position, like that of the pacifist, is difficult to support. For instance, if you accept that it is sometimes okay to kill people in a 'just' war or to kill those who have a different ideology that allows them to harm or kill others, then your sacrosanct view is compromised. As we know from history, many individuals and groups can experience a threat to their own existence from those who have different beliefs. From the perspective of a nonsocial/human level, we could probably conclude that the person holding these views is, at best, highly insecure, cognitively limited, or in some kind of delusionary state (as used in our somewhat metaphorical manner).

We could consider the person holding these conflicting views as seeing self as above the physical limitations of being human in an effort to deny the reality that they are insecure, inconsistent in their thoughts and feelings, and self-absorbed. *Or* we could see that this person is 'not human' because he/she doesn't hold the values that we think the 'cultured', 'civilised' human should hold. Ironically, it would seem that the person is also most likely to hold a narrow sacrosanct view of human life and sees themselves as above or 'heavenly'; the person is actually dominated by midbrain (SC) 'earthy' functions like fear. This person may tend to react in an intolerant, defensive manner in response to any questions about personal beliefs.

So even though we don't know what any of these positive human terms really mean, we know that, at best, they are highly selective and contradictory. Let us return to our symphony orchestra analogy to see if this can help address the situation.

To adequately integrate our discussion of necessary and sufficient conditions with holism, cells, neurons, conditioning, symbolic dualities, humans, human insecurities, and basic beliefs in human/nonhuman distinctions, we need to apply these terms to our orchestra.

In no special order, let's assume the following:

- Musicians are nonhuman. (That's pretty well accepted anyway.)
- There are individuals and sections of musicians in each orchestra, and they may not have any individual identity or importance in themselves. (They are not soloists.)
- Musicians can survive by playing in different orchestras and can actually survive playing on their own.
- Musicians can be taught to respond in a conditioned manner to stimuli.
- New musicians need to have a compatibility with other musicians in an orchestra to survive.
- Musicians can individually and collectively play sounds that represent symbolic dualities.

What is missing from this list is a consideration of the composer, the conductor, and the unlimited number of ways notes can be expressed and the dynamics of expressive influences. Let's try considering the composer's and conductor's creative and structuring influences as analogous to those influences that give some kind of human organisational qualities to the collective expression of these nonhuman musician entities. We have discussed the composer as the creator who could integrate a vast number of dualities in a structured manner and that the sources of inspiration could have come from different places. His/her composition could be an expression of Atman (an expression of the universe of all energy and all time but also nothing) or something like an Atman or even atman, depending on how we address what influences the composer.

Some of you may think of atman as godlike (for the moment, i have given that impression), and you may also make a kind of atman/spirit/ soul/mind/human connection. A typical association that many of you might make is that the composer is representative of some godlike entity/ force that has taken these nonhuman pieces and organised and structured them in some higher-ordered manner such that it gives these nonhuman building blocks the essential features of being human. This view would be consistent with a holistic one, but also, it would be consistent with most religious points of view; however, whether composing a symphony or designing and defining the human, one's starting point allows us to differentiate between Atman and atman.

Look at the organisation of the same number of dots below. Our metaphorical Atman and atman can be distinguished by looking at direction. If one goes from left to right, one starts with entities that seem unstructured and transforms them into another structure, which in our example looks like a stickman. In this case, we will assume that the form has emerged and has not been predetermined; this is akin to Atman.

If one goes from right to left, one starts with a stickman outline and sees physical structure as being consistent with the predetermined outline. The far left is simply unstructured chaos; this is akin to atman.

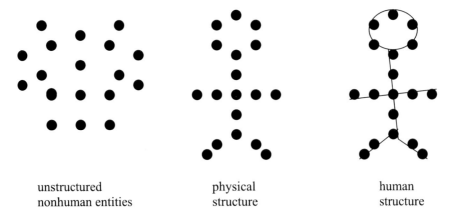

| unstructured nonhuman entities | physical structure | human structure |

Warning: Just to complicate our discussion, i will have fun of sinfully mixing metaphors.

Our concept of the Composer could be considered as someone who moves from left to right. The Composer organises unstructured entities (Atman-like) in a manner that could end up looking like something familiar, for example, the human form. It could be that the composer has established a creative journey that structured dots in a unique manner, which end up being similar to a human form. Some music critics (remember, we are mixing metaphors) may discover the essence of the structure of the composition by joining the dots and appreciate the creative product but also discover that 'Aha! It is organised like the human form!'

However, we could assume that some other critics might see the human form as the structuring goal state (from right to left) because the dot organisation looks like a stickman. And yet some others (the right only) may only see a stickman that is representative of a human. For them, there may not even be any thoughts about the process or the creative elements in the expression. It's a stickman. Think of how many people look at 'modern art' in this manner. Some of our above critics may see that some variations of this assumed 'stickman theme' could be made and would involve moving or changing the number, size, colour, or placement of dots; but since the stickman/human is understood to be the creative end, it would not involve making a change to the structure. In a sense, they would be making the false assumption that the stickman structure is the essential purpose of the composition, rather than it being the outcome of the emergence of a unique structuring of unstructured entities. In simple musical terms, does the Composer write a piece of music to fit a musical form, for example, a symphony? Or can music just be composed and have the resultant form based on what is expressed?

Our 'inimical composer' would be one who would start at the right, maybe move a bit to the left but not very far. What i suggest happens here is that the composer doesn't create out of the unknown but starts with the line that has joined the dots because it is familiar to those on a social/human level. From a musical perspective, it would be like deciding on a key and time signature and writing in a verse/chorus that is not concerned with enhancing some unique creative expression but is written in a manner that can be easily enjoyed by most people.

Think of the Composer as the embodiment of an unlimited universe (a kind of Atman sense) and not as a god that has also been created by joining the dots in a more limited human qualitative sense. Any musical form or structure that is used by a Composer could be seen as a function of the creative process and his/her resultant artistic expression.

We could say that a godlike social/human composer could be given human qualities, like good, father, all-powerful and forgiving. Atman (representing the heaven, god-type side of different dualities) in the lowercase sense could be given these attributes; but in the upper case sense, Atman would have none of these but all of these.

I mention these here because my reference to a god-type concept of the composer that is the creator of mankind, who are created in his image, makes it easy to define 'human' and would be comfortable for many. If we take an abstract, nondefinable term like Atman, our challenge has only just begun. A composer that represents all the universe and all time doesn't give us closure. We are still left with having to describe what makes the human with no comfortable answer. This could be an easy place to stop for the faint of heart. You have your answers, thank you very much. *Or the curious may ask, 'Where is he going to go now?'*

What is our purpose here?

In our previous discussions, i have considered the Composer in a nonhuman, universal manner and have also considered the Composer's relationship to the social/human listener. Some of you may have found some or many of our discussions interesting but may be looking for some sense of purpose, concrete direction, something that holds all the pieces together and maybe even offers some closure, a climax, and a denouement. In simple terms, this won't happen. But these thoughts have generated some questions.

1. Should these ramblings simply be descriptive of different points of view?
2. Should these ramblings help each one of you clarify what you believe while giving you some exposure to what i or others believe?
3. Should these ramblings pursue some sense of truth?
4. Should these ramblings help you see the limits of your points of view and find some different perspectives, knowing they too will be limited?

My intent in these ramblings is to address the four questions above. I feel we need to go to the route of trying to see the ultimate essence of the composer both cognitively and experientially. However, if we attempt to step into the unknown and reflect on some kind of 'all things at all times', which we could contend is beyond social/human comprehension of our humanity, we are left with a reasonable, though not very satisfying, conclusion. We know that we live in a vast unknown. Remember, Alan Watts has written about the wisdom of insecurity.

The popular alternative for dealing with the unknown is to create our own definition of _self_ and _god_. But we know that most are aware of, and probably never think about, the fact that we live within an unlimited universe that the social/human has no clue about. I think the irony here is that the more we accept that we know very little, the more open we are to seeing. As a result, we can see and understand more than the person who knows. The one who knows doesn't see beyond or below.

So a lot of this discussion may seem pretty confusing or questionable from your perspective. In most books, the author gives you an answer or at least a statement of his/her point of view. In this case, i feel that an articulation of where you see your own threshold of acceptance is important. Using our metaphorical terms, i could ask you to consider where your concept of the Composer is grounded. Does the Composer start on the left, or does the composer remain on the right? Some of you, like our composer on the right, will need to accept a simple set of human beliefs that account for your view of the world and humanity. There is some kind of god, there are good guys and bad guys, there are things we have to do, etc.

Others of you may 'know' that everything is relative (an inherent contradiction?), but disciplines like mathematics and logic are universal or at least the best tools we have for understanding. Your thoughts about humanity may be clearly articulated or even appreciative of scientific limits and, therefore, somewhat uncertain.

And others of you may simply have a 'who knows' sense. If you have this 'who knows' perspective, i think you could have different experiences in holding this point of view. In not having an answer, you may have a laissez-faire, 'it's all too much for me' perspective. You could have a feeling of being overwhelmed and distressed just thinking about it. Many of you may remember, even as a child, trying to take the concept of 'infinite' and trying to experience a universe with no end and finding you couldn't do it. You may also see yourself as one small speck in a world of billions of people on one small planet. This one small planet may or may not be the only one with 'human life', but either way, your speck status may remain the same. You may see yourself, as in our analogy, as a vast number of cells, molecules, atoms, and subatomic particles all put together in some ephemeral form. You may agree with all or some of the above, but 'who knows?'

A needed short digression to define the universe

If we don't limit our perspective, we can expand our understanding beyond each one of us to the universe, or we can at least expand our understanding from our own internal limits. Either way, we have an expanding universe. So where do we start? Let's start with some contradictions, some more dualities. Antithetical gyres?

On page 11, we had ▽

On page 49, we had △

On page 167, we had △

It looks like △→ wins. It's 2 to 1 but not exactly. W. B. Yeats, for the same but different reasons, combined them.

Our first step is to establish two open-ended, vertically opposite triangles (see U and D in the next diagram). These are triangles in which one side has not been completed. Maybe these become angles, not triangles. But let's keep them as symbolic triangles that may theoretically have a common third side that is somewhat infinite in space but whose end we can't define.

From a social/human plane, we can see a universe that expands upwards and downwards. (Isn't the number of dualities we can use amazing?) A third side to either one of these 'angles' will imply a limit; that's all there is—interesting that a singular verb works here. However, for some of you, a large cube, the new Jerusalem, some 3.375×10^9 cubic miles may offer an upward limit.

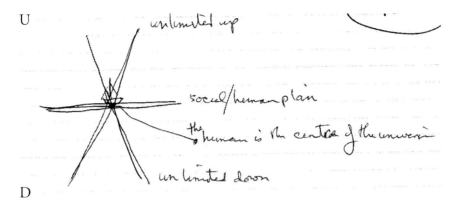

The approach in the above diagram, which goes from 'me' to an ever-expanding universe, seems to make some intuitive sense (see the sailboat on the surface). Whether we look to the sky, the heavens, the energy that encompasses an expanding or contracting universe, or the earth and the physiological nature of things, we can see that it seems to go on forever. Here, we have another duality, but both are unlimited and, upon reflection, could be considered the same. Does the universe actually have an up and down?

The momentary challenge for me at this point is to find some diagram that might show our understanding of the 'known unknown' and the 'unknown unknown'. Is this logically possible? Not really, but consider the following:

Aristotle, in his triangle, saw an apex that represented no physical form but ultimate structure. Poets like T .S. Eliot and W. B. Yeats saw the whirlpool, the gyre, the still point.

Let's add these to our diagram.

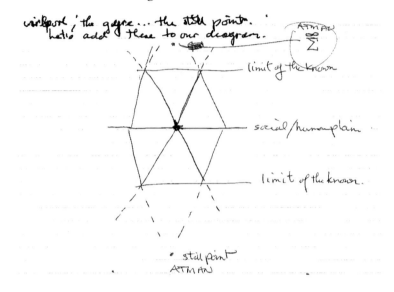

In this diagram, i have used broken lines to represent the hypothetical region that is beyond human, empirically based knowledge. From three points of view, we could consider god, who is within the boundaries of the known, as = (analogous to) some single highest possible number, like the new Jerusalem or maybe all numbers. But maybe numbers don't actually fit for this god. To conceptualise the nature of some kind of ultimate structure, our creative thinkers have developed analogies that logically progress from less structured, more chaotic states on the human plane to calm, focused single points. To our poets, this still point is down; and to Aristotle, it is up. But in both cases, this single point = 0. And just to confuse you more, these single point apexes don't move, have a physical mass of 0, and represent a 'timelessness'. Yet at the same time, using the expanding broken lines that start with each one of us (which could be considered as an apex of 1), we can expand our understanding both up and down. What we can't reach, but approach, is an 'unlimited all', which we could see is just another way of expressing 0, which mathematically could result in the following expression:

$$\infty = 0 ?$$

But we know that these abstract conceptualisations are not even a concern for most of you, and your brain might get sore even trying to think about them. For this problem, the solution is simple: create your own limits, depth (an exploration of all things physical, whether cells, nuclei, or subatomic particles).

The limited world of social/human

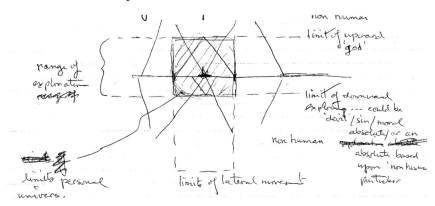

As i define these factors in these diagrams, i have this interesting conflict about scope. It is certainly well accepted that circles/ovals/eclipses are more natural forms than triangles or quadrilaterals. But i find that a box, like the shaped area above, is a better representation of different human experiences. Remember, the early Christians formed the new Jerusalem into a box.

For instance:

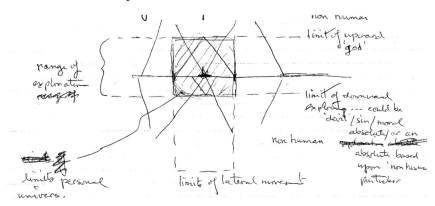

And as noted in our example, a person's personal universe may be different from another's. Some may have a clearly defined universe (it's in the box) that encompasses varying degrees of combined vertical and lateral movements, which could be above or below the social/human plane; and some others, like our Composers, may not be enclosed in a limited universe. What they experience is open, not definable; it is all and nothing at the same time—Atman.

In an attempt to incorporate more of these factors in a diagram and give us an interesting visual that isn't too confusing (like a mandala), i have incorporated circles, squares, and triangles from a three-dimensional perspective. Of course, the limitation here is that this visual is built with geometrically formulated structures.

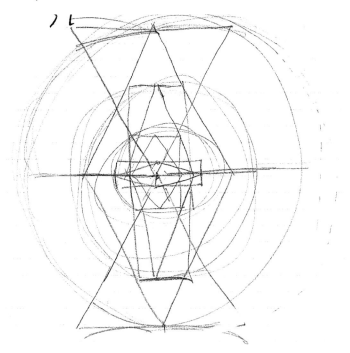

As i draw this diagram, i feel circles make it complete not for conceptual reasons but because it 'feels' better. I also, in a post hoc manner, find that any attempt to complete a triangle that is expressive of an absolute could be understood as a straight line or seems like a short segment but could also be seen as such a small arc of an infinite circle that it looks straight. Is straight really straight? *Or* who cares? This may help define the limits of a universe and the problems of sketching something limitless.

Isn't space curved?

Stephen Colbert, in one of his 'interviews', asked a scientist (astrophysicist, i think) why some people have very fundamental views of god. He paused for a second and responded, 'Because they have lazy brains.' I think there can often be a 'lazy brain' factor, but there are also people, maybe most, who don't think in a scientific or tightly structured, inquisitive manner. Life is too all-consuming. There is, i think, also a fear factor for many because security and comfort of 'knowing' is needed. For the 'outlaw' comfort comes from not being 'trapped' by social/human dualities by one's own psyche seems to be imprisoned by upper and lower limits.

Now that i have either confused you more or added some clarity to what looks like growing complexity, let's return to our Composer/conductor analogy.

It seems that our discussions about the composer have taken some different shapes. Some references define the composer as some type of theoretical absolute, and at other times, the conductor is a Vaughan Williams, Ives, Schoenberg, Stravinsky, and more contemporary Composers like Pärt. In these cases, they are real people, real Composers who have created works that are both loved and hated on the social/human plane. In any discussion of the absolute, like Atman or laws that seem to be universal, we are always entangled in conceptual complexities. As the reader can appreciate, i have attempted to define an absolute; but in doing so, we end up with nonabsolutes because we are attempting to define the nondefinable. Here, we have another duality. They are certainly difficult to get beyond.

Let's accept that we could have this ultimate, beyond-time-and-space something (ultimate composer), which is too abstract to be practical. But we need some kind of composer that creates a work with order and structure. We could have a composer that has an expressive foundation that integrates a vast universe of vertical (upward and downward) inspiration. We could also have a composer who draws solely from a social/human plane.

Let's check your level of comfort based on your musical tastes. How deep is my composer, or is it how deep is my love? What range of music do you enjoy? Does the music you enjoy have different creative forces, structure? If you say that you like different genres—pop, rock, country and Western, easy listening, or whatever—you don't understand the questions about range. Except for a few possible exceptions, all these types of popular music have a similar underlying structure, key, and time signature.

As you may have noticed, jazz and some other genres are omitted here. What is important to note is that some genres like jazz (an american genre) have an expressive range that can go beyond the familiar/comfortable. In fact, jazz offers a different creative paradigm. The free-form expression of a jazz musician may take a small c composition and transform it into spontaneously expressed new large C piece that may drift a long way from some simple melody. In this genre, it could be that the artist is the Composer. Keith Jarrett takes four minutes to get to the simple melody line of 'autumn leaves'.

Some of you may listen to music that you don't really understand, and you may be curious and want to explore or may be uncertain and avoid. As a selected default, your taste may be limited to a user-friendly composer and artist. At least musically, we could conclude that you exist on a social/human plane. In fairness to many of you, our musical analogy is just that it's an analogy, and so it may not suggest anything more than you having a limited interest in music.

If you accept the human/nonhuman distinctions we have made earlier, your level of understanding the Composer could be quite different for each one of you. If you accept that there is no such thing as human other than in the thoughts of people (our social/human delusion), then your Composer is probably drawing from deeper waters.

I would see these ramblings as the work of a single composer who, like Ives et al., is drawing from the vertical and some lateral aspects of their world.

What about the conductor? As discussed, we could see the conductor as a bridge between the work of a Composer and an audience. The conductor is also the creator/artist who can be at one with the Composer and conduct a work as he/she feels expresses the Composer's creation, or he/she can transform the Composer's work to a degree that gives it audience appeal (social/human).

The conductor/translator of music could also be seen as similar to the film or stage/director, religious teacher, art critic, sea captain, or anyone who is taking the work of others with special insight and bringing it to the surface. Let's also consider this conductor as an aspect of self. What do we do with energies/thoughts/feelings that are moving up from our own nonhuman world? Of course, this could be considered as a function of the symbolic composer within us. In our analogy, we could say that the conductor can only conduct what has been composed. Early on in this work, i have spent some time talking about the experience of being different and what that means. I have talked about my friend and how typical ways of describing her are limited and inadequate. I have also discussed the sense of potential. Can all people achieve or live on a plane that is like that of the 'outlaw'? I have suggested that most people are not able to achieve such a state; however, i would qualify this statement by considering our internal conductor and the possible variability in how this conductor can mediate mind/body and vertical/lateral dynamics. Our internal conductor, in a sense, consciously or unconsciously orchestrates mind/body dynamics that are influenced by the Composer and the social/human world. As you orchestrate your life, you could vary your life experiences by mixing the vertical and the lateral.

Let us say that when considering your own conductor, your understanding of life, and your own comfort level, you may be confused by the distinction being made (which means you are lateral), or you may be able to describe yourself as more lateral than vertical, vice versa, or possibly a mixture of both.

For those of you who are uncertain about the nature of your thinking, wouldn't it be nice to have some test or measurement to assess your type? 'Am i lateral, vertical, or a bit of both?'

We know that accurate methods for measuring physical phenomena are essential for the advancement of science (well-disciplined lateral thinking); however, we also know that our understanding of the nature of things will only advance if questions and hypotheses—ones that have not been thought of before (creative vertical thinking)—emerge from the Composer or Thinker. It is only after a newly found insight has been somewhat formulated that some questions about how one writes the score in music or finds a way to measure establish some type of proof in science.

If we were able to explore some type of physical/psyche spiritual/intellectual potential (which we actually can't), it would seem that we could determine your 'composer potential'.

Important cautionary reminder here: Measurements of high IQ and test scores may show some degree of 'smartness' but may also be signs of limited vertical potential. They are measuring your social/human ability, not your ability to think beyond.

An interesting irony is worth considering here. You may decide to measure your intelligence and see if you can meet the 'intellectual criteria' to be a member of a selective group. However, a somewhat ironic intellectual limitation is evident with tests that are used to determine how smart you are. You may miss an important variable. Can a test measure abilities that are beyond the limits of those who have created the test?

To some of you, it may be seen as somewhat ludicrous to suggest that we could create some measurement of creative potential, even though i suggest that it may be logically possible to approach theoretically, but i don't see it as a practical possibility.

Let's reconsider that each of us has a personal conductor who balances Composer expression and audience (yourself) acceptance. Our personal conductor may protect us from the unknown or expose us to some distress or openness to the unknown. Consider the following possibilities:

Possibility 1: Let's say that your potential is vast, but your experience is limited. Your conductor is working in a very vertically narrow plane because that is all your experience has offered you. You could have an openness and excitement about new ideas, you see things others miss, and when exposed to new ideas or situations, you're excited and incorporate these into your personal universe. You have been exposed to a vertical range of music, literature, and maybe even fantasy but have had very little lateral experience. You enjoy being at home and are not a very social person. You find that you have different experiences than relatives and those with whom you are friendly. It may simply be that you like to listen to music not just as a background, and you like to read literature, not just popular fiction. You hear new or different music, and you experience new nuances and hear new sounds. Your life experience is enriched by the insights emerging from literature. To others, your experience may seem limited; and to you, others may seem boring and limited.

Possibility 2: Your potential is the same as the person above, but you either have been traumatised or have learned that any ideas, thoughts, or experiences outside the social/human plane are weird, bad, sinful, or whatever. If this possibility applies, your conductor may feel anxiety about moving downwards and becoming open, one part of yourself simply says no, and questions without obvious answers are not even considered. You have very clear boundaries for your tastes and are not open to new experiences unless they have popular appeal. Your simple response when exposed to new or different genres or something that just isn't popular would simply be 'I don't like that!' and walking away.

Possibility 3: You are at a human stage where you are comfortable, have your own sense of how the social/human world works, and can see its flaws and strengths but don't see any need for venturing any further. Your day-to-day responsibilities and some needed breaks, including some holiday trips and socialising with friends, encompass the range of your experience. Your musical, reading, and television tastes would be fairly clearly defined. You are not opposed to other kinds of music, literature, or media expressions that are more esoteric but just don't enjoy them or understand them.

Possibility 4: You are the student/teacher (to me, any good teacher is a student) of an academic discipline that is focused on the 'history of', the 'philosophy of', or the 'science of', and your factual knowledge is very comprehensive. You understand the concepts that compose your discipline and are intellectually curious and open, but you are not moved or changed by learning. It is as if knowledge could be listed on a blackboard but were not integrated into self. Your musical taste, as well as appreciation and enjoyment in other creative expressions, may be eclectic, and knowledge of these may be great, but your passion for them is limited. Your movement vertically above a social/human plane is much higher than your movement below.

Possibility 5: You are like the person in our first example, but you have had the experience and opportunity to explore other levels of life; you have had more lateral movement. But like the sea captain, your lateral movement has not just been that of the surface traveller but you have also experienced the sea and its many states and have developed a rapport. You don't just see; you also do. You may feel at peace with contradictions and the unknown. You are able to be a part of the social/human world but also separate at the same time. You may see yourself as being academic in your interests yet see its limits. You may be physically active but see its limits. You may see yourself as spiritual in some manner but do not have any religious beliefs and do not have a belief in any god. Your musical taste and appreciation of creative expressions would be eclectic with passion and curiosity but would be attuned to those expressions of that which encompass the essence of the 'Composer'. You have the ability to hear, see, and experience those expressions that come from the unknown.

The essence of beauty is hidden by a social/human malaise.

These listed possibilities are just that—'possibilities'. If i consider my friend, she could be described as having had some of the qualities of possibility 1 as a child and young adult with some built-in limits of possibility 2 (though easily dismissed). In fact, her possibility 2 defensiveness could be seen as the result of having teachers who could be described as possibility 4. Over the years, she has developed some of the attributes encompassed in possibility 5. She is a good example of someone who could be seen as having moved from showing the characteristics of possibility 1 to showing the characteristics of possibility 5.

Reflections on the Social/Human and the Emotional Nonnegative

My consideration of my friend and her feelings leads me to another important point. This work, if read from a social/human point of view, is an implicit criticism of the limits of a social/human level of understanding. However, what is important to remember is that i do not see the social/human level negatively. It is the reality that humans have created. It's the plane we all dwell on. Its limitation exists for those who believe that it is some kind of objective reality and not as an expression of an underlying pervasive structure of which the human species is only a small part. For some, their belief in the importance of humanity could be more like a delusion than just some unquestioned assumption. To use our metaphor, we could consider humanity as a symphonic expression. Is it good or bad? Does it contain different variations and different musical expressions that, on one level, may not seem harmonious and consistent with normally accepted rules of harmony? But we might find that, from a nonsocial/human perspective, the Composer may have actually enhanced the dynamics of the overall musical expression.

My experience and that of my friend are different from each other but are also not normal (whatever that means). And as we have described them many times, not normal lives are often misunderstood and responded to negatively.

'The essence of beauty is hidden by a social/human malaise.' I see these words as ultimately descriptive, not judgemental. Ezra Pound writes similar words near the end of his poem 'The Rest'. He notes, 'I have weathered the storm, I have beaten out my exile.' He realised that his survival required not only acceptance but also learning to cope with being the swan/poet (someone who is different). He could somewhat accept that the world doesn't understand him or the beauty he treasures.

As i have discussed, there are different states for different people. Being judgemental about the social/human world can be a meaningless activity since it doesn't change its existence, nor does it enhance the life of anyone. Though, the social perception of the life of someone like Ezra Pound or the lives of many who are different and creative people, like my friend. Their lives may be seen as more difficult because their ways of thinking and behaving seem to be driven by influences that are outside social/human norms. It seems like they don't know what they are supposed to do. The assumption by many seems to be that they probably don't fit because of their social insecurities and limitations, and from a psychiatric perspective, they may be seen as having a psychopathology, possibly coupled with poor social skills. In fact, it is interesting to consider the number of creative people (scientists and artists) who have been given, sometimes posthumously, a psychopathological label.

But label or not, i think it is very unfortunate, but it is also a social/human 'reality', that numerous creative people need to find a symbolic exile or retain a social defensiveness. I think some of you may have the opinion that 'there will always be weird, creative geniuses, and some of them do lots of neat things. It's just that we may not understand them or know why they are different.' However, i have had people ask me, 'Why can't you just be normal?'

Let's consider this from another point of view. Let's assume that the regular, everyday person, our possibility 3, describes what most people present and are contented with in their state. My view could be that everyone should be at a possibility 5, but this is equally value laden. If we accepted this, we would hold the position that we don't like ducks. Everyone should be swans! Then the weird ones are ducks. The reality of social perception is that we live with both. Yes, even the reality that we consider a delusion is part of the way things actually are.

Moving away from values is very easy but very difficult. I have introduced the outlaw (Robbins) at the beginning of these ramblings so we could have some type of conceptualisation of a state that one 'ought' to be in (value judgement) so that the person does not get stuck in social/human value judgements. However, here, we have a problem. Can we have a nonvalue judgement point of view that is supported by a value judgement? Can we achieve this?

In my experience as the different kind of person, i have found that i don't have the ability to feel a personal dislike for anyone, though sometimes i may find it difficult to understand why some 'normal' people can display such high degrees of hatred for other people and races. Many people behave unethically but are often not aware that they are doing so, and others with whom i have discussed such topics as the inadequacy of simple diagnoses and treatment approaches of some complex people may resort to what i call 'an arrogance of ignorance'. These people portray an unwavering confidence in their knowledge of a particular situation, but in reality (both social/human and below), they have limited knowledge and ignore important variables that they don't understand or don't know what to do with. Though these situations and people can sometimes be frustrating to me, i know that they are representative of how people cope with challenges in day-to-day life. But a question i sometimes ask about these people is an ethical one. If one has limited knowledge of a particular field, let's say in some area of human health, is it unethical for this person to insist that he/she has an answer and not work with or refer the situation to one who has more expertise? Or is their position ethical if they believe (delusion) they are right?

I have had many opportunities to express dislike, or something stronger, but haven't been able to experience it. One personal experience where some negative feelings might have been expected has occurred a number of years ago. In fact, this experience raises the ethical question i have just raised.

A family friend, who was also a fellow sailor, at my request, helped out with one part of my business. I asked him if he would be interested in being a board member for a not-for-profit society. He was experienced in business and knew i didn't have a clue about how to run a business (though i had done so for ten years before his involvement). After a year, he became chairman of the society; and during his tenure, he always expressed great confidence in how things should be run.

Even though he did things that i felt were mistakes, i initially made a point of expressing my views, which he sometimes responded to very aggressively; so to keep things calm and since he and others knew he was an expert on dealing with life on the social/human level, i followed his lead in making business decisions. However, his views about management and the society's mission were very different from mine and the staff's. Since he had no understanding of what the society actually did (which was to treat children and adolescents with complex psychiatric disorders) or even the culture of the society, he resigned after a number of years. His parting was very positive, and i thanked him sincerely for all his help. Though i knew he never understood the nature of the business, its cultures, and the nature of its successes, he was very sincere in all his efforts, and his desire to help was unquestionable.

However, one of his strategies, which he was obviously confident would work, backfired and resulted in harmful long-term consequences to me and to my business. Unknown to me, he had made contacts with our bank and tried to solicit their help by focusing on the fact that the business was going to fail if they didn't help. (This was not the case; he simply wanted the bank to give a donation.) And since we treated children with complex health and mental health disorders, he felt that his approach would put more pressure on them to be supportive. His approach didn't work in the short term because they didn't donate any monies, and it didn't work in the long term. After he left, we approached the bank for short-term financing, which had always been required because of the way government funding is distributed, and we were refused. What he had done, we found out, had made the bank question our financial viability, and they put us into a 'high risk' account department. As a result, the bank refused to offer us any help even with supporting evidence that all monies would be covered by guaranteed government funding. To make matters worse, because the society had no substantial assets, the financial institution made it clear that, no matter how stable cash flow and profit and loss statements looked, the society had no way of getting rid of its high-risk status.

He had also 'helped me out' personally, against my better judgement. Cost to me without his help was $0. Cost to me after he helped was $50,000. If i hadn't found new sources of business financing, the business would have failed, even though revenues were increasing.

These details are not ones that he is even aware of; i mention these to give you some sense of the nature of a realistic social/human situation. In this case, there is a combination of contributing factors, including separate perceptions and a need to follow 'the way things need to be done', that have resulted in an outcome that has even overlooked the viability of the business from a financial growth potential.

The benefit for me from this situation is a confirmation of my understanding of the workings (and nonworkings) of the social/human world and my own experience. I have realised that even the outlaw, the not-fitting person, could handle the challenges of the social/human world and do so with more insight, possibly because the outsider can see how such variables as egocentric thinking, different expectations, learned patterns of behaviour, different points of view, and different people following different policies, rules, and procedures can all be integrated if everyone is on the 'same page'. But if not, outcomes may not be successful or not understood from one perspective and may be seen as successful and clearly making sense from another perspective.

Should i have let him know that he didn't understand the nature of the society, which would have been okay if he hadn't tried to change it, and he messed up in his fund-raising strategy, which i was able to put right by changing banks? What i have found and continue to experience is that i have no desire to inform him of the details or even that, after several years, the society had recovered and was doing well.

You may ask, 'What about the above account? Will he not be informed by it?' That is not a concern. This may sound priggish, but i can't imagine any of the people he knows reading this work. I feel that, for them, it would be like listening to music that they don't understand. Typically, they are not motivated to experience anything that is not within their comfort zone. I feel that if they were to start reading my ramblings, they may last a few pages at best.

Anyway, back to the point at hand, i have no feelings of animosity, and i realise i can't even find any. He is a well-meaning guy and has done his best to help. We continue to see each other and be friends within my 'being different' limitations. As i have said, he's a good guy on a social/ human level. He is our possibility 3.

What about my responsiveness to adverse social events? Is my natural response to this situation

- a weakness?
- a strength?
- not applicable?

If we consider 'not applicable' as the right answer, we would be taking a point of view that is inherently contradictory to a nonvalue position. Is it 'not applicable' or 'right'? I worry that our use of language and what we focus on as relevant shifts our focus and distracts us from inherent contradictions. For me to say 'not applicable' is the right answer, in the context of getting away from values, is an inherent contradiction.

Even though N/A is the answer that best suits my direction, it is important to be aware that the values of probably anyone who lives on a social/human plane are always there. For me, it is something i want to be aware of. I will make judgements, i have points of view, and i can be opinionated, but i can also put all these in perspective. They have no long-term influence on my psyche, though they can momentarily affect my emotional experience.

So do you accept that your experience in life and your perspective is limited because you get stuck in some value-based, emotional experience? Maybe you don't see it as stuck because it is justified. Whatever your position, it can be viewed differently from different perspectives. It is also important to note here that having an outlaw point of view and experiencing life differently does not necessarily mean that the social/human level should be regulated differently. For instance, it's pretty evident that laws and legal consequences need to be there to keep civil order. There are going to be good guys and bad guys, there is going to be love and hate, and society has to deal with these. *But* it is important to remember that these are all expressions of a species that has existed for a very short period, even when considered from the history of the earth, and whose individuality, when considering the earth or the universe, is not significant. Its history can be seen as momentary in time and insignificant in size. Will it last? Who knows? Social/human life is ephemeral, pretty meaningless in itself but filled with the delusion of self-importance.

How do you respond to the above statement? Does it make sense? Does it not make sense? Does it seem spiritual? Does it seem anti-something? Does it seem pro-something? Does it seem? Did you see it simply as a statement to be read cognitively? Is there an emotional element to it?

Reflections on the noncognitive

The example of my friend who helped in my business and my reactions to him are a way for me to experience my feelings in a situation where negativity or anger could emerge. What is essential here is the acceptance of our own feelings and our evolving sense of detachment (a Buddhist term). This detachment is really the retention of compassion for others, coupled with a nonpersonal involvement in what one individual or a collection of individuals do, feel, or believe.

This detached point of view and how to achieve this has been discussed in many Buddhist texts. If you have read some books or articles on Buddhism, you may have found them interesting but impractical—too much work, and following its tenets would certainly interfere with living a regular life.

However, i'm going to try to make some aspects of Buddhist thinking and point of view more user-friendly. Have patience. We have to go through some discussion that will possibly not seem relevant but is essential for developing an understanding. In fact, i will use detachment in a somewhat contradictory manner, at least from a social/human perspective, as you will see if you keep reading. It is hoped that you will start the process of detaching from a single 'one' and attaching to a 'one' that is all.

Let me start by considering some of the possible dynamics that can constitute one's cognition, experience, and physiology and how they can be integrated. Maybe i will start with some cognitive/experiential examples first. In these examples, i am going to use the orchestra as an illustration of an evolution in one's listening ability. With understanding and experience, one can go from hearing a single orchestrated sound to hearing a weaving of multiple sounds, timbres, harmonies, and melodies all creating an integrated oneness.

Though we have many instruments and parts being played, we will assume that our nonexperienced listener hears one sound. This could be a wonderful lyrical melody or a whole bunch of noise. Our nonexperienced listener decides to study this whole music thing and learns about the unique timbre of each instrument, scores, arrangements, the ways in which different conductors express, and so on. As the student, this listener learns to hear different parts, how key influences the sound, how different intervals affect our listening experience. We could say that the listener now, with a mixed cognitive/experiential sense, hears many different sounds with different timbres coming together. Here is our expanding gyre.

However, with time and listening (and possibly even playing), our person's experience becomes less cognitive and more integrated into his/her own self. The sounds become united as a whole, the listener hears a sound with a myriad of elements, and the 'all'—the one—is experienced in a profound new sense. Here is an antithesis and paradoxical state. The 'all' is now 'one'.

This transformation from a single sound to the multitude of variables in the orchestra is consistent with our broken-line gyres on page 135. We have more and more defining stuff. This is consistent with the way a mandala works.

elements of experience

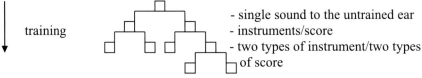

training

- single sound to the untrained ear
- instruments/score
- two types of instrument/two types of score

What brings about this transformation? To answer this, i will use a number of examples.

I have mentioned at the beginning of this work that i have been a ski coach. Part of my job was to improve technique, knowing that every muscle and bone of the body needs to be in 'right positions' at each moment of a turn. Often, for the athlete, there needs to be a cognitive awareness of what needs to be done. Unfortunately, a list of all the right things to do can be a hundredfold, and then these 'right things' need to be modified continuously because of snow conditions, terrain, type of course, etc. This, of course, would be cognitive overkill. Here is our wide point of a gyre of factors. But fortunately, after a while, all these variables become automatic as if they were a natural part of self; they become a dynamic sensation. They become a single feel that is part of a fluid feel of skiing. Here is another move to some unity.

For the person who is learning to play the piano and read music, there are many steps required before one even goes from manuscript to played notes.

 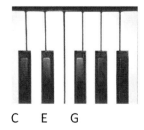

(Please note the incorrect musical notation.)

It is a long way from these beginning skills to sight-reading and to the integration of playing well technically and then incorporating feeling. The goal of practising is to develop a mastery of the skills so the experience of the music can be expressed without requiring any thought about which note is which or what keys need to be played. Once all the skills are mastered, and one has developed the skills to play with technical ease, and then one can use these abilities to express one's own feel for the music (which, of course, can still be a challenge). When everything works together, a single beautifully integrated expression can be achieved.

If i consider my listening habits, i am aware of my conscious listening and, upon reflection, can also be aware of my nonconscious listening. (This awareness, of course, happens after the fact.) Some music or musical expression that i may not have heard before, which might include a new arrangement or music that i may have difficulty appreciating, could leave me in a somewhat cognitive state, which would limit my overall experience.

What is interesting is my awareness of the mistake in a piece that is well-known, which could be a very small part of the whole. I find that the expression of oneness while listening to a piece of music i know can be profound and be somewhat beyond consciousness. You may say, 'You said that already.' You may ask, 'Are you aware while you're not aware?' The irony is that if there is a note or phrase that doesn't fit or a musician makes a mistake, it can bring me to awareness. I jump. My awareness of a mistake or an unfamiliar sound made within a piece i know has also made me aware that an experience of oneness in an unthinking manner does exist for me. It's like the dream from which i have awoken.

What is interesting is that my experienced reaction is an 'oops!' The cognition comes afterwards.

So let's consider that our gyre—like our mandala—can go from a myriad of variables to oneness, but of course, this oneness is a qualitatively different state from our beginning oneness.

Here again, we have 'all' being equal to 'oneness'. It is a simple example of Atman.

<u>elements of experience</u>

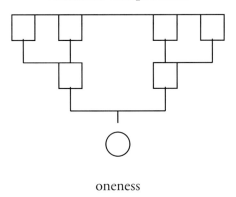

oneness

In this situation, the whole—the integration of all pieces—and each piece by itself are all experienced as a dynamic 'one'. It is also leading us to an understanding of how we might approach the essence of detachment.

Since this 'one = one' to an 'all = one' is such an important transformation, it needs to be felt by you. Please indulge me as i consider some other examples. Since the very beginning of these ramblings, i have referred to water and have used sailboats throughout. What better analogy than sailing to make the transition from oneness to oneness.

Boating is simple; you start at A and go to B—oops that's a 'stinkpot point of view'. (I apologise to any real seamen who realise that the powerboat person who believes this knows nothing about the sea or boats/ships.)

Here are some fun realities for nonsailors to consider that have nothing to do with how you trim your sails. Consider the following three examples about going from A to B under sail.

Example 1. A circumstance may arise, given that the water isn't too deep, where you temporarily anchor your boat and improve your overall rate of getting from A to B.

Example 2. Going in a southwest direction and then north may be the fastest route for going west.

Example 3.There may be no wind (sailboats need wind), and your auxiliary motor is not on, but you are going from A to B at six knots.

Like i have discussed in my reference to skiing, there are so many variables that knowing all 'what you are supposed to do' becomes unmanageable without learning, practice, and experience. I have an uncle who has held that there is only three degrees of tolerance in sail trim either way, and that could be high. As you can possibly appreciate, the irony is that even if you are a perfectionist, you cannot achieve some type of best state by following rules; it has to become a 'oneness of feel' that results from the integration of multiple ever-changing variables.

In my practice, as i define it, i need to consider an unlimited number of variables that have been observed over time. I know that these many and different perceptive variables come from different environments and many points of view—parents, family physicians, schools, psychiatrists, psychologists, and others. I know that they may all feel that they have an accurate perception of the person and often overlook their limited points of view.

As i review numerous reports and compile data from many sources, i need to consider if there is any dynamic commonality within all these. Having done this for many years, what becomes important is that the developed (or whatever) sense of a dynamic oneness hypothesis emerges. For many of us—whether you are a scientist, mechanic, physician, artist, or sailor/seaman—the understanding is established. An important result of applying this awareness is that you get to B; you find an answer that works. Here, we may see a distinction between those whose experience is more or less dynamic and multifaceted. One may accept that getting to B isn't possible. 'We've tried and nothing works.' For another, it might require an exploration of the vast universe of ideas, points of view, these myriad of variables. From this, you may express something that seems to be revolutionary or innovative and may be timeless. That ability to intuitively understand and synthesise and then to have these actualised in some new scientific discovery, making someone better, or just getting you safely and efficiently to B is something that we may often describe as talent or genius. As i write this, i am reminded of an interesting social/human distortion of this oneness i have just addressed.

For the athlete and the musician, achieving a disciplined, fluid openness is an essential feature (necessary) for performing in a manner that expresses excellence. This expression is beyond themselves since they are doing what others have defined as excellent, they are not expressing unique aspects of self, they are the embodiment of what society wants them to be. In fact, it is somewhat ironic that, on the social/human plane, society extols the individuality of those who excel at expressing the nonhuman/nonindividual abilities. For many of you, this may not make sense; but if we consider perfection in sports techniques, our measure for some sports might be time. From a coaching perspective, the fastest time is considered a function of technique, conditioning, rhythm, and timing, all of which can be defined in terms of biomechanics. If we considered our use of nonhuman, then we are really defining the best athlete as representing this state. In simple terms, the best athlete is the one who can repetitively behave in a manner that is expressed by nonhuman factors (i.e., biomechanics). Personal instincts or questions about the meaning of life need to be put aside. Their fame as a person could be considered as not based on their human individuality but based on their nonhuman individuality.

It is interesting that, at this moment, i have a tendency to editorialise; this is my momentary 'emotional response', but it passes quickly.

Talking about athletes is useful because it is an example of the integration of many factors in an unthinking manner. How the social/

human world views them and how they respond to this are not relevant to our discussion.

What we can say is that the ability to express comprehensive dynamics in a united manner is necessary for good playing in the orchestra and on the sports field.

As i have alluded to, transformations can also be made by those experiencing some art form. The student may start with developing an analytic awareness of some of the features that constitute 'one' artistic expression. One has gone from one to many. As we have discussed, with time, the experience of the listener of music requires less consciousness and a greater intuitiveness. Like the musician and the athlete, an integration of many aspects of physical self-regulation are necessary for high achievement; but in these cases, self-regulation is important for achieving an openness/selflessness to do everything with maximum biomechanical and utilisation effectiveness.

If we are attending a musical concert (not the same in sports) and are aware of our own thoughts and physical comfort or discomfort while listening, these become part of our focus—a distraction. And as we have considered, if a person is learning and analysing, this too will distract. In a sense, as the listener, we want to achieve a state of noneffort—a nondoing.

So when is attentive effort a noneffort? Or maybe more to the point, when is nonattentive effort really like effort? The importance of the distinction is one of socially defined emphasis. It is like trying to relax, trying not to think, being aware while not aware. It is the loss of innocence and original sin and consciousness described by Dylan Thomas in 'Fern Hill' (see pg. 126). It is beyond the push/pull, strong/weak forces experienced by my friend. It is being the duck and the swan. It is accepting and discarding everything. I have written about this point before.

Not Another Review

Let's take a few minutes to review the process of my ramblings. I have started out describing myself as the one who doesn't fit, who is sometimes respected but not understood, and who is sometimes discriminated against. I have expressed difficulty in dealing with the surface but have also described the need for the conductor who can express the creative work of the Composer to those on the surface. Am i akin to a Composer, or am i akin to a conductor?

In the early part of my ramblings i have mused on the importance of my relationship with my friend and my need for human connection. I have shared my feelings as the fragile human but also as being someone who has discriminating taste, which is seen as priggish and perfectionistic.

From these humble emotional beginnings, i have ventured into life below the surface and considered how symbolic dualities can be used and also their limitations. And until using my orchestra analogy, i have not offered any framework for approaching answers.

As the reader, you may feel that you have followed along with what has been said but may be uncertain about any logical progression. You would have been aware that, in many pages, i have made references to myself or my friend, but these have become less frequent and less personal in their impact. This perception is certainly correct and intended. However, the new challenge for me is keeping a personal feel to your reading experience. If your experience becomes too cognitive and filled with many details, ideas, and instruments, the essence of my expression of oneness and being aware of the importance of being able to become less consciousness can easily get lost.

It could be that you are interested in my writing and feel that what i am saying is kind of interesting. But how much more will i keep your interest? If there are only 50 pages to go, you'll finish it, but what about 250?

It might feel that this work has been interesting and that it actually has had an influence on your feeling/thinking. Then my responsibility to keep you engaged cannot be taken lightly (interesting how a cliché can reduce personal responsibility).

At this point, i am left with two dilemmas. To move forward, i cannot simply share my experiences and perceptions. I can no longer reiterate Pound's lines as an expression of something outside what i am writing about because my focus is going through a transformation. It is going from a single sound to a single sound. It is making that transformation from the surface to multisymbolic to the beauty Pound has described. My writings will need to help engage you in this reading experience or offer direction for experience. This could mean that lateral and vertical movements may be required, if, of course, you really want to enhance and lessen your experience. This offering of direction for experience is very sutra-like, which leads me to my second dilemma.

There surely have been tens of thousands of self-help books, seminars, courses, retreats, and other personal development programs that have offered instruction on how to have a holistic life, become enlightened, learn to relax, or become in touch with yourself. There are thousands of religious texts, scriptures, and spiritual/philosophical dialogues that have addressed the nature of religious truth. You may ask, 'How can you even begin to address such a vast literature or even feel that you could do a better job explaining what has been explained repeatedly throughout history?' My response can be a personal one. What i can do is not just be another philosopher/thinker/scientist/human/writer, but i can write about my experiences, being different, and my travels into uncharted waters. I hope that this glimpse into another world will touch some of you and give you new perspectives.

It is important to note that writing, though highly self-indulgent, is an activity that some people 'have' to do, like others have to breathe. I also feel that the mixture of ideas that i am writing about should be seen as one humble expression of a universe. It is not of a person. It is not of an ego.

Some Thoughts about Reading as Closure to This Section

So let's return to approaching some kind of oneness and consider what might be a necessary condition for approaching awareness without conscious experience. Here is a contradictory description. Can we follow a cognitive path to a noncognitive state? Is consciousness influenced by physiological states? Earlier, i have made references to SC and PFC and how they work both independently and together. What state will work best if our goal is to *not* have our physiology adversely affect our openness to internal thoughts or external stimuli but also be able to integrate these with developed personal understanding? Our H and L used below are describing the intensity/dominance of functioning, not degree.

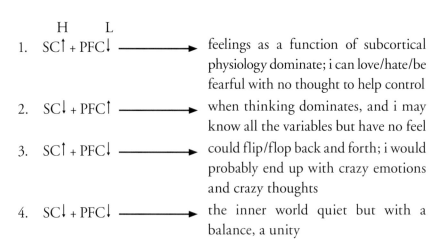

	H	L	
1.	SC↑ + PFC↓	⟶	feelings as a function of subcortical physiology dominate; i can love/hate/be fearful with no thought to help control
2.	SC↓ + PFC↑	⟶	when thinking dominates, and i may know all the variables but have no feel
3.	SC↑ + PFC↓	⟶	could flip/flop back and forth; i would probably end up with crazy emotions and crazy thoughts
4.	SC↓ + PFC↓	⟶	the inner world quiet but with a balance, a unity

Whether reading poetry or science, a number 4 state is required. One Zen haiku considers the relaxed mind as the still pond that is open to thoughts and experience. Thoughts are like drops of water that ripple the pond. If we consider the oneness of experience that we have discussed while listening to music and combine that with our haiku, we could describe the music as a progression of raindrops. Consider this modification of a Matsuo haiku.

> An old silent pond
> A single drop of water
> Water ripples the pond

For you who are not readers of literature or science and tend to read popular novels and enjoy the story or who read the newspaper or Internet to get the facts as presented, you need to stop and reflect. If you wonder why i suggest that you stop and reflect and if you have an impatient 'i get it' reaction—we know that you probably don't—your SC and PFC are probably both too high. You may be thinking too much. You may be feeling too much.

Reading these words is for reflection; they slow the process of getting through the material, but if reflected on, new ideas and thoughts can enhance inner experience and, interestingly enough, even distort your experience of time. However, for some, it may feel that reflection is a waste of time, like waiting for a red light.

Here are two possibilities to consider. Do you find enjoyment in reflection and curious contemplation, or are you driven to keep moving on in your reading?

What did you do with my three sailing examples?

- Did you just keep reading on to the next paragraph?
- Did you stop and think for a moment and then move on?
- Did you stop and answer the questions and move on?
- Did you stop, come up with some answers that may or may not be correct, and then move on?
- Did you stop, come up with some answers, ask others, look for answers, and then move on?
- Did you realise that you don't sail and, besides, the questions are dumb and then move on?

Here is another possible measure of your natural sense of stopping to appreciate and enjoy.

Think about the mind as a still pond. Are they simply words on paper, or can you visualise and physically experience a still, quiet pond in your head?

To experience this stillness, a number of controls over physiology are necessary, but let's leave them for a moment. What is going to be essential from this point on is a different balance between reading and reflection.

Let's look at some ratios.

Reading a popular novel, newspaper, or magazine may be 99 percent reading words and 1 percent reflection. I'm just reading the story. This is probably a 100:1 ratio. Reading a text that requires some memory of facts could be 70 percent reading and 30 percent checking comprehension and retention of facts/concepts. Reading an instructional book may be 30 percent reading the instructions and 70 percent practice. Reading the directions on how to put together some product made by a non-Western country could be 1 percent reading the directions and 99 percent figuring out how the pieces go together.

Reading poetry, philosophy, or science has a different balance and variable ratio. To me, it is like drinking wine. I read a line and savour its rhythm, concept, or idea. I need to digest, to experience, to feel, to contemplate. With reading and listening to recorded music, i can stop the flow and experience a specific moment, phrase, or idea again.

If you are not able to stop, reflect, experience, and become one with what is expressed through me (remember, i am expressing in my own very humble manner what has been written about for centuries), you may be like my helpful friend. You may want to get through the content and surely get the point, maybe learn something, but you cannot see the importance or personal significance of following some type of instructional manual that doesn't really seem to have any practical purpose. Your point of view may be different from the ones we will discuss. Your beliefs and care for others may be well intended, but you are probably not ready to experience 'outlawness'.

If the above is descriptive of your approach to reading, is consistent with how you see yourself, and is representative of how you like simple, straightforward content, then there is no need to read any further. End here.

If you are reading this, you either have not listened to my direction or are ready to move on and are curious. My feeling is that you could be a nonreflective reader who has kept reading even when the personal message to you is to stop. If you didn't pick that up and stop, then you have made some assessment of your ability to respond to what you read. Of course, it could be that your reading momentum and possibly your skimming over details has resulted in you missing the point. You, of course, could be somewhat curious or don't want to take direction from others and, therefore, have kept reading. If you are about to stop at this point, i hope that you have gained something from the experience. You have had some cognitive descriptions of oneness in music appreciation and in physiological balances. One day you may venture further and return to this or some other work to experience the oneness that you have not explored.

Maybe one difference i can possibly offer from my own perception and the myriad of works that are read by various people is that most courses, books, and instructions may not offer the essentials of dropping below the surface and living on a different plane, as well as exercising the body and mind. If you didn't see that the above statements have some inherent contradictions, that is okay. *Just stop reading* at the end of this section.

The rest of this work will require a desire or curiosity on becoming a misfit, weird, or possibly even delusionary as defined by the social/human sense of reality. An interesting question arises here: we have a social perception that we have defined as delusionary and see outsiders as having a delusion. Does that make the outsider's (outlaw's) not a delusion or just a different one?

You are invited to read the rest of this in any manner you like, but becoming weird or even understanding the weird point of view takes time and nonwork. There may be times when you can read quickly, but there are times when the 'reading/figuring it out' ratio may be 1 to 1,000 or even 1 to tens of thousands. It can be extremely difficult to have something become part of your natural way of seeing and responding to life and not have to think about it.

For you who are leaving, i hope my ramblings have given you something to think about. Maybe one day you will return to read the rest. Remember, even though i have presented this in a personal manner, i am doing this as a humble person who realises my own human needs for a human connection but cannot place these ahead of the best of human thinking and its limits. As i have mentioned, i am not ready for complete separation from the human.

For you who are leaving, we hapless few, thank you for coming this far.

For you who are going on, i hope that the voyage is rewarding.

Please note that my discussion of antithetical gyres will be included in this next section. I apologise for not giving cognitive closure.

PART II: BECOMING THE MAD OUTLAW

Becoming the Mad Outlaw—a Brief Introduction

These next ramblings will take on the task of assisting you in developing a more self-aware state and will use an instructional format. I feel that it is important for me to share these with those of you who are interested. I want us to explore some different ways of experiencing life that are not just 'mindful' but lead also to the acceptance of an 'outlaw' perspective. In the following section, I will use descriptions of some thought exercises that have been used for years. It is hoped that your experience in reading these writings will assist you in making up your mind about whether some of these strategies will work for you.

Where do I start? There is so much to consider. Maybe lateral movement will work.

In one sutra, the student asked the enlightened one, 'What is truth?'

The enlightened one responded, 'Take fifty lean and sickly cattle up into the mountains and return when you have five hundred. Then you will know the truth.'

This may be somewhat impractical for most of us.

Hermann Hesse in <u>Siddhartha,</u> in a more Western sutra, envisioned Siddhartha as the boatman taking people across the river. It was metaphorically interesting but maybe not too practical.

Could we just have people learn to relax, take yoga, meditate, or take mindfulness training? These are all beneficial, and as we will see, relaxation and being calm is an essential piece in the evolving process of becoming (whatever that means), but I don't think this is the best place to start sharing a timeless point of view through written language. As you can probably guess, without some instruction and experience, even telling someone to relax or breathe more effectively may, believe it or not, actually result in increased muscular tension, biomechanical stimulation, or poor, exaggerated respiration.

A question about writing content is also something that I needed to consider before working on this section. Do I throw out to you or throw away some more cognitive instruction, philosophy, science, literature, or music? I think, for the moment, I need to throw them away.

There is, however, one skill that brings the above together. From my experience, the ability to visualise is an essential piece in enabling the person to achieve another or other perspectives. It may take some of you a little while before you will see the relevance. Be patient. It is important to appreciate that developing new perspectives requires personal experience. A cognitive description won't work. You need experience, but not everyone has the time, ability, or space to raise a bunch of lean and sickly cattle.

Visualisation, Experience, and Transformations

I am going to consider visualisation in a multidimensional manner. On the simplest level, you may be able to see some image from your past, and you may be able to read a book and have an image of the characters, where they live, and what happens. In these cases, you are the observer. You can see something, but you may not experience yourself as part of the situation. On another level, you may be able to visualise the still pond in our haiku being in your head. Can you see the inside of our head as a pond? You can possibly even experience the drops of water and their influence on thought.

Check your own experience:

- When I read a book, I can see and hear the characters, and I can see locations.
- When I remember things that have happened in the past, I can see them clearly.
- When I remember the past, I can literally reexperience the situation.
- My memories can be triggered by something I read or something someone says, by music, by smell, or by taste.
- I can visualise an abstract idea, like our still pond.

Try the following:

First, consider the experiences or any other experiences you have had that stand out in a whole-experience-type fashion. They don't have to be profound or moving, and it is best if it is not a negative one.

Next, consider your own state of being at this moment. Are you energetic, impatient, ready to go? Or are you somewhat relaxed?

It is best to find a memory that you will be open to in this moment, and in these cases, being more relaxed is a better state.

Finally, sit in a comfortable chair, if you are not already, close your eyes lightly, breathe slowly, and allow yourself to visualise!

I can visualise.	I can't really visualise very well.
- Carry on with the present text.	- I don't really get it.
	- Move to appendix A.

For you who are moving on and don't feel like looking back to appendix A, I'll let you know what is covered.

- the physiology of visualisation
- other views of internal experience—Huxley and Leary
- the nerd to virtual reality
- some practice exercises with feedback

On one level, you may be able to visualise (that is see and experience something internally); and with practice, visualisation can be accompanied by very real physical sensations and activity. For the athlete, visualisation can be a powerful performance-enhancing strategy. In ski racing, the skier can actually run a course and have all the sensations that accompany muscular movements and experience these in a realistic time-based manner before skiing the course.

Unfortunately, good visualisation ability with integrated physical sensation can also influence the less functional side of the person. For instance, someone may have a fear that is accompanied by panic attacks. This good visualiser would be very adept at integrating visualised experience with a dysregulation of physiology. These people are very good at taking what they think/hear/see an associated symbolic visualisation physiological changes that are the same as their real-life panic experience. In a sense, their 'real' physiological state may be driven not by a real occurrence but by a visualisation. Typically, these 'panics' are partially a function of social/ human perceptions. I will address this further in our discussions.

We can consider visualisation from another perspective. Consider the person who may not have a strong visual associative ability but may have a strong relationship between a thought experience and the physical sensation that is associated with different situations, people, or words/phrases. For these people, many of whom may be also known as musicians, the visual piece may not be a significant part of experience. For them, the association is auditory. Remember that Beethoven was able to finish a score while deaf.

If we consider these people, we could say that they have the same dynamics without the visual modality. What they pick up is the overall sensation, which may affect all experienced systems except vision. I guess we could say that a blind person could be a good visualiser. Certainly, if we keep our rigour of conceptual language, to say that would seem ludicrous; but if we move away from simple visualisation to a total internal experience, we could set our visualisation goal as the ability to experience, in a complete way, a wide range of inner experience that is triggered symbolically or vicariously or anticipates reality-based events.

As I am writing this—it could be *righting this*; in fact, I made the mistake of using the 'writing' homonym. Is my writing right?—I have come to the sudden realisation that once I have moved into the integration of physiology with what I visualise, I have opened a big 'can of worms'. It is my concern that I clearly separate the technique/ability to visualise and its integration with total physical experience and some assumed vertical insight. But isn't this obviously an important skill to master for the potential outlaw?

What about its content and influence? What about its value? You might be somewhat confused and ask, 'Where is the problem? Where's the can of worms?'

Anyway, let's consider the problem. For many of you, this will seem like a complete non sequitur, but the philosopher in me drives my need to address this visual/auditory/physical distinction. I am illustrating the importance of integrating the visual and the physiological, certainly a useful skill and of great value. I have also discussed, at length, the value of vertical movement and where that leads. What I haven't said, because it is not logically connected (but typically is), is that visualisation doesn't make me panicky, or something like that; but in essence, it works as some kind of door to more reflection of self and to vertical expansion. Unfortunately, this is not always the case. We could have great skill in visualising, but we could also have an emerging, hidden social/human value factor that, as I have mentioned, can become a traumatic experience to the person with panic attacks. These states can be adversely influenced by the fact that the person may have a strong sense of social judgement and expectation that requires them to do something that they can visualise as traumatic. The problem could be huge or not much at all.

The extreme

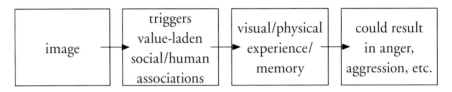

In the above, the visualisation mechanism is working well. *However*, it could fuel racism, intolerance, nationalism, and a myriad of 'isms' if these social/human values are ingrained in the person's psyche.

The moderate

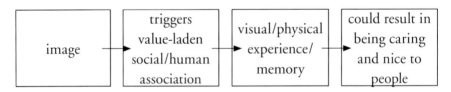

In this situation, there could be a confusion between an ability to visualise well and the experienced outcome. The false assumption is that if I visualise well and I care, then the outcome of this visualisation is desirable. Unfortunately, there are many caring people who believe that their empathy is enough to help others and, in doing so, overlook ways in which others can be helped.

What is essential here is that

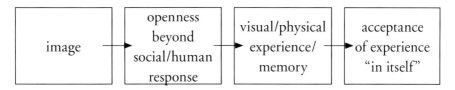

Probably the best, simple test of the purity of your visualisation comes from the nature of your own experience. If your experience is profoundly insightful or nonhuman experientially, that is desirable. If your experience is judgemental, says something about others, sees good and bad, connects with a higher being, or is what your meditation class taught you, then you are, at best, mixing the skill of being able to visualise with how social/human influences have directed you.

There are many important aspects of being able to visualise experience. We cannot always have firsthand experience; in a lateral manner, it's not practical, but we can expand that experience base with visualisation vertically and not go anywhere. Lateral movement may be beneficial. We can say, 'Been there, done that.' We can remember the facts. From a vertical perspective, experiencing something has an impact on us overall. It has timeless significance.

Consider the social/human lateral experience of the traveller, one who is on a tour visiting a resort or exploring a new part of the world. Travellers may experience the natural beauty and wondrous sights; they may also experience a separation, a sense of 'this is different', and with this some discomfort, or maybe even a sense of threat may be evident.

Consider the social/human experience of the person who experiences the world differently. There may be wondrous natural beauty. But to some, the physical world is seen as combinations of basic physical structures. For instance, the geologist (obviously an organic person) may find 'beauty in the ugly', like some synplutonic dyke, and 'nothing special in the beautiful'. In the same way, the people who populate the social/human plane look different in some respects but are of the same classification of mammal— live and die, have beliefs, eat, breathe, move around in similar social patterns.

I feel that whether you accept or are uncertain in your response to reading my ramblings, it is important to experience. In the beginning, I have talked about stormy seas and contrasted these seas with a quiet underneath. This could be seen as a metaphor, which it is. But it is also part of my life experience and moments of awareness far before I was ever introduced to any metaphor of the sea. Let me see whether I can explain this so that you can experience this contrast.

Let's assume that you are snorkelling or swimming with scuba gear just below the surface of a rocky coast where the waves of five to six feet or bigger are breaking against the rocks. As you come close to shore, the waves that are breaking against the rocks are tossing you around; you have no control and could be destroyed when you hit the rocks. This is not a surfing beach with reefs and shallow water. So instead of fighting these breaking waves or swimming further offshore, you try a different perspective and go down to the bottom—which, let's say, is twenty to thirty feet below—and find a calm, protective spot. If you have not had this experience or if you have been in this situation and it was traumatic, then your visualisation will be different than mine. What I now visualise is calming. One looks up to the surface and sees an up-and-down movement of a transparent horizon above, and at the shore, there is a lot of white, but it is distant. I can still remember the first time I experienced this phenomenon; it was a moment of 'epiphany', not just because it offered safety but because it said something about life. If I am going to have you feel/experience a sense of separation between life on the surface and what's underneath, a visualisation of this type of experience would be essential.

- This image may not make sense to all of you, so what blocks your positive visualisation experience?
- You may feel it, but your fear of being underwater may make this visualisation scary. The good thing is that you're feeling it. We just need to find another visualisation.
- You have been through this so many times, and so it has no importance. What's the big deal? That's okay. It's part of your psyche.
- You find it so removed from your own experience that it is difficult to feel. Maybe some other examples may work.
- You don't see the relevance. Find something else to read!

As you may be aware, I have brought in another variable here—the whole idea of how past experiences may influence perceptions. With this example, I am considering an experience with a positive awareness outcome. But ironically, experiences that are seen as negative can become equally positive.

In a sense, this experience variable could also present a difficulty even for the good visualiser. You may be able to vividly remember events that have a strong visualisation impact; however, their profound literal impact may make it difficult, if not seemingly impossible, to 'get into' certain new experiences, whether actual or imagined.

And let's say our goal, from a self-development point of view, is to offer some direction for a visualised experience that offers a sense of being part of a more fundamental perspective while being open to experiencing insightful new dynamics. It is hoped that expanded awareness may transform the nature of the experience—once again, I will use my experience as an example. Two transformations of this simple underwater experience are evident to me. I would consider them as 'literal' and 'metaphorical'.

In my illustration of the undersea experience, I had a sense of safety while being immersed. Often, safety may be thought of as being away from the water (i.e., onshore). While looking up to the surface, I could see water moving up and down against the rocks and whiteness. It didn't really look chaotic or threatening. I could not hear any sound. But having been at the surface, I knew the reality was different. But the surface and where I was reclined were both aspects of the same reality.

As I have experienced and thought, I have realised that since waves are simply water being shaped by the wind, the water (as long as there is no tidal current or undertone) just moves up, down, and around; it doesn't go anywhere except where there is undertow—but it looks like it does. Additionally, in my literal transformation of this experience, I have considered current. We could have a current that is moving water around but is not obvious from surface observation, especially if you're in open waters. So from my safe perspective, I have played with my thoughts and considered the fact that water that isn't moving laterally may look like it is and that water that is actually moving may look still.

My next thoughts could also be seen as symbolic or metaphorical. Does my experience have some kind of generalised application to life?

It is this type of generalisation that is the essential final step in transformation. The experience *is* the source of a visualisation that is 'beyond me'. But it not only develops insight but also enhances one's ability to express it.

This visualisation, which I can now experience sitting at home, can be transformed into an experience that has symbolic significance; then this understanding can be applied to life. It is like an epiphany, a heuristic moment.

Consider what this visualisation says about some dualities and how they can be understood in a contradicting manner.

> danger ~ safety
> strong ~ weak
> What is moving possibly isn't.
> What isn't moving possibly is.
> The social/human is a lateral traveller.

Life has its up and downs.
Here are some more random thoughts:
safety ~ being onshore now!
The strong is fighting the waves to get to shore.
The weak is giving in.
This person is trapped in an either/or universe.
What about the vertical traveller?
danger ~ in the waves at shore
safety ~ in sinking deeper to calm waters
~ moving farther out to sea where the waves aren't breaking
Does the bigger ship/boat bring more safety?
~ finding a best place to land onshore, which requires moving out to sea (away from land)
The weak is fighting the waves.
The strong is giving in to the sea and going with it.
Maybe this person is less trapped.

Another, I think, interesting insight is the misunderstanding of water movement. We have waves and no current. We have currents and no waves. And we have combinations. But from a lateral/vertical confusion, popular beliefs may hold that waves always suggest lateral and vertical movements. What we know is that there is vertical movement.

Conversely, calm waters may have no vertical or lateral movement. What we know is that unnoticed lateral movement may be evident. I once listened to two powerboaters talking on channel 16 (shouldn't be), and one was experiencing a technical problem because his GPS and knotmeter didn't agree with each other. His friend (?), after some discussion, thought that maybe there is a current or something like that. (They were motoring an area where tidal currents can be significant.)

Forget the literal sea lessons; consider these constructs and how they can be applied to social/human life in general. The application is endless!

The final step in this and any transformation is seeing how even one visualisation and its insights may be representative of how life can be viewed on different planes. Equally important is affording the reader the opportunity to visualise some new experience that takes them beyond what they have encountered in their day-to-day lives. These experiences may start with more consciousness but can lead, as with our gyres, to expanded nonconscious states.

We live on the surface and think waves are going somewhere. We may not clearly appreciate that currents, that we don't see, are actually moving things around (back and forth).

Those things that seem life-threatening, chaotic, or beyond our control or even calm and seemingly safe can be seen as only surface manifestations that do not necessarily represent underlying realities.

The essence of reality could be seen as the body of water and all its elements. It is the ephemeral behaviours of water that often affect them, which are often what people focus on, not its underlying structures.

Are the seas a threat or a friend? Are they an origin of life or a threat? Is it social/human behaviour and its desire to control that have made any threat more 'real', or is it simply how the waters behave? A simple answer emerges here; it could be that the social/human species, as discussed before, is defined by its own sense of self-importance and its fear of not having control (a delusion), and these needs are seen in very simplistic terms.

In this short description, I have described an example of one of my vertical transformations. I have gone from having a practical experience, going through the dynamics and momentarily seeing life from a different point of view and then integrating that experience and its significance with myself. It becomes part of my psyche and influences future perceptions.

For some of you, who have had other experiences that adversely influence your openness to this visualisation, consider these two possibilities.

- Some lateral transformation may be required. In this case, it is exploring the universe of experiences that can meet our goal. You may remember an occasion where the circumstances triggered insights similar to what I have just discussed.

228

- Some vertical transformation may be required. A significant part of this transformation is making a negative/positive shift. For instance, is being scared a positive or negative experience, or is it neither? Let's start with descriptors such as interesting, overwhelming, painful, not painful (but should have been), fear of loss of life, fear of the unknown, being totally alone, anger at someone else, anger with oneself...

Anyway, no matter how we describe being scared, it is an experience that tells us about how we react. It tells us something significant about ourselves or even the nature of human reactivity. If we can see what it tells us, we can help transform the negative into a neutral. The neutral can set the stage for fruitful visualisations and the opportunity to get beyond the negative. Remember our discussion about dualities and their limitations.

A profound transformation from negative to positive insight occurred with a policeman I saw years ago. He grew up in a small Ontario community, was a reasonably good student, played junior hockey, and achieved his childhood desire of being a federal police officer. His life had been straightforward without many crises or adversity. After working for several years, he met and lived with a fellow police officer—in this case, a female—and they planned to get married. She had a very different background and had definite emotional swings. One day he returned home to discover that she had shot herself with her service revolver. As you can imagine, he had no way of dealing with this; the image of the body of his lifeless girlfriend haunted him. He couldn't eat, sleep, work, or focus on anything. I saw him regularly for over half a year, but in that time, he developed incredible insight about himself and life. He did not find God or some magic cure. He understood the different realities of surface and underneath. He ended up feeling a strange sense of 'I should feel guilty but I don't' because the image of his deceased girlfriend represented a positive (at least neutral) opening to a universe that he never knew even existed.

From our brief discussion of visualisation and its qualitative features, including experienced transformations, I hope that you will be able to spend some time to revisit some of your previous experiences or be ready to expand new experiences in a visualised manner. But it is important to understand that it is a skill that takes practice, is easier for some than others, and can be applied in different ways. Like any skill, it can be beneficial; but in the short term, it may inhibit your development of understanding and movement towards 'oneness'.

Visualisation without experience

Now that we have tied visualisation with experience, let's consider visualisation that is not simply based on a memory or experience. I see two types here.

First, there are those of the athlete. I mention the ski racer who can learn a course by walking it and then can practise it by using visualisation. It is interesting to note that the sensation of doing this is very real and has been shown by neurological research to result in an activation of motor/mirror functioning neurons.

Second, of more interest to us in our journey, is the use of visualisations based on symbolic structures, like the artist, poet, or creator. Oscar Wilde considered that life/nature imitated art. The auditory example here is the composer, the free-form jazz musician.

Consider the visualisation of the artist as vertically free. It comes from the depths, it wanders above, it is articulated in an art form. It is then presented on a social/human plane, which can result in others seeing life differently.

A simple example, for me, of this phenomenon occurred when I was about eleven or twelve years old. I had seen Van Gogh's painting of the sunflower. Sometime later, I saw some flowers (not sunflowers) in a garden, and my moment of epiphany was 'These colours are like Van Gogh's.'

Relaxation/Arousal

Relaxation is a term that has many experiential states. What is relaxation? You may ask, 'What does this have to do with developing some type of understanding?' As mentioned some pages ago, my first thoughts about where to start in teaching a new perspective are with relaxation and meditation. But as I have mentioned, I have started instead with visualisation, experience, and transformation because I think it is more open to written instruction and self-check. Relaxation is more difficult to address because there are very specific measurements of 'relaxation', but these may not coincide with your human experience.

In one class I instructed years ago, I tried using 'progressive relaxation' with a group of pregnant women. This was an established way of getting people to relax their muscles, but I found that it didn't work well for a significant number of people (probably >20 percent). One particular woman reported that she was completely relaxed. When I lifted her 'relaxed' limp arm, it was like lifting a thirty-pound weight; and when I let her arm drop, it almost went through the floor from her muscular tension. She knew she was relaxed.

Getting people to breathe in a relaxed, deeper, slower manner is also not always effective. It usually results in a nonrelaxed manner. Instead of breathing diaphragmatically, most people move their upper chest and raise their shoulders but do not actually improve their breathing efficiency. Many may even make their respiration worse. We have many measures of physiology that can, in combination, give a sense of how relaxed you are. Unfortunately, the fact that you have taken yoga classes, are very flexible, and have been instructed how to meditate tells us little about your ability to actually relax as measured physiologically.

Unfortunately, many approaches to achieving a relaxed state and developing an understanding of relaxation have no way of measuring one's state. In fact, the degree of one's relaxation could be determined by such measures as heart rate and variability, respiration, muscle tension (EMG), or brain activity (EEG). You may question the practicality of the above discussion since it would seem that you won't know if you are relaxed or not unless you get some measurement, and to get all this data would be impractical. My response to this reasonable concern is to avoid giving an answer at this point, though I would agree that the question is a valid one.

Experienced Arousal: What is Relaxed?

Even though relaxation may be an important ability to have, I am going to start with looking at 'experienced levels of arousal'. In this way, we can—at least subjectively—evaluate and record your changes in state. To do this, I am going to consider your overt activity level, as well as your internalised experience. Let's look at two personal thermometers.

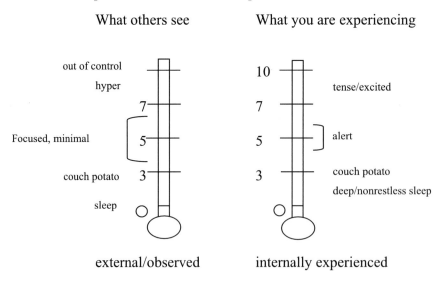

The first mode to consider is how your body is expressing itself externally. In very simple terms, this would be a measure of whether you are moving or still. On our scale, 5 could suggest some movement, and arousal levels above 5 would show higher degrees of movement. You could be typing on your computer (let's say a 5), you could be involved in an active sport (let's say a 7), or you could be running away from some fearful situation (let's say a 9). At the bottom end of our thermometer is 0; this shows that you are not alive. And 1 would suggest that you are sound asleep. As our diagram shows, higher arousal states that don't involve movement may be evident. These states are based on levels of concentration and alertness.

How others see you may be more difficult to determine since their observations may be more judgemental and generalised; for instance, someone might see you as being lethargic, hyper, lazy, never changing, boring, or never getting excited.

However, there is another factor that we need to consider. What is the relationship between inner experience and external expressions of arousal? For some people, what you see is what you get. The person's body is in a high arousal state, and it is expressed in degrees of movement. Others may be in a highly aroused state, but they look like a 3 or 4. They may not move and may even be noninteractive.

As we will see, the control of experienced arousal is essential for change. However, it is important to remember that we are dynamic organisms and that different levels of experienced arousal are functional and also expected. There isn't any absolute right or wrong.

There are times to be relaxed and times to be tense or excited. These are two ways of considering our physical states as we move on the social/human plane. These also apply to those who have more vertical experiences. The balance of these dynamics in different situations is probably going to be the best experiential measure of your arousal range and your ability to functionally regulate.

What about emotions and arousal?

Before we can go any further, we need to consider 'affect' and 'emotions' and their relationship to arousal since they can often be seen as connected. If we return to the world of dualities and define emotions as positive and negative, we could conclude that they, of course, could be experienced in probably any arousal state greater than 1. We know that arousal could describe the degree in which an emotion is experienced. What about an intense ennui?

From the outlaw perspective, self-awareness is important, but what others think doesn't really matter that much anyway.

Time to do some self-generated recording

In each of the following situations, we will consider the 'observed' and 'experienced' intensity over a four-hour duration. We can actually graph what this might look like.

Example: You are going to have some stressful event in your life that is known about ahead of time. It could be that you are going to be tested on a subject/activity, you have some work pressures that need to be completed and presented on a particular day, or you may need to make a speech at a wedding or funeral and you don't like public speaking. It is important for you to do well, and you have studied, practised, or prepared yourself for some time. But you are anxious, and you don't want to mess up. The stressful event is on a Friday morning at eleven.

Let's consider some patterns:

First, consider assessing your general response to our example. For simplicity, use H (high), M (moderate), and L (low).

THE ACTUAL ME

- degree of importance
- confidence of knowledge
- test-taking confidence
- degree of anxiety

Second, graph your overall arousal levels at the time stated. Next, graph what you think another person who doesn't know you well might see.

observed _____

experienced - - - - -

	7				
	5				
	3				

7:00	8:00	9:00	10:00	11:00
get up	have something to eat	drive to the event location	talk to some others who are or have been in the situation	event begins

Third, consider assessing the cliché 'strong' social/human. How would this person react?

THE STRONG OTHER

- degree of impact
- confidence
- test behaviour
- degree of anxiety

Fourth, graph this person's pretest status.

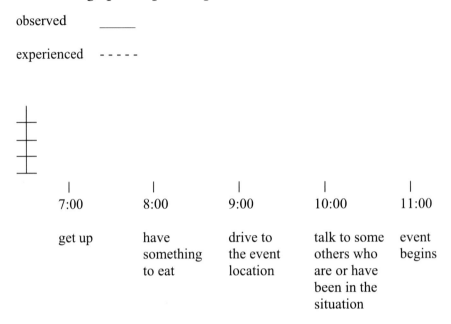

observed   _____

experienced   - - - - -

7:00	8:00	9:00	10:00	11:00
get up	have something to eat	drive to the event location	talk to some others who are or have been in the situation	event begins

Finally, consider your own ideal state.

THE IDEAL ME

observed   _____

experienced   - - - - -

7:00	8:00	9:00	10:00	11:00
get up	have something to eat	drive to the event location	talk to some others who know	event begins

As you thought about your responses to the questions and considered your own patterns, you may have found that there wasn't enough information or that the example didn't work. If it didn't work, that would tell us something.

Let's assume that you know that these types of events don't get to you, and considering the strong and ideal doesn't really come either because they will all be the same. From this response, we could conclude that either you are immersed into a social/human value position that assumes that only some kind of distress is recordable and you don't have any (which is probably a defence) or you are highly defensive. Since you are still reading because it isn't stupid, then it is unlikely that you are highly defensive.

If these situations don't get to you, that could be fine, but your state is still recordable. Quite often, people forget that changes and no changes can both be recordable. It could also be that you feel that reacting is 'bad' and that you shouldn't react; therefore, you don't. This, of course, would be defensive, which ironically is probably accompanied by increased tension.

When it comes to patterns of reactivity, my friend and I react very differently to the same situations, but we will both have changes in physiology. Since I have practised relaxation for many years and measured my states, I am able to achieve a relaxed state by regulating my breathing. I can do this in almost any setting but may have to change my expectations or use visualisation to change my point of view. I sound pretty ideal, don't I? Actually, even though what I have said is correct, I live on a social/human plane and confess to be highly perfectionistic in all areas of my life; but ironically, I am enthusiastic in doing well in areas where I am developing my skills but actually humbled when I offer something that is accepted but is outside this social/human plane.

My friend can have a more difficult time changing in some settings. She has more difficulty keeping a consistent reflective sense of self. Her experienced arousal can increase when she realises that she has given in to social/human expectations that conflict with her spirit, but sometimes that allows her to experience vertical movement. As we have discussed, she sometimes is desperate for lateral movement ('I will go somewhere and experience freedom') but ends up in the same social/human plane.

However, for both of us, thoughts have a significant impact on physiology and physiology on thoughts. But this relationship I will discuss later. For both of us, our observed arousal would probably not change with the internal stress; and for many of you, that may also be the case. Another factor to consider that brings about changes in arousal state is one's degree of self-awareness. My friend will sometimes lose her openness and self-awareness when tense; she can still be influenced by the social/human need to be a duck. This is a factor influencing her state, and that is okay.

Just in case you may not see yourself as others see you, check out your own observed/internal dynamics by asking a close friend to describe how they see your observed arousal and how they read your inner experience in different situations. If you are talking to a friend about his/her view of you or even when considering your own view of you, it is important to be descriptive. Your states and changes in state are not good/bad, right/wrong, weird/normal; they just are.

We could make a self-contradictory judgement. It is bad if you or your friend is critical or complimentary about your changes in state or degrees of self-awareness.

For further clarification of the many possibilities of state that can exist, here are a few.

- You are extremely physically fatigued because of some prolonged distress, and you go to bed. What happens?
  - You fall soundly asleep and sleep well.
  - You cannot sleep. You keep thinking.
  - You cannot sleep. You feel physically restless.
  - You fall asleep, only to wake up a few hours later.

- You are bored. What happens?
  - You veg out in front of the TV.
  - You find something to do that is rewarding.
  - You find something to do.

- You find yourself pacing and unable to settle.
- You feel tired and are able to sleep.

- You feel tired but need to concentrate to complete some task. What happens?
  - You take a break—veg out.
  - You persevere and work very slowly.
  - You realise that the task was stupid anyway.
  - You take a break to adjust your physical/mental self.

- You are practising some musical passage or some skill and are not getting it. What happens?
  - You take a break—duration is based on knowing what it takes to get your concentration back, though you have no strategies but time.
  - You take a break, knowing how to change state.
  - You keep going—practice makes perfect.
  - You give up. 'It's not for me.'

All these above alternatives seem to have a value-laden best response. From a social/human point of view, it is obviously better to sleep, do something rewarding, take an appropriate break, or persevere and to not quit.

However, if you want to move toward being able to relax, you need to start where you are, no matter where that is. You need to understand the dynamics of your state. As you are probably aware, being fatigued is probably not a relaxed state. The direction you go is based on you, not on an imposed set of 'you-musts' or even 'shoulds'. The irony is that following your own path will result in a better state for you; following 'the musts' would most likely result in less relaxation. (Here is a fun contradiction. To relax, you 'must' not respond to 'musts'.) Your first experiential measure of 'is what you are feeling working?' is that you feel better balanced. For instance, you think that if you are bored, you may feel better walking (though others may define it as pacing). It may not sound very socially correct, but most likely, it is a better expression of your physiological state. We would probably find that if we measured your physical state while walking, your respiration, muscular tension, and heart rate would all suggest a far more relaxed state than if you became self-judgemental, sat there, and thought about finding something more rewarding.

You say to your restless self, 'I must do something rewarding!' You say back, 'I don't know what to!' As a result, you are less relaxed, have poorer respiration and more muscular tension, and are less able to think of an alternative that works. Your thoughts at this point are tied in knots because you don't have an answer to your dilemma, and your *i* is in a lowercase.

The outlaw and Buddhist response to this dilemma is 'Do nothing' (as defined in a social/human context). It just means going with your natural flow, stepping back, letting your being express what it feels. Once again, there is the contradictory 'must/should' challenge. 'Must/should' must not be the driving force. What?

Of course, the critical social/human response to this is 'We can't have people just do what they want to do.' I will leave an editorial comment aside for the moment. Let us respond to this concern by saying that, at this point, we are only looking at being able to approach relaxation. There are, however, caveats. If someone does not have a demonstrated ability to relax, we cannot tell the person to do so. It would be like telling someone to perform a particular skill without practice or instruction. We also know that relaxation can be physiologically measured. We might think that it should be easily achieved by everyone; unfortunately, it is not a state that most people achieve as a natural expression of their social/human existence. One needs instruction and practice.

I am reminded of the old joke about the person who had been in a serious car accident. The physician gave the patient the good news that the prognosis looks good. With that good news, the patient asked with a cautioned sense of hope, 'Will I be able to play the violin?'

The physician answered yes. The patient responded, 'That's great because I couldn't play it before.'

As I just mentioned, if we look at the physiological measures of relaxation, it is not something that most people seem to be able to do without guidance.

So why is this relaxation thing so important? I would reframe this question. 'So why is this ability to self-regulate so important?'

The regulation of self?

To answer this, we need to consider the integration of a number of factors. As I have mentioned earlier, we are dynamic organisms whose physiological states change, though I would suggest that the ability to relax is an essential part of functioning.

In fact, from a general-health point of view, being relaxed (as measured) requires respiration to have an efficient balance of O_2 and CO_2, well-regulated blood flow, reduction in the demands on all organs, minimised muscular/skeletal demands except those required for breathing, and a dominance of slow wave activity neurologically (typically alpha or lower). We know that humans, like all species, have functional, adaptive dynamics that are homeostatic experience stressors but also require ongoing periods of relaxation (a midbrain calmness).

I have a race car and enjoy racing, but it needs to be able to idle and change its revs. Its revs need to meet the demand of the situation. It also needs time to be turned off and cool down. In fact, with a dedicated track car, it stays turned off most of the time. Yet if it were relaxed and running all the time, that wouldn't be practical, even in traffic or on the highway. If it were high-revving all the time, that wouldn't work either. In fact, there are effective times when the brakes are 'hard on', and the engine needs to keep its revs higher but not too high. It's all about balance.

But now I am going to go one step further. What about the driver? It could also be the musician, the ski racer, the golfer, or just the regular you. These people are controlling their equipment. Control requires concentration and effort, making the equipment do what you want it to do. This does not seem to come from relaxation. It comes from vigilance, concentration, and control; it comes from effort (social/human?) *but not entirely.*

Piglet and Igor went to Pooh's tree house to visit; they noted that the more they knocked, the more he wasn't there.

What we know is that there are many times in life where the more we intensely try, the more we limit our success.

Barry Stearman tested the sustained attention of fighter pilots, and he noted that they modulated between attention and relaxation as measured neurologically. They were attentive and then relaxed and showed this variability in seconds, not minutes or hours.

What about relaxation or even an experienced lower arousal level and its influence on point of view at any given moment?

Here, we are back to the initial concerns of this section. What is important? Is it achieving a relaxed state, self-awareness of arousal, or the ability to change arousal? Ultimately, it is all the above; but for the moment, it is helpful if you become aware.

As I write this, I am reminded of a very important distinction. I am thinking about my good friend whom I feel very connected with and her developed self-reflectivity. I may be more self-aware in all situations than she is, but it doesn't mean that I don't indulge my own feelings and do things that may seem inconsistent with someone who is self-aware and self-disciplined. What I can do is keep my awareness, even with high arousal. What I can do in talking to her, even if my arousal is high and coupled with a serious or negative affective tone, is decrease arousal and change states. Even in the triggering event that has given me the impetus to write this work, I have adjusted my arousal and focus. It has triggered humility. It has triggered a need to express. What can sometimes happen with my friend at this point is that her level of arousal can affect her openness to other points of view and self-awareness, and there are times when she can't make the adjustments, at least at the moment. Once her arousal decreases, openness returns. For many people, a single point of view can be so dominant that any questioning could increase arousal.

high arousal ⟶ highly rigid thinking with little openness + low or no self-awareness rigid thinking with low arousal + rhetorical questioning ⟶ high arousal + low or no self-awareness

The distinction we need to be aware of is that arousal, point of view, and self-awareness are all distinct, but they are tightly tied together and mutually influential. What I am aware of is I have not given you any sense of how to see/measure whether you are able to relax as seen by others or as measured, and I have not given you any specific steps for achieving this. But I have realised that I need to consider point of view first. As I have mentioned, for both my friend and myself, thought influences physiology, and physiology influences thought. But let's consider the first relationship.

Arousal, Visualisation, and Point of View

A while ago, I have described how going to the bottom of the sea is quieting and peaceful. But I have also considered how this may be distressful for some. The object of my writing is to have you visualise this calm point of view. If you couldn't or can't, it is probably arousal, in conjunction with either visualisation or thought, that is the enemy. I could have an idea, thought, or particular point of view that is quite changeable or very rigid. Rigidity requires tension, which requires high arousal. You may be able to visualise (experience) this. Here's visualisation without a visual. Tense your shoulder and neck muscles and think rigidly. Think of some type of social injustice. Feel the high arousal.

I have a friend who could become easily stressed by specific social/human events that he felt strongly about but were really insignificant. In fact, I would speculate that some life-and-death situations would be easier for him. Anyway, there are two events that I felt would kill him if happening simultaneously. If his favourite hockey team was scored against in the last seconds of an important game with a resulting loss and he simultaneously opened a bottle of tonic water that had been shaken, which resulted in the spray of tonic water being propelled into his face, this would result in such an instant and high level of arousal—all systems would stop, and he would die.

I used to kid him about his reactivity to each one of these events. Consider the spraying tonic water. He would jump, raise his arms, yell, spin around, yell, bang his fists on something, yell, and then slowly achieve a calmer state while questioning in a somewhat baffled manner, 'Why would people shake the tonic water? Why would they do that! And why would the hockey team allow a goal like that to be scored against them!' The whole event might last twenty to thirty seconds. He would then go back to a regular arousal and life. Fortunately, these two events never happened together.

If we return to the less dramatic, we have considered that our point of view could be influenced by a belief, assumption, hypothesis, value judgement, or something experienced. It could be grounded in social/human thinking, philosophy, or some other realm of thinking or feeling. We have just used a couple of examples of the possible influences that high arousal has on thinking and vice versa, though we know that there are many other factors that influence one's ability to think and change point of view. We would expect that cognitive and intellectual abilities, as well as education with science, philosophy, or mathematics, would result in better logical and conceptual thinking. Some education in religion, literature, or anthropology would help in understanding symbol, theme, and belief. Some education and experience in the arts, developing self-awareness, identity, and standing in another's shoes can all help in integrating thinking and expression.

But just to keep things in perspective, my tonic friend is intelligent, educated, and appreciative of the arts and sailing. His understanding and appreciation of life and spirituality is beyond that of most social/human-focused people I have referred to at the beginning of this work.

Henry Miller, whom I would describe as an angry mystic, had what could be seen as a social/human tension or a lack of connection in his works and as inhuman and not caring; yet his understanding, I would suggest, was profound. In his real life, he was certainly not liked by all. He was seen by a friend of mine, whose father was a friend of Henry's, as intensely self-centred, egotistical, and obnoxious. Of course, as my friend was describing Henry Miller to me, I noticed an increase in his physical tension and rigidity in his opinions.

So who is right/wrong? What about rigidity? Is getting beyond it the answer? Is it relaxation, a point of view, both, or neither? If we consider rigidity of thought, a high arousal state, and getting beyond, can we get from details to a fluid/intuitive oneness?

What we see is that arousal can create a false transformation of our 'elements of experience' into a 'one'. Since I am not able to have a feel for you as the reader, I don't know if you have reflected on how your own experiences of high arousal can result in a limited, restricted oneness—one sound, one idea, one level of intensity. We haven't interacted. I know what I want to say and how it all ties together, but I know you may not have a feeling for a sense of 'oneness' in the way I have discussed it earlier. Remember, oneness is not really oneness in the way we normally think about it, so using 'one' in two different ways may not make any sense.

For instance, if you reacted stressfully to being underwater, it could result in a single dominant, personal experience of fear or distress. It is not uniting elements. It is only picking up those elements that are associated with a fearful response. Conversely, if you had the sensation that you defeated the sea, arousal would probably be still the enemy. However, both of these could be considered as a single, one-type experience—in essence, single focused. These are somewhat like the single sound heard by the nonmusical person experiencing the orchestra. In this case, high arousal may result in a 'single' like or hate. I think that we can all agree from our examples that high arousal can often be associated with a limited, possibly rigid point of view. We may wonder about Henry Miller. Was he really as tense or uncaring as he presented? Could he be an exception?

Let's consider the possibility that there could be tension and openness. We used to have fun playing around with phrases like *intense ambivalence*; it's not quite an oxymoron, but it may describe a human state. If it does, is it a functional one? Ambivalence, which we could consider as akin to an uncertainty that is coupled with some awareness and openness, would not be seen as associated with intensity. I guess an image of this might be a person at a crossroads who has the strong feeling that a decision has to be made 'now!' We see the person standing rigidly with a fixed gaze, staring at some space in between the two roads. It's hard to tell whether the person is even breathing. Can you visualise this? Can you visualise this by standing in this person's shoes?

I think that we can end up with a person being stuck.

Let's try another openness with intensity. In the <u>Tropic of Capricorn</u>, Miller reflects on his relationship to the social/human world as a child. What we see is a disconnection, which has some of the same elements I have discussed earlier in this work. If we use my image of the sea, we could consider his point of view as being below the surface, looking up. But instead of just accepting its existence, he sees and strongly experiences the inadequacy of life on the surface, and this is in dramatic contrast to his experience of life below. But rather than moving down vertically and letting go of the surface (the social/human), he has continued to remain on the surface and below and, in a sense, describe two levels of experience, at least in this writing.

What we have is a body of work that continually reminds the reader of his disconnection and lack of respect for the social/human level. At the same time, he explores a wide range of spiritual ideas. I see his tension as a function of the juxtaposition between these two realms and his desire to remain in a rebel-type state (tension driven?) and not accept the social/human. His tension may not have influenced his ability to think creatively below the surface, but it has prevented him from going beyond and becoming the 'outlaw'.

If we accept my hypothetical treatise, we could continue to hold the position that a lower arousal level is essential for enhancing experience that we have discussed.

Let's say that, on a more practical level, letting go of intensity opens up our senses. If we become less fearful underwater, we can see the surface, experience the calmness below, and even reflect. I can remember going to the symphony as a child wearing itchy grey flannel pants. My experience is my itchy pants. We could go home and listen to a scratchy 78rpm record, be comfortable, and really hear the music.

Let's put these dynamics into a learning condition. There is a Buddhist saying that suggests that once you believe one thing, you can't believe another. (This, at face value, could be considered a belief but really acts more like a higher-order principle.) I have spent some time discussing the social/human aspects of belief/delusion principles at the beginning of this work. I have even discussed some aspects of neurophysiology that can influence these beliefs. However, before we consider the influence of arousal, let me consider a Buddhist teaching that addresses the teaching of this concept.

The student asks the master, 'What is Buddha?'

The master points to a bird in the sky.

'Is the bird the Buddha?'

'No,' the master responds. He then points to a rock near to them.

'Is that the Buddha?' the student asks, pointing to the rock.

'No,' says the master.

This dialectic could carry on forever—asking, pointing, asking, and responding with no satisfying answer given. So what does the student learn? What is the point of the exercise?

Let's look at some arousal and point-of-view influences.

Student I: The student asks a few more times and gets no answers other than more things to look at, to which the master responds with a no. This produces an increased level of impatience and arousal.

Is the student open to learning? On one level, no.

Is the student able to put pieces of experience together? On one level, no.

If this impatient student doesn't know how to change point of view or arousal in an insightful manner, he would probably become stuck, which could result in a nonproductive transformation in point of view. For instance, if the student gets somewhat defensive, there could be a shift from open student to cynical observer. 'This is stupid. I don't have time for this!'

If this impatient student could change point of view and is able to step back and relax, what would he learn? He may learn that there is something broader that could explain contradictions. The answer is not one thing but many. He may understand that no is an answer; it isn't the absence of an answer. But more importantly, he may also have a moment of insight that actually is part of the answer he is seeking but doesn't know it. If he became aware that his arousal rose and declined, that his own impatience was preventing his openness and blocking his understanding, and that he was not being able to see the reality, himself, his need for simple variable answers, his anxiety, and his insecurity, he would learn a lot.

The experience of the student who will learn something from this situation needs to be one of stepping back, even move outside himself, so he can see himself and what he is doing and observe with a kind of calm detachment. Here, we have a change in point of view, arousal, and with this the probability of an awareness not experienced before.

Visualisation can help us experience the state transformation of this student. We could try making a transformation using our contrasting visualisation examples starting on page 164 (also refer to the appendix, 'Primer on Visualisation').

Let us consider the impatient student who wants a simple answer and has rising tension because the master seems to be playing head games, and the student has become defensive. Try to get a sense of this situation, increase your arousal, and then see if you can make a point-of-view transfer from the student to an impatient observer who has things to do. You may even feel this sometimes if I lose you in my stream of consciousness. As the observer, you may experience self-talk or feel one or all of the following:

- 'Give me the answer! Give me an appropriate answer! Explain!'
- 'This is dumb!'
- You feel your arousal increase!
- You ask yourself, 'Do I express my impatience or walk away?' You have other things to do.
- You are reminded of other situations that have made you frustrated.
- You become stuck. You don't get it.

How do you get unstuck?

Let's consider the impatient student who can change in an open, accepting manner. To do this, try stepping back. Can you see yourself stuck? Not getting anywhere?

Then reaffirm your visualisation of you standing there impatient and tense, and then visualise yourself stepping outside yourself. It could be a stepping back so that you can see yourself and the master, and you can watch the interaction—this is just like dropping below the waves. If you can experience this different point of view, in which you are not engaged, you can then become calmer and be able to see. It is at this moment you can have that heuristic 'Look at me. I'm impatient. I couldn't respond to the master's teaching because I was trapped by my own tension. I have learned. I've learned about me.'

In this exercise, you could also visualise calmness; but from my experience, this is often a more difficult first step because you may still feel a sense of being stuck with a momentary calmness and then feel increased distress as you attempt to step back.

What is important is that you want to transform your state. How you do that is based on what works. Works require an openness to experience and an integration of an expanding sense of self.

This visualised plane of receptive openness could be our still pond or even the experience of expansion or of nonanswers, a light rain, a rain, a vulnerability. This can expand to a 'Wow! There is so much!' I could not think of a better visualisation for beginning to integrate the skill of visualisation with vertical movement.

The test of your visualisation is that your personal reward comes from an awareness of your limited self within a universe of no answers. If you need a definition or an answer, that is okay, but its truth is your own insecurity, nothing more.

Since some time is needed to try these visualisations and it is nice to know you are making headway in your reading, the next page allows you an opportunity to practise your visualisation and still turn a page; however, it could be that it takes longer to read a page with no writing than one filled with copy.

●

Visualisation page. Focus on the dot.

Student II: The student continues to ask questions, and every time, he gets a different answer that is inconsistent with previous answers, or at least it seems that way. But the student stays calm, reflects, is open, and experiences a sense of music in all these pieces. He understands that these are all instruments, they are all teachers, they are all Buddhas, they all are expressions of the same. It could be that in learning and developing a point of view, the student, session after session, has no new insight. The student has just experienced a trusting sense, knowing that one day something unknown would be experienced as long as he remains open.

In this student's shoes, you can visualise yourself as calm—you listen. What is being said makes no sense at first, but you remain calm. The objects and words are like the drops of water on the still pond. You look at nothing/everything—the flower, the smokestack, the orca swimming in a bay, the orca at Marineland. You have an image of a New World pond—a computer disc. Every image goes on the same plan. Images are differentiated by megabytes, not by content. From the master's 'point of view', one image is the same as any other. They are all aspects of the Buddha, but none are the Buddha.

In writing these last few sentences/phrases, I have experienced some conflict with the temporal/experiential requirements of understanding and telling someone. I am reminded of two experiences in my life that address the need for the ongoing impact of experience and its generalisability. It needs to become part of you. In essence, in the social/human world, some written visualisation exercise in a book you are reading rarely has any long-term impact. You finish this book and go on to read yet another. What remains?

Experience, insight, visualisation, and time needed to become

First, let me recount some of my personal experiences that consider the need to integrate experience with self and its relationship to learning. In the late sixties, I, with three other people, spent a couple of hours talking to the Dalai Lama. All of us were academically and spiritually connected with Tantric Buddhism. At that point, we were transliterating and translating ancient Tantric texts. In our discussion with the Dalai Lama, we talked about his view of Western culture's commitment to the disciplined study of mysticism, meditation, drug use for spiritual purposes, and approaches to life. We touched on LSD. This, of course, could be seen as a bad drug, and many of you may know little about it. The point that was of concern in our discussions was that it is a hallucinatory drug that was initially used for researching schizophrenia in Switzerland, and it was shown to give an experience that had similar qualities to meditation.

The Dalai Lama wasn't concerned about the possible physiological effects; his concern was at the social/human level. To him, the drug represented the Western need for everything to be instant. If he was right (which I think he was), you could have an interesting experience. Take a pill to get it, have it wear off, and go on with your regular life.

Visualisation, like calming and adjusting your point of view, can happen a lot of the time, daily, or once or twice in your life. You don't need to use a specific location, attire, or drug; it needs to become a part of you.

A good test of having a calmed, visualised new experience comes when you go through something you have done many times before. From this new perspective can emerge an experience that is totally different.

Second, let me consider experience, insight, and time. The development of insight with calmness, which can have a generalised effect on a person, can take months or even years, not hours or days. It comes from a natural openness to self and others and not from a planned desire to see differently. Our Student II discovers the nature of the Buddha by being open to what isn't learned. He learns by not learning.

There are other approaches to developing insight that have become popular. Mindfulness is one of these. It focuses on the principles of being calm, living in the moment, doing nothing, and being self-aware. It accepts that some time and practice are necessary for achieving a more meditative state, but personal success, at least in developing personal insight, can be achieved in a relatively short period.

For many years, I practised different forms of psychotherapy. For me, the goal of this process was not changing social behaviour (cognitive/behavioural) but first to have the person obtain some insight into self and learn how to think, feel, and experience how the body and thoughts behave and then teach some self-regulation skills, given the nature of the person. My outcome goals were to help the person's life improve without having to just act like a duck. This treatment, typically once a week, had variable degrees of success. For those who were ready for generalising what they learned about themselves, these sessions worked effectively; but for children and high-risk adults who were not functioning with day-to-day life, this hour a week was ineffective.

The degree of this ineffectiveness hit me in a totally unrelated incident, which—as you will see—started with an insight about therapeutic effectiveness but resulted in triggering an experience that I realised lacked awareness, which later resulted in insight, which led to visualisation and also to a transformation of self.

I live on the seashore of a fairly large bay that can become quite stormy. At one point, we had a little protection from the sea; and if we had a high wind and high tide, the waves would hit our small seawall and shoot up ten to twenty feet in the air. As a result, huge sheets of waves would come crashing into our garden. During many storms, I would go out and try to sweep out water from the garden. Though it would seem ridiculous to do so (which it was), I felt like I was doing something—ten thousand gallons in one gallon out. Fortunately, the tide ebbed, the waves lessened, and our property could begin to dry out.

Once the threat of the storm was gone and a personal calmness prevailed, I reflected on the futility of many things we do that we may not be so vividly aware of. I also thought about the futility of talking therapy for some. It was clear that, for these people, one-hour weekly sessions, even if effective in themselves, were not going to be significant enough to influence someone's life in a generalised manner.

I could also see that there are ebbs and flows in one's life environment that can influence one's state in a positive or negative manner. Someone may show improvement or get worse. Are these changes a consequence of the therapy? Or are there other forces, which are not obvious, that have affected their situation? For instance, if I didn't factor in the ebb tide and the tide was going out, I might conclude that my hours of sweeping out the water actually improved the situation. I swept, and water stopped filling the garden. Or conversely, it could be that the tide is still rising, and I have no knowledge about how high it will be and when to expect the worst. In this case, it could sweep and feel a sense of futility. Fortunately, at least with the tides, there are tables that tell us the times and heights of all tides. Unfortunately, there are no tide tables that inform us about all the ebbs and flows of life.

I realised later that my circumstance here was somewhat like that of Sisyphus as described by Albert Camus in his book The Myth of Sisyphus and Other Essays. While I was sweeping, I was contented because I was too busy to reflect on the futility of my tasks (Sisyphus rolling the rock up the hill). The tide ebbed (the rock rolled down the hill), and at that point, I was able to understand the reality of waves, tides, winds, and where I was. I knew that my sweeping had no effect, but accepting that these were the energies, forces, or whatever that we needed to accept gave an important understanding of my social/human self and its relationship to the sea.

The sea has power beyond our ability to really comprehend, but we do know that there will be another high tide and another storm. By the way, I don't sweep anymore, and my experience has been transformed, but more of this later. However, man (excuse my sexist noun) often has the need to engage in 'futile' activity because he is doing some something focused.

Sometimes it often helps to forget man's vulnerability. Many of you, if you get a sense of the ongoing vulnerability that humans may feel, might suggest to us that we build a bigger wall for more protection or move away. Interestingly enough, a new wall has been built to help us—a wall three times higher and stronger—but we have still had many other storms that have filled our garden. In fact, two storms have flooded a lower part of our house, and one of them has destroyed two cars. (They didn't float). So as many have asked us, 'Why not move?' This is our life; this is the relationship we have with natural forces. It is important to remember that we are presented with calmness, mild winds, and lesser storms, but there is always weather. There is always the sea. They are always present. We cannot live inside and feel protected or be away from it. We are always part of these forces.

So how do we accept this? We do so with calmness and acceptance. We know that every day is different, but they are also the same. They are all expressions. Each day 1 is experiencing the unknown. It is not battling, sweeping with futility. It is listening. It is being symbiotic with the elements—every day. It is not just reading a book; it is also living it. In our situation, this has been going on for over thirty-five years.

Most of you may not have had the seashore experience, talked to the Dalai Lama, read thousands of books and lived some of them, and spent hours and hours talking about and contemplating the nature of human existence. These are simply some of the experiences from which I have learned. It is important to remember that experiences can be personally profound or significant to the person and may have an 'always present' influence on an one's life, but neither my profound experiences nor yours need to have a relationship to some type of social/human measure of what is supposed to be significant.

Consider the following example: You may have won an Olympic gold medal or had been a world-class athlete in your youth. This level of achievement, of course, required talent, years of training, and complete dedication. At the time of your successes, you were elated. It was a dream, an almost unrealistic one, that had come true!

But it might not be until years later that, at some seemingly insignificant moment, you have a moment of epiphany, and this happens to a number of athletes who were once very successful but may have become somewhat lost. After years of retirement and with some possible uncertainty about where life has taken you, you may come to a somewhat bleak realisation about the past and present.

What does the past look like? Those years that had been dedicated to training and competing were very satisfying, but they could be seen like Marlow's dreams of sailing a ship to the east in Joseph Conrad's novella 'Youth' and could also be seen as not unlike Sisyphus rolling the rock. They were times when awareness was totally absorbed in rolling. Wow! They were times of naivety or limited awareness with an almost 'nature of innocence'. Yet there were times of angst and times of joy. During these times in your past, you may now have become aware that, at the time, time felt timeless; and ironically, you realise that these timeless times are actually very ephemeral in nature.

The important point to remember here is that, for those of you who have experienced these moments of epiphany even after years have passed, it is these reflective insights that become the profound moments of one's life, not their athletic predecessors. Does your need to define yourself on a social/human plane have personal importance? Can you define yourself by who you were or who you are at present? Though I would contend that these moments of insight are essential for making changes, these changes could result in states that could range from depression to elation. You might ask, 'So what do you do with these thoughts?'

Alternatively, you may have had some experiences that have the potential of being personally significant in an insightful manner, but you may have ignored them or been told by others that they are unrealistic and that all experiences are somewhat the same anyway. What's important is how many you have and where you had them. 'Where have you travelled?' one might ask you. However, you may ask yourself, 'Can't experiences come in different forms? I'm always somewhere all the time. What does travelling have to do with insight or personal significance?'

One exercise that may help begin answering these questions, if you feel pressured to do so—which, ironically enough, does not answer anything—is to establish a different personal foundation.

What we are going to consider is to visualise with calmness a changed point of view and possibly a new understanding of connectivity between the unconnected. A visualisation that has worked for me both literally (I have done it in a real setting) and metaphorically (I have done it elsewhere) has a number of elements to it. Consider being in a small boat in a quiet bay with no one else close. The boat is firmly anchored, and you are peacefully reclining, moving slightly with some small waves, and looking up to a clear sky. Your only conscious thoughts reflect a sense of calm, peace, and security. After some time has passed, you see a passenger jet fly overhead miles above you. Its presence draws you into thoughts about its journey—going from city to city, busy life to busy life, times and places where there is no time to reflect or to experience an inner sense of self. It's all external. For a moment, it may draw you to it but also away.

To expand your insightful experience, a time to reflect is essential. This reflection could follow the approach used in mindfulness that emphasises the need for living in the present, or you could visualise images that establish a calmness and a connection to underlying order. Or a time for reflection may be triggered by some social/human event or some discussion about an accepted point of view. In these cases, three aspects should be considered. First, be calm. Second, take the view of a neutral outsider, one who is not part of the social/human world. Third, consider the situation by not looking at the details of who is right or wrong, but consider what the situation says about the species.

To have these times become effective and influence what you see, hear, and experience in your thoughts, they need to be experienced every day but not for long. Soon it will become second nature.

So what about experiences and insight?

What might one consider as a profound learning experience? Should one expect to have a single experience that results in ongoing changes in insight? A single moment of epiphany? Or should one expect to have ongoing experiences that result in the manifestation of new insights continuously that could actually change one's view? Are metaphoric and symbolic insights equal to real experience?

If we follow my use of the waves on the sea, they can be literal, as seen in my last example, or symbolic of the social/human condition (Sisyphus). You may be—in fact, probably are—flooded by social/human demands. There are the 'must-dos' and the 'have-tos' and with these the advice, the commitments, etc. Work that could be going really well or that is not satisfying produces 'symbolic waves' (the work that comes at you), and you are responding. On the perceived positive side, you may see the waves, handle them well, and as a result feel that your work is successful. You know you are getting ahead, making things work. You may believe that it is not like trying to sweep out a thimble of water against a storm breaking waves.

But let's look at this from different points of view. If I measured my sweeping task by social/human criteria, I could consider the rate in which I swept and the volume of water I could push out with each sweep, which could be compared with a researched maximum for each sweep. And if I did it well, compared with some benchmark, I might be able to report that I swept with 90 percent efficiency. From this point of view, I was doing well. I could possibly be the best in the world.

It is only if I consider the bigger picture—in this case, my efforts in relationship to the power of the sea—that my efforts look inadequate. Would some other approach be better, or does it not really matter because there is nothing I can do anyway? At this point, I could default to my social/human voice and proclaim that I am the best! I could feel empowered.

There is, of course, the positive outcome that has nothing to do with me. The sea always recedes, and the threat will be gone, though there will be another high tide, so it could happen all over again. If I leave aside this last piece of information and focus on my reflection on my recent challenge, I could have a number of perceptions. If there is no damage, except everything getting soaked, I can wash off the house because it is covered with salt, rake the lawn that is covered with seaweed and pieces of wood, and feel a sense of relief but also achievement. I could feel that I did it.

Think of the different reactions one could have. One could feel something akin to shock—feel anxiety, tension, calm, worry, spaced out, maybe even shaky. One could feel vulnerable to the sea and lucky that everything turned out all right. One could feel a vulnerability that is balanced by a belief system; for example, God has helped and has listened, and so one feels less vulnerability. Or one could be calm and digest the elements of the experience, including oneself. It could even be similar to hearing a moving piece of music, though probably more like Bartók's 'Concerto for Orchestra' than Debussy's 'La Mer'. This last response would represent that kind of experience that unites a myriad of variables into a oneness.

If my response had been 'I did it', my experience of oneness would have been a false one. It could be characterised by that high arousal ⟶ rigid egocentric thinking + no self-awareness.

As we have discussed, relaxation could be seen as a specific measureable state, with functions like heart rate, respiration, and muscular tension all having stable and low measurements. In recent discussions, we have used 'calm' instead of 'relaxed', and we have combined this calm state with certain visualisations. We have found that this combination of foci have helped people achieve a measured relaxed state. But at this point, it is important to understand that this state of calmness is necessary but not sufficient and that an understanding of an outlaw perspective requires an openness, an absence of rigidity in thought (need calmness), experiencing a different point of view, and not resorting to beliefs or platitude (God will help, or God comes from bad).

A Rationale for Accepting, Being Self-Reflective, and Visualising

Be cautious of your understanding of success.

You are getting ahead. You have more money, more success, more people know about your work. I am reminded of Ulysses and the attraction of the Sirens. You could be flattered, but the attraction can trap you in false praise and really bring about your demise. On a real-life level, you end up needing praise and success; and if it's not there, you have nothing else. You become addicted. It could be that you feel like you are changing things, making things better in your own work environment or maybe for all the social/human plane. Whatever the case, that good feeling is self-rewarding, and that's okay, but you would need to accept that it can easily become blinding and limiting.

Has there ever been an individual leader/thinker whom everyone has accepted as all-knowing, meeting social/human perfection? It seems to me that there will always be that group of individuals who will disagree or even rebel. As we have considered, it seems that one of the needs of the social/human species is the need to define oneself socially as being part of a group, but it seems that an important way for each group to define itself is being different, a.k.a. better than another or other groups (religions, nations, football sides).

In the early 2000s, there was a well-meaning politician (we'll give him the benefit of any doubt) whose personal perception of his success was very positive. He was sweeping well, but some questioned his sweeping. To many, it was felt that his sweeping wasn't necessary or possibly in the wrong direction. Was he actually just filling the garden more? But right or wrong, he could still feel success when the tide ebbed and one set of problems seemed reduced; however, we know that winds come and go, and tides flood and ebb, so nothing is really achieved. As I write this, I am reminded of the Peter Sellers's character Chance, the gardener, a.k.a. Chauncey Gardiner.

You could have work challenges that are exciting and successful, or you may feel that you are just trying to survive. Success and failure could be seen as composed of some of the same factors and defined by social/human ups and downs and richness and poorness. T. S. Eliot, in 'The Waste Land', describes Cleopatra and a lower-class woman in London. One is surrounded by opulence, and the other has a single bed in a small room, but both are the same—alone.

Of course, everyone's experiences are different, but all could be seen as akin to dealing with the waves of life. Are these simply waves flooding you? Are you sweeping? Are you rolling the rock up the hill?

I think that my discussion of personal experiences and consideration of metaphors, visualisations, success/failure, sweeping, and the futility of human efforts may be somewhat confusing or possibly depressing to some. You might wonder why I would want to put a negative spin on feeling success and being successful. Remember, we 'don't do either/ors'. I enjoy doing something well. I am competitive. I can sweep the waves. But I can also calm, visualise, and open myself to new perspectives. Being open isn't being positive or negative; it just is.

I also understand that you may feel that this doesn't apply to you or that you know all that I am discussing. If you are not a monk, mystic, creator, or outlaw, either you don't understand because I didn't explain it well enough or you are defensive and are hanging on to a broom or a rock. Remember, even though these ideas are my own expression of my experience and my perception have been partially shaped by the wisdom and thinking of others, I am simply sharing my humbled personal view because, as I have described at the beginning of this work, I have had an event that has triggered my selfish need to explore my own psyche and to address my desire to make some personal connections. (Sounds like sweeping to me. It is.)

A good personal example of my need to enjoy the positive experience on the social/human level is the enjoyment experienced with my friend. I am not ready to let go of her, and it is because of this that I can experience my strengths and weaknesses. I can see that I have weaknesses as defined at a social/human level, and I have discussed a lot about that, but I also know that I will never be the monk and don't really want to be the reclusive mystic. So reading this doesn't need a defensive response since the person writing doesn't fit and is simply redefining himself and sharing this voyage (for whatever it's worth) with you. These ramblings are simply another expression of the Buddha. Are they the Buddha? No.

I will assume that, since you are still reading this, you are not highly defensive and are open to playing around with different points of view.

In this work, I have described many personal experiences that could be used for self-reflective purposes, including visualisation, calming, et cetera. As I started to write this sentence, I stopped. I was starting to write, 'In this work, I have *shared* . . .' I could not use the word 'shared'. In my life, it has been used by people who lived entirely on a social/human level but felt they were insightful. It goes back to my experience described on pages 71-73, where neither the trainers nor participants understood the dynamics of meaningful individual relationships, at least from a nonsocial/human perspective. Thus my response to my thought was defensive. 'I can't use that word!' My functional reflection was 'No one else really cares if I use "share", and those who use it superficially are having an interesting time exploring my psyche, haven't thought about it before, or have given up reading.'

If I step back and take a calmer point of view and start with a rational perspective, I can see that my sensitivity, based on my experience, could make sense. But from a rational social/human point of view, probably the percentage of English-speaking people who have the 'share' connotation that I have would probably be one in five million. (Actually, I have no idea, so I made up a ratio.) But gosh, darn it, I can still feel this nauseating, touchy-feely association. If I am calm, visualise and vicariously experience my own reactivity, and look at myself from below the surface, I see a person who is sometimes conflicted. Strangely enough but not really giving my perspective, I am typically more about ideas, thoughts, and poor thinking than about real-life situations.

If I can experience my arousal decline and change my point of view and ignore my statistical uniqueness, I can still be aware of its general use by the touchy-feely crowd but realise it is an English word that is polymorphous and can also have metaphorical uses. Maybe I will just use something else. We are talking about an English word; it's not a big deal.

However, Stephen Dedalus, in <u>A Portrait of the Artist as a Young Man</u>, had a difficult time accepting that 'god' and 'deus' were the same. Another word just couldn't be 'god'. God is god.

Wow (that's *mom* upside down), even the choice of one word can be enough to trigger a number of associations. Is your use of language a self-expression that has an impact, or is it simply sweeping?

Let's leave this language digression behind us and go back to the need for defining your own waves. Can you visualise yourself as calm, listening, having a visualising experience? You could be hearing good things or bad things, future things or past things, or something that works or doesn't work. These are droplets on a still pond. Are they the same as waves on the sea?

- You keep calm. Intuitively, you experience the all-encompassing nature of the Buddha. You experience that no one object, experience or idea has exclusivity.
- You become aware that wanting an answer (cognitively) does not seem to give an answer. It is sensed, not thought. An answer will come. Be patient. Be calm.

There is now a time to reflect on your own waves, though I think another reminder is needed here. These ramblings are not suggesting that you change your direction in life or what you do. My desire is to help others develop an openness and appreciation of different points of view, which are not necessarily iconoclastic but, in fact, are ones that underlie the (structural) similarity of almost all social/human perspectives but may be differently perceived and not typically experienced. The answers lie elsewhere.

- Be patient.
- Be open.
- You don't have to change what you do, but be aware!

I would expect that you have, at least from the perspective of an interested reader, taken on the point of view of Student II, which could mean that you are aware that learning to become somewhat Buddha-like will take years and that you could consider yourself as being the student forever. And being a student is also full-time commitment. Though it may not change what you do, it will assist you in being able to continuously change your perceptions.

Here is a good opportunity for another visualisation exercise. Since some of you may not feel as calm and safe in even shallow, protected waters as you do onshore, try the following:

In this visualisation exercise, consider your own seashore. It needs to be one that is calm and tranquil on a sunny, warm day, but it could also be threatening in a storm, but you are continually safe since your human movement allows you to be in or close to the sea or further back in a storm. But whatever the weather, this visualised seashore and its changes are always present in your psyche. Step back and 'observe with calmness' its different characters. You know that, whatever you do, you will not 'sweep' away the influence. The sea is not wonderful or terrible. It is always a source of wonder. To assist you in transforming the terrible to wonder, think of a specific storm. Don't sweep or interact but become an observer. Move to a close place that feels safe and reflect about what you are experiencing.

Here's an example of how perception can change with time. Consider that you are the gold medal winner as a younger person. And now years have passed, and you have a new understanding. Let's say that you revisit receiving your medal but now with a new perspective. As you look back, you may see it as moment of great pride and elation and may also feel a sense of calmness and relief. It is a momentary experience of relief, a pause. It is a successful completion of all the stresses of training and competition, and for some, it may be the beginning of what is next. For most, we would expect that the experience, at the time, would be all-encompassing. But how would you see yourself in retrospect?

'O youth! The strength of it, the faith of it, the imagination of it!' Yet you may see that its strength is its limitation. You may ask, 'Was I aware of anything else?' It could be that you can see yourself as a person of the surface of the sea, as Sisyphus getting his rock to the top first, but whatever. You were unaware at that moment of any other perspective. You didn't question what you would do next. What is the significance of what you have accomplished? Does it become a single moment of glory, or is it a moment that helps define the ongoing moments of your life?

Stay calm and visualise a memory from the past or even our hypothetical one. Can you see yourself as elated or even challenged by a life event? At that point, it is all. You are unaware of its context or the life that follows, its different perspectives.

●

So here we are at a new page with a number of possibilities.

- You may not have really understood my point but are going to read on.
- You may have spent some time actually visualising a past experience and kept as calm and relaxed as possible and may have even taken the perspective of a neutral observer. In doing this, you may have found that the experience has a completely different sense to it from what you have remembered.

If you did have some success visualising, you probably have had some experience with visualisation, changing points of view, and relaxing. If you tried but it really didn't work, well, that also makes sense.

I am saying 'Visualise.' I am saying, 'Allow your point of view to be transformed.' In fact, it is almost as if I were asking you to be the actor because I may be suggesting that you try to 'stand in someone else's shoes' (e.g., 'Be the impatient student' or 'Be the patient one'). I am saying, 'Be calm, relax, and accept that you are asked to learn,' but it might seem as if nothing concrete were actually learned and like the child who is asked, 'What did you learn at school today?'

'Nothing.'

On page 220, I introduced visualisation.

On page 232, I introduce arousal and relaxation.

On page 244, I introduced arousal and point of view.

As the one writing, even with my content/experience disclaimer, the assumed level of the reader's (your) ability to change point of view, arousal, and visualisation may be 'I feel unrealistic,' but your ability to appreciate is essential at this point. Having two blank pages without a time frame or specific goal expectation could result in you flipping over these because you are uncertain about what to do, even though you are open to learning and are interested in experiencing a move below the social/human plane. It could also be that you may have to read more. I have made references to many writers who have had a profound influence on me, and these writers may do the same for you. But first, see if the next section helps.

Optional Read for the Uncertain: This Is Written for Those of You Who Are Still Uncertain about This Whole Approach

I have considered putting this in the appendix but felt that if you are uncertain, you wouldn't be an appendix reader, so here are some additional paragraphs.

For you who are reading this and not convinced of the effectiveness of calming/visualising and don't feel that you are defensive, you may have a difficult time separating social/human values and the need for some type of externalised control of human behaviour. There is a learned sense, for most of you, that it is the structure (rules, expectations, etc.) of the social/human level that believes that social control is essential. Without this control, we have chaos. Remember, back at the beginning, I have spent a fair amount of time considering the nature of reality and that it could be seen as the creation of man (a delusion) and that, in some cases, the socially accepted requirement of following the rules of society may actually result in an increase in behaviour that is considered wrong or bad (think of the priests, think of wars). Even though you may accept that sometimes the pressure to conform may make some people worse, no matter what, it makes you feel safer. You may find that when you think about experiences that are metaphorically below the surface, ones that seem to have no established limits, it may seem that the result would be a loss of social/human control and maybe even anarchy, though many other mammals function fairly well collectively without a controlling church or state and don't kill one another because of ideological differences. However, you may feel that you need some type of externalised control; or at least, even though you don't need it, society does. It makes you feel safe. Another factor to consider, if you believe in some higher power, is that you may not understand that many people who 'don't believe' do good things without any ulterior motive (one aspect of good karma).

An important caveat here for the uncertain is one could obviously not have a social/human, functional world without church, state, principles, laws, rules. But think about having a foot in two worlds (oops, another duality). There is the social/human world, but there is also that underlying, limitless world of the creator, the artist, the Buddha. Things may not be exactly the way they seem.

You may feel that you are okay with the possible contradiction of social expectation and human control, but you perceive an unstated expectation that you would have to change, which would require some type of Student II long-term life commitment. But I have also said that you don't have to change. 'So what is it?' you may ask. What I am concerned about, which does develop a contradiction, is that my expectation is that there isn't one. First, you start where you are. Just begin to be aware. Second, don't change what you do—think about the usefulness of calmness in your day-to-day life and see if that leads you anywhere, even though it may seem to have no useful purpose. Though it may be interesting or pleasurable, that is its purpose.

For you who may see all this as unrealistic, you may believe that there are the 'have-tos', that things need to get done, and that there is no time for this calming stuff, especially if it doesn't accomplish anything. For instance, this whole approach of calmness and experiencing different points of view obviously wouldn't work! One needs to be assertive and not openly trusting of others to function in society. Take policemen, for example (excuse my stereotype example). If you're a policeman, you can't be calm or be 'wishy-washy'; you have to be alert and ready for the unexpected and enforce the law. That's the job.

I have spent many years, as I have mentioned before, working with police. Let's say that a good policeman from a social/human point of view is someone who arrests bad guys, does it with the least amount of damage, follows arresting procedures, has a good and accurate memory, and writes reports that are precise and thorough. From my experience, the good cop can follow through with the arrest and legal consequences of the 'bad guy' but does this with no intense negative energy. Intensity messes up the process. As one undercover officer and I have talked about, policing really has nothing to do with good guys and bad guys; it has to do more with enforcing the rules of the game and keeping in control of the negative impact that some selected people have on others. The law is the framework for being able to do damage control. Of course, there are many policemen who focus on the law. Good guys follow the law; bad guys don't. Their job is to arrest 'lawbreakers' who are 'bad guys'. The calm, more reflective officer knows the good guys/bad guys, and lawbreakers/nonlawbreakers interact in an interesting manner. Here are some more dualities.

<h2 style="text-align:center">lawbreakers nonlawbreakers</h2>

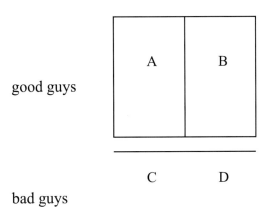

good guys

bad guys

Let's consider these from the calm/reflective officer's point of view (C/R) and from that of the officer who is more intense and focused on catching law-breaking, bad guys (I/B).

A. C/R – There is a wide range here. The obvious example is the somewhat naïve person who makes a mistake. There is another group that the undercover person may find. That is the drug-dealer/mafia-type guy who is really a good guy at heart, loves his family, is trustworthy, and has the attributes that are considered good but grew up in a family or community culture that limited this person's experience. They don't know anything else. For the policeman who weighs what is important, he/she can still arrest the drug dealer because of what he is doing, not because of who he is.

I/B – For this group, life is much easier; they are lawbreakers and, therefore, bad guys. Arrest them all.

B. 'Don't need to worry about these guys, I guess?

C. C/R – There are going to be those people in whom the calm/ reflective officer cannot see any redeeming qualities of attitude, ethics, or whatever. The interesting irony here is that, from the C/R point of view, many socially recognised criminals fit this category, but so do a large number of policemen.

I/B – They cannot make a distinction between A and C. They may actually see some of the wimpy C/R policemen as a different type of 'bad guy'. They are bad because they are too good.

D. C/R – We can ignore this group since this could include anyone who has a different set of value judgements from yours.

I/B – These types can have considerable stress with some of this group as long as they don't have to deal with them. They may be obsessed with finding something criminal so they can have the upper hand. But from my experience, the I/B officers are wired, angry, and overfocused on putting 'bad guys' away! The somewhat tragic irony here is that they are, in essence, 'bad guys' themselves.

Another irony is also evident here. If we compare the C/R and I/B from a somewhat intense social/human point of view that wants 'bad guys' punished, the C/R officer makes better notes, does his/her homework better, and increases the probability of a conviction in court. Their point of view is not distorted by high levels of arousal.

The experienced sea captain/sailor, who knows from years of experience what to do in all situations, remains calm; the sea captain/sailor intuitively reads a vast number of variables and responds magically (if you don't know what he/she is doing). Years of experience focus with calmness. With the experienced surgeon, it's the same thing; focus with calmness is essential.

What about the student? There are some important needs. One needs to listen, see, be open to many new variables, and integrate all these pieces. Here is our oneness to oneness. And even though confusion and uncertainty may prevail at times, a settling period of visualisation and calmness is essential for developing an integrated new insight and responsiveness and becoming experienced.

What might seem somewhat paradoxical is that calmness (which isn't necessarily the same as relaxation) for the very experienced person can actually improve one's ability to focus and, at the same time, be open to other variables presented to them, which to the unexperienced would seem an unexpected 'oh no!' Calmness also decreases the possibility of fatigue, influencing concentration.

As I am addressing you who may have been uncertain, I can feel an interesting social/human conflict in myself. I can feel the urge to give you a long list of other examples of the benefits of calmness. Once I had that thought—guess what?—I have realised two things. With the strength of my urge to give you a list came an awareness that I was starting to lose my own calmness at that point.

I need to shift the task to you. Consider your life—your dialogues with others and self, your activities, and your times alone and with others. Can you get a sense of your own range of arousal? Do you think you have experienced calmness? Can you think of a time when calmness could have been, or had been, beneficial in enhancing your ability to communicate, understand another's point of view, or even enhance your abilities?

Your answer:

_____

_____

_____

I don't want to put you on the spot. Anyway, there is no one here to judge your response except you. From my point of view, I see this question as possibly presumptuous since it makes a social/human judgement about your performance and calmness.

My somewhat paradoxical insight

My rationalisation of my social/human urge to give you multiple examples could be that, to make a point to those who don't understand calmness, I need to give you answers. However, in doing this, I would be an inherent contradiction; it would be inimical to my whole Buddhist need for experience in developing insight. It is interesting that even my response to this rationalisation is 'Wow, what a mistake,' which in itself is a noncalm response. There are ripples on the still pond—a moment of epiphany.

Since it seemed so easy to be trapped in self-contradictory points of view and how they are expressed, I have decided that the best way to approach this is to be a calmness evangelist. The answer can be found in the following short advertisement:

(visual)

To assist your reading experience, visualise a person busy at work with demands. Then visualise the same person walking on a beach on a warm, sunny day with small waves lapping against the shore.

(copy)

ARE YOU LOST, TOO TENSE, AND NOT CALM?
THERE IS AN ANSWER!
LONG-TERM SUCCESS – 100% GUARANTEE
AFTER THOUSANDS OF YEARS OF SUCCESS,
YOU WILL FEEL GREAT FOREVER
NO COST
NO MEDICATION
NO THERAPY
NO COURSES
NO NEW JOB OR CAREER
(side effects and treatment limitations)

Please note this may not work if you are very ambitious, have children, have no children, have a job you don't like or maybe even have one you like lots, are of average intelligence (somewhat below or above), are not a risk taker, have no interest, are using psychotropic medication, or are too old, too young, or in the middle.

The answer is 'calmness'. Accept calmness in your heart, and you will be at peace forever.

I find it interesting that even writing these last few sentences with a fun, sarcastic tone is somewhat stimulating. Calmness requires a different sense, and in fact, even writing this last sentence is calming. My fun desire to rewrite (or re-right) my earlier ad campaign is, by being tempting, stimulating. It is almost as if the experience of calmness could not even be suggested with enthusiasm, and it becomes an inherent contradiction.

For you on the social/human level, I would suggest that calmness, even in the face of adversity, is a rare phenomenon, but it is one essential component of understanding yourself and your relationship with the social/human world. Consider it as 'letting go', not 'holding on'.

In essence, a certain level of calmness can enhance social/human performance, as well as developing a deeper understanding, maybe even wisdom.

I Would Like All Readers to Rejoin Us Here for a Moment of Self-Reflection

As I was anticipating my next topic, which considers calmness and self-regulation from a physiological perspective, I had an interesting experience. I had a déjà vu + déjà vu 'déjà vu all over again' (Yogi Berra). As we know, Berra's use of language showed limited or humourous insight but a good understanding of the concept, which resulted in a wonderful *déjà vu* definition. I thought of his expression because I had a different déjà vu.

I experienced a two-level awareness. I felt that I had already written the piece, which I may have; it's been six months since I started this work. I could also clearly remember a dialogue I had with a close fellow academic. I had been there before—déjà vu—but at the same time, I was watching us knowing I had been there before as a watcher as well. The triggering context was that I wanted to fine-tune the accuracy of the science I am going to describe. I wanted to make a scientific point but knew I would have to compromise it to make it understandable. He had expressed that my supposition wasn't totally accurate from his point of view, which was correct, but as I mentioned, it also wasn't accurate from my point of view either. I also realised that I haven't given him this manuscript, so he hadn't read it, and he wouldn't know that what I was experiencing couldn't have happened before.

What I did have was a momentary visualisation based on a conflict between my friend and myself about the need for the rigorous use of scientific thinking and how it is applied. In these ramblings, I have taken some scientific licence by expressing some concepts in simpler terms or by describing some concepts in a symbolic manner. My fellow academic didn't really understand my use of symbol or metaphor because it would compromise the intellectual integrity of the point I wanted to make. What I saw was that the use of literary devices can assist others in getting a feel for a concept that they may not understand scientifically. This was reflective of my conflict—my need to communicate ideas in a user-friendly manner but with scientific accuracy. Sometimes a compromise is needed. What is interesting here is that this déjà vu experience has a combination of visualisation, symbolic thinking, and projection (giving someone else my own attributes).

Here, we have had a digression from calmness, or have we? In a sense, calmness and going with the flow of thought produced a personally insightful experience.

Appreciate calmness.

Now for Something Completely Different—but Not Really

For the moment, let's forget about any kind of new insights or self-awareness and focus on physical health and well-being. This is certainly popular at the social/human level these days. Everyone should be healthy! In fact, I think we could assume that there is a general social/human promotion for people to be healthy. It seems to me that this is usually considered as a function of a good diet, exercise, not smoking, moderate alcohol consumption, and control of stress. From a social/human intuition, this sounds great. But why be healthy? The proponents will say that it is

- for longer life,
- for more energy,
- for less sickness/disease,
- for weight control,
- for a better quality of life,
- just better to be healthy!

Let's say that you are driven to exercise. You strictly control your diet. You don't smoke, and you drink moderately. You would expect that this will help you achieve your goal state—which could be seen as any or all the above. However, the <u>driven</u> (you will make this happen by your efforts) aspect could chronically influence the benefits of your disciplined regime. If your stress level is high, it could adversely affect your respiration, heart, and muscular tension. It is somewhat like having a car that you like to drive quickly. You put in high-octane fuel, and you change the oil, but you never clean the air filter or fuel filter (consider that these filters restrict), and you never allow the car to idle. As a consequence, the engine is always under some stress. Over a long period, the risk of failure becomes high.

The car, like the body, needs fuel (diet that meets physical needs) and air to function (remember my fellow academic).

The following is not scientifically complete, but I think it works nicely in describing some biomechanics.

With the human body, respiration and the heart have a relationship that is not only essential for life but also highly stress producing if not effective. When we breathe in, we use some muscular activity. That activity requires increased blood flow that delivers O_2 to all parts of our body. Like our car engine, it will not work without air. If it doesn't get oxygen, we die. If it's restricted, it puts significant stress on the body. Of course, every organ, tissue, muscle in the body needs O_2; and the more active they are, the more O_2 is needed by the body. So let's say that we all agree that respiration is a fairly important function. The relationship between O_2 and the exhaling of CO_2 is also important, but that is something you can look into if you are interested.

All this seems pretty straightforward and obvious. But in practice, it isn't. From my experience, I would suggest that almost all the population do breathe functionally. They are all living, but they are not necessarily breathing effectively, at least from a biomechanical point of view. As a result, they are not able to relax/calm their bodies and idle efficiently. And similarly, they may not able to effectively increase O_2 delivery and exhale CO_2 when needed even while exercising.

How do I know this is the case? I can measure it. The person who can regulate well physiologically has an interesting relationship between respiration and heart rate. This person will show a slight increase in heart rate when breathing in. Muscles required for breathing need more fuel/air mix while inhaling and less while exhaling.

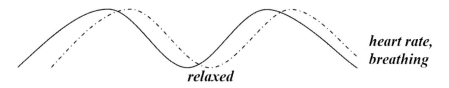

relaxed

heart rate, breathing

To achieve this type of measured state, other systems in the body need to be calmed/relaxed and not needing increased fuel/O$_2$.

I am going to make a metaphorical shift here. Here's my rationale. First, I have found that, for some of you, the use of symbol or metaphor can be confusing, even though I can guarantee that you experience life that way. Second, I have found that some metaphors work better for different people. So if I use different ways of describing the same phenomenon, it is not to confuse but to reach each one of you more efficiently.

What I would ask is that, after reading the next two physiological metaphors, you can decide what works best for you. Ideally, I hope you will be able to relate to both.

Air demand and its effective use could be considered with reference to running air-conditioning or heating or less obviously could be seen in relationship to the use of energy and the electrical demands of one's home.

For some of you, our car reference may work; for others, it may not make sense. So here's another way of considering the functioning of your body and respiration. The changes in one's physiological state associated with respiration and other body demands may be described by thinking about an electric utility meter in your home. If you are using no electricity, the meter doesn't move. If you have every electrical appliance demanding power, the wheel on the meter will be moving at great speed. So let's consider what would happen in two contrasting situations.

First, your electrical use is very high, and the meter is going quickly. You then turn on two additional lights, but because these lights require very little power, especially in relationship to all the power being used, you don't notice any differences in use. (But of course, there will still be increased amperage.) Your whole body is working and demanding energy, the activity of breathing isn't even noticeable, and so your heart rate doesn't change noticeably with the mechanical effort of breathing.

Second, your use of electricity is very low, and the meter is hardly moving at all. You turn on two lights, and you notice that its rate has doubled the use. You turn them off, and the meter slows. Your body does the same thing. When it is relaxed, there are no demands on your heart. You breathe in, and there is a demand. And it is easy to see the increase in heart rate; you breathe out, and the heart rate declines.

There is another factor that most often affects breathing and heart rate and that gets overlooked. When asked to take a deep breath, many people move their chest, shoulders, and other muscles that are <u>not</u> required from breathing. As a result, breathing for these people can take a fair amount of work. What we may see with these people is more dramatic variability in heart rate, and because they are working too hard, we don't see a nice exhale decline. What is also evident with poor breathers is that the O_2/CO_2 inhale/exhale dynamics are poor.

Okay, so where are we? We have been discussing the need for calmness to experience a different point of view. We have also considered that the ability to be calm can be an asset in the social/human world. I have introduced fitness and overall health from a social/human perspective. Since these ramblings have often focused on the shortcomings of social/human values, you might ask, 'Are you suggesting that the popular focus on health and fitness overlooks the fundamental needs of the body to function?'

This is certainly not the case; though popular, surface perceptions can be highly variable and changeable. As we are all aware, the media may contend that certain foods may be bad for you at one time and then, later on, report that they are okay and maybe even good for you. Of course, this does not suggest changes in the quality of the food; it is simply an indicator of the limits of knowledge and social attitudes.

Another interesting observation I have had is one of personal physiological awareness. If you ask people what good health is, they typically never mention basic physiological or biochemical functioning of the body. They may consider good health more in terms of diet, exercise, and lifestyle. And of course, there are others who don't want to be sick but who really don't emotionally connect their life habits (e.g., drinking too much, poor diet, smoking, and not exercising) with some of the physical aspects of personal well-being.

There is this belief (maybe another delusion) that these health foci improve basic functioning. In a way, social/human pressures can make good health or bad health a source of stress and can be manipulative. What it lacks is not a concern for health but the measure of what good physiological health and personal well-being is all about. Ideally, if someone is attuned to their own body, he/she will be more aware of his/her own unique physiology and sense of self and guide himself/herself accordingly.

I would suggest that if you can't achieve calmness physiologically, the rest of the stuff (unless you just enjoy it) doesn't really matter.

Once again, this could be read as critical of those who are concerned about their health and work at being fit. From reading this work, you would realise that I have an obsessive interest in sports and fitness. How can that be if calmness is what I'm promoting? Probably the first point I could make is that I have always enjoyed sports and exercise. I am competitive (more with self than others). It is fun. It doesn't define me. It is one aspect of my social/human role. It is part of me. If I denied this, it would be an indication of being too serious, too defensive, too closed, and too tense.

I went into a classical record store and heard an Arvo Pärt composition for cello and piano. It was an incredible piece from my point of view, very minimalist. And I hadn't heard him before. When I talked to the salesman, who was a music student, we discussed a wide range of music. We both had very eclectic tastes. Some was fun and energising, some really had no redeeming musically defined qualitative features, while others were profoundly moving for the person who is attuned to the dynamics of the 'oneness' of sound, which we have addressed before. The enjoyment of one type of music does not preclude the other.

I started this work expressing my need for human connection, the closeness I felt with my friend, and my diminished desire and ability to achieve a compassionate distance from others. I was feeling a sense of 'either/or'. It seemed that I could remain calm and detached or be engaged with the social/human world.

I have found 'sweeping' satisfying, and still can, though I have new strategies for dealing with storms, but the exercise is still equally futile, yet there is something about the movement. I am aware of what I am doing at the same time, unlike Sisyphus rolling the rock up the hill. Even though it may be stressful for many, I enjoy risks and challenges. It is not an either/or. It is not just living on another level either but it is living with the understanding that what is seen on the social/human level as defining individuality, politics, and importance exists when you come to the surface. Leaving calmness, you are engaging in the waves, the yin/yang, the good/bad, etc. This vertical movement is not a transformation in the way we have used it previously. It is more akin to experiencing two worlds at the same time with a clear awareness. Thus it could be seen as single- and multifaceted. Ideally, we wouldn't have unconscious influences determining what we see or how we experience; we would simply experience. If you go back to my discussion of Joyce and my futile attempt to use these dualities to explain the psyche of my friend, we can see that these are inadequate in some absolute sense. As we further explore a sense of calmness and how we see the world, we can begin to separate our perspective even from symbolic dualities.

I can visualise myself looking up to the surface of the sea on a sunny day and seeing an interplay of light and dark, white and blue and green—a constant interplay that is never exactly the same. I notice the rising and falling surface. That does seem to repeat. It's hard to tell from this perspective whether each wave is the same height, though I do notice that there are some that are obviously larger. Above the sea, I can actually see the blueness of the sky, the sun, and some clouds. As I look around me, I see a very different world. The water is reasonably clear, but my vision is limited by what looks like cloudiness. I see that it is a mixture of the sand colour at the bottom, the diffused light coming from the surface, and the colour of the water. I have always found it interesting how the colour of water is created by the interplay of light, water, and depth. I see some rocks to my left with sea life but no fish at the moment. The bottom around me is just sand with a few rocks and lots of small shells, but these are all covered by light and shade.

By simply writing about my visualisation here, I have calmed and changed my point of view. I like some kind of distorted checkerboard. I can feel a sense of wonderment, like the child discovering something. Here is a 'oneness'. Here is an orchestra of colour, movement, shape. Here is a canvas. Is it like virtual reality? I ask as I am looking for something that might be the same. I can sense that it is beyond virtual reality. It is the experience of the creator in much the same way as my writing is an attempt to share an experience.

The Conscious/Unconscious: Opening the Doors

In the recent discussion, I made reference to my desire to get beyond an unconscious influence and the need for transformation. If we consider how I used conscious and unconscious on page 116 and in the next section, we can see that they were discussed from the perspective of structured dualities, and also included were some of the following:

- swan-duck
- creative-social/human
- aware-not aware
- salient–not salient
- attached–not attached
- real–other than real
- bad-good
- elating-depressing
- lateral-vertical
- integrated–not integrated

Let's consider these from our new perspective.

We are calm and observe. We see a swan and then a duck; we see some fish. From our underwater point of view, we can see the shadows of all of them on the bottom. They are of different shapes and sizes, and if we look up, we can see different colours. We can see the feet propelling the two birds. The fish has great acceleration, not feet, but has far more speed. We can see and experience. If we reflect on our experience and then look at our list of dualities, we can see that they are not applicable—N/A.

The style of the above paragraph may be something unfamiliar to many of you. It is the style often used in sutras and poetry. It is simple. It is childlike. It is open. It is.

In this simple experience, we are open to a wide array of stimuli without any particular modality or focus. In a way, we are absorbing. We are becoming one with . . .

If this experience had some specific conscious or unconscious associations, the experience could be quite different. The following example is a single illustration of how we can develop unconscious associations that influence our perceptions.

Let's say that you have a conscious interest in ducks. You know all the scientific names for all the varieties. You are also aware of the range of weights and sizes. I can't say that you enjoy pigeonholing them, but I can say you like duck-holing them. What then is your experience?

You saw a particular type of duck that you guessed weighed two kilograms and could be defined very specifically using correct terminology. The duck was swimming on the surface. For the duck lover, this reaction made sense; however, with it came several other changes with respect to being calm, absorbing. Physiologically, you could have a change in EEG wave patterns; they would most likely become faster with lower amplitude (essential for thinking). In essence, you would be more alert. You would probably shift from a more global response to a more specific cognitively based one. There would be greater involvement of your own factual duck memory.

In fact, we could consider the possibility that the self defines the moment instead of the moment defining the self.

We could see, using a similar explanation, that an unconscious association could have the same type of influence. Let's say there was this kid at school; let's say an older peer who was highly abusive in nature and who always got into trouble in school was aggressive in nature, was unfriendly, and was often abusive to you and others. Even though he had no friends, everyone knew him. The one thing that everyone knew about this older kid was that he loved ducks or at least killing them. He was a duck hunter, and it was believed that he had many trophy ducks in his house. (We'll assume he is male). For some reason, you and your friends were very aware of this kid, even though you had very little direct contact with him. You felt and maybe would still feel great anxiety and fear thinking about this person. He was a scary guy!

On a conscious experiential level, you know he was a mean guy who liked ducks, and let's say that you haven't even thought about him for years. But the question remains: Does your past experience influence your attitude about ducks? Can the memories of this one kid influence your feelings about hunters? Or are your thoughts about him still somewhat negative but really have nothing to do with your present experience? Or is your attitude a 'so who cares?' one?

What this hypothetical example is illustrating, and one may not have been realised, is that it is common for people to develop very specific physical responses to experiences that are associated with very positive or negative past experiences. Think of PTSD (post-traumatic stress disorder). Thus in our example, someone being close to a duck or even seeing a duck could likely have a reaction that is influenced by associated experiences and memory, especially if there are some reactively induced internal changes in physiology. For instance, changes in functions like heart rate, respiration, and muscular tension could have occurred without any conscious awareness. In a sense, your body knows and remembers, but you don't.

From a personal perspective, if this type of experience were yours or something like it, then a present situation, like the one in our example, could result in your feeling uncomfortable. This could be the case, even though you would consider yourself as someone who likes ducks. In very simple terms, your body has learned to react to ducks as if they were associated with sources of abuse (a typical conditioned response). Also, you may not have even been aware that you tend to simply move away or avoid ducks. So here you are in the water, below a duck, and you feel significant discomfort, and it dominates your experience. You may look around, not knowing why you are feeling the way you do, and even experience some panic and want to get out of the water, but you may have no idea about why you are feeling anxiety and may look around for some source. You could have fleeting images of this person but also not know why. We don't even need to address the physiological changes that take place, but this can be an expression of the nature of the unconscious.

In this case, your experience is defined by the self.

The important point here is that when it comes to being open, calm, and accepting, it doesn't really matter whether it's conscious or unconscious; they both influence. One thing that is common to both is that they both change your physiology, though we could also consider that one of the barriers between the conscious and the unconscious is a built-in, somewhat protective physiological reactivity that you are not aware of. As you approach some unconscious thought or feeling and go into that inner circle, as I have defined previously, you may find resistance, which is a function of physiological arousal.

Could we say that with calmness the conscious/unconscious distinction becomes less evident?

Let's visualise our psyche. But you might rightfully ask, 'How do we do that?'

Before we look at an image of doing this, let's consider two types of explorers. One is the person who is unable to sustain calmness and reacts to many situations or thoughts. The other is one who can remain calm, even in the face of adversity.

If you would like, please take a moment to review page 57. On that page, I used a diagram to explain what I saw as the dynamics of a child's inner experience and social role. On pages 62-63, I illustrated some other complex relationships between the variables we have considered.

The use of visualisations to experience these states could be quite different for each one of us. Let's look at one more factor before we proceed.

- The reaction of person 1 could be alertness ('What's happening?') or panic ('I'm not going there! I don't know what to do!').

- The reaction of the other person could be one of calmness ('I'll go with the flow. Let's see what's there.').

Okay, we have two explorers and some human dynamics. So what is next?

There are yet some other influential conscious/unconscious factors to consider before we move ahead. First, let's consider the person who is 'quiet, unconscious/intuitive' and expresses insight with calmness. This could describe the wisdom we see in the person who has had many years at sea, who knows what to do, and who has experienced every condition but may have no idea how to teach it to others. It's not really part of his conscious experience. He just does what is needed.

Second, let's consider the person who is very open to learning and new experiences. It is not that conscious/unconscious factors are still important, but they don't inhibit learning; it is just that they haven't had the experience yet.

Again, it is important to explain and understand that there is no good and bad, or is there? You may get the sense that, from my point of view, being calm, visualising, and understanding self are better. But don't forget that the whole intent of these ramblings is to express my own view of how to develop an 'outlaw' perspective or at least give you an appreciation of how I see the process. Being the outlaw is meaningful to me. But it isn't good or bad. You may feel that, to me, good could be seen as learning from me and bad would be not accepting what I say. This, of course, is not entirely incorrect. My hope is simply that hearing and reflecting on the personal expression of an outlaw will give you some appreciation of those helpless few, those lovers of beauty, and that you will be open to vertical movement.

If we return to our exercise of approaching the unconscious with visualisation, we need to find an image that makes sense to you and has some inherent symbolic conscious/unconscious qualities. I have often found that using the image of a storage room that you don't go into very often is a good starting point. In this closet, attic, basement, or whatever storage-type room you would like, there are things that you are not certain about (need to get rid of) or things you want to forget about.

Just a reminder to you, literal thinkers, who might say that you have no extra stuff or no room in your home with things you don't want to think about. You may add that you deal with everything and never let anything get hidden away. For you, we may need to use a different image, or do we? We know that to have this 'nothing extra' point of view, you need to have a certain degree of intensity, which would need to have a number of hidden (unconscious) drivers. Your home may not have the 'hidden away' room, but your psyche probably has lots.

This metaphor of the storage room seems to be a good one for describing those memories, thoughts, or feelings that are always there but not thought about. But then I have thought about the fact that here is yet another metaphor that really has nothing to do with previous ones, and then I have sketched a house with an attic, basement, and closet and become almost immediately aware that the image fit perfectly with what we have discussed before.

There is our social/human plane, and there are the threats of the unknown moving both directions, laterally and vertically. In fact, we could use this house to imply (though I thought it to be somewhat rationalised at first) that lateral movement may have its own 'closet' of unconscious influence.

Let's first consider our house with a closed-off attic, basement, and closet. We can see that there could be very different ways of dealing with these areas, and since I like 'irony', 'paradox', and 'contradiction', we will be able to see them used once again. Let's look at the following examples.

Some of you may have some kind of 'fear/angst' that you can't explain or a memory that you don't really want to dwell on. There is no point in thinking about it; it's best just to leave the doors closed. Besides, you 'kind of' know that there really isn't anything of great importance there anyway and that maybe someday they'll get around to clearing it out.

Here, we have a typical human coping mechanism, using rationalisation. However, in these cases, we could conclude that the influences of unconscious fear/angst are always there. Strangely enough, these influences may typically be evident in chronic levels of physical tension.

Some of you may have had a similar sense of angst about the world, yourself, and life in general, but some of you may have found a 'truth' that brings order to the uncertain and the unknown. You can open the attic door briefly and know that whatever is there is unthreatening because there is a higher being that protects and saves. Those of you who are like this may experience a better sense of comfort and may symbolically be able to open the basement door, knowing that what is there is earthy, maybe even evil, but doesn't have to be a threat, though evil is always there. Remember our symbolic dualities and J. Edwards and his essay 'Sinners in the Hands of an Angry God'. The closet may be more readily opened because whatever is there in memory can be forgiven by their newly found order. In this case, physical tension may be lower.

However, here, we have coping with fear by using belief defensiveness. In these cases, we could contend that conscious fear is reduced. But what is actually happening? We could contend that the influence of unconscious fear is still there. With this coping strategy, there is a focus shift. A feeling of safety from fear comes from a belief in a protective-type parent, not from dealing with the fear. As a result, the fear is shifted to the fear of any threat to your belief! Ironically, this safety founded in belief may actually result in a greater magnitude of unconscious fear. In essence, 'the more we believe, the more calmness isn't there' (A. A. Milne for the structures). 'The more one believes, the less one knows.'

Some may be fearful and possibly depressed/anxious about these closed doors. But they also know that these fears won't go away. They may need to look for support, take things one step at a time, or use other strategies. Medication can be a double-edged sword. It may make it easier to open those doors, or it may make it easier to close them and not deal with whatever is in there.

In many situations, the person may have some difficulty dealing with fear/angst. Certainly, dealing with some fears may be very difficult, but there is an important first step. Some may be naïve, curious. This is well depicted in horror- or suspense-thriller-type movies where the female who is alone in a dark, isolated house hears noises from the attic or basement and goes to find out. There are, of course, a range of outcomes. It can go from 'nothing' to 'death and dismemberment'. In these cases, the movie plays on the audience's fears of the unknown, darkness, and personal threat. Sometimes in these movies, light has symbolic power of adding clarity, making something more horrifying. And sometimes, as with sunlight, it can destroy evil.

In these films, we have a good illustration of how people cope with their personal fears in a somewhat symbolic manner, though it wouldn't be much of a thriller if the protagonist didn't even address the fearful situation. In day-to-day life, the opening of a door to some unresolved thoughts or stresses may be the same as that experienced in the scary movie. The problem is that many people may never consider that opening the door to the uncertain may bring in light because they have no alternate perspective for their insecurities or angst.

And there are some others who are curious, open, and maybe somewhat uncomfortable in opening unpleasant memories, hidden thoughts, and so on; but they have learned, maybe little by little, that this opening up can be fascinating and be filled with discoveries and epiphanies.

For these people, the house would need to be open vertically and laterally.

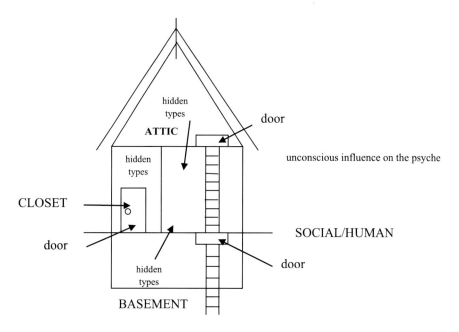

ATTIC/CLOSET/BASEMENT – These could be memories that are physical, sensory, or symbolic/literal. They could also represent a sense of 'mess'. There's too much stuff to even sort out.

The other important benefit for those who are curious is that when these people are exploring or encountering some socially disturbing event, they do not have unconscious influences that disturb their stability. Think of the difference between an 'oh no!' reactive response and a calm 'That's interesting. I wonder what is happening.' The curious person might look at situations, experience them in a less personal manner, consider what they might say about the nature of social/human existence or themselves, integrate these thoughts with other underlying structural hypotheses they hold (which could require some transformations of assumptions), and then carry on.

Let's say our discussion of the benefits of curiosity and calmness and that having openness makes sense to you. But of course, achieving calmness can be difficult. It requires an understanding of your own thoughts and the regulation of your physiology.

We have many measures of physiology that can, when combined, give us a measure of how relaxed a person is at any one moment. I need to go through those at some point, but for the moment, we will just focus on diaphragmatic breathing, relaxation, meditation, or some other techniques that decrease personal intensity. In fact, just relaxing your body can open you up to new experiences. As you can imagine, if you are physically comfortable, have no intense memories, have nothing that distresses your physiology, are experiencing your present state of relaxation, and have no direction, you have left yourself in a very limited state. It might seem pointless, but it is a necessary first step. It establishes a fundamental calmness. Once this state can be achieved, two interesting experiences emerge. You may have some interesting insights that just seem to come on their own, or with time, you will be able to explore your psyche and retain you calmness. Remember, calming techniques come first.

When looking at your inner experience, openness, and maybe even your readiness to confront your psyche and, in particular, those closed-off areas, I am going to use two concrete metaphors. The first metaphor that comes to mind is one of the faddish approaches used to help people understand their pasts. The metaphor had people consider their memories as tapes. If I remember correctly, that was popular in the '70s. Tapes worked on the principle that you have an auditory memory at both a conscious and unconscious level of things people had said to you and about you and that you have a similar memory of those things you had said about yourself and to others.

To use this, the therapist might ask the client/patient about what memories can be heard in their head, almost as if they had been recorded; and of course, therapists are generally looking for some negative, nagging, or scripted memories, though positive ones could be also evident. There are phrases like 'You can't do that. You were never very good at that. You were always the perfect kid, always wash your hands after being in public, eat your vegetables. Why did you do that!' You will have hundreds if you think about them; most may be fairly innocuous. But they can also be very limiting because they become a focus of attention, and depending on how you react to them, these scripted memories can influence your physiology.

Can therapies help achieve these more open, calm states?

The purpose here, of course, is to open up the person to memories and explore their influence not necessarily to erase the tapes (our old metaphor for memories that can influence our present) but to assist the person in developing an understanding of their influence!

A second more dynamic approach to dealing with these memories is to consider how they affect one's ability to be calm. In doing so, the therapist is addressing psychophysiology and physiology. Memories can be physical in nature. There may be conscious awareness, but there doesn't have to be any. A very common phenomenon in the therapy world is evident with people who have high degrees of reactive anxiety or agitation. (In these cases, we see measurable changes in muscular tension, heart rate, and respiration.)

Several conditions can emerge here, and these are influenced by three factors: an (1) anxiety-producing, (2) learned (3) associative condition, like my example of the learned fear of a duck. Actual physiological changes occur with 'anxiety' and the conscious experience of feeling anxious. In each case, one could have awareness or no awareness of each factor or the whole experience.

	anxiety association	physiology changes	anxiety experience	the whole chain
conscious		→	→	→
unconscious		→	→	→

I won't list all thirty-two possibilities and all the learned physiological connections that can be made, but to achieve calmness, a therapist would need to establish a profile, bring all factors to conscious awareness, and then desensitise and reduce physiological reactivity. This more dynamic understanding would require the exploration of many possible sensory associations that, in reality, may be not practically possible in all cases. In fact, even a physiological sensation that is associated with some normally expected past event may trigger high levels of physical reactivity.

Let me share a few personal memories of some modalities. Over looking my wine nose, which has a memory of special wines and undrinkable ones, I can remember that many years ago, before I had a diesel car and a sailboat with a diesel engine, I would smell diesel exhaust and instantly be transported to London. I could see, feel, and experience London and the smell of taxi exhaust. The car and a sailboat simply replaced that olfactory connection.

A good example of a visual memory and its learned influence on physiology would frequently occur when there is a noticeable bump on the road while driving a car. The driver's reaction should be to slow down and go over it slowly. From a ski-racing perspective, one doesn't slow down but lifts one's legs to either prejump or absorb the bumps. For me, the connection at one point is to see the bumps on the road ⟶ lift my legs.

There are, of course, an unlimited number of associations that stimulate and are normal and learned, but they can all influence one's ability to be calm (not stimulated). Oops, there's another term, 'stimulated'.

For most of you, there has been some food that, for some reason, didn't agree with you, and the thought of having that food may make you feel nauseous. This can happen even after *one* experience.

For any of you who have developed some 'bad habits' in some sport, you know about muscle memory. For others of you, stressful thoughts may result in painful biomechanical responses (e.g., tense shoulders) and distressed thinking. We can see that therapy and coaching may help those 'bad' habits. But what about the positive?

Beyond therapy

But as some of my illustrations demonstrate, these sensory system associations and memories are just that—memories and associations. They could be anxiety producing, but they could also be calming. I remember landing on one of the Tongan islands at night, and there were maybe fifty or sixty people standing on the shore. As I looked at these people, I was calmed in an almost unreal manner. They all seemed calm, no one moved, and no one made a sound. There was no breeze, and the water was calm.

	calming association	physiology changes	calming experience	the whole chain
conscious		→	→	→
unconscious		→	→	→

In this case, we can reconsider our thirty-two different possibilities. We are not trying to get 'rid' of negatives but instilling a complete experience of calmness on both a conscious and unconscious level. In other words, there is no unconscious/conscious conflict. We are simply in an open structure.

An Exercise in Memory Exploration

Now that you have some appreciation of calm, let's go back and explore some other states of mind and memories, some of which may include the unsettling. Though our goal may be to have you able to achieve a calm state, it needs to be the function of a different perspective that is all-inclusive. It cannot be achieved if it is accompanied by denial or avoidance of stress. Like our *oneness*, it needs experience, insight, and the ability to embody all.

Separating memory sources and finding some apt metaphors

What about tapes? Those recorded scripts?

We have, of course, moved on technologically from the world of 'tapes' and their use as a metaphor for auditory memories, though some audiophiles still condend that the reel-to-reel tapes still offer the best recorded sound. But when considering our new technologies, I have realised that there isn't really a simple replacement. We could assume that more modern is better, but is it in the world of metaphors?

The first thing that comes to mind is the adequacy of the tape metaphor. The tape is a metaphor for one's internal thoughts. These tapes are not the source of these thoughts, but the idea that they are like a recording makes sense. They are a single modality and play in your head. These thoughts come from a 'real' life experience.

My next thought, though somewhat a non sequitur, is that in the age of small televisions and limited coverage of world events with no Internet, Facebook, or YouTube, the world of television content was 'very limited'.

In this 'old' world, there was a very clear distinction between real personal experience and vicariously experienced life as seen on television. Now these boundaries are blurred or maybe even nonexistent. In fact, I heard the following statement the other day: 'It's unbelievable! I'll never forget it! I saw . . .' In this case, the source of seeing was on YouTube. This person could say that it was a real experience since it really happened, and I felt it.

On television, the images could be bigger and more defined in colour and clarity than 'real' life experience (HD). It's like being there! Or is it? Let's assume that many lateral travellers see the world while on a tour or even backpacking; they have experiences that are meaningful.

This meaning as a memory could be 'I saw this! Can you imagine?' *Or* it could be 'I didn't know what to do. I was overwhelmed.' (The person was out of their personal comfort zone.) From these expressions, personal involvement is not necessarily clear. Was the person watching something on YouTube? A passenger in the experience? Or the driver of the experience?

I guess the questions I am approaching about the sources of personal memories relate to the dynamics of the situation. For some, memory may be a stream of images. They were there and saw this and that.

For some, meanings could be composed of a stream of media impressions and images. Their personal experiences may include sports teams, media personnel, religious leaders, the conquests and failures of politicians, none of whom they have met or been involved with.

For some, memories are composed of skipping your own boat, writing one's own computer program (not using someone elses), or creating something.

For some, when age seems to take over (one is too old to do), memories are stories of the past. Some may stop creating new memories.

For some, memories can be very 'real' in nature, but they are of a very different sort of reality. Some draw on the unconscious and actually expand conscious awareness. One may remember a line of prose or poetry that changes the psyche and results in vertical exploration and opening doors and the unconscious, doors of perception and heaven and hell. Was it a drug or the reading experience that altered consciousness?

What is interesting here is that for those living on a social/human plane, all these types of memories can be joyous or dramatic. The difficulty is that these memories for many may not promote any vertical exploration. They are prisoners on a 'darkening plane'. Blake calls this the world of 'experience'. To him, this was the world of factories, cities, and populations that dominated the industrial world of the 1800s. We could consider his 'experience' as similar to the negative aspects of our social/human plane, though it is important to rememmber that the stage of 'experience' is one of his four stages that go from innonence to Eden.

It would seem that, in all the arts, there are often expressions of vertically different perspectives. The memories of these new perspectives expand one's experience to other works, other creations, and abstract forms that in themselves offer a reminder of profoundness of expanding conscious awareness. It's not just more of the same. It's interesting in a somewhat contradictory manner. It is like stepping inside one's psyche, but in doing so, the outside world is changed. It is like being inside and outside at the same time.

Why is that Goya print here? It could be that it reflects what is inside, or it could be that it disturbs what is inside; either way, the image works. This could be an expression of who you really are, a need to get engaged. You should not be calm at this moment or any moment. You need to be excited, fearful, or confused, but you see and feel.

Now that you are confronted with another's created image, I know you can't ignore it. In fact, whatever you sense, please note that it is not the image per se but your own psyche because it moves you vertically. This is a very important point! It is really the limitations of our own point of view that you should consider first. We always have them. Now approach your memories.

Becoming a conductor or sea captain

Before you do that, we need to consider another factor that I have overlooked. To even begin to explore yourself, you may need to have a level (I can't define it, mind you) of social/human experience and confidence but not too much. But as we have considered, too much or too little can be paralysing. In Hesse's <u>Siddhartha</u>, which I have alluded to before, Siddhartha experiences many different lifestyles and is successful at a social/human level at all of them. But he is not fulfilled. For Hesse, it is stylistically important to develop social/human success but lack of fulfilment to make his point.

What is important here is that your self-exploration of social/human successes could be influenced by a number of factors. It could be that you have been successful and felt fulfilled or kind of fulfilled or not fulfilled (whatever *fulfilled* means). It could be that your successes are measured by your own or other social/human criteria. Is the businessman, lawyer, doctor, or successful athlete more successful than the starving artist? What is important in exploring memories from a self-evaluative perspective is the need to be humble and to accept your level of social confidence and personal drive. *Drive* may seem to be the wrong word here, which it could be; it is too lateral in its use, but it also works, I think. Maybe this is just an example of the use of words and how a contradiction seems evident, not because of a word's definition but because of how it is used. One needs to work hard over time (drive) to be successful. But we could also consider that to get beyond social/human drive, one needs drive.

For instance, one could look at their experiences with a certain humble and somewhat distant perspective and ask, 'As I was at the wheel of the boat, the tide was ebbing to the south, and I was heading to the north. I needed to get north. There was time pressure. Was I learning, or was I stuck in the circumstance? Did I have confidence? Had I taken time to learn? Did I need to learn more? Did I need more years of experience to be able to play with all the variables intuitively and calmly and accept the reality of the interplay of forces?'

Maybe the irony here is that to experience calm, you have to not only be open but also experience fear, anxiety, distress, or high arousal, even that intense, single-focused oneness. Without these, you may not have developed a differential awareness necessary for really feeling 'calm' when it is experienced.

Some exercises in memory

Remember that the experience of no distress and calmness requires experiences of distress.

You may find this section a bit confusing, especially the part about distress and drive and their value. Here again are the limits of dualities. We have been talking for pages now about being calm, visualising, changing point of view, and considering the conscious and unconscious. Couldn't one achieve a desired calm state by just remembering the positives or having a life of little distress?

Then we could begin with a visualisation exercise that is supposed to be looking into ourselves, remembering calmness. I would agree that this seems fairly straightforward; it may be harder to do than you think.

Memory no. 1

Let's try several calm memories. The typical relaxation exercise might be to have someone place themselves somewhere where they are sitting in the warm sun with nothing that has to be done. (For almost all of you, this is not going to be an underwater image, like the one that I have used.)

Or consider an experience that should be relaxing but may not be as relaxing as it should be because of fatigue or the result of a busy day, yet your experience is enjoyable.

Make a note of an image that may work best for you, one in which you can feel calm and any busy thoughts are distant at best.

Memory no. 2

Consider the calm-after-the-storm-type memory. In this memory exercise, first consider the 'storm', the 'tough day', or the 'journey' needed to reach a calm state. In this case, an important variable is that you have made it; you are successful. Next, consider the experience of being calm. In this case, the immediate memory of the 'storm' is there; it is the sense of it being over that creates the sense of calmness.

Make a note of this image or one like it.

Memory no. 3

Consider a memory of a time(s) of self-reflection, a stream of consciousness, a time when you may have thought about the purpose or meaning of human life or asked a number of questions you couldn't answer. Were you able to step back and reflect about circumstances or about whys? Did you find that you didn't end up with an acceptable social/human-belief-based answer? Did you cling on to some type of scripted social/human answer that didn't feel satisfying?

Some of you may not be able to retrieve a memory like this, while some others may recall a moment or many moments like this. However, the nature of these experiences could be very different for each one of you.

Interestingly enough, the presence or absence of memories like these may both suggest questioning that is vertical in nature. Having them would, of course, show conscious thought, but not having these reflective times or memories doesn't mean these questions have never existed. It could be that they show an unconscious conflict that has been suppressed.

See if you fit one of the following:

- ▪ *No necessity to ever experience self-questioning (doubt)*

Were you 'saved by beliefs' in childhood by parents or other adults? They answered the question before I asked it. There were latitudes like 'You're okay,' 'Get on with life,' 'Get real,' 'Everything's okay,' or 'Forget about that stuff.'

Beliefs that were religious or political may also have given you answers before you asked.

Result: no awareness of questions (all the answers were there) no angst

- ***A necessity to experience (maybe only once)***

    Did you find that the beliefs that you found quickly protected you? As a result, any moment of self-questioning or doubt was answered by belief.

    Result: awareness of questions (all the answers were there) limited angst

    One's possibly frantic search could involve a search for a mentor, saviour, belief system, or ideology.

    Once found, life became calmer.

- ***A necessity to have experiences but don't know what to do with them or how to give them meaning***

    Did you find these moments distressing? But they keep coming up, and you have searched in vain for some belief or platitude, 'other' political party, or religion. It could be karma, it could be that others are worse off, or it could simply be that you end up feeling like a victim of life.

- ***A necessity to experience but realise that it isn't personal; it isn't a function of karma or political/religious belief***

    Do you find that these moments are interesting and worth researching or analysing? Your questions are open-ended but are focused on a social/human plane.

- *A necessity to experience the unknown, especially in your thoughts about self or your exploration of the thinking of others, and with questions that have answers and others that have none*

  Do you continue to ask, resolve some, ask more, see limits? Do you find these moments essential to your being? Even though you may know that you are trapped by your own human limitations, there is a freedom. You can move above or below the social/human plane. See the species as an outsider and insider.

Memory no. 4

Consider a memory where calmness, like our skipper, exists even with multivariant adversity. Of course, a successful outcome of this situation could be the result of 'dumb luck' or a belief in some higher power with 'dumb luck', or success could be the result of calmness based on knowledge and experience and accepting the vastness of the unknown.

This kind of calmness may not be part of everyone's memories because this involves calmness and engagement. It could be experienced by the talented musician who plays an ethereal or free-form piece that gives an overall calmness. A personal calmness in body and spirit could be experienced by the person who possesses a degree of wisdom. It could be the philosopher-teacher who can offer a sense of calmness and overall security to others, at least in an interacting setting.

I think that this discussion of calm memory has become a bit more confusing.

It's clear that we have to accept some different types of 'calm' experience. It does make sense to accept that some people look inwardly with variable degrees of comfort. And it may seem that experienced calmness can have many different faces, and each one may look like a state of calmness that is an experienced *oneness*. Look at your own memories and how you understand them. Our memory exercise may help illustrate your personal dynamics.

	can't do, have done	can do with difficulty, have done	understand but can't do or don't do	don't get it, would like to do	can't do, no desire to do
Memory 1 – calm/ relaxed (away from)					
Memory 2 – calm after storm					
Memory 3 –					
1. reflection and before?					
2. found belief					
3. futile – doesn't go anywhere					
4. necessary for life					
Memory 4 – calm with environment control					

So what are the right answers? Are there any?

From my perspective, there are no wrong answers; however, if you didn't follow my thinking, it could be that my explanation was poor. I admit that this is actually possible since my explanations may be unclear and confusing, or it could be a level of personal defence.

Understanding all these different memories in themselves isn't important, but accepting your own 'this is where I am' is important since it helps define yourself, your own limits, and what it feels like to be comfortable. But this honest reflection could be experienced with a vast number of responses.

What is obvious is that no one vertical column offers a set of desirable responses.

So where are we now?

Maybe one way of looking at personal readiness to be calm at all levels is the ability to be open to all conscious and unconscious sources of stress. However, it could be that you are aware that there are some things that are hidden away. You may have a sense that there is something but haven't ever opened the door. All you know is that thinking about this 'something' makes you feel uneasy, and you don't really want to find out what's there.

Here's another contradiction. *Out of all stresses comes calmness.*

Some Considerations of the Impact of Stress: A Stressful Interlude

Before we move ahead and return to considering improving our understanding of the conscious/unconscious and its eventual integration, I think we should consider the following:

- All people have stressors, even if the stressor is that you believe you have never had one.
- Stressors are uniquely individual and may or may not have a specific relationship with real life-threatening stresses. They may simply be related to social/human perceptions. For the European or North American, which is more stressful? The death of your old cat/dog that has been a family member for years or ten-thousand-plus people, none of whom you know, killed in some distant war or natural disaster? There, of course, is no comparison. And of course, it's the same everywhere in the world. It is the personal experience we feel.
- There is, however, an irony here. If the same North American has unconscious fears about personal safety, it could be triggered by many objects. For instance, one might show a fear response to 'Middle Eastern–looking' people (who may be possible terrorists), even if they were seen on television.
- There are aspects of ourselves and our experiences that we are aware of, and there are others that we are not.
- All experiences, even those we don't consciously remember, influence our physiology, thoughts, feelings, and behaviour.

I think we can all agree with the above.

Can we go back to our visualisations of these inner rooms, the recorded messages, the images, and how you feel? Not quite yet.

Before we address achieving the calm with a typically stressful content, I feel that we need to make sure that you understand the need for feeling some distress or angst first. We can achieve the calm next. Remember, we simply want to open doors and develop a feeling that the unconscious that is influenced and possibly felt in some nonarticulated manner is not to be feared or hidden away.

I am reminded of one person I saw (another water example, I apologise for the consistency of the symbolic references) who had a fear of water that actually resulted in a pattern of significant panic attacks. In fact, I often use this as an example of how the therapist can change the past. Boy, that sounds a bit presumptuous! But it isn't. By using clinical hypnosis with visualisation, we were able to have this person relive the situation. (We opened an inner door.) This person could remember experiencing fear. He was going to drown and die. This was especially interesting (from a therapist's point of view) because he grew up in a fundamentalist Christian family that convinced him that there was divine retribution for his sins, and as a child, he was convinced that he was a sinner. From a social/human perspective, he would have been considered as a quiet, perfectly behaved, bright little boy with no friends (a nerd). He was a sinner because he was 'caught' a number of times playing with his genitals when in bed. All these social/human factors let him know he was alone and had no hope. So for him, the terror of his drowning experience was magnified by guilt and knowledge that he was obviously deserving. (As an aside, he wasn't just a nerd but also a swan whose parents wanted him to be a duck.)

Changing the past

In reliving this situation in a constructive, therapeutic manner, we needed to consider several things. First, he had developed a trusting relationship with me, which included a sense that I really understood him and also that I had an ability to deal calmly with adversity. Second, he was able to experience his trauma and express it. As you expected, his verbal descriptions were minimal; but once he opened that door, his overall expression was psychophysiologically profound. Third, I was able to enter his memory and be part of his visualisation. I could be seen as someone above the surface with a hand down to him. He could hold on, and I could pull him up. He could visualise my presence and felt safe. It was almost as if he could reprogram the memory and eliminate its trauma.

Of course, the actuality of the event didn't change, but the memory of the experience did. From this changed experience, we were able to slowly reduce his feelings of guilt and anxiety and help him feel a sense of calm using similar types of strategies. From a therapist's perspective, it was necessary to be completely calm in the face of the adversity of his memory.

For this person, a guide, coupled with some sense of security/support, was needed to explore his psyche; and in doing this, he was able to open the doors to his unconscious and make them part of his conscious experience.

For most of you, this exploration of memories will be much easier or at least less traumatic.

So let's return to those inner doors and how these can be opened by expressing them.

Some of you may be good visualisers and will be able create an inner room that has stuff in it that reflects your experiences, and one piece leads to another. Some of you may be better at remembering past incidents in an almost daydream manner, going with the flow, and letting your own thoughts and feelings lead the way. You may find that the 'listening to old internal recordings' approach is easy to do. And for some of you, none of these may work easily. If you have difficulty finding these recordings from your own past, think of some of the social scripts that are evident in society that tell you what to do or not do. You could try expressing some of these in a 'subvocalisation' manner or discussing these with someone else. This expression does two things. It helps aware people make a distinction between social platitudes and their own introspective thought, which is an expression of themselves, not society. It also helps open up the less aware person and can give them an opportunity to express their own thoughts, feelings, and questions about life.

For this second group, we are really approaching the opening up of a person to the 'stream of consciousness' thinking. Even following this approach to thinking may be difficult for some. If so, my next recommendation is to simply start writing down anything and everything that comes to mind. I have done this with many groups in the past, and typically, I will observe a number of people with a blank page, even after several minutes. Of course, they will say, 'I don't know what to write.'

As you can predict, I would respond, 'You just told me what you should write.' Usually, they don't get it at first, so I have to dictate to them.

'I don't know what to write.' They write that and then stop.

'Now what is happening?' I ask.

'I still don't know what to write,' they respond.

'Write that down,' I say.

Usually, after a few false starts, they get going. They may even repeat 'I don't know what to write' for a whole page, but eventually, they begin to be somewhat reflective. They may write 'This is stupid' and then maybe 'I feel self-conscious about what I write.' With this exercise, the process of opening inner doors is beginning.

In this process of opening inner doors, I have had one person in therapy sketch very simple images. It was interesting that even the shapes and lines she drew showed her feelings. As she began drawing more pictures, she started to become more comfortably aware of her own past and her present feelings and then drew more.

Note: In my suggested ways of approaching the integration of the conscious/unconscious, I have purposefully left out meditation, which, with years of practised discipline, is profoundly influential and can be somewhat appreciated and achieved to a certain degree by 'mindfulness' strategies. However, it is used to achieve calmness and to integrate body, speech, and mind; it is not used just to explore your own psyche in quite this manner. Its outcome is the achievement of a calmness that integrates all self.

So what about personal expression?

The neat thing is that whatever your form of personal expression, it could be seen as being artistic in nature. It becomes a unique personal expression that cannot always be defined as bad or good; in fact, social human good can be bad.

I once clinically worked, for a little while, with a chap who attended a workshop i was giving. He was in his early twenties, very bright, and successful academically and socially; but when asked to draw whatever came to mind, he confessed that he couldn't draw. Not that that should really matter anyway, but he agreed to try to draw something expressive. He looked at his blank sheet of paper for some time, and then he drew a checkerboard figure and started to fill in the squares with these different colours. About a quarter of the way through, he stopped! He wrote a title at the bottom—*Insecurity*.

This one simple exercise had a profound influence on him. He saw it as highly symbolic. He realised that it expressed the way in which he ordered his life based on social/human norms. It wasn't the drawing exercise that was the challenge for him; it was his own insecurity and his discomfort about expressing himself as a person.

A consideration of practical expressions

Okay, now is the time to begin your own process of discovering the conscious/ unconscious. Forget about calmness for the moment. In this work, I have given space for these exercises. At the beginning, I have asked that you listen to John Cage. More recently, I have dedicated two blank pages with a focal dot for practising visualisation. At this point, I will simply recommend that you make some notes about what will work for you to begin the conscious/unconscious voyage. Remember, you may find one, two, three, or four modes that work; or even better, they may all work together.

Are your memories of calm or stressful events clearly visual? Are your memories of calm and stressful events connected to other sensory stimuli? You may have memories that are clearly driven by smell, taste, or even touch.

If you were asked to express your memories as you remember the experiences, you ideally could have a single modality of expression and write, draw, compose a musical piece with or without lyrics. Keep it simple. You could create a multistimuli expression that involves many sensory modalities; however, simple expressions may be lost if one attempts to use too many expressive modalities. The high-tech irony here is that the more you, as the expressive person, consider some expression that includes every modality of your expression, the more the essence of your expression may be lost since others may not make the same multimodality associations.

Like the expressions that compose this work, the process of becoming the outlaw requires an awareness of the vertical and lateral influences on one's psyche. With these exercises, we are attempting to assist you in exploring and expressing your inner conscious/unconscious core in a nonjudgemental manner, knowing that whatever you discover is fine.

Reception and expression

A number of years ago, many young people played a game called dungeons and dragons. The game was played on a graph paper, and all directions and what a character might see or hear were given orally by the dungeon master. With this game, a very vivid imagination and ability to visualise was essential. Someone reading a novel may find that the words guide their experience. In a sense, the words become incidental. If we follow these ideas, we could make the point that as a number of sensory/media expressive modes increase, there is a decrease in inner conscious/unconscious emergence.

Let's say that a single-visual-medium artistic expression, like our Jean-Goya print, can alter the imagination and open all sorts of emotional and experiential doors. And surely, we could contend that this is also the case with music and writing. Let's also say that these experiences are not only opening doors but also triggered personal memories and are being integrated with personal consciousness and unconsciousness. Thus we wouldn't expect that this Goya image would promote calmness. But we could also ask, 'Why not?'

What about these ramblings and your inner involvement?

Let's say that you may frequently be impatient with just reading these ramblings, though you may be most willing to read and digest some of the ideas. Yet you may not bother with any of the suggested self-reflective activities. Anyway, here is another concrete suggested exercise.

The stressful

1. Select some stress-producing, dislikeable images (e.g., artwork, architecture, interior design). Select some stress-producing auditory work (e.g., music, acting, sounds). And finally, select some stress-producing written work that affects your imagination in a number of sensory ways.
2. Use an expressive mode that works best for you. For most of you, writing down your reaction may be the easiest.

> For instance, you may look at an image, and actually feel fear, anger, or something like that; however, your conscious feeling may be 'This is dumb.' So you write that down, but then you need to keep going. You need to keep writing down whatever you feel. You will know when you start to move vertically and into your unconscious, when you start to experience a shift in judgement from outside imaginings to descriptions of self. Within the microcosm of self is the macrocosm of the universe.
>
> You could even repeat the above with different expressive modalities. Explore and see where your thoughts take you.

The calm

Simply repeat the above by stepping back and experiencing yourself with calm-producing stimuli. As above, express your thoughts about this person's experience by writing a number of lines or thinking for half a minute and see what changes exist. How about another reflective thought? Unity of thought and experience requires detachment.

What may become evident is that your memory and experience of calmness may be like memory 1 or 2 and not representative of a conscious/unconscious openness.

Where are we now?

Are you now more self-aware, and do you feel that your consciousness has been slightly changed? Could simply reading these notes or taking a course result in a state of continuous peace? Will the sea never have waves or tides again that will disrupt you? Are you able to be in a state of continuous calmness? As you are probably thinking, this is not achievable or even desirable. Even though we could accept that we all live in a world that is always the same in its underlying structure, we know that it is also always changing on a social/human level. As a result, we need to have a wide range of adaptive responses to function, though more calmness might be nice.

From these last comments, it might seem that all the efforts to expand conscious awareness, explore self, and understand and accept our memories in some esoteric manner may be worthwhile on some level. But it would seem that these new insights may not change anything and don't seem to be very practical. You may question why one might spend all this effort exploring self, knowing that we still have to function in the 'real' (social/human) world.

If you have this point of view, you may also be questioning or may not actually understand our discussion of that single state that combines *all*. You may agree that calmness might be hypothetically desirable, but you may also question the belief that one can be completely self-aware or even achieve that state. Wouldn't that be a delusion? Don't some schizophrenics feel this way?

However, all this self-exploration could help you see the relative and limiting qualities of social/human values and states of understanding. Consider the following:

There are many occasions when we feel excited, when we can also feel anger, when we can feel fear, when we can feel ennui. From a vertical perspective, ennui could be considered as a high/low-arousal conflict and may not be a bad state. It could be a good beginning point and worth exploring. From the same perspective, we could view all our experiences and appreciate that they all have value.

Before going any further, we need to consider a social/human caution. The personal value of being excited is often seen as better than negative experiences. But is it? In fact, some positive feelings may be misleading, like the Sirens who enticed Ulysses and his crew, strong sexual desires, the humour of a racist group, or even the elation that accompanies victory. In a sense, positive emotions that require a negative view of others may be seen as somewhat scary. These may be more trapping and more difficult to step back from.

I was recently speaking to a father whose son had a high level of performance anxiety. The child's need to perform well, coupled with a high level of physiological arousal, had resulted in what appeared to be 'socially aggressive' behaviour. If he couldn't do something well, he would often hit others or have a tantrum. He was not having positive feelings.

His dad's solution was to find an activity that he was good at so he could become the best or at least better than most of his friends. This is an understandable parent strategy, but unfortunately, this approach, as you can imagine, would most likely result in increased anxiety and reactive arousal in another area. But isn't there something more?

I don't know whether the tragic flaw in the dad's approach is obvious to all of you. But I bring in this example because it is a good example of how social/human value judgements may shape how you explore your own psyche.

We could say that the son is a prisoner of his own anxiety, which could be the result of his need to do well, or it could be the result of a number of other human traits. Should the dad be concerned about finding success for his son or focus on the nature of his anxiety? We could conclude that the dad is 'missing the point' since a major influence could be parental pressures. But of course, the dad's approach could have been seen as successful if his son did well in another area. Therefore, his approach worked, or did it?

So we could also conclude that, at a social/human level, being successful and happy may not require any self-reflection. In fact, self-reflection may mess things up.

I saw a male in his late twenties who had done everything correctly. He had been popular at school, he had played sports, and he had received good marks in university. He had become a chartered accountant, got married, bought a house, and crashed. He didn't go crazy; he went sane. We decided to explore his past.

He had done everything to be the best duck possible. The only problem was he wasn't a duck but didn't know what he was. Upon reflection, he realised that there was something wrong; he often experienced an angst that he didn't understand. He knew it should not have been there because everything in life was great.

There was an emerging conscious sense that he had lived for others and that he needed to separate his own instincts from those seen at a social/human level. He realised with a sense of panic, as he was settling into a career and marriage, that he had never considered his own nature or questioned social/human values in all his life. Like Sisyphus, he had been fulfilled rolling his rock; and as in Camus's essay, he had reached the top of the hill.

I can give many more examples of other points of view, but if you see yourself as happy or successful, have had lateral movement in your life, and have experienced different social/human points of view, it may be difficult to consider yourself as someone who has actually missed anything. You know that you can see differences and would be able to say that you are like this or like that and that the culture you grew up in is like this but also like that. Certainly, any descriptions of cultures are okay. But you may have described your cultures of influence differently. Most of you probably started with family and maybe ethnic background. You may have considered regional influences. You may have grown up in South America, Northern or Southern Italy, or in the Far East as it was once called or wherever. But from my perspective, you could be missing something.

Define yourself as best you can, but also consider the culture(s) that you have lived in and your family genetics. Can you define some or all your attributes and values from these sources? Do you feel that some of your attributes are actually reactions to these influences, or does it seem that you are completely different from these influences? You may consider yourself a unique person.

I would take the risk of contending, given the nature of the human species and its evolution, as considered throughout recorded history, that ideologies may have been useful in their attempt to control some expressions of human drives; however, they haven't changed them. Ideologies have often just rationalised them. As I write this, I can feel a level of distress. The human/social world is run not by leaders per se but by the mass of people who need not only security but also a tribal-type identity that is based on an 'us' that is different from others. With this comes an intolerance and tolerance of others. And as we know, the species will kill others for many different reasons. Is it simply fear of the unknown or differences? Is it to improve tribal identity? Is there a need to control others? But enough of this. I have spoken about this before.

I am able to calm and move below the surface. I realise that waves on the surface are natural phenomena as are the different social/human views. I speculate that neither waves nor values will ever change as a result of human effort. As we know, our metaphorical use of waves (challenges) and social/human values are a function of the species. However, as we have discussed, a different perspective can exist for some. In fact, this understanding is one of the defining characteristics of the outlaw. Typically, social/human efforts require trying harder and putting in more effort to control others and sometimes the self. But what is missing is a changing of perspective and establishing calmness. Could we conclude that man's noneffort is necessary for calmness?

Sinking below, we can see the futility of human efforts. They end up making more waves to bring about a calm. Instead, they perpetuate the storm of believing the cliché that there is always a calm after the storm.

A learning note for some and a cognitive anticlimax for others

I would like to think that the above discussion about the nature of the species and the need to have another perspective have assisted you in realising the benefit of having some new insights and calmness, like drops of water rippling the pond.

Hopefully, you have been reading, reflecting, and maybe even getting lost. For some of you, these few lines may have given you a moment of insight—an epiphany. Yet for others of you, this may seem like the same old point is repeated again (which it is). To you, I apologise. If we consider that these lines are the concluding ones of a section about calmness, memory, and insight based on vertical/lateral perspectives, it's the same old point, nothing new.

Revisiting the Human/Nonhuman and Ephemeral Individual Life

Let's try another point of view, one that we can visualise and that may assist us in understanding ourselves in relationship to this surface world. A while ago, I have talked about considering what we mean by human/nonhuman. If you remember, we have concluded that musicians are nonhuman. But they are the building blocks; they are like individual sources of musical energy. We are going to play around with life, death, and identity using musicians and orchestras.

Here is an image that we can visualise, though its image is literal, and its meaning is metaphorical. Picture a large field with thousands of musicians milling around. If this image isn't specific enough for you, you could visualise these musicians at a golf course with a large open area and maybe with some trees here and there. You could use the City of God/New Jerusalem or maybe the Elysian Fields. But whatever image you use, you need to visualise some open space that feels comfortable, with musicians wandering aimlessly.

After a short period, these musicians group together. All of them establish a clear, organised structure based on 'instrument families'. All the woodwinds, all the brass, all the strings, all the percussion come together in their family group, and each group is separated from each other. Next, to create an orchestra, members from the different families are picked by a conductor. It is almost like the kids pick up different teams for a sports game; team members are picked based on the captain's consideration of who would be best at each position. Like the kids' game, sometimes the conductor gets who he wants, and sometimes he doesn't; and sometimes, in this situation, the musicians seem to know where to go to fill in the

318

structural requirements of each orchestra. And in almost every case, each orchestra ends up with a range and numbers of instruments required for each orchestra grouping. However, we could also visualise that a number of musicians have no obvious place to go. As a result, there could be some groups (orchestras) that might end up with missing instruments, having too many of one kind or having too many of one kind and not enough of another.

Anyway, they play together, are given a name, have their own unique sound, and are each clearly individual. At this point, try visualising a number of orchestras, maybe ten or twelve, each playing some piece individually. Wow! It could be pretty overwhelming. This would even make Charles Ives and his *Symphony No. 4*, using two orchestras, seem small. However, we could also consider them all playing together but with slight individual differences.

It would be helpful to take some time to visualise the different orchestras so that they have their own identities. They are like people we know and have grown to like and love. They have their own sound, look, et cetera. As I am writing this, I have realised that a rock/jazz/small combo visualisation would also work for you who would relate to this image better. For this exercise, both will work, though I will keep with the symphony orchestra reference for consistency and because of its more multivariant composition.

Okay, you are seeing different groups playing together. Try to visualise.

What about orchestra identity? Do they (orchestra groups) all look the same, or are they different? Like people's names, name has nothing to do with the nature of the person. So could we conclude that an orchestra that retains its name but is composed of completely different musicians and a different conductor is a different orchestra? We have lots of Bobs in the Western world.

At this point, I will take a little poetic licence and create some unreal developmental stages.

Life, Death, and Identity

First, we have the birth of an orchestra as we have described. This is real and pretty easy to visualise.

Second, we could have an orchestra with some changes. Some musicians leave and are replaced by others. This is also real and easy to visualise. Here, we have the same orchestra.

Third, we could have the 'death' of an orchestra or several orchestras. All the chairs are there but are empty, and all the musicians have dispersed back out into the field. At this point, we would have a lot of 'out of work' musicians wandering. This, of course, doesn't typically happen (the Vancouver Symphony Orchestra (VSO) had a year where they didn't have funding and had no season) but does. At this point, we have an image of empty chairs on stage and musicians wandering around our field.

If we consider that orchestras, like the VSO, return to the performance stage, we are back to where we started from. We have our unemployed musicians in the field. So what happens next? They could possibly return to the reborn orchestra, or they could possibly regroup with a different set of musicians and create new orchestras. Others may fit into existing ones, and some may remain wandering. As a result, many may have a newly formed identity and collectively become new individual orchestras or have an identity that fits an existing orchestra.

So with our extended metaphor, we have four stages in an orchestra's existence:

- Birth
- Some internal transformations
- Death of the orchestra
- Rebirth

But some important identity questions arise here.

- Does a musician's identity only exist as part of an orchestra?
- Does the individual musician add anything unique to the overall sound?
- Is it the musician's job to play any piece exactly as the conductor desires?
- Can the unemployed, wandering musician have any personal identity?

In a sense, we have an interesting dilemma. However, our dilemma may not matter in the whole scheme of things, but it is relevant to our understanding of the relationship between underlying structure and social/human perceptions.

Let's consider the orchestra and its socially defined identity. We could easily envision a new orchestra and appreciate its efforts to establish its own identity, but what about the orchestra that has died and is reborn? Is it different or the same as before? What we would surmise is that its identity still remains, even if its musicians and conductor are different. The London Symphony, though it hasn't died and been reborn, could be seen as having an identity that exists independently of the personal identity of its musicians or conductor. Here, we have an interesting perceptive confusion. Does the collective identity, the London Symphony, exist independently of it musicians, or is the London Symphony's identity really a function of the musicians and conductor?

What I find interesting about the above considerations is how identity can be conceptualised. Is your own identity or human identity like that of the social/human perception of the orchestra? You may contend that 'my name, my identity, and the fact that I am a human make me important.' Or you might see that your identity is really the collective expression of nonhuman musicians who are playing together and held together by a conductor. This personal conductor could be passionate about Stravinsky, Schoenberg, Bach, or maybe only Muzak and pop music. But where does this leave your identity? You can still hang on to something more permanent, but it isn't going to be you. It's going to be the nonhuman, the non-ephemeral, the underlying *all*.

It has always seemed to me that the human need to hang on to one's own identity and to live forever is a symptom of the developed insecurities and anxieties of the species. There is that need for a specific orchestra (with the same musicians) to last forever.

Though some sense of longevity may exist, it may be that the music an orchestra has played will be enjoyed and even extolled like the expression of any creative person. And of course, music can remain in written or recorded form. If communicated through the airwaves, it may last 'forever'. However, we would probably have to accept, though somewhat ironically, that the unimportant nonhuman musicians, as well as the structures that bring them together, will continue to exist, where the existence of the individual human doesn't last.

Hanging on to some kind of everlasting 'identity' could be seen as a social/human delusion. Experiencing the music as composed, structured, and played is lasting. It is the way things are; we are not going to change this. We just want to be able to step away (or under) and watch calmly.

This kind of visualisation is not an answer, but it does give another way of seeing our dot-to-dot pictures on page 178. These images took a similar perspective of the structure of the person.

If we consider individuality as an ephemeral organisation of some type of building blocks that have a more permanent existence, then we could see ourselves as part of a whole and not just as separate individuals who have some sense of permanent identity. I guess we could say, 'Boy, that combination of musicians that lasted for a number of years really had a great sound.' We might even ask, 'What did they call that orchestra?'

This kind of thinking—with calmness—can help us let go of our need for identity and ego as it is generally used.

For the moment, consider the assumption that human identity is nothing more than an ephemeral manifestation of a 'human form' structure of nonhuman entities. *Looks like a human, must be a human*. For some of you, this conceptualisation may be very difficult to integrate with your thinking or feeling on a literal level. Doesn't being human imply that the human is greater than the sum of its parts? Couldn't the missing part be like the conductor? Maybe the missing part is one's ego and identity.

In this short section, the images and discussions of musicians and orchestras are used to give you another metaphor to consider when describing how physical reality may actually work in creating unique people over time. This section has also addressed that our building blocks, the musicians, last longer than we do and are not just ours. In fact, the identity of the ephemeral human (orchestra) could be described as a function of 'energy sources' and their unique structural organisation (conductor arranged).

The goal of this section is to have you consider, at least hypothetically, that the individual is not an entity that is superior or separate from the underlying, nonhuman, timeless world but an ephemeral expression of its energies.

Having Feelings beyond Tolerance: Instructions on How to Achieve a New Point of View

We have discussed tolerance before. Remember, tolerance is not acceptance. It's not tolerable. It may not ideally be a desirable human quality. Think of a situation where you would say, 'I have a great deal of tolerance for this situation or person.'

Given that you are experiencing a level of tolerance, you will probably find that you are not calm but putting on a calm face. And what about different points of view? There are yours and the one you are tolerant of. Do we have tolerance when the other person is 'correct' from their point of view but are wrong from our point of view? Or would we expect that our position is more correct, though theirs isn't bad? A third factor here is that we may be tolerant because we have a positive human connection/feeling for the situation/person. You may say, 'I don't agree with what you are doing, but I can really understand how you feel.'

Let's say that our experience of tolerance probably has a connecting part to it. We feel a degree of empathy, but there is also a separating part. We know that we are right and that the others are not quite right or maybe even wrong.

Can we experience something that is beneath the surface of social/human tolerance in a situation where there are conflicting or different views? To do this, we need to leave the security of our own beliefs first and then see their relative nature. We need to understand that they are not correct in any absolute sense. They are simply mine or yours and understood with humility. Probably the social/human belief systems that best exemplify tolerance and even intolerance are those centred on religion and church.

A non-Jesuit Catholic priest once explained to me that their ideology was the correct one, but they tolerated different churches and religions. This is the same as our above example. So how could this priest achieve a different view?

Rather than giving a simple 'do this', I am going to spend some time exploring perspectives and states of mind. We will consider some of your personal experiences, some different aspects of the human experience, and some needs of the species and will even reflect on the whole scheme of life and the universe (or at least part of it).

Step 1: Find a calming nonpriest environment and relax. Be open to any thought.

Step 2: With acceptance, reflect on that religious ideology that gives answers that meet our social/human needs. It offers meaning. It offers security. It offers a set of rules to live by.

Step 3: Follow a number of multifaceted steps. The goal here is to create some experiential, possibly visualised situations that will give you an opportunity to feel secure and not secure, to understand and not understand, and to compare what it is like to have rules and direction vs. no rules and direction. Review those early pages of my ramblings or explore your own life. In your reflections, see if you can find some experiences, in a visualisation-type manner, that contrast two conditions. First, relive the feeling associated with a situation where you don't know what's happening and you don't know how to bring it back into some type of order. You might be able to get a sense of being lost. You might be pacing, looking around, anxious. You are asking yourself, 'What do I do? Where do I go?' Second, since you are now reading this, you have found a way out, an answer. And as a result, your body has calmed and felt better. Make sure you feel the calm. It is important to feel that need. However, if you remain relatively calm in the situation you have visualised, you should be able to get a sense of the need even if you are not over-engaged by it. You may even experience yourself as the observer of you. But also understand that it is a feeling you can experience, but it isn't the only one.

Reflect on the fact that our understanding of the universe is very limited. There are so many things we don't know, and we can be fearful of the unknown, but we can also be wonderfully intrigued by what we can't explain, though it can be seen as a function of our limits. The unknown doesn't have to be encapsulated in some entity we have created; it can just be.

In your reflection here, see if you can achieve two types of experiences. First, consider an experience of 'awe'. You see things that are incredible, unbelievable, serendipitous, and all-encompassing. At the time, you don't even try to make sense or explain them—your experience is magical. You don't put them under the heading of science, religion, or even some type of coincidence. See if you can still feel that 'Wow! What about that!' You leave it open. Remember, once you have an answer (a belief), that belief prevents you from having any other questions or answers.

Second, consider yourself as living in a physically 'limited' environment where you can't get out. Since limited can be seen in many different ways, we need to define it.

Let's say that many people in the world live in a rather restrictive environment in the sense that they may never travel very far from home. This could be true for many in poor countries, as well as rich ones. And there are many others whose environments are less limited. They may go to another home (summer/winter); they may go on tours or cruises, which allow for lateral movement. In most cases, these travellers keep some connection with the security of their own social milieu (i.e., the cruise ship, tour group, hotel, area of town, or activities). In some ways, we could say that these people observe but don't get involved. In these cases, one is not actually travelling 'out' or 'away'; one is staying within a defined limited environment. It is almost like being in a protective bubble of social/human values. But typically, these people don't feel limited; they are fulfilled by their experience, though they might complain about service or other such things. For others, being told that one must remain with a specific group, not visit certain neighbourhoods, or not do certain things might be seen as highly restrictive. Yet there are those people who do things on their own. They sail their own boat. They don't just visit the famous car racing track but they also race it.

Let's take these experiences one step further or backwards and consider—as you just did a few moments ago,—that, for most people, there is the need to feel safe and at home, even in a symbolic sense. With this feeling, everything is okay.

Finding your own limits of comfort may be fairly easy for most of you. But sometimes being too limited can be stressful.

Being physically limited

Now imagine three different restricting situations that could result in different degrees of feeling trapped and contained.

Consider yourself at home, where you feel safe and comfortable. But because of some environmental event or some type of quarantine, you must not leave the house for an undetermined length of time. You are not allowed to go to work, shop for food, or even open an outside door. For some of you, it may not take long before it feels like you will *never* get out; in fact, you may even feel trapped just thinking about the idea. In this case, you are in a comfortable and safe environment but still restricted. You may feel like an animal in a small cage or someone in prison. Yet for some of you, not being able to go out may seem positive because you get time off from work or don't have to take on responsibilities that you don't enjoy.

This leads us to a far more traumatic second example. Consider the experience that would, I think, be difficult for all of us—being a prisoner in some foreign country for unknown reasons. And as news reports and films on these conditions say, being let go is often difficult to determine.

Our third example has different dynamics. In this case, consider yourself in a desirable location of your choice. You are out at sea, hiking in the mountains, or skiing in an open alpine country. There is a sudden change in weather—an avalanche, rough seas—and you suddenly feel trapped, and it seems that there is no way out. A somewhat tragic irony with these possibilities is that one could feel safe on a one-thousand-foot cruise ship or in a lodge in some alpine village, but on rare occasions, these too are vulnerable to natural elements.

In the above, we have considered different situations where you are physically restricted. In each case, your thinking may be restricted to thoughts about the situation; but in essence, you are hypothetically free to think whatever you like.

William Golding, in <u>Free Fall,</u> writes, 'Free will cannot be debated but only experienced.'

Being mentally limited in freedom

Maybe there is a more imprisoning state than the ones already discussed. You might experience a restriction that also takes away our freedom, and it could be one that you may have had before. In Kafka's <u>The Trial</u>, Joseph K. becomes a prisoner of his own need to find an understanding of personal guilt based on an imposed truth that he has no idea about. He is just a regular guy who one day is found guilty, doesn't know why, and is not physically imprisoned or restricted, though he is required to appear periodically in front of some others to prove why he is not guilty. I will not elaborate here. It may be a novel some of you may enjoy or have enjoyed.

There may be some other experiences that have given you a sense of being trapped or restricted. You may even recall times when you didn't feel trapped at the time, but upon reflection, you can now experience the sense that you were trapped.

For those of you who were grounded by parents as teenagers, you may remember what that felt like. Did you accept or rebel (still social/human)? What we would like is that you can feel what it is like to be a prisoner or closed in.

There have been a number of popular movies, not just the foreign-prisoner ones, that may have given you, at least vicariously, a feeling of what it would be like to be trapped.

Wow, this step 3 is certainly a long step. Steps 1 and 2 are only a couple of lines. And this step, at least at this point, seems to want our priest to feel somewhat distressed, not calm, trapped, and not free to think. And this is correct; we want him to feel these trapped experiences in a calming environment. It is almost like feeling trapped in a nontrapping environment. It seems almost contradictory.

For Kafka's Joseph K., his being accused of being guilty of some unknown crime could be seen at another lateral-level challenge. What was his crime? What had he done wrong? Is this some type of existential dilemma? In very simple terms, Joseph K. needs to look at himself and life. Hopefully, using some of dualities can make an important point about perspective. For Joseph K., answers are not going to come by looking for answers on the social/human plane or from his personal experiences but could come from looking at underlying realities. What emerges, and possibly for you too, is an awareness that results in a moment of epiphany (a la Joyce). You have been trapped (a prisoner) many times and maybe are still trapped, but you haven't even been aware that you were!

In essence, what I would like you to experience here is that the whole social/human plane and the security and beliefs it offers are like a prison. They impair one's ability to move outside vertically.

Step 4: Find some contrasting experiences. Imagine and feel some experience that includes the angst of being captive. Think of your own limits that could be a source of frustration to you or others. Then experience the comfort of being captive and the comfort of being free.

In this step, we want you to be able to have some contrasting experiences. There are moments in everyone's life where it feels good to come in from the unknown. Yet at another moment, it feels good to experience the unknown. At yet another moment, it feels terrible, panicky, or whatever being a prisoner, even at home.

What we want our priest (who tolerated other beliefs) to experience is parallel to our own visualisations. Feelings of security can be good, but one's need could make one a prisoner. Having an established meaning of life and rules could become one's focus, and one would not be open to the unknown, though the astute 'believer' could contend that any understanding of the limitless is always defined by the limited.

In illustrating the nature of this step, I will return to our 'tolerant' priest. For him, his Catholic view (could be any view, of course) makes him an unaware prisoner, a caged lion born in captivity that has never had the experience of an uncontained life. If we follow the logic of the priest's view, the captive lion should be tolerant of the lion living freely and also tolerant of the other zoos who approach captivity differently.

Strangely enough, we have a number of people who think zoos are bad; but ironically, they too are trapped in an ideology, though they are probably openly intolerant of the other points of view. Same difference? (I don't know where I heard 'same difference', but I always liked the expression.)

Let's assume that our priest says, 'I can see that I could enjoy the unknown and exploring. I also understand that my most profound realisation might be that I have been caged and I didn't realise it. I understand now that I have always enjoyed feeling safe but also being imprisoned.' This certainly would be a profound realisation.

However, some interesting contrasting reactions could happen here. Does the need to explore, be curious, and question move someone away from being trapped, or does the desire not to be trapped drive the beginnings of curiosity? Of course, you could, like Joseph K., become trapped by an obsessive desire not to be trapped.

For our priest, he could visualise himself below (outside) of his church and other churches and observe. What might he see? He could consider that human security is a dominant human need. And if this is the case, then different thoughts, beliefs, and ideologies are all meeting the same need. It could be that the 'truth' is defined in meeting human needs, not some religious absolute.

He may first consider these speculations in a cognitive manner from a changed point of view. He might start by reviewing different religions and their institutional entities—the church; in these cases, he could consider some aspects of their theoretic structure. He may be not interested in the nuances of their culture but may start by looking at structural similarities:

- All have some god-type figure.
- All have religious dogma.
- All have a book or books of divination that are open to interpretation.
- All have different, often charismatic religious leaders who expound their own understanding.
- Most popular religions and churches have a certain amount of religious zeal, not calm.
- Most have an articulated or implied moral code.
- Most have a significant son of God–type figure.
- Most have built a sense that their beliefs are the words of God and that other's beliefs are not as good.

After exploring these thoughts, he might ask the question, is there some kind of inherent need for people to belong to a group but at the same time define individuality (or group identity) by being different from others?

What we would expect our priest to see is that tolerance doesn't make any sense since all these views are the same. They give a home for people who need to be captive, but just as importantly, we can see that they are not aware of their captivity. Upon seeing this, he is ready for the next step.

What is also important here, from a calm setting, is an experienced awareness that these are some of the defining qualities of the species. There is no good or bad; that's just the way they are.

What he might consider as interesting, in an ironic way, is that many people are unaware of their captivity, have not integrated the conscious and unconscious features of themselves, are not calm, and are tolerant at best; but they know they understand the truth and need to 'share' it with others. My question to the priest might be 'Could these people who define themselves as being right and just actually be able to define themselves as "bad" using their own judgemental criteria?'

For you who are reading this, I feel it is important for each one of you to be aware of where you are in a very general sense. The priest doesn't have to leave his order. We want him to not only experience his new awareness but also realise that he has believed in a specific set of beliefs that meet his needs and that others could have a different set of beliefs that meet their needs. That is all that he knows; they are both the same.

His view could go from tolerance to an acceptance that all beliefs are meeting human needs. But we could speculate that, in a way, he is still on a social/human plane. Our priest could also hold that his church meets these human needs but does so in a more biblically correct manner. Oops, if this were the case, we would be right back where we started. He hasn't changed his perspective.

Step 5: This step involves not only looking at the world from a different perspective but also understanding and accepting where you are. As step 4 illustrates, what we would hope is that, once our priest could step away from his own perspective, he could see that all believers are the same, meeting the same need. As a result, tolerance wouldn't apply because everyone is the same. We did, however, consider another human trait emerging here. The priest may still have found it necessary to define his group (his church) by their differences from others. If this were the case, then his perspective and his tolerance would not have really changed.

For you who might be somewhat defensive and react strongly to these last steps, your arousal would have to go up, and that simply means that you are threatened. Aren't you? You may want to ask, 'What about terrorists or racists? What about threats to democratic or religious freedom? Do we simply understand and say that's fine?'

Before going ahead, we need to make some distinctions. Consider the following:

We can accept that the underlying thought structure and basic human needs are the same across the species.

We can accept that we are all mammals (please appreciate the humour) with a delusion of self-importance.

We would accept the value positions that it would be desirable if all peoples could experience a sense of inner similarity with all others and also understand that there are many observational differences (phenotype) that can distract us from experiencing our perceptions of sameness. We know that there are females, males, and some in between. There are differences in colour and race. There are some who are short and some who are tall. There are others with a whole range of different physical characteristics. There are those with high energy and low energy. There are those who are happy, sad, and mad. There are those who are sensitive and those who are not. There are those who show aggressive and violent behaviours and those who don't. To carry on with our differences, we know that there are many nationalities, many political ideologies, many religions and sects, and many cities and sports teams.

Rather tragically, these perceived differences can trigger extremely reactive behaviours in some; and from a social/human perspective, these reactions can include feelings or superiority or hatred, seeing others as evil, or just being completely wrong. However, the degree of intensity of their beliefs and their inability to see any other point of view would show that these attitudes are more akin to fear, even though there may not be any actual rationally articulated social/human basis for such fears. What we could speculate is that these fears are the result of underlying conditions in certain people or possibly inherently evident in the species, but they are not the result of the reasons given.

However, we can also appreciate that some of these beings may feel threatened (like our fear of the unknown or different) by others and become extremely reactive in an aggressive manner. Like present-day terrorists or racists, their actions may go beyond what our social/human values can understand or even condone under any circumstances. Yet these groups can attract some people who could be vulnerable, needing some type of social fit or feel a greater sense of empowerment and strength of character. If we reflect for a moment, we can see that these needs are much like those of the people who find a more fundamental religion or political ideology to find some meaning in life and improve their emotional well-being.

So where does this leave us? This discussion offers some background information, which I think most of you would agree with, but the above points don't address the fundamental question of our acceptance of all that is more open than tolerance.

Let's go back to where we started with, cogito ergo sum, and consider for a moment that this is our prima facie position. As a result, we could consider that beliefs are a function of the species and their needs. It is not some objective statement of beyond human truth, but it is often believed to be that truth.

If your beliefs are supported by the argument that they are true because you believe them to be true or because you believe that others are wrong, your position is a tautology.

If you accept our history of science, philosophy, and disciplined thinking, you are stuck. You need to reject that thinking to get unstuck. If you are not open to accepting our priest's new view, you may meet some of the fundamental diagnostic criteria of being delusional. Here's my opportunity to make a value statement.

If you find this discussion difficult to follow or understand but are contented with just believing and feeling secure, you are probably not ready for my ramblings in any absolute sense, but that is okay. What is important is to be aware. You could say to me, 'I have these needs, and I believe X.' You have different needs, and you believe some type of complex X, Y, Z, or something. Then you could ask, 'Aren't they kind of the same?'

You would be literally correct in not accepting differences. You would have, by default, accepted an important piece, a sense of sameness. We each have a point of view. But you may actually be questioning critically and aroused in a defensive manner. As a result, you would probably have lost your ability to ask any meaningful questions. In essence, you don't know, don't want to know, or maybe don't understand.

A digression, including some editorial comments about my personal state of mind

I could feel a slight increase in my own arousal as I wrote the last somewhat editorial comments about those who know the 'truth' and know that no supporting arguments are required; they just know! As I have confessed, I still enjoy life on the surface; sometimes that means challenging others' beliefs that seem to be more a function of a closed mind, arrogance, and an inability to be self-reflective.

For most of you, the above digression does not apply. I must confess that sometimes the editorial comments are kind of fun. Is that tolerance or intolerance? What I am doing is tolerating my own lapses in perceptions. It is my way of coping with the fact that the perspective I experience can never influence the direction of the species, for there are moments when I can feel stuck on the surface and become momentarily disillusioned by the continued lack of insight and the impact it has on the social/human level. I could write more editorial comments here, but it would be giving more importance to the present, which I don't see as any different from the past.

Some of you may be getting impatient because I still haven't addressed the concept of acceptance that is beyond tolerance. We will get there, but we have some more to discuss.

SAVE THE EARTH/PLANET

What does this really mean? Does this mean that humans need to do things that will prolong the earth's existence so it will last billions of years? Does this imply that the earth is a living entity that has feelings? Does this mean that humans want to keep the earth in a manner that will allow for some living entities—including viruses, bacteria, other living cells, some plant life, and other simple organisms—to retain their existence? *Or* is this desire really about sustaining the world in such a manner that is friendly to the human species?

Humans are concerned about global warming, but the planet probably doesn't care.

So here is one last perspective to consider. If we look at the earth from some 'whole universe', Atman perspective, we could describe our existence as a species that dwell on a small planet in one small galaxy, and this particular species has existed for a very short period. So how important are they?

I had an interesting discussion with a philosopher friend of mine concerning moral decision making. His contention was that anyone taking a perspective that is, in essence, outside our social/human real is also outside the boundaries of moral or ethical decision making.

Finally, some closure—acceptance, not tolerance

Our voyage through your personal experiences and our consideration of different points of view and events that trigger the good and bad feelings that different people may have illustrate the wide range of various experiential differences and limits. These are all expressions of the species, and understanding these differences, especially at different levels, allows us to see that these are all similar expressions of the same underlying structure; it is just that they look different when simply observed on a social/human level.

If we take a more universal perspective, we could see that human life, like all entities in the universe, is controlled by nonvalue-laden structures, many of which we may not understand. However, whether they like it or not, those people who see our species as beyond the laws of the mechanistic universe don't understand that this are still controlled by these universal structures. And as we have seen throughout history, their behaviour and intolerance, and sometimes even their tolerance, supports that they are driven by basic drives, not by ideological social/human principles. As we have seen, often, those who embrace superiority may define themselves in social/human terms that include the dualities of good and bad and right and wrong but ironically don't behave in a manner that is consistent with their ideologies.

As one looking at these people, do we

- show intolerance of these people and react in punishing manner,

- tolerate these people and hold back some animosity, or
- simply accept that these people are typical of the species and leave it at that?

Do we tolerate or simply accept the ebb and flow of the tides and the fact that a high tide could be coupled with high winds and big waves? Do we tolerate or simply accept that the human fear of the unknown or strong beliefs can drive aggressive behaviour?

However, accepting the above does not preclude doing something about these situations. Do we sweep the waves out of the garden? Do we need to find ways to control aggressive and violent behaviour that affects others? Of course, it is just that we know that these conditions exist. They are not good or bad in any absolute sense. They simply 'are'.

Let's return to our perspective. Could being calm and humble and looking at the social/human life from a different point of view leave some fundamental human needs unfulfilled?

What about personal meaning, security, order, and belonging?

In some ways, I am not sure how to answer these since the stronger your social/human needs, the less able you are to approach being 'the outlaw'. But that is also okay.

Things are where they are. (Please note that, in seconds, I have calmed from my social/human editorial comments.) The human species exists or doesn't exist. In the whole history of the universe, social/human life is pretty insignificant. Oops, not pretty insignificant. What about 'very'? Let's say it certainly would be far less significant than the death of a single ant from our point of view.

This is still pretty editorial in style, I guess. The social/human perspective hasn't totally left. I'll try again.

Things are as they are. In the whole scheme of things, there is the influence of human dynamics, values, religions, politics, technology, movement of information, wars, or intolerance. That is the state of where things are and always have been. They are all expressions of the species.

You have your own perspective, experience, nationality, religious beliefs, political ideology, views of the world, what you are doing, family, and relationships.

All these are descriptive of where you are. The acceptance of these is of utmost importance. Without accepting where you are in a nonjudgemental way, you can never change your state or experience life differently. You either accept in a very superficial way (remember, everything is instant in North America) or reject some idea because you are not ready for it. If you accept where you are, you can be open and can begin to develop new points of view, be calm, visualise, and even move away from a need for being tolerant of others. You realise that you had better start by being tolerant of yourself first, and then you can move to acceptance and then development of new meaning, security, and belonging.

It may not be about denying these human needs as much as it is about changing your focus. In the early pages of my ramblings, I have discussed my point of view in a very social/human and academic manner. I have expressed my feelings for my friend and human connection and then moved to philosophy, mathematics, literature, and music. I have used the word *cathexis* to describe a sense of psychic importance. Here's what I think happens.

For the person who lives on the social/human level, relationships, family, political trends, what's on TV, income, social status, sports, the economy, wars, terrorism, etc., all dominate what meaning is all about. If meaning is based on these factors, then life could be seen as pretty bleak. Very simply, if you pick the negative aspects, life is a downer. If you pick the variables in your life that are positive, life is great. Your reality is created not in any absolute sense but based on whatever you pick. For most people, your reality will not influence the world, but it can certainly influence yours. Social/human reality is based on some underlying scientific principles of all aspects of existence. Things change and don't change in the grander scheme of the universe. These are probably beyond your control, and as a result, the world and your world need to establish some type of harmony to find some piece of mind.

For many of you, these collectively defined entities like country, church, or economy do not really give you meaning, security, or belonging; but it may seem like they do, doesn't it? However, these entities cannot address your personal/human needs of being cared for, loved, or whatever. A love of your country doesn't work as a substitute for human care and relationship. You could believe that your country is the best, the political party you support is in power, and the economy is going well, at least for you. But these are all conceptualised collections of social/human factors and dynamics; they are not 'you'.

So make a shift, a kind of lateral one, and focus on the individualised human. If you just focus on your health, family, close friends, and relationships (given that some of these are going well), you may find that your most important needs are met. If you focus on work, you may find the same satisfaction. Or you may focus on personal faith. In both cases, the dynamics of human support are different.

From one perspective, support comes from social/human phenomena, not personal one-to-one coexistence. From a very human perspective, two people may connect at a vulnerable, open level but have different political and religious beliefs. This is a great starting point. Others may need a political or religious belief in common that helps make a relationship work. Those contrasting relationships should not be confused with any vertical and lateral movement but are probably more symptomatic of a lack of being able to connect on a 'human' level.

Two ironies are evident here. First, probably the more that one rigidly believes in some religious ideology, the more one is incapable of a loving acceptance of another (especially if they are different). Second, the 'outlaw' perspective, which could be seen to be very distant from a social/human perspective, is based on open, complete, accepting relationships.

A couple of pages ago, I have made some editorial comments about my own stresses with living life on a social/human plane. This is, of course, where we are. If this is the case, we need to find a balance. In a sense, we need to find the nonstressful in the stressful.

Here is another opportunity for a visualisation-type exercise.

1. Come up with a list of stressors.

2. Consider a few very fulfilling situations.

3. Place yourself in the world of stressors. Feel yourself having to respond here and there. 'Do this! Do that!'

4. Move away from all these to one of those fulfilling times. Be calm and enjoy. Immerse yourself in your fulfilling experience.

5. Take a moment to reflect, if you were able to do this effectively. I think most of you would have felt a sense of belonging and security. This experience, I would suggest, is a function of having a contrasting experience and contrasting physical/emotional state. You can feel good and don't need a belief or higher-order being.

6. Can you now consider your experience as complete in itself? Can that good state be independent of the triggering context? In a sense, since I have suggested that you go through these visualisation steps, you may actually be separating a real (physically happened) situation from one you are thinking about. Yet a further aspect to consider is about the real. We know that a real outcome of an event or even a thought (still real) does have a real physical response.

You fall and break some bones (real). ⟶ You have physical pain (real physical response).

You hear some distressing news (real). ⟶ You think about it and feel it (real physical response).

You think about some distressing thoughts (real?). ⟶ You think about it and feel it (real physical response).

RAMBLINGS OF A MAD OUTLAW

You have a relaxing massage (real). ⟶ You have a great physical sensation (real physical response).

You receive a wonderful gift (real?). ⟶ You have thoughts and feelings of excitement (real physical response).

You hear that you will receive some great gift (real?). ⟶ You have thoughts and feelings of excitement (real physical response).

What would be helpful here is that you can begin to see that your feeling doesn't have to be connected exclusively to any specific condition or something real/tangible. Often, we confuse the relationship between the real with the perceived and the perceived with the real. Unfortunately, at the social/human level, this confusion is accepted, especially if it is of negative quality. It doesn't seem to be accepted as realistic if it is associated with a positive feeling, even though it too has certain physical characteristics.

Get real! (I mentioned that restaurant earlier; see page 58.)

Face facts!

Get with the program!

You have to!

If we look at our six statements above, we can see that, in each case, there can be something physical happening. (It is real.) But it is also interesting to note that the nature of one's physical response may not be specifically a function of what really happens in the outside world or even the perceived reality. Our body doesn't typically make that discrimination.

One person has a life with socioeconomic nothing and is happy/contented.

Another person has a life with socioeconomic everything and is miserable/discontented.

Let's then consider that there is the physiological reality of the universe, of which you are a part, and there is also the physiological reality of yourself, which is made of the same building blocks as the universe. Does there have to be more? Yet this thought could be distressing. You might feel you need a belief.

But what about starting with your body? Be calm and then see if you can continue to experience a physical calmness while contemplating a social/human world that has no meaning beyond itself.

Let's also assume that the above is difficult and that you need to experience some personal meaning, security, order, and belonging to calm your physiology. Let's say that you also become aware that your experienced feelings of stress or well-being determine what you decide to do and how you plan your life. This underlying motivational structure is referred to as 'future psychological hedonism', which is probably the most common description of how most people are motivated. In simple terms, it holds that people are motivated to do things that will bring pleasure in the future. As supporters of this position would hold, even the religious martyr could be seen as holding this view because the reward will come in the afterlife. But as we will discuss, to the outlaw, there is a thinking that goes beyond these limits. In fact, there is another important reality that influences our own physical experience, and that is . . .

The Reality of Thought and Thinking

The aspect of the real, which is missing from most lives, is the acceptance that there are certain tenants of thinking that have been essential for the development of mathematics, science, conceptual analytic logic, and ethical philosophy. In the study of philosophy, the strengths and limits of thinking have been historically addressed. It is with this thinking of the above disciplines that academics accept or reject the credibility of research or new ideas, though it is important to remember that new ideas and questions need to come first. But more importantly to the public, it is this disciplined, innovative thinking that introduces new technology, improvements in health, etc. And one may highly regard the benefits of these improvements. Let's say that new discoveries require not only innovation and creativity but also good, well-disciplined thinking. However, from a real day-to-day life perspective, there is an ironic appreciation and understanding of thinking, what it produces, and how people use this thinking. The social human reality is that the thinking is not only not understood and not used but also 'mistrusted', defended against, or ignored.

Are making social/human changes in touch with the real? From more established conservative values, sticking with what has met the test of time is reality, and just because one doesn't like the established way doesn't mean that things should be changed. Americans have their Constitution; churches have their beliefs and catechisms. From a somewhat fundamental view of life, one could conclude that all this new liberal thinking stuff just distracts one's attention from what is 'really real'. In fact, from a somewhat cynical, fundamental view, they may describe present attitudes and thinking as self-indulgent, ignoring traditional values, and overlooking fundamental truths. Their contention could certainly be correct. However, if they are correct and this is the way the world works, then this would be 'reality'. Ironically, from what we have discussed, we could easily show that traditional social/human values were once new ideas that were also self-indulgent. So maybe this new thinking is just another 'really real'.

We might all agree that making a change these days is what people do. It's okay. Thus this new approach could also be seen as making more sense and being more rational since it's open to change and questioning.

Could we conclude that people who are self-indulgent and open to change and hold this 'more' rational view are more rational?

Here's a situation that happened some time ago that addresses rational thinking within a limited context. An employee who had a demanding job and was poorly paid from his perspective (though consistent with the field) wanted a change. Without informing his employer, he decided to open a retail business to make more money. Note that his employer appreciated his work but was unable to pay him more.

In his initial approach to his employer, he informed them of the new business venture he was considering and offered a couple of initial options: 'I need to be paid more so I can pay someone to work in my store while I work here. I could work part time and modify my store's open hours, but I would like to keep my wage.' To this, he added, 'I'm not really needed in the afternoons anyway.'

A review by the firm of their needs concluded that they could, at best, pay him a bit more but not a lot and that, more importantly, it would be ludicrous to pay someone more who showed no corporate-based motivation. They also looked at their staffing needs and realised that they needed someone full-time employees and not part time.

So now where does he go? What feels right?

The company conveyed the following: 'We're very pleased with your work. We also support your desire to open your own business, but that is your thing, not ours. We are stuck because we need someone working full time. We thought the position could be shared if you know another suitable candidate. We can't pay you a full-time wage for part-time work.' Here's a 'focus shift'.

Even though the firm's review of his request was supportive, encouraging, practical, and fiscally realistic, his response could be seen as emotionally threatening, a kind of 'oh no!' with no self-reflectivity. What the employee could see, at this point, was another set of variables that were not anticipated by the employer and that resulted in his becoming somewhat defensive. One fact about his role emerged as highly relevant to his new perspective. In the past, he would frequently need to help 'cover' for staff who were absent from work. This was true and appreciated. It was also accepted by the employer that staff absence can sometimes be a problem. The employer had developed specific strategies for dealing with this; in fact, one staff member who had been a major contributor to this problem had been dismissed and replaced.

So his next request followed along with the above details. 'Every day I cover for staff who are away, and no one seems to care if they take time off. So when I ask for time, you say no. That's unfair.' Here's the shift. 'It's not that I am asking too much. It's the fact that you are unfair.'

What is important for you to get a sense of is that there are a number of 'reality' factors that make sense from the employee's and employer's points of view. All of them are pretty obvious, and they are social/human realities!

Staff member's focus-shift point of view as a victim of corporate insensitivities (Typically, this is not a conscious manipulation but a sincere feeling of 'injustice'.)

- Staff are always away.
- This staff member may be needed to fill in.
- Filling in did not offer optimal service to the clientele.

At this point the employee, with his 'focus shift', can see that the employer doesn't care about the clientele. (They will compromise their service.)

'They obviously don't care about people in general.'

'They don't care about me.'

The bottom line in this case was the employer says no to his requests for

- more money
- part time with full pay.

Company's point of view

- Company policy allows five sick days with pay per annum.
- This averages about six hours per week and is part of his job description.
- Filling in did not offer optimal service to the clientele.
- The employer says no to his request for part time with full pay but open to job sharing.

What happened to the employee's thinking in this case, and could also happen in the employer's position, is that the discussion starts with the employee's desired outcome, and the perception of 'reasonable' roadblocks is transformed into social/emotional negatives. My purpose is not to put him in a negative light but to illustrate how thinking seems to work for most people and how it can work if its rigours are not adhered to. What we have in this example is a loss of the *reality* of thinking, coupled with the reality of circumstance. Unfortunately, if you have not been schooled in philosophy, you may not know how to address this dilemma, even if you can intuitively see the problem.

Remember, the employee approached this dilemma by holding on to a fair evaluation of himself as a hardworking, conscientious person. He helped by covering for staff who were absent from work; they got time off with pay. Therefore, he should be given the same opportunity. Otherwise, it's unfair because they can miss and he can't.

What's wrong with what he says? Is it not accurate?

The employer could present a number of arguments, which include limited ability to pay, the desire to have no absenteeism because it is unfair to others, and the need for giving some people paid sick days.

All the facts don't offer a solution. Both sides could bring in other social/human or political perspectives.

- If you want more money, get another job.
- It's the responsibility of the employer to pay staff fairly.

As you can imagine, none of these statements in themselves offer the right kind of direction for finding a solution. Others, when asked about their opinions, sided with the employer; but when asked why, their answers varied and were not based in any sound, ethically based thinking.

This kind of everyday dilemma cannot be resolved without first understanding some important ethical distinctions.

A momentary outlaw digression

As the outlaw, personal needs and views cannot override ethical thinking; only clear, rationally developed argument can change this. If it can't and it does not meet our emotional needs, then these needs cannot be indulged. If we do so knowing that we are putting our personal needs ahead of rational thinking, we would not be able to be the outlaw (though the outlaw could do some goofy things, but we would expect that they would not compromise ethics).

From an outlaw perspective, we can see that calming, visualisation, and changed point of view are necessary but not sufficient to give a new perspective. However, coupled with these is the ability to use sound ethical thinking. My present bias is that a grounding in ethical thinking is also a necessary component.

You may be asking, 'So what do we need to understand about ethics?'

A consideration of ethics

In the 1920s, G. E. Moore, an English philosopher, made a distinction between 'is' and 'ought'. A similar distinction was made in the '60s by Paul Taylor, an American philosopher, between what he called 'non-normative' and 'normative' language. For the purposes of simplicity, the is-ought distinction is probably the easiest to understand.

What we find is that, throughout history, people have explained human behaviour by saying that this is what people do. It's reality. However, for the ethical thinker, even statements that sound like self-evident truths and their application need to be questioned.

Many people may contend that everyone is different; therefore, everyone should be treated as individuals. A parent may tell their somewhat lazy adolescent, 'Everyone needs to do something. You need to go to school or get a job.' Here's our 'Get real. Face facts!'

But rather than just accepting this at face value, let's look at these platitudes in a good-thinking academic, philosophical manner. Remember, you either accept good thinking or don't. If you decide not to accept it or accept it selectively, you are destined to remain on the surface, fighting the waves.

Before I start this next section, I apologise to all ethical philosophers for my attempt to cover a discipline that has evolved over decades of thinking in two pages. Okay, let's go back to the 'is-ought'.

Let's consider some examples. Moore addressed the difference between statements that are descriptive or naming and those that are moral or ethical. 'This *is* a person.' 'Today it is raining.' These statements include all those we might consider as factual. Factual is another problem as we know. It could be a delusion, but we won't discuss this here. But for the moment, let's consider these factual or descriptive statements as 'is' statements.

However, other statements can be judgemental and state how something 'ought' to be. These statements include value judgements, morals, and all those views that encompass the realm of ethics and also aesthetics.

As I mentioned in an early part of this work, we considered some of the challenges in defining words and their referents—the tangible, the conceptual, the real, and the delusion (see pages 52-55).

But let's be intellectually lazy for a moment and consider that all those concepts discussed earlier are descriptive and could be expressed as 'is' statements. 'This is Toronto.' 'This is a house.' 'This is the sky.' 'This is life.'

'Ought' statements are a different kettle of fish, a different animal. 'What ought I to do?' To answer these questions in the best possible manner, one needs some education and training in a fairly extensive field of philosophy. Since this is beyond the scope of this work, I will highlight a few important points. For you who know how to think but have not studied thinking, logic, philosophy of science, or ethics, this could open a door to learning. If you decide that your thinking is as good as it can humanly be and study is not needed, then you are the greatest genius ever, defensive, or in a delusionary state. Being the outlaw requires learning and thinking (an 'is' statement assumption). More people should become outlaws (an 'ought' statement).

Let's look at the staff member who focused on the fact that he felt put upon because he had to fill in for others. As we know, he used this as a basis for his request to work part time. He felt that he 'ought' to be able to.

Let's accept his 'is' statements. As I see it, there were three of them. 'Staff are sometimes away from work,' 'they get paid,' and 'he fills in for them.'

Let's look at his 'ought' statements.

Others are away and get paid.	I ought to be able to be away and get paid.
'is' statement	'ought' statement

In a very simple way, ethics works on rules or various levels of principles and logic and ultimately an ongoing intuitive validation when these principles are applied to hypothetical and real situations. Ideally, a well-structured ethical school of thought would require the support of an 'in every case' argument that would support any moral decision to be made. In a consistent manner, the outcome of any decision would need to meet the test of intuitive correctness in every case. This may be too abstract, but I would like to leave this here (see appendix for more information). One thing we do know is that we need to use examples to test a hypothesis. In essence, any school of thought, ethical approach, or academically established perspective requires a thinking structure that will have consistency throughout a range of decisions and will always work (given any ethical outcomes). Let's test this with an example.

Over centuries of recorded history, humans have killed one another for many different reasons; two of them are over the ownership of land and conflicting religious ideals. This is the way the species behaved and still does. Can we conclude that because this is the way we are, we cannot just conclude we *ought* to be able to kill others for these reasons? If we accept this *ought* conclusion and accept that a logical and rational consistency is fundamental to good thinking, then we are left with the fact that anyone's desire for land or any religious sect (for ideological purposes) has the right to kill others. We could easily acknowledge that some blanket acceptance of this is-ought connection would result in presenting some big problems.

Let's try another. When a child is upset with a brother or sister, he/she may hit their sibling; therefore, a child ought to hit a sibling if upset. As you can imagine, there are an unlimited number of examples that clearly state that we can't accept a connection between *is* and *ought*. This disconnection between these two types of statements is often called the fact/value dichotomy or the naturalistic fallacy.

Though there are many problems with our example of the employee's position, we can see that he is supporting his *ought* statement by stating what *is*. If we accept the need for logical consistency and consideration of ethical principles, we cannot accept his position based on this connection.

So how does one approach this dichotomy? In ethics, we end up having rules, principles, and even higher-order principles; and these have been discussed, written about for hundreds of years. I find myself thinking of Kant, Mill, categorical imperative, utilitarianism, and beyond. All this is beyond what we can even begin to cover here but essential in developing a good understanding.

Let me try this: back to Moore and some emerging complications. As we have noted, one cannot ethically say that 'people do *x*; therefore, it is okay to do *x*.'

Collectively, people kill one another in the name of God (or religious ideology). As we know, there are the ethics of war that might seem somewhat inherently contradictory. Anyway, let's say that, from a political point of view, it has been concluded that one (a collective, nation, etc.) ought to be able to kill others during a religious war. Therefore, we might conclude from a consistent ethical position that it is correct to kill anyone in the name of God—but not exactly.

In society, a separation is made between the 'ought to be able' of the individual, groups, and the politically organised groups. As anyone's experience would show, killing others based on religious ideologies with certain restricting limits is supported if the entity is a nation or a group of nations that are fighting inhumanity or protecting their nationhood, but it is seen as inhuman or criminal if the act of killing others is committed by an individual, group, or faction within a nation. What we have here is an ethical mess.

Let's consider another approach. Rules are established to guide human behaviours so people behave how they 'ought to'. As a result, it is considered good or right behaviour if one follows the rules and bad or wrong behaviour if one doesn't.

Rules are generally consistent with some overriding principles. For instance, most driving rules (e.g., speeding, drinking and driving) are based on the principle that rules need to be established to protect the personal safety of others and self.

One major challenge in testing ethical principles requires answering the question 'Are there any or even one ethical principle that when applied to every possible situation will always seem to meet the intent of the principle?'

Let's leave this circular logic and try something that is easier to follow. Certainly, calmness, visualisation, and establishing a different perspective can help, but I contend that clear and precise thought is also needed for achieving an outlaw's understanding.

Ethical discussions need to follow a different set of references. They often start at a simple rule level. Rules include laws; religious rules, like the Ten Commandments; rules of clubs, schools, reports; etc. Life could be easy; we just need to always obey all rules. As we know, rules can be a problem because people don't follow them; and besides and as mentioned, rules are not always consistent with one another and sometimes may not be considered as 'right'.

All of you will have had occasions where a rule seemed unfair because it didn't account for other factors or contingencies. Let's consider this questioning as a social judgement. Someone is speeding as they are rushing a seriously injured friend to the hospital. Knowing the situation, would policemen hold the person up and give a ticket for speeding? In essence, follow the rule of law or make a social judgement and accept that the best thing to do in this situation is to get the person to the hospital as quickly and safely as possible.

In ethics, we can illustrate the dynamics of this in a very concise manner. At a basic level, we have

- a social judgement that says, 'Get this person to the hospital as quickly as possible,'
- a rule that says, 'Do not speed.'

Let us say that, meeting our social judgement, we come in conflict with the speeding rule.

Rule level:

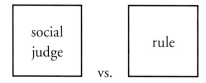

We have a very special way of resolving these types of conflict. To do this, we go to a principle level. Principles are those generally accepted values or social outcomes on which rules and laws are based. For instance, in the above example, we could consider that one makes social judgement and rushes an injured friend to the hospital. This judgement would be based on a generally accepted principle that one ought to do things that directly affect the health/safety and well-being of others.

But as many driving safety advertisements say, speed kills. This is actually an exaggerated 'is' statement that sounds like a social judgement. At a literal level, it makes a conditional relationship between speed and death.

if speed ⟶ death

This is not an ethical principle! It's attempting to sound like one. In fact, one might accept this as a reason for driving more slowly because speeding, which results in death, is in direct conflict with saving the injured friend. Others may argue that speeding is against the law! We don't want people to speed because it increases the risk of people getting hurt.

In a sense, a social judgement could be seen as 'why I decided to do what I did'. To the philosopher, the structure of their decision is far more precise. One interesting test of the structure of the speeder's social judgement, which may not make sense at face value, is to ask, 'Was your speeding wrong?' If the person says yes, the person may see themselves as making a human mistake, but they had to do it. If the person says no, then there is an understanding of the importance of principles, at least intuitively.

In the speeding situation, some principles can be considered when making the decision to speed while rushing someone to the hospital. There is the principle that values human life and human health as a primary guiding factor in ethical thinking. Thus the prevention of someone's dying or having some significant physical disability would be considered as the reason for speeding. Since the importance of human life and well-being and the safety of others underlie many driving 'rules' or laws, it would be important for our speeder to drive in a manner that has increased speed but also uses good social judgements about speed and safety. Thus this behaviour could be considered as morally correct. These same ethical criteria need to be considered by ambulance drivers and police.

An ethical decision: speed or don't speed

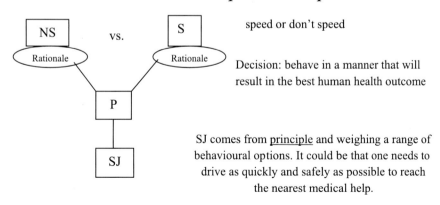

In more specific terms, we could ethically explain that one's behaviour is consistent with the principle of doing something that is essential for the continued health and well-being of one person while not adversely risking the health and well-being of others. This is, of course, consistent with an underlying principle but not with the rule.

As you can imagine, I could give numerous examples where a rule may seem to be in conflict with another rule. These can generally be easily resolved in the manner as we have just discussed. Ethics becomes a more challenging discipline when we look at principles and higher-order principles.

Sometimes a rule and principle can be confused, and a pseudoconflict can exist as seen with those who responded with a 'yes' to the question about the 'wrongness' of speeding. They do not have a formalised structure for distinguishing between rules and principles. I will use an example developed by M. Chandler to illustrate this type of false ethical dilemma.

Let's suppose you want to join some organisation that has very restrictive rules or expectations. This could be a sports team or a religious order. In each of these cases, you are required to live by a set of specific rules that limit your opportunity to make free choices and do what you want. Let's assume that these thoughts about the absence of free choice are a concern because you have grown up with the belief that making free choices is the right of everyone in society.

The dilemma could be experienced as 'does one join the organisation and give up free choice, or does one not join and retain free choice?' As you may have noted, there is a problem with this dilemma. Following rules is obviously rule based. That sounds very obvious, doesn't it? But what it implies could be seen as a conflict.

Is there a conflict?

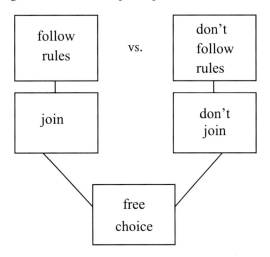

But making a free choice is a principle.

You could make a decision to join the organisation. It is your free choice. You could also make a decision to leave the organisation. As a result, every time you comply with the rules of the organisation, you are making the free choice to do so. The decision could be difficult, but it is not a conflict; it's a dilemma.

In this case, you would be making a decision personally. It does not require moral or ethical thinking beyond your personal needs.

I was going to give you more and more complex situations, but I feel that building this from the ground up is too lengthy; instead, I am going to move to some of the higher-order principles that have been used over centuries.

One of the searches in ethics has been to find one principle that might be considered as the highest order—one that could be validated by universal human thinking and morals, would meet any moral test, and would be logical and consistent. As an aside, for you who may consider some religious association as 'highest order', forget it. Any religious truth is either created by man (and that's okay), a personal belief (and therefore, cannot be applied to ethics in an ultimate sense), or for the extreme fundamentalists seen as the unquestioned Word of God (a delusion). In philosophy, this is referred to as 'formalism' (based on undisputed assumptions) and is not supportable because these assumptions (beliefs, delusions) are not open to rational discourse or evidence.

A few pages ago, I have talked about a test of intuitive correctness. In essence, it is looking for a principle, like a law of physics that works in every case.

In the 1800s, Immanuel Kant considered the concept of the 'categorical imperative'. This is, in essence, a self-defining principle that articulates the need for an ultimate principle from which all others could be supported. The most important feature of his imperative is that any principle of a lower sort must meet the test of higher principles. In ethical philosophy, principles are tested by considering any number of hypothetical situations that one can come up with. Some of these situations may seem a bit of a stretch, but they are necessary to test one's view.

For instance, let's say someone you know holds a pacifist position as one of their fundamental principles. His/her position is 'Do not kill another human under any circumstances.' You might ask that person, 'What would you do if you were confronted with a person who is going to kill your family of three and you have a way of killing this person? Would killing that person be the right thing to do?' Typically, any person holding a specific view will try to find a way out of having to make a decision. The pacifist might suggest he/she try to talk the assassin out of it or whatever. However, the hypothetical dilemma can be adjusted until the person is forced to kill or not kill or let his/her family be killed.

This pacifist might decide that not killing is an important principle, but there is another principle that would be of a higher order (more fundamental) that would consider that saving the lives of three people would outweigh the killing of one person. Some of you may consider not just numbers of people but whether the people are good or bad. This unfortunately is not necessary here, and as you might imagine, defining good and bad requires another set of rational decisions.

What is important here is that, from any consistent/logical/human perspective, holding on to a rule or even principle that overlooks outcome may be shown to be logically inconsistent with a rationally developed value system. Consider the antiabortionist who supports war or even killing the abortionist.

Probably the most influential higher-order (fundamental) principle, but still flawed, grew out of the workings of J. S. Mill. From him came the principle of 'act utilitarianism'. This principle held that any act could be morally supported if it could be shown to contribute to or result in the greatest good. Though at one level this seemed to intuitively work, it had lots of problems. Besides being very socially misunderstood because of how people rationalised its application, it had, as you can appreciate, significant analytical, philosophical problems with definitions. What is good? How is it measured? How does it deal with quantity and quality? Number of people? Who they are? What they do?

Over the years, philosophers have considered thousands of hypothetical circumstances and definitions of 'greater good' to see what might work. As a result of this, ethical philosophy has moved considerably; however, I think this is probably the best starting point for most of you, though I apologise to any ethical philosopher who wants to inform you of where things are now. Unfortunately, this is beyond these ramblings.

What is important to appreciate is that there are some very systematic and logically developed ways of considering ethics and morals and arriving at well-formulated conclusions. But there are still many situations in which the discipline is challenged. If you find this brief discussion interesting, read some more. I would recommend university bookstores or bookstores that carry used and collectable books. You will <u>not</u> find much philosophy in the big modern chain stores.

<u>Warning</u>: For most people, reading primary source philosophy is very boring!

However, there are some limitations in moral philosophy from our outlaw perspective that need some discussion.

Two possible reader reactions may be evident here.

There are those readers who may not be reading this now who are uncomfortable with the unknown, have definite beliefs, and defend their beliefs with what I have called a focus shift (like our unhappy employee).

Another look at our focus shift

A good example of this can be seen in discussions between the fundamentalist Christian who believes in a creationism myth and the person who understands evolutionary principles. Since the Christian has *no* supporting evidence for their position, their only defence is to find any flaw in evolutionary knowledge. The Christian then attempts to 'support' the creationist myth not by debate (because there is nothing to debate) but by shifting the focus off their own belief to alluding to any weakness that they can find in the evolutionary position.

The adolescent who is in trouble for doing something wrong can refocus a reprimand from self to parent. 'Mum, you used to get into trouble when you were a kid.' In a similar manner, a reader may contend that reading these ramblings is a waste of time and that they have better things to do. However, any reader would need to make a distinction between my ability to craft an interesting and readable work, which could certainly go from good to bad, and the thinking and ideas being expressed. The way these ramblings are written is the outcome of my efforts. The ideas are not!

To reject the history of creative thinking, as well as disciplined thinking and concepts, from many disciplines that might be difficult to live with can certainly be criticised by the absence of having <u>all</u> or even any specific answers. If this is the case for you, your need to use a focus shift to protect yourself would probably be quite strong and unfortunately leaves you stuck on the surface.

The same type of approach can be seen with their formulation of moral positions.

There are other readers, ones who are still reading this, who appreciate not only the challenges we have discussed, the human inconsistencies, and the need for disciplined ethical thinking but also the need for different perspectives, a calmness, and an openness to the limitations of the species.

There is, I think, an interesting flaw in moral philosophy, and that is its limits, which I have discussed. It is concerned with social/human behaviour, codes of behaviour, and right/wrong with reference to others. It always returns to 'human well-being', sort of 'species centric'. If we take our ephemeral view of individual human life and identity, as we have visualised, then we can't just assume that each human life is sacrosanct or that the well-being of life has anything to do with socioeconomic status, religion, race, behaviour, etc. On the surface, we have winds, waves, no winds, and calmness. We have hurricanes, typhoons, and doldrums.

Remember the question we asked (which may not be moral in nature) about the species and concerns about global warming. Is their concern about the earth, rocks, water, bacteria, viruses? Or are social/human beings concerned about the well-being of the species and its existence on the earth? One could hypothesise that the species will self-destruct through wars or whatever and that the earth could live happily ever after, though there would still be global warming and cooling.

Can we consider the ethics of the nonhuman? What about all our nonhuman musicians? Are they part of our 'ought' judgements? Could we arrive at a moral conclusion that would support their existence, knowing they would never form another orchestra? If we held the principle that all forms of human violence are undesirable, could our ideal state have all the social/human beings self-destruct and the crazy nonsocial/human beings remain? <u>King of Hearts</u>?

With both of these questions, we are stepping below the surface, looking up.

But before leaving this discussion of thinking and its influence, we could ask here, 'Is ethics real? Is thinking real? Does it influence real life?'

Typically, I think thinking, like thoughts, in our equations used in the past, are nontangible but real. But I don't think, in an ideal sense, that they should influence real feeling (real physical response) as we have seen in our other examples where there is no calmness. Yet their influence may offer a change in feeling and outcome.

(I have thoughts and feelings about doing *x*.) + (I may ask the question 'what is it the right thing to do?') + (I consider some ethical variables.) ———————▶ (I make an outcome decision.) ———————▶ (I act accordingly.)

A simple case

- My thoughts about what to do in a particular situation are self-evident; they have no impact on initial feelings, and I experience no physical change (e.g., increased tension). My response is made without contemplation (no transformation or resolution needed). Outcome has no ethical thinking needed.

   ### Though the decision was easy, it may not be ethical.

The more complex

- My initial ethical questioning is adversely influenced by a fearful physical sensation associated with a formulistic belief. Let's say that, in this case, there is no ethical consideration, transformation, or resolution. ———————▶ Outcome has not been influenced by ethical thinking.
- My ethical thoughts could have an impact on me, and I experience a physical change with some distress. I may struggle to find a resolution (it could be that I have a very negative feeling someone or something), but I don't compromise good ethical thinking. Transformation takes place. ———————▶ Outcome is consistent with ethical thinking.
- My feelings are neutral. I experience no adverse physical sensation, and follow a well-formulated ethical thought process. In this case, there is no transformation, but there is a resolution. ———————▶ Outcome is consistent with ethical thinking.

My concern is that the ethical outcome of decision states, for most of you, may not be the result of calm ethical contemplation but that of personal feelings or some formalistic tenet that gives specific direction (i.e., in specific situation *y*, one must do *x*) . In fact, the opportunities where one might think that ethically structured thought is needed are probably fairly rare. However, where I think it could be used is vast. One area in particular is that of mental health, where unquestioned value judgements dominate. One formalistic tenet that is unquestioned is that all people need to be social and have appropriate social skills. Here, we have a social/human value judgement that is inimical to the essence of these ramblings.

I guess I could say that only the last two examples represent real ethical thought, and unfortunately, so few drink of its fountain.

What we also see here is the way in which human emotions and changes in physiology override good thought. There's that SC (subcortical) and PFC (prefrontal cortex) dynamics again. What I think we have, if we look at the most ethical and moral decisions people make, is people tossed by the sea. They want the best for themselves but are uncertain, anxious, or whatever. They are unable to achieve calmness in adversity, and they are also unaware of the structure of good thinking and have not cathected it with any real importance.

As I have mentioned, the understanding of the thinking that has been required for good science, mathematics, and philosophy is essential for being complete.

Take a readjusting short break here.

dort

Awake slowly. Stretch. Breathe. Get ready for some new thoughts. Remain calm, though.

Some More Thoughts about Thinking and Thought Support

Remember that, on the surface, we may have big waves and stormy seas, no waves and doldrums, light winds and moderate seas. All these are really happening, but the reality of each one of these is a function of the person.

Many years ago, I skippered a forty-three-foot yawl. Our trip started in Palermo, Sicily, and one of the crew was seasick while the boat sat in the harbour. His physiological reality was that he felt some movement and felt sick. His reality was his own physiology; there was no boat movement, and we sat in the cockpit.

So let's make the bold move and assume that most of what is considered reality is defined by the conscious/unconscious experience and physiology of the person. If this is the case, then the focus of our thinking and visualising could adversely influence our human sense of meaning, security, and belonging needs.

Let's try two visualisations that trigger a stream of consciousness, one on the surface and one below.

But before we go any further, here is a *repeated caution*! What we experience individually, from a calm point of view, does not mean we 'cop out' and do nothing. Instead, we do it from a different point of view. The composer composes, and the conductor conducts. One does not stop conducting.

Visualisation 1: You are watching news reports that fifty-three people of your nationality were killed by 'terrorists'.

Let's assume that your physiology changes and produces a high level of tension, you have feelings of anger towards these bad guys, and you are ready to kill them or know they should be killed. Your sense of security is momentarily lost. You feel threatened. You feel anxious. You know that killing bad guys will reduce your anxiety. Waves or maybe doldrums exist on the ocean, and you feel powerless.

Visualisation 2: You look up from below or from a detached perspective to the surface of the sea. What do you see? You see waves, and you reflect. There have always been waves and no waves, winds and no winds. There have always been wars and probably, at some time, no wars. Both sides are right. Both sides are wrong. Waves can destroy ships. They crash against the rocks. They can overpower, be destructive. We have nation against nation, ideology against ideology, group against group, individual against individual.

Let's play with this visualisation. From your perspective, let's say below the surface, there is calm. You go to the surface. There are rough seas, and you feel some anxiety. Fall below and feel the peace.

Here, in this calm environment, we are fulfilling your human needs and establishing a different *real*. It is the *real* that underlies. It is also the *real* of our own calm physiology.

To use a metaphor we have used before, it is like the small Joycean ship. It is well anchored. It is not the invincible-looking ship with an inadequate anchor.

If we consider the above, can we find security and meaning on the surface? Will joining the biggest/best navy give us security? If the navy was 'God's navy', can it sink? Could there be two God's navies? Oops, we're moved back to the surface. Onward, Christian soldiers.

What would be helpful to experience in those two visualisations is an association of calm physiology with something other than the social/human surface and ideological, political, or institutionalised beliefs and attitudes that are evident on a social/human level.

Think of calmness and being below the surface or other perspective that is safely removed from the social/human level. Don't try to define this perspective; it is just not tied into the social/human plane. Let it be somewhat circular in a self-reinforcing manner. No thoughts and calmness create a peace, which creates no need for social/human thoughts, which creates calmness.

You should be able to reflect and experience that you feel calm because you are calmed.

If you have always accepted the importance of life on the surface and the institutions that have given structure and meaning to the world to which you belong, you may have found it difficult to go to a no-thought state as discussed earlier. Think of a mantra or any phrase you can repeat many times. It could even be repeating the counting of your breath. It is the speech that distracts your thinking and makes it easier to integrate the body, speech, and mind. Give it a try.

———

At this point, you could have several questions of yourself or me. 'Could I actually feel more secure and calm if I let go of social/human beliefs and thinking?' 'Doesn't it seem counterintuitive? Everyone has to hang on to something, don't they?'

For you who are still uncertain, these might be of a concern.

'Could we actually hang on some kind of Atman?' Hanging on to the lowercase god or atman makes sense, but hanging on to something that has no meaning seems impossible.

'Could we actually hang on to the whole universe?' It might make our existence meaningless, unless we could see ourselves as the 'masters'.

If you are asking questions, you may be experiencing some anxiety and may not be able to accept this position on an emotional level; it may feel like you are losing something, but you don't know what. As I have mentioned with the priest, he doesn't have to lose what he has; he just has to approach it from a different perspective.

Feeling anxious may trigger an experience of needing to 'hang on' and an inability to let go or a feeling that all this visualisation stuff doesn't really work because it doesn't change anything. If you feel like this, you may not have an openness to integrate new vertical experiences with your own self. You may know that they will not replace the ones you have. To make this vertical move, you need to be ready to take that calculated risk, but you don't have to let go entirely.

I feel a need to hold this process for a moment. Let me explain.

When we discussed lateral movement, we considered movement from A to B, maybe from North America to Europe and then looking back.

start   finish (Looking back, A still exists.)

'How do ya keep 'em down on the farm after they've see Paree?' (post-WWI song)

When we discussed vertical movement, we went from A to B, from the social/human to a creative, different perspective to one below the surface.

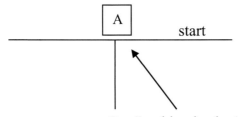

B – Looking back, A still exists, but one's reality has shifted to B.

But what is B? It is our new vertical perspective of A, and it can be seen from many perspectives.

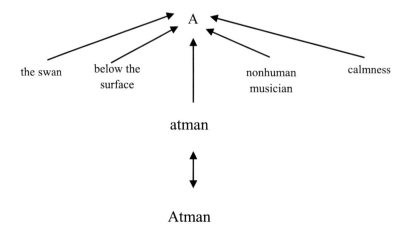

However, this multivertical perspective can go in different directions. We have more, not less. But as we will explore, more is less. Be patient.

As I hope you may now see, these different vertical perspectives are still limited by their own definitions, but the inherent qualitative features of all these non-A points of view is to assist you in

- developing the ability to see A differently;
- developing an acceptance that 'all' can be seen as a 'oneness' (like our symphony orchestra), which can be seen as paradoxical;
- developing a readiness to be comfortable with a universe that has no meaning—it just 'is'.

It is important to see that calmness is a physiological state. It is not a vertically defined position. It is like a door. In the same way, being below the surface of the waves doesn't define a point. It is only a relative position. It could be seen as not on the surface or above.

It is possible that your ability to be calm and visualise can give you a kind of protective state whether you are on the surface or below. It will probably not be understood by others. You're view of reality may be seen as 'not real', so ongoing support from friends and family may not work. And these few short pages of discussion with suggested exercises can only, at best, be the impetus for change, given that you understand and are interested.

A real-life contrast in perspective, A or B?

I had a meeting some time ago with a small group of schoolteachers. They were motivated to learn and to help an impaired child. They wanted to know 'what do we do?' They needed to know how to instantly control this child's behaviour. 'Just tell us what to do,' they asked. What seemed evident to me, from what they told me, was that this child could improve in all aspects of functioning; but this would require knowledge of his physiology, his sensitivities, the structure of his individual dynamics, and some understanding of aetiology. However, they had no knowledge of any of these variables. It is important to note that what would typically be required would be low stimulation (calming) and a 'feedback, feedforward' approach to interaction that would be sensitive to internal dynamics and improved regulation. Here is our B perspective.

It was evident from our perspective that any attempts to control his challenging social/human behaviour in the short time, within a nontherapeutic, stimulating school environment, would most likely make him more reactive and more dysfunctional. It was clear from our understanding of this boy's self-regulatory functioning and dynamics that the teachers' and school's <u>need</u> for a single 'do this' approach for correcting behaviour would actually be detrimental to his well-being and would not achieve any desired outcome. I explained that any effective approach would require considerable knowledge about underlying physiological mechanisms, development, and this boy's underlying dynamics; and to be effective, they would need to be able to respond differentially to his expressions in a constructive manner.

If we return to their question about controlling social behaviour, we could also explain that their desire is misplaced. Our goal is to improve the unique inner dynamics of the person at B so they work; it is not to control social/human behaviour so it looks good. Here is A.

'A foolish consistency is the hobgoblin of little minds' (R. W. Emerson).

One might make a request: 'I don't know much about music. Can you just tell me how to conduct the orchestra and make it so people will like it?' They would not meet their social/human needs. Unfortunately, they had no interest in understanding what would really work; and in fact, they really didn't think it was necessary.

Like these teachers, you may want an answer. What is realistic is 'Get real, will you!' Unfortunately, to really understand and live these different perspectives, some kind of ongoing training and direction would be needed, and this is beyond the scope of my ramblings, but it is not beyond what you can accomplish.

You may have a strong sense that you don't want to spend the rest of your life reading these self-reflective ramblings. You are not up to the task and are not intended to do so. But I know that being open, curious, and patient in your approach to life will be very beneficial.

Our next-door neighbours had a bathroom book on the fifty fundamentals of golf. The I Ching could also be a bathroom reading, though I must confess that, years ago, I did read the I Ching in its entirety over two days—a futile task, but I didn't know any better. The first lesson I learned was keenness was good, but it didn't help learning the purpose of the text. I didn't try, but I could have found my divined hexagram and found its message, which may have warned me about being young and wanting to learn. For you who are golfers, there are fifty fundamentals, according to one book. I guess we could assume that if you mastered those fundamentals by practising over a period, you would become the perfect golfer. Find your hexagram for each day, and you will be guided to the perfect balance.

There are, of course, an unlimited number of books, courses, experiences, therapies, trainings, or whatever that can help you develop a more fulfilling understanding of self and the world. Yet there are some common elements in all guides to life and sports. They all require a degree of internal calmness, balance, and self-regulatory body rhythms that become the foundation for social/human success.

My question to myself as the writer is, do I attempt to give you an extensive list of books, courses, etc.? Or do I wait and give you some other thoughts first, with the result that you will explore your own experiences and what you have learned from different teachings? Remain calm and patient. Do not be overwhelmed. And like I have mentioned, when looking at ethics, start with the more timeless. Experience the beauty, and there is beauty in science and academics.

Dispelling Ego by Having One

As you will have noted, I made a change from *i* to *I* and also changed my use of lowercase letters for proper nouns some time ago. Did my use of one and then the other give you a sense of either my view of self or how I symbolically considered or consider the use of uppercase? You may ask, 'Why did he use that lowercase *i*, and why did he change?' As you have travelled with me, you will have experienced a range of my personal expressions. Initially, I presented myself as a humble, different, alone person. I expressed my desire for connection with another human, but I also referred to connections with beauty, with writers and artists, and with a nondefinable Atman. I also felt separate but connected with the social/human plane. I felt a need to speak to others from a position of social/human humbleness. It isn't what we know; it's what we don't know.

At a shared experience level, I referred to other writers and artists. I made a point made by Kandinsky on page 57, which to me meant that it is important to engage the reader (you), not just overwhelm. And of course, for most of you, this might have seemed unusual and even possibly unrealistic. It was also important to me that my expression of self and the nature of the social/human world in comparison with Atman and of *all* with *one* required the selection of a lowercase *i* and the use of lowercase letters for proper nouns to illustrate the relative lack of importance of the social/human world in any absolute sense. It seemed to be the right choice.

On the other side of your possible perception is that I seem to have confidence, have done lots of things (and I am still a doer), and have had some success; and in fact, I have even developed a rationale for why it is important for being successful and working hard. That obviously means that I have ego strength, and an uppercase *I* would seem to be more appropriate.

So what is ego strength anyway? Isn't too much of it undesirable?

Years ago, I did a whole individualised graduate study course in philosophy in which I wrote a long (can't remember how long) paper on defining 'ego'. Since I have already put you through some of the rigours of thought in defining terms, I won't do that again, but remember that ego is a concept without a specific referent that probably has many commonly accepted properties. See if these work for you. It is generally assumed that the ego requires

- a certain level of social confidence,
- a certain belief in one's ability to do or know something,
- a sense of one's social role and identity.

These, as you may or may not be aware, are very different from Freud's use of ego and very different from some twentieth-century English authors who understood his view. There is an author I have not mentioned yet, but he is a writer who has influenced my life and perceptions. His use of ego is very Freudian symbolically but he does not use Freud's psychosexual stages in any literal sense. The author I am referring to is David Herbert Lawrence, who I think is one of the most talented British writers in the early twentieth century. Just so you don't think it is my ego saying this, F. Leavis (head reader of literature at Cambridge for many years) agrees.

I found it very interesting when I realised that I had not referred to him in this work until now. This was especially significant to me since he had had an influence not just on thinking but also on some aspects of my writing style when I was in my twenties. I'm not sure what that says about my ego. Anyway, I hope that question triggered a response in you, maybe a couple of or even several responsive thoughts. Here's what I thought some of you might ask:

- What is Freud's defined use of ego?
- Who is the author you are referring to?
- Could it be that you don't really care about others and get lost in your own thoughts?
- Could it be that your ego is so big that you don't acknowledge that you have learned from others?

When I first wrote this, without even thinking about what I wrote, I realised that I may have made an unfair assumption about your knowledge of Freud. It would certainly be reasonable to assume that his name and who he was is common knowledge, but it would be unreasonable to assume that a direct knowledge of his work is common knowledge. I also realised that it would be somewhat presumptuous of me to assume that you have an interest in him or in evaluating the accuracy of what he wrote. In my own naïve way, I listed four questions and realised that I did this in a very 'ego defined' (whatever that means) manner.

After the above moments of reflection, I thought about the fact that the first response for most of you would probably have been a practical one.

What is Freud's defined use of ego?

or

Who is D. H. Lawrence? How does he use ego?

Since we have considered the importance of visualisation experience, I am not going to attempt to define ego, but I will use a D. H. Lawrence image. This, I think, does a good job explaining a Freudian sense of ego. Remember, I am using one of Lawrence's images because it can be visualised and experienced rather than just being defined. In this image, we are going to consider two human factors. There is a factor that describes an underlying human/animal force that could be defined

- as SC (subcortical; see pages 30–31), a biological driver that exists in all mammals;
- as 'blood consciousness' (Lawrence);
- as base biological drives, the id.

Metaphorically, this could be seen as the 'horse' in its natural state and its tendency to follow natural drives. However, for man, there is also a social goal, a direction, an ideal where we should go. Lawrence has used the railway as a metaphor for this. The railway is seen as representative of the drive of the industrial social/human world. He sees this as linear, as controlling, like a social direction that overrides nature and natural instincts—the superego. The ego could be seen as the rider who needs to balance these opposing forces. Does the ego control the basic drives and follow social/human ideals, or does the ego allow natural drives to be expressed? In <u>Women in Love,</u> this image has some other dimensions to it. The rider in this image is a person, Gerald Crich, who wants/needs to control the biological/natural/SC, the horse. Lawrence portrays him as having an almost desperate need to control. He is the industrial magnate. He controls people, mines, trains, and certainly horses. His horse, however, is fearful of a train going by, and Gerald must hold his horse in line. Much like we have seen in other literature, we have a duality. In Freudian terms, we could see it as a conflict of the 'id' and 'superego'.

This definition is very limited if we consider all the uses ego has in everyday language, though Lawrence, in this novel, does develop a clear sense of how he believes these forces should be balanced. He does this more symbolically, literally. He does give the reader a sense of these seemingly opposing forces.

My own view of this balance is consistent with Lawrence but described differently.

Consider these questions:

Is a strong ego a good thing?

Yes.

Is a weak ego a good thing?

Yes.

Is a strong id a good thing?

Hard to say.

Is a strong superego a good thing?

I don't think so.

Let's consider this in terms of our last section. Let's start with calmness and then look at these strong extremes. These extremes are not compatible with calmness. However, a strong middle is something interesting and different. It's like our strong ambivalence but different; it is not paralysing. If we use our horse metaphor, let's see what a strong rider might do.

Does the strong (experienced) rider overpower and control the horse or have an understanding of the horse's character and know how to work with its energies? Which approach gets the horse and rider to work together?

Here is a good visualisation exercise. You can take a horse, a boat on the sea, or even another person. Your goal is to have control. See if you can feel a difference in the following:

- Do not listen to or see other forces. You are determined to hold on to what you want. Reflect on your level of tension, your focus and need for success.
- Listen, experience the state of the forces, and try to combine your needs with the other's state.
- Give in to the power of the other forces. You end up being controlled by them. You give up.

Next, consider the following:

- What happens to your focus and measure of success?
- Reflect on your level of tension and your speculated experience of success.

You may need to make a commitment here. If you were able to find a suitable visualisation and could experience the variables, only one experience would work. It would require being calm or at least being balanced in your experience.

Without going into lengthy discussions of ego, let's just use it as we have done in this visualisation. It is a balancing energy; it needs to experience the SC (subcortical, id) forces at the same time as it experiences the PFC (prefrontal cortex, cognition and control, not really superego unfortunately).

Ideally, I think it would be beneficial to have you think of ego in this way. See if you can move away from our more popular social/human view of 'big ego' being akin to arrogance, not thinking of others, being full of oneself. If you could do this and move away from a popular point of view, it would be desirable to have 'no ego' in a personalised sense.

I think we could postulate that ego, as we have discussed it, could be considered as the absence of 'I am important or great' in some absolute sense (which I will explain), but I would humbly suggest that this aggrandised sense of self could exist on a social/human level.

Boy, that certainly sounds like a contradiction. Is it okay or not okay to have this socially defined ego?

Unfortunately, two pages of written description with your visualisation (I hope) will give you a different experience, but this will not change years of popular use of the term. So let's return to its popular use.

Social success as a source of ego strength

Let me start with a discussion I had with a friend many years ago. We had just finished listening to an interview with Bobby Fischer at age seventeen (one of the great chess players of all time, I think; I don't really know, though, since I don't know that much about chess other than playing it as a kid). I think it is correct to say that, at that point in his life, he was by far the best chess master for his age in the world. I would also suggest that his social skills were not the best, probably PFC with SC; in fact, he could sometimes be somewhat autistic sounding. Anyway, in his interview, he was very matter-of-fact about his ability; he was the best. After the interview, my friend's comment was 'Boy, is he ever egotistical!'

I questioned his position because I felt that Bobby Fischer—who expressed himself in an almost flat-affect, atypical manner—was factually correct. I suggested to my friend that being humble, a.k.a. false modesty, may really be more highly ego driven than being honest about one's abilities. As an aside, my friend was very much a false-modesty-type guy. He studied hard but never admitted it. He always got good marks but never wanted to admit that he cared. I saw him as someone who had a strong ego need. He wanted to be seen as the very capable person who never had to work. I, on the other hand, didn't do as well but didn't really care in the same way. To be honest, I cared as much as he did, but my learning and struggles in life took a different path.

Over the years, I have learned from this and other experiences that there is this incredible irony to ego, especially when considered in terms of social perception. For instance, someone who only drinks the best wines, has to have the best of everything, has read all sorts of books, has to do everything well, and is perfectionistic obviously has a huge ego. Bobby Fischer was the best chess player in the world. Are these ego functions based on individual expression or developed as an expression of social/human reality that one chooses to make to be better than others? I think that, as I had discussed before, a certain amount of social/human-defined success that could be seen as ego developing (at least in Western cultures) is essential for having a measure of oneself on a social/human level. If one doesn't have at least some social measure that reinforces the belief that 'I can do something' and some socially defined ego, then that person could be left with a sour grapes view of success, a rationalisation, or even a fear of success. Views that hold success as dumb, a trap, 'I don't need it' could simply be delusions or defensive reactions and are actually accepting social/human values and definitions of success. Their success and their 'ego' are based on 'not falling into the social/human trap', but the reality is that 'ego' is based on social/human criteria. They are just on the flip side.

So all this seems to say is that ego may not be ego and that non-ego may be ego.

It sounds like this popular view of ego could be somewhat ironic. Could some expressions of ego not really be expressing ego as we know it? And do nonexpressions really express the ego need?

To better explain this irony, I would like to approach ego from yet another perspective. First, I think that, like our Bobby Fischer example, we would expect that if someone is *observed* as having 'ego strength', it should be based on social performance. However, in retrospect, we can see that Bobby Fischer was (and is) certainly not a regular social/human being. Those people who we see as having a 'big ego' but don't have any social status may seem to be somewhat a contradiction in terms or, as my kids used to say, legend in their own minds. If we accept this premise, we could then see ego as partially influenced by how one is seen by others or how people see themselves from a social point of view. Typically, we see a strong 'I' component in this performance-fed ego. It is not 'we are the best'; it is 'I'.

Society accepts that world champions are highly capable.

Being highly capable supports one's individual ego strength.

One is a world champion, and therefore, it is understandable that that person could have ego strength—a big ego.

Social success and low ego strength

Ego strength or lack of it could be established by another source(s). Let's say that some world champion in something grew up with a belief that he/she was 'no good', can't do anything right; even their best performances seemed flawed. We could now have two influential aspects to this person's ego. One is performance driven, and the other one is driven by development and sense of self. Let's consider this from an above/below-the-surface point of view.

Expected ego strength based on performance   HIGH

Expected ego strength based on self-belief   LOW

Possibility 1: Negative self-belief never allows good feelings about performance to get established. Ego strength remains low.

Possibility 2: We have a flip-flop. In some environments (i.e., performance contexts), the person shows confidence; but in a nonperformance context, the person is withdrawn and has poor social confidence. Ego seems variable.

Possibility 3: We have a mixture of these two. The person is seen as humble in his/her expression of self in all areas of life. Ego is seen as low.

Possibility 4: The performance feedback is strong enough to overcome earlier negative feelings of self. Ego becomes high.

So in this, we can see two obvious forces at play. Are there any others?

If we return to our sea analogies, our gyre on page 8, and my expressed relationships with different writers, painters, and composers and in our views of nonseparateness, we can use the same dynamics described above and come up with an ego of a different sort—a non-ego ego.

Let's assume that when we consider the influence of the creative people throughout history, we see a socially defined performance that is rare and individual. For some, their work is highly respected. Even if these people may or may not have had ego strength as we have discussed, we could say that the social perception of these people is one that has the qualitative features of strong ego. There are also those creative people who don't achieve socially recognised success in the short term but still create. In both cases, we can see a drive, a possible confidence, a sense of personal belief, or a belief in self that is required to produce. But in these cases, it is not the result of socially defined ego strength. It's defined by some ideal. In fact, we could probably accept that they are responding to some internalised sense of ego ideal. In simplistic Freudian terms, they could be seen as representative of the superego; they have established an ideal.

The essence of beauty is hidden by a social/human malaise.

This should not be confused with an apartment block manager. They are supers. They must have superegos. I just felt like throwing that in.

I need to shift gears here. I need to begin to approach another understanding of ego/no ego. We have a poet who became connected with creators and had a feeling of oneness with them. In T. S. Eliot's 'The Waste Land', the lines, quotes, and references are almost all someone else's. He didn't plagiarise. He created a new work, but his work was the result of his own need to express something profound with respect, being open, listening, and reading others before him and then being calm, visualising, working, reworking, and creating a profound work of his own. So how does our social/human view of ego fit or not fit here? From a performance point of view, he could say, 'This is my creative work. I'm the best!' But if we look at Thomas, this view doesn't fit. This could be a social perception. But in fact, for him, and considering his mythic method of writing (combining words, phrases, and concepts of many others who have gone before), we would be led to believe that his ego is partially strengthened by those creators who had existed before him, not just himself.

From an ego development perspective, one might wonder what he was like as a kid, whether he had developed ego strength, which, of course, is not really relevant. Paradoxically, we could consider the possibility that part of his ego strength could be based on his not having to have social/human fame or notoriety.

However, we do know, like most creative people, that there is something else that drives his behaviour, his need to create. What is that? Even though I am not a Thomas Stearns Eliot, I can see that his style, like mine, tells us something.

The profoundness of the literature that had come before, coupled with personal experience, could have influenced him to a degree that they shaped his creative expression. He may even have felt that there was no one influence or writer who could be considered as the sole creative force underlying his self and work. But there were many. He may also have realised that there are no specific aesthetic benchmarks for any new work, and for all the works in the past, there are and were no socially established benchmarks to guide the Composer, the Writer, or the Painter. Most likely, he understood that the influences of creative expression come from some undefined depths within the person.

As we have discussed, most creative people would accept that it is essential for them to have their creative works expressed at a social/human level. The composer needs a conductor, the writer a publisher or a manner for sharing their work. From an ego-building perspective, the poet may feel that he/she is a wonderful, creative person. And even if a publisher doesn't like it or if no one else seems to like it, it doesn't matter. The writer who knows that their work is good and that they are great may be self-absorbed and tied into a self-rewarding loop that doesn't respond to social/human feedback or underlying creative energies. Is this an ego based on a delusion?

There are also the less ego-driven people who feel the profound influence of a certain 'spiritus mundi' and who are one with those helpless few who may have shaped science, the arts, and spirituality. They may or may not be responded to in a positive way by the publisher or others, but their response to their work is different. They are not affected. They just need to express but don't know why. And from the outside, who can tell?

Unfortunately, there are others like David Foster Wallace, whose stream of conscious mind created great works that were well regarded on a social/human level but whose sense of self and thinking was overwhelming to him, and he could not find peace and calmness. He took his own life at age forty-seven.

When I consider my own ramblings, I know that ego in a social/human sense is not a factor in my need to write; however, I do have a need to write but also a sense of uncertainty. And as a result, I will sometimes question why, but I need to express my thoughts on paper (compose). On one level, I see it as a social responsibility. I have indulged myself in years of reading and studying; and rather than just keeping this experience to myself, I feel it should be shared. On an academic level, I see writing one's work as a way of getting insightful criticism and an opportunity to share ideas with colleagues around the world. There is also just a need to have some social/human communication (conductor).

So you may, once again, get the impression that I have taken something that seemed to be fairly straightforward and complicated it, which is true. Maybe the most important added feature of ego that we have discussed is the distinction between a purely social/human ego and an ego that underlies one's emergent being and is necessary for creative expression that may or may not get social acceptance.

Could we attempt to make a similar ego distinction between different readers? Probably not. But here is a possible litmus test. If any work you read offers an experience or ideas that are not consistent with your individual point of view and these ideas question your social/human sense of self—your ego—it may suggest that your socially developed ego is threatened. Like the ego of Gerald Crich, the industrial magnate in D. H. Lawrence's <u>Women in Love</u>, his need to always be in control in the social/human world prevented him from accepting that his type of control adversely affected the human spirit and the emergence of a more 'natural' expression.

I feel the need, at this point, to make another editorial comment. It's another irony, though it has nothing to do with ego per se, but here goes. People living at the social/human level want the best that science can offer. However, many don't want to understand the rigours of good scientific thinking or the thinking that has given society all its technology, especially if it does not support their view (e.g., stem cell research). For instance, their expressions may support a positive health outcome (make us healthy, solve our problems), but they typically don't understand or care about understanding the science. They just don't trust it and don't like it. There are also times when science has been disproved because of poor scientific design or falsified data (e.g., autism and vaccinations), but many continue to believe in outcomes. They have established a belief and will not reconsider it. These inflexible beliefs, coupled with a degree of intensity, which I sometimes refer to as the 'arrogance of ignorance', could be indicators of a strong social/human ego.

If we consider the strong and weak forces we have discussed in the section entitled '<u>My Friend and Others: The Nonduck Realities</u>', we can see the paradoxical nature of how weak is strong and how strong is weak if we apply these to the nature of ego. Also, take a moment to review the section on transformations and the essence of change.

I once again need to offer a few cautionary remarks about social expression that is described as non-ego in nature. Is non-ego weak or strong? What is its influence on transformations of perspective?

Keep these questions in mind as you read my more personal perspective.

As I have just discussed, my experience, my sense of ego, and my desire to editorialise and write this work have come not really from my need to connect on a human level but from my need to express some important aspects of the history of creative thought and expression. This is clearly not my ego per se but an expression of self that is founded on the expression of others. As I write this, I am once again concerned about the misinterpretation of such expressions because the same expression of ego could be used by any evangelist. He/she could state unequivocally, 'I have no ego. I am expressing God's Word!'

In this context where belief dominates, the line between what is seen as psychosis on a social/human level and what actually could be considered as psychotic is confused. We could say about the nature of obsessive belief, in a somewhat tongue-and-cheek manner, that what isn't psychotic is and that what is psychotic may not be.

Some additional personal thoughts about ego

What I can see by my own digressions is that my ego strength on the surface has many facets, but its most important expression, as I have repeated, has nothing to do with me, but it does. I have also suggested that my editorial digressions are more a function of my experienced oneness with thousands of years of universal creative expression than myself, but it is still about me. As you are aware, I have a passion and intimate connection with these creative energies and what they have expressed, those lovers of beauty. But also, I find it discouraging to note that even though these great creators are well acknowledged socially and their names are highly respected, few connect with their spirit, their essence by meeting them many times in their works. I often allude to the fact that everyone knows Shakespeare, and most British and North American adults have studied some of his plays or poetry in school. But very few have actually read many of his works and developed an understanding and appreciation of his point of view.

The expression of my ego in these ramblings is a desire for a social/human outcome for some. I do wish that people could hear. I sometimes see myself as a conduit, a conductor, and maybe a composer to some degree. This work is my own (ego-based) orchestration of an approach to hearing and experiencing those creative works that you may have overlooked.

Given the above, my I-ness could be seen as a vehicle of the expression of a myriad of timeless figures, of their energies, of an all. It's like the small boat with many anchors. Ego then could be seen as a kind of collective; a combination of individuals, ideas, or expressions that are timeless; a oneness that is beyond self, that shows no separation.

So the irony that emerges here is that one needs to have ego strength to be an achiever in the social/human world, but that surface ego is given its essence not by having a personal sense of being great but by having a sense of *no personal* ego. The ego is the other. (This is not alter ego!)

As we have experienced as an outcome of our discussions, we need to achieve some experiences that illustrate this underlying sense of self, some visualisation or other experience.

Before we take some time to contemplate, there is a fun regression argument used in philosophy that may help you in this exercise. Its argument is actually looking at free will. To clarify, let's consider the popular notion of free will as being demonstrated as the result of rational thought. The notion is that one can freely decide what to do at any moment in time. And this decision is not simply determined by genetics, physiology, development, etc. In a sense, free will assumes that there is a 'me' quality that can function independently of these possible determining conditions. In a way, it is consistent with our Gerald Crich 'ego'. The person is not only unique but has also the ability/responsibility to make free choices and not use 'determining' factors as a reason or excuse for any choice.

Here is the fun regression. Let's assume that your response to any specific situation is partially a function of two factors: first, *all the aspects of yourself that exist at any one moment* and, second, *all aspects of the situation at that moment.* We will know that people are dynamic in their adaptability and that changes can occur all the time. But no matter what happens, your response is still a function of what's inside you and the outside situation.

(all aspects of me) + (situation) ⟶ response

Let's say that the particular time we are looking at occurred at 8:35 a.m. At that point, all physical systems are in a particular state. One could be groggy, alert, hungry, not hungry, worried, not worried, excited, distressed, etc. The situation could be with family, with the spouse, at work, while exercising, etc. Let's conclude that the dynamics are unique to that moment.

Now let's go back in time. We could go back a second, minute, hour, day, or whatever. What we know is that, at any prior situation, we have the same two influences—aspects of self and influential situation. We could go back to 8:00 a.m. on the same day. Again, we know that the number and types of influences will vary and how the body and experience are influential will be highly individual, but they are still *inner* and *outer*.

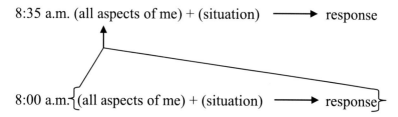

8:35 a.m. (all aspects of me) + (situation) ⟶ response

8:00 a.m. {(all aspects of me) + (situation) ⟶ response}

What we know is that what happened at 8:00 a.m. and 8:01 and what have you all influence me and how I respond at 8:35 a.m.

If we follow this in an infinite-regress manner, we are left with species' primary functions, individual genetic makeup, epigenetic developmental factors, and environmental conditions.

In a logically consistent manner, we are left with the fact that individual uniqueness is really the result of genetic- and epigenetic-type influences and the continual interaction with moment-to-moment situational conditions.

Following this argument in a regressive manner, we could argue that there is no independent 'me'. Your 'me' state at any given time is not independent. There is, of course, an argument for a unique 'me' and a self that is not completely understood.

As we have discussed, the free will question is based on the assumption that some 'unique' aspect of the person is independent of these two conditions. What is the part of self that can make free decisions that is independent of other factors?

What is hoped is that these ramblings, coupled with your predetermined state, can have an outside influence on your ability to change the nature of your experience. Are you experienced?

Here's a trial visualisation exercise. *First,* you need to put yourself in a situation where you feel a positive sense of self, you are involved in some activity in your immediate world, and you are accomplishing something or you have just finished something successfully. It could be that you did well at work, were successful academically, or did something positive that was appreciated by your own family. It could be that you are winning a debate with someone else, you could have just mastered some new skill, or whatever. Take a moment, be calm, and visualise yourself in the location where you experienced this state. Allow your feelings, your thoughts, and your physical self to experience. Just experience; don't try to interpret and don't read on yet.

visualisation space

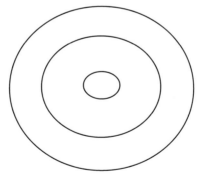

Second, you are going to explore some of the pieces of your visualisation. For instance, you may say that it's pretty simple and that you felt good doing well. You may feel physically up or exhausted in a positive manner, and you may have even expressed how great you are, at least to yourself.

So what are the sources of this experience?

As we have already discussed, your feeling about doing well may be directly related to social/human measures of success. It may be that you are not the world's best. It could simply be that what you did was good for you. See if you can 'script' the message or messages that underlie your feeling, like a parent saying, 'Good job. Well done!' You may also describe yourself from a social-value point of view.

Third, see if you can find situations in your past where you can feel, see, or hear these scripted messages: 'You're trying your best', 'What you did was great', or whatever scripts you can remember. Look for their sources. Is it a value held by a parent, friend, teacher, or whoever?

Fourth, see if you can get a sense of how the above get transformed into personal experiences. It could be that you processed other comments in a positive manner. It could be that there were strings attached to some positive feedback. Others wanted you to do something. It could be experienced as condescending. Someone gave you very positive feedback for doing something that anyone could do. 'Oh, good job!'

This time, see if you add physical sensation to your experiences. Remember, a very important part of what you experience is physical, both at the time it occurred and when you remember or visualise.

Visualise the ultimate social/human positive state.

A history of external positives and resultant physical sensation all lead to a positive sense of self.

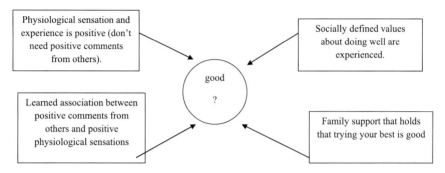

What you will see through this exercise is that what you feel good about is entirely driven by a social/human connection. It comes from somewhere other than yourself, and with this comes a good physical sensation.

Here is a perfect state, or is it?

Let's try a different experience, one that may have realistic and variable-associated experiences. For some of you, as a child or adolescent, you may have had times when you were carried away with your own feelings of momentary empowerment, new awareness, trying something new, or achieving something that adults don't quite understand. You may have been excited about some experiment you did with chemicals or electricity, or for those of you who were risk-takers or driven by adrenaline, you may have made a big jump with your bike or climbed something that was dangerous. In these cases, your recollection of your excitement may also have triggered an image of a disapproving parent, a phrase that tells you to cool it, or even parental anger.

So what are some of the possibilities we could have? Let's say we have an under-the-surface expression of positive energy and that a parent may or may not understand but is accepting of your enthusiasm.

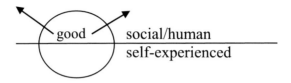

In this case, there are good feelings with a positive integration self and the social/human.

In this next case, the feedback is negative because it doesn't meet social/human expectations. Let's say that the desired outcome from a social/human perspective is to change the underlying desire to express from positive to negative. Parents want you to stop doing things that make them upset or to stop doing things that could hurt you, though you may have felt that they were overreacting. Anyway, what does their reaction do to your positive sense of achievement?

Here is the possible downer. As you visualise a situation like this one, consider two outcomes.

1. The whole experience becomes negative.
2. The experience becomes divided, a positive sense of self remains, and a somewhat rebellious reaction to others emerges.

This parental feedback could also shape expressions of self.

So here, we have experienced some different visualisations all based on the relationship between personal experiences and social/human influences. We have also discussed their relationship to ego and free will. Ironically, we can see that the most ego rewarding (a la Gerald Crich) and empowering sense of self and free choice may end up being the product of one's responsiveness to social/human conditions. Look at Lawrence's Crich; he is the industrial magnate!

From our vertical perspective, we can see that his 'feeling empowered' state is one that is based on his not being aware of his ephemeral existence and his ability to establish control based on the social/human norms at the time of his existence. As we know, financial empires can come and go. And as Eliot wrote, people 'come and go talking of Michelangelo.' These unaware people can live on the surface and may have actually abandoned their own underlying nature.

Conversely, the experience that is conflicting in a vertical sense within yourself and your parent may allow for a more rewarding experience and help in the development of a more self-expressive ego, like my friend whom I have discussed earlier. Somewhat ironically, we could postulate that having an understanding of the limits of self and the social/human world may actually allow you to be more open to experiencing life in a manner that is consistent with how free will is seen on a social/human level.

For the person who experiences the complete 'downer' and feels oppressed by parental judgement, some ego support from those hapless few, those lovers of beauty, may be needed to establish and to achieve a balance. From our Hans Christian Andersen perspective, we could conclude that this person should not attempt to develop the ego of a duck but instead develop the ego of the swan. Maybe we could refer to this as a non-ego ego.

Some notes on physiology and associated memory

What is important here is that associated memory could be a controlling one. It could also be a learned physical one. There are many situations where you try something, even once, and with it comes an associated physical experience. It could be that it was something you were frightened about, and your body has learned to connect even the thought of the situation (fear of something) with a specific physical fear response memory, or it could be a physical memory connected with parental negative judgement. Once this connection is established, it can take on its own life. You could have some occasion that triggers a similar physical sensation, and with that comes the same feeling you had with the original fearful experience. That relationship works both ways. These are not learned as a function of something like ego; they are learned by the body.

But once again . . .

If we follow the logic of these examples, we might have to conclude that you may have an ego, but it is really the creation of 'non-you' building blocks. When the Zim was asked in an interview in recent years (early 2000s) about where his songs like 'Blowin' in the Wind' came from, he really didn't have an answer. His somewhat default response was that it was from that well stream of creativity.

For our metaphorical Composer, we might conclude that their personal ego is partially based on what is expressed through them, not just the self. So maybe the ego for the creator offers a combination of the strong and the weak. The strong holds the creative pieces together, and the weak transforms this created entity into a social/human expressed form.

The nonhuman musicians create ephemeral orchestras and then dissipate.

So this may sound kind of unrealistic to some of you. You may say that everyone has to have their own ego. You need it to deal with life, to feel good. It gives you drives.

If we consider just your own gut feeling that sounds good to me, remember my suggestion that successes on the social/human level are essential for doing, expressing, and becoming. And that could be seen as a function of ego.

To address this confusion of ideas and feelings, let me use myself as an example of how all these factors may be explained. I am very competitive, especially in reference to doing measurably better. For instance, I enjoy developing skills, pushing the envelope in riding my free-ride mountain bike. I enjoy improving my time over a downhill section, riding along the top of logs, doing bigger jumps. I enjoy racing my car and practising my skills, improving my feel of the car, and improving my time on a track. These activities may seem very foreign for someone writing this kind of work. Shouldn't I be going for walks in nature? Watching birds? Doing something that is non-ego, noncompetitive, and maybe tied with nature? I have always sailed, and as we have considered, sailing requires a special rapport with 'nature'.

If you think that the activities that I enjoy don't seem to match my perspective, you may still not have grasped the whole idea of the outlaw. But I may have confused you because I have spent a fair amount of time discussing ego and non-ego states, and the delineation between them may not be clear.

In fact, you could ask, 'Isn't your competitiveness and some of your activities ego driven? And if so, doesn't that make you somewhat of a hypocrite?' To answer this, I am going to combine a few concepts that we have discussed. Let's start with our nonhuman musicians and impose a popular view of ego on them. This could be that they express a sense of social confidence because they do well playing music and play without perceived hesitation. Their perspective could produce behaviour that, from a social/human perspective, looks highly ego driven but doesn't have to be.

Glenn Gould could be seen to have ego strength. He had strong views and expressed them; however, he was probably never influenced by social praise in an ego-building sense. In fact, at the social/human coping level, he was just the opposite. In his case, we could consider him to be very 'fragile' in his physical and social life. He had a passion for music and how it should be played and what it conveyed. When he discussed music, he displayed a strong 'non-ego' ego that was sometimes in conflict with social/ human views that he felt lacked insight. Like many creative people, 'ego' is really the combination of the strength of the non-ego of artists that offers inspiration and expressive drive as seen from a social/human point of view.

Charles Ives was not only a successful insurance executive but also a creative composer.

Before discussing these figures of bad and good further, there are some other personal factors that influence me. Here are some personal drivers:

- If I am physically active, I have more energy, can concentrate more, and have more life experience.
- I spend many hours concentrating on academic and creative thoughts and expression. I need some different foci.
- I have always been physically active and involved in sports and have never changed that enjoyment.
- I have fun practising and pushing my limits (but based on my skill level). I have an incredible feeling when learning and pushing that edge of control, but this is not being out of control. It is right on or just over the edge. This is a feel that, for many of you, may not make sense. But for me, it is important. It is fun, exciting. It expands my sense of self and firsthand experience.

As I finished writing these digressionary points, I realised that I have focused on what could be seen as the less personally significant and maybe not so ego involved. You may think back and question my feelings of being alone, not being able to connect with others in a meaningful way, a possible sense of importance in what I do. Aren't all these representative of some kind of ego function?

Can we put human relationships and one's work as being less important than just feeling healthy and pushing the limits in sporting activities?

Bill Cosby, when taking the athlete's point of view, asked the esoteric question 'Why is there air?' His humourous response, as seen from an athlete's point of view, was to fill up basketballs and footballs. Of course. Albert Camus considered all human behaviour as somewhat misguided. It is our 'absurd' thinking that creates the belief that humans and their purposes are important.

Living on a social/human plane is where we are. Having fun doing something adds to its enjoyment, not its significance. In fact, sharing stories with fellow bikers (pedal), sailors, or car racers is also enjoyable. And on the surface, it is certainly ego driven (in our social/human manner). But for me, these activities are on the surface only and do not conflict with anything. It is just that they are different. If I use my 'dropping below the waves' visualisation, I can see myself from my calm position below riding the waves, crashing through the waves in my boat, getting wet, having a good time. But I also know reality is below. It is connected differently but also play in the waves.

My desire to connect with others or another on the surface has diminished since i began writing this. My desire seems more remote. It is almost as if i have been able to settle comfortably below the surface again and anchor myself with an ego that isn't me.

In some ways, I can see that my desire to connect, which could have been seen as a vertically connecting one, was one that would bridge my underlying state with another social/human being with the same 'non-ego', a strong force being.

As you can appreciate, my desire is inimical to someone like Gerald Crich in <u>Women in Love</u>, who has the need for control not only of the social/human world but also of self. From his perspective, there are no vertical distinctions that matter. His horse (those aspects of self are characterised by Freud's id) can be controlled by a strong social/human ego, which Lawrence and ourselves would see as false.

In my case, my social ego is more like a sauce or dressing; it adds some flavour, but it doesn't offer the nourishment of what is underneath. My approach to these activities that look ego driven is that it gives me a balance between levels of life that look vertically distinct.

My desire for some all-encompassing human connection does not seem necessary at this point.

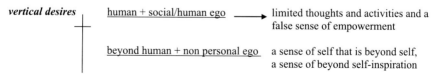

vertical desires   <u>human + social/human ego</u> ⟶ limited thoughts and activities and a false sense of empowerment

<u>beyond human + non personal ego</u>   a sense of self that is beyond self, a sense of beyond self-inspiration

If one always keeps these states in mind, one has the freedom to dwell in both.

So what is the point of all this discussion about ego? Can't there just be a good and bad?

Consider the following:

- We accept a beyond-individual-influenced ego, like that of our creative artist.
- We can appreciate that having different egos that combine self and context can also be desirable.
- We can appreciate and understand, when calm and visualising, that being influenced does not preclude the value of enjoying the challenges of life on a social/human plane.
- I can accept that my social/human ego can come and go, be above the surface, and then drop below.

Before finishing our discussion, we could confuse the whole topic and look at all these ego expressions from a conceptual, analytic point of view. But in doing so, we may be simply questioning all we have said so far. We would have to accept that ego is not mechanistic in nature. It is defined phenomenologically. Thus we could conclude that there is no such thing as self or ego in any physiological sense. It is strictly conceptual. And if we accept Wittgenstein and his investigation of concepts, we would also surmise that there is no aspect of self or even self itself that can be defined as some type of independent, autonomous, functioning entity.

Though this final insight would seem to be conceptually correct and undermine our efforts to define phenomena like ego, it could also be considered as another perspective that doesn't undermine but illustrates the limits that exist in any statements that are descriptive of an assumed truth.

Here's another visualisation that might be interesting to try. On the surface, see yourself as the compilation of social/human 'scripts'. Different people are all around you. And at a slight distance, there is somewhat like an Ives composition where sounds are coming from different sources, and they are all incorporated in his music. You hear all these social/human platitudes; the must-dos and don't-dos; the expressions of ego, of belief, of ideology; the expressions of love and hate.

Next, move below or away, like the mast of the sailboat. See and hear, but do not be drawn in and lose your perspective. See if you can experience how easy it would be for someone immersed in this social/human world to be overwhelmed.

I am reminded of a Yeatsean image, which can work. He writes about youth as being like a tree with branches reaching out, and then with age and wisdom, the tree withers into its roots.

Here, we have an image that could equally represent an expression of the transformation from individual importance, separateness, or grandeur as seen by social/human values to an ultimate state where we are one with the roots that are one with the earth. We become part of the earth and have no separate importance or grandeur. We are part of a Jungian-type collective unconscious.

We could also consider the living tree and its need for roots, as well as branches and leaves that reach upward. I think we can consider ego in the same way. Anytime we feel our sense of self, our egos, we know that it is always grounded in a nonseparate, non-ego root structure.

Undoing Separateness

Throughout these ramblings, I have considered my point of view as being different, as one of a hapless few, as alone, as being the 'outlaw'. These associations would certainly imply a 'disconnection' with others, a separation.

At the very beginning of my writing, I described myself as being humanly frail (as seen in a social/human manner), as having a loss of grounding, and also as needing some attachments. Your impression of my writing would most likely have to conclude that I felt separate and wanted to connect. And that impression would certainly be correct as seen from a social/human perspective.

However, as we have seen over and over again, what seems straightforward from one perspective can be seen as very different when discussed further. So let's consider the above as a type of separation, which could be used to define my experience. But what was that experience?

For the purposes of simplicity, let's agree that what I experienced could be defined as feeling separate and not connected. But this reference to separate raises two questions. What does separate mean to me? And what did I feel separate from? (Excuse the dangling participle.)

Before going ahead, I would like to consider the feeling of being separate and not separate (connection) in four different ways:

- One feels connected to some people, group, friends, etc., but also feels separate from other groups.
- One has no close friends or family or no emotional attachments and feels alone and separate from others.

- One is just different from others (could be a swan), is not accepted by others, and feels separate.
- One feels separate from the day-to-day workings of the social/human world and their beliefs, their loves, and their hates but has a compassionate, nonjudgemental, nonseparate connection with all the nonhuman musicians who form all these different orchestras (to use our orchestra metaphor). The separation is experienced when listening to the music played by the social/human orchestras and seems limited and lacking any creative expression. In essence, one is connected with the underlying nonephemeral *all* but feels distant from its often transformed popular musical expressions. Aldous Huxley had the 'feelies' movies to entertain the epsilons.

With these distinctions in mind, let's return to the beginning of this work. I described the underlying dynamics of my expressed sense of separation as a very specific one. It was clear that my feelings were no longer retaining the compassionate, more enlightened (from a Buddhist perspective) point of view that I had accepted and lived by for many years. What I experienced, upon reflection, were two emerging factors. First, as I described at the beginning, I had become too cognitive. This single-aspect state seemed very similar to the state of Stephen Dedalus at the end of Joyce's A Portrait of the Artist as a Young Man. In a sense, I had neglected my feelings of compassion for the *all*. I didn't take the time needed to immerse myself in the beauties of creativity and the arts. As a result, I had a great desire for connection and attachment to another who would understand my cognitive views and thinking and who would also embody those passions and connections I had had for the 'beyond', the 'nonhuman'.

In fact, before my moment of epiphany that inspired me to reevaluate, I had spent a great amount of time with my friend with whom I felt a strong attachment. The connection between us was especially rewarding for me because she embodied a compassionate view of life that was akin to the one I had held but was neglecting. I would have to suggest that our friendship was more complicated for her, but for both of us, I humbly felt that it offered a good basis for moving on without losing the benefits.

Considering her from our present context, we could also describe her essence as similar to the Composer, whose sense of self (ego) was an expression of those beyond-human energies and unknowingly had the same outlaw potential that i felt was essential for making sense of human existence.

I will leave this quick example of separateness and connection, which could actually be seen as a mixture of a couple of types of separateness mentioned above, and I will move on.

Some general thoughts about different types of separateness

Let's consider some other types of separations. We could say that separateness is purely conceptual—a product of our delusion? For instance, one person is Canadian, and another is American. Or one is standing in Canada, and the other is standing in the United States. They could actually be touching each other while standing at the border, but they are in separate countries; the border separates them. So they have separate nationalities and national identities, yet in this situation, they would not look physically separated. They are separate people. But we could define *separateness* as a separate conceptual classification, let's say, based on some physical quality. In this case, we could separate them based on physical attributes. Though we could support that a physical difference (separate classification) exists between, let's say, males and females. They have different physical attributes. However, we can't support that all Canadians have one set of physical attributes and that all Americans have others. We could conclude the separateness, like nationality, is conceptual and a product of man's psyche.

As we have discussed in this work, we wanted the priest to understand that there are separate churches and beliefs. But if we look at them from another point of view, we can see that they are all the same. They are the same underneath but separate on the surface. This too is conceptual.

We can see separateness. One object ends, there is space, and another begins. Here is visual separation. This is easier to understand. It's tangible.

Is physical separation easy to define? A case for the physical and nonphysical

We can also define a state of physical separation that is like the above but is seen from a scientific perspective. This goes from very easy to understand to less seemingly real. But for purposes of distinction, i am going to call this physical separation. However, separation can be seen from different perspectives. 'Seeing' can be assisted by microscopes or other enhanced ways of seeing physical reality. In these cases, we can end up with physical and conceptual (theoretical) questions. The challenges in understanding what we see and what we hypothesise increases the need to find a conceptual/theoretical scientific answer. In essence, logically developed and mathematically supported hypotheses can leave common sense behind. But all this is for another day. You may have initially wondered about the difference between visually perceived and physical separation.

I have always found the old black-and-white newspaper or comic book pictures as a good example of this distinction. If you look at the picture or illustration at normal reading distance, you can see different figures, you can see foreground and background, you can see separateness. However, if you look at it more closely, you can see that the whole picture is made of equally spaced black dots and white dots. In this case, the physical separateness of the dots is equal. The subject picture, as seen from a distance, isn't even discernable.

If we consider the real physical world, we have another level of confusion. Does the background in these old newspaper pictures have no dots, or is 'space' between objects simply not visible? Think of the dusty place with the sun shining and the dusty place without the sun highlighting the 'empty' (?) space. Is there 'nothing' because we can't see it, or is there just a change in density? In fact, we could take this further and contend that everything is composed of molecules, which are all composed of atomic structures. If this is the case, then it would make sense to consider that it is the density of collective atoms that defines the boundaries between what we see and don't see. However, from a regressive point of view, we know that subatomic particles (separate entities) could be seen as bigger than they are because they are moving quickly in a limited space. They give the impression that they are actually bigger. The old Bohr diagram of the atom is a simple representation of this. From a regressive argument, we could contend that even the smallest particles seem to be composed of yet smaller particles and that their perceived size is a function of their movement.

My fun hypothesis is that if we did an infinite regress, we might assume that the world is composed of nothing moving quickly.

'Full of sound and fury, signifying nothing.'

So what do we do with all this?

First, as you would have noted by previous discussions, these types of questions require a calmness and emergence of conscious/unconscious, contrasting experiences, sameness not separateness. By doing this, you are at least starting the process of becoming.

Second, my discussion of the human and nonhuman becomes important here. If we consider the visualisation of the musicians and the different orchestras that they form over time, we can see that the human orchestra is simply an ephemeral organisation of musicians. We can certainly visualise a mass of musicians moving around and organising differently, but it is important to remember that the musicians remain the same and that they are nonhuman.

Third, if we look at what we see and consider what we know exists but can't see, we can have a new experience. However, for some of you, it could trigger a panic. Centuries ago, it was accepted that space was not emptiness but was composed of ether. A question arises here. Was the presence of the ether a well-founded hypothesis, or was it considered because it met a human need for not having emptiness? What is plasma as discovered in space? We know that the CO_2 and O_2 are pretty important for life. These are molecules and have mass, but we can't see them. We also know that the ether has structure. Do these elements exist?

If they do, we are left with the fact that molecules are everywhere. The atmosphere is just less dense than humans. I guess that means that humans are pretty dense. It is also important (here's the panicky piece for some of you) to remember that the body isn't in a protective bubble. When we let O_2 and CO_2 into our body and when we eat, drink, touch, or simply move in different environments, we open the door to other molecules. These could be outside or inside. They are not necessarily separate. We need to understand that all sorts of foreign molecules may become part of us and that many are essential for life. Unfortunately for us, it could be that dwelling in a human environment may be good for some cells and their structural formations, but sharing our body with these cells may not be so good for us. Some of these cells may take over and live off the molecules that compose us; cancer cells may just be looking for a home. Bacteria is good for humans but also bad. Viruses may live forever.

Consider all these cells that we can't see and may or may not feel. What we know is that they may not be separate from us. They could be required for our conscious existence but also our demise, our lack of human movement. Consider John Cleese. He thought that the lack of any physical movement was a sufficient criterion for supporting the conclusion that the parrot he bought was not alive. He described it as demised, no longer with us, gone to see his maker, dead. So is that death? Death can be debatable anyway. Is an intact physical form sufficient for something to be alive, even if it doesn't move? Are some cells still living? Does the body that is no longer with us offer an environment for the regeneration of other 'foreign' cells and other living organisms?

So we have a number of different relationships—conceptual, visual, and physical. In some ways, we would need to acknowledge that our consideration of the physical may best describe what might be understand as real, at least as seen by what sciences are pursuing and by what our conceptualisation of an underlying nonhuman reality. But we can also accept that these thoughts are not very personally satisfying for most. What emerges here is an interesting irony. From a value position, we may contend that being separate from others in our world isn't desirable; however, being separate from some of the cells in our body, especially the ones we don't like, is desirable and necessary for life.

Of course, one way to cope with this physical vulnerability is to create a meaning to our social/human existence. We are surely highly important, godlike beings and have spirits that live on the afterlife, and we are not separate from this fact.

Or does meaning really matter? The rhetorical questions that the anxious social/human being would ask may look upwards: 'There has to be some meaning to life, doesn't there?' 'We have to hold on to the sacrosanct importance of human life, don't we?'

A momentary review of what we have discussed so far

In a sense, I think these questions have the implicit quality of wanting to combine our four types of separateness. Humans have relationship needs that bring them together with like people. They may have some type of unifying god figure or ideology. As a result, visual separateness is not questioned because a single-belief system seems to bring people together, and physical science is interesting at best. Ironically, this single-belief unity can result in two significant types of separation. There is a separation between man and the nonhuman and a separation between those who hold this single belief and others who don't hold their beliefs.

Some further considerations of separateness: reality and created realities

My view looks at these types differently. I know that, in any description of time/space continua, there is energy or forces. (I don't know if either of these terms is the best word or not.) Anyway, we know that some scientists have developed theoretical models, like Hawking's Theory of Everything. But for most, these theories are not relevant to their lives, and they have little interest. And I think it would be ludicrous to assume (at least from my point of view) that, in the whole scheme of things, any new insights into the underlying physical reality, whether about the nature of the human species or the universe, are experienced as separate from the self and offer no personal meaning or sense of secure connection. As a result, the self-created beliefs in ourselves (our delusion) continue to dominate.

What is important to remember is that one can live on a social/human level, enjoy sporting activities, have friends, have a successful career or no career, and feel connected and separate but still dwell in a vertically experienced reality. Life is not an either/or.

I can accept that I have found it very rewarding having a good friend. Having someone who shares some of the same understandings and with whom I have an emotional tie is very desirable. I am also very attached to my immediate family, especially children and grandchildren; they too are rewarding on many levels, though I do feel that these relationships meet a selfish need, which I enjoy indulging. What I see is my own needs, though these relationships are clearly reciprocal. I could explain or rationalise these personal connections as an expression of species-specific behaviour, which in turn could be seen as an expression of some universal truth. But to me, they are rewarding but selfish. What I don't do then is try to define what is important to me as a way of defining the universe. My position is 'I can often experience a separation with others because of my frail individual need, which I like to indulge. + I sense/feel/know that this is a species desire. + Everything is simply connected energy.' But what emerges in my thoughts is that there is no separation between me and undefined, universal, timeless energy/forces. Here is an essential connection. What about the following?

> Be connected with an underlying reality that accounts for *all* (which includes all those who live on a social/human level).

> Be connected with a created reality but separate from *all*.

Some further thoughts

In finishing the above reflections, which considered my feelings and my general cognitive understanding of separateness, some additional insights floated to the surface. Our considerations of connections and separateness brought to mind feelings about human touch, expressions of care, and closeness.

Though I won't belabour it, my initial thoughts about how touch is seen by many in Western cultures are that it is 'strongly ambivalent' and somewhat disheartening, even from a social/human point of view. First, there is the institutional perspective. It seems that, out of legal necessity, any human touching another—whether it be a client, student, or fellow worker—is simply taboo. 'Under any circumstances, do not touch!' Second, there is the group therapy context. From this perspective, giving others a hug is encouraged. It is used to enhance human connections. Does it? I don't know. It doesn't work for me.

How do I generally feel about human touch? Touch is certainly an expression of nonseparation. It's togetherness. It meets personal needs. One doesn't feel alone. One feels emotional support.

If you felt alone, you could reflect and visualise the cuddle from your mum or a close friend and feel calmer, safer, and not alone.

At this moment, the thought of this physical/emotional connection feels distant to me. It is almost as if I have made a shift to something else. It could be, as I visualised, giving a hug that I initiate to my friend, spouse, or child. It could be that I am expressing a need for dependence and something from them, at this moment, that feels as if that is unfair to them. I am imposing. If I consider returning a hug that feels good, I am being supportive to another. That feels okay.

At this point, I can't think of a situation where a meaningful hug feels reciprocal; but just after writing this, my emotions have made another slight shift. I have visualised myself holding a resting infant and both being very calm. I have realised that I have been and could be fulfilled if my connection with another is clearly reciprocal.

Maybe what is important to convey here is that openness to our own feelings and thoughts illustrates a human frailness not just in me but also in everyone. There is the strength of risking openness. Remember, I once considered that one's weakness can be his/her strength.

I found this personal digression interesting since it was unexpected. But it does make contextual sense if i considered that I do have some very simple human-relationship desires, possibly some developed defensiveness, a sense of self that seems to be influenced by some aspects of reflective contemplation, or possibly a need for control, being better than others, or maybe feeling humble. You may have some other personal evaluative ways of describing what you see.

The question that is fundamental to becoming the outlaw isn't so much the variability in human day-to-day emotional experience; it is its acceptance. It's the manifestation of universal forces and energies that compose the *all*. We are unimportant not because this position expresses some possible depressive, underdeveloped symptoms but because that is the reality of *all*! The social/human being hasn't understood that it is okay to be unimportant, at least in the whole scheme of things.

If you accept the above, then you need to consider some calming visualisation exercises. The challenge here is that knowing or learning how to get beyond yourself does not require some kind of unrealistic intellectual or spiritual state as a starting point. It can start with the desire to undo separateness.

To get a feel for this, and one that some of you can visualise, I will use a sailing/boating visualisation. The sea is the physical reality, and if we are in a small boat in the roaring forties (southern hemisphere where there is little or no land), we may feel somewhat separate from the sea, but we know that we are part of it. We are only separate because we feel that we need to be. We feel safer. It is as if the boat were protecting us. Remember, the sea is just being the sea; it isn't trying to do anything.

Okay, so we are on the boat now being tossed by the sea. And of course, the boat requires a highly skilled skipper and some crew who understand the relationship between the boat and the sea and how to interact. It requires working with the waves, the wind, and their magnitude. It is challenging and hard work, but it is not fighting in the sense of opposing. It is not like Camus's Sisyphus. It is a constant loop of reading, responding, reading, responding. It is not to be separate from; it is being part of. The skipper or crew would need to be completely attentive to the sea and boat and be completely connected (not separate) with one another even though they are in different parts of the boat and have different roles. On one level, there would be little or no interaction with one another. In a sense, they are collectively hugging the restless sea.

Here is a kind of symbiotic afterthought to consider. If the skipper hugged the crew by giving support and letting them know that everything was okay and, in doing so, ignored the sea, that would not establish a connection with the crew or the sea. It would establish a separation with both. In this case, we could consider another example of being connected. For the conductor or the skipper, there needs to be a symbiotic-type relationship with the musicians or the crew. At the same time, the conductor or the skipper needs to symbiotically connect with the composer's music or the sea.

Here, we have a nonseparate relationship among the sea, composition, boat, orchestra, crew, and musician.

Body, Speech, Mind:
The Experience of Integration

This is nothing new. It doesn't require, I think, much elaboration. It is an understanding that has been around for thousands of years. It has been one of the basics of many forms of meditation and is consistent with any Western approach to self-regulation and all the topics we have discussed so far. It's what we have discussed in considering calming and visualisation. It's an exercise; it is not imposing any new insights.

Very simplistically, the goal could be to relax the body; it could also be to integrate all aspects of the body and mind to improve one's focus. As all of you are aware, the mind (thoughts) can interfere with achieving a desired state. You can't get to sleep at night or even perform well at a task.

I once worked with a golfer whose thoughts produced high levels of right trapezium muscular tension that messed up her backswing. For her, like everyone, I could control her right trapezium by talking to her about stressful and nonstressful topics, and she had no awareness of the change. So how do we control thinking? If we repeat some neutral verbalisation over and over—such as a sound, mantra, words, or phrases—we can actually focus our thoughts or concomitantly limit our thinking of 'other' thoughts. This way of controlling the mind can be coupled with focused breathing (body), and an integrated state can be achieved.

Years ago, we found that the biomechanical reaction to repeating *aum* resulted in a slight vibration in the lower back, which reduces muscular tension. We were able to measure it by using EMG (electromyography).

Throughout this work, I have considered 'self' from numerous points of view. I looked at my own needs in a very self-indulgent manner. I am different. Then jumping way ahead and looking at the other end of a self-focused continuum, I considered the view of separateness and delusion. We have also looked at anxiety, connections, beliefs, religions, ethics, nonhumans, atoms, forces, energies.

I hope that it is becoming clear that all our discussions have led us to a fundamental social/human (I guess) need. People seem to have a need to believe in something or some things. Is this pathology of the mind? Can the body and speech change this mind domination? If the influence of this mind pathology isn't reduced, would that make one a prisoner of belief or even result in a delusion?

Here's a contradiction for you, some thoughts that have come to mind.

As I am writing this, I am feeling some human functioning, possibly rhetorical questions. Here is that interfering mind again. I am wondering why humans see themselves as so important. A Freudian term, which then became part of the developmental psychology language, that seems most apt is egocentricity, or maybe we could call that 'species centricity'. I don't know what it is mechanistically, but it is probably the best word for phenomenologically describing 'something' in the species that impairs their understanding of the *all*.

As you walk around, try to be aware that what you see is not the world per se but somewhat preselected based on what your eyes find of interest and how images and colours are interpreted. It is often a strange experience. Here, I am looking out. What do you see? What do you not see? Is the sky a limit or an openness to something endless? Is all this influenced by the mind?

I think this simple experience of seeing promotes separateness, ego. Earlier, we have looked at transformation and ego strength. One needs strength of character/ego to do things, but one also needs the ability to fall below.

Here endeth our reading, at least this phase.

We have a number of rests in this section. You could think of them as blank pages, if you feel that you need to turn pages to move ahead.

So you may ask, 'Where are we? How do all these ramblings fit together?'

So we have had lots of exercises in calming, visualising, and changing our points of view so that—even with our many different states—we retain a constant perspective. We have a sense that dualities are really social/human expressions of the same thing—conscious/unconscious, tolerance/intolerance, captive/free, human/nonhuman, good guys/bad guys. We have looked at dealing with life/the real (your own experience), and we have considered the importance of good ethical thinking and beyond it and then discussed separateness and nonseparateness. I wonder if we should have an outlaw acronym, but maybe not—that sounds too much like the fifty fundamentals of golf. Maybe we can't have a nice, tidy 'do *x, y, z*' (oops, ran out of letters) approach. Does this section give us all we need to achieve a more profound experience? Is this a pathway?

There are important questions that have important answers, but I realised partway through writing the next section that I may have missed a very important piece. I looked back to see where I put it and realised I hadn't addressed it. I felt that it would work best here, so I have put it next for a number of reasons:

- It tells something about my perception of self and my thinking and what i may have forgotten about or taken for granted.
- It is an essential factor in what I have written so far, but I have not specifically addressed it as something that would require your awareness.
- Your present reading experience, which is now, has actually come from my future. In essence, your now is my future. And as you reading this, you are experiencing my future. I have just moved it to the past.
- It is also something that can be understood by applying some aspects of perception that we have developed in this section.

So what is this missing piece? See the next section.

An All-Pervasive Missing Piece: It Integrates All, and It's Essential and Fundamental

It is the smiling Buddha. It could be seen as an expression of humour, a lighter side, a calming compassion. It is knowing that seriousness may be destructive to the human psyche. But it is also important to remember that humour can be a double-edged sword.

I think that having a sense of humour is extremely important, but its essence is very fragile.

- It can be connecting and calming and can lessen the intensity of human experience.
- It can also be disconnecting and intensifying and can increase human separateness and intolerance.

My feeling is that humour is based on a number of different associations, but for it to be beneficial to the human psyche and be consistent with our views as the outlaw, it needs to have some very special qualities.

Frequently, humour makes fun of others. And even though it may look the same on the surface, it could be very different in its intent and how it is received. The differences in this humour can be extreme; they may affirm a relationship or may start a world war. In fact, I can remember spending many hours over many months with a friend trying to explain an important difference I could see. He is a well-meaning person who has a good heart, is experienced in life, and is bright, but he doesn't understand the nuances that I feel are obvious. His view is that humour is great because it brings people together and transforms negatives into positives.

One day he was telling me about an English beer that was making fun of Germans and their WWII planes as part of their promotion. He felt that this was good fun and was positive because it made light of a once-serious condition. From his point of view, he was correct. Certainly, the Brits and the Germans could tease each other, and it could all be in good fun, but what I wanted him to appreciate was that his positive view was egocentric and would not shared by everyone. He hadn't thought about the possible perspective of others and those who may hold on to bitter feelings. My challenge was trying to convince him that there are others who may have less positive perspective and that humour may trigger intense and even aggressive responses.

I suggested that there may be some other possibilities. Let's suppose that the person making these promotional jokes or someone laughing at these is someone who still holds animosity towards the Germans, and this promotion has simply fuelled his already negative feelings. It could also be that the promotion was well intended but could be seen by some Germans as negative and insulting. So instead of having good feelings, we have intolerance fuelled by humour. What is happening here is that we are not laughing 'with'; we are laughing 'at'.

He eventually accepted that, unless you clearly know your own feelings and motivation and the feelings of 'others', humour that makes fun of others could be separating, not uniting, and intensifying, not calming. My discussion with him about the double-edged nature of humour was before the Danish and French jokes that were made about Islam extremism, which unfortunately illustrated my concern.

However, I have a young Mexican friend whom I initially met at a bike shop some ten years ago. He worked on my bike for a number of years until he moved away. He is now back. Anyway, from a business point of view, he offered great customer service, he was always sincere and positive, and he knew his clientele and their needs. He knew the families and made everyone feel respected and understood. He was excellent at standing in another's shoes. He organised a downhill bicycle racing team and did all the behind-the-scenes work. For his future, he had plans to do something positive with people. He has a great sense of humour and has an energy that is deeply positive. We have joked over the years about the fact that he is my Mexican son since he is the same age as my kids. Our relationship is such that he can joke about himself or about being the little Mexican, or we can both make critical comments generally with a national Canadian/Mexican theme without any sense of negativity. Here we are laughing 'with'. We each can intuitively feel what is humourous and what isn't and change gears from the fun to the serious in a very natural way.

Jock: This type of humour is frequently evident in a range of environments, including sports (of course), policing, armed forces, or other environments that have been traditionally male dominated. This typically involves 'putting down' teammates or fellow peers in a way that may be offensive to many. Put-downs are usually exaggerated criticisms of performance, sexuality, or just general competence. For many women who have been and are in these environments, this type of humour is often considered as abusive and not tolerable.

Use of stereotyping: Though these are simple, self-evident examples, I have used them to illustrate one specific dynamic feature—stereotyping, which not only is often used in humour but also could be racist or mocking in nature. It also helps reinforce that sense of group or personal identity that is based on feelings of separateness, which we have discussed before.

My examples of 'humour' have considered stereotyping based on nationality, which as mentioned could go all the way from an expression to mutual affection to possible intolerance. I may use a stereotyping-type teasing with some mental health staff, though in a somewhat ludicrous manner. This could be based on where they were born or grew up, on their sex, or on some aspect that I know the person would feel a positive sense from the personal attention. It should be noted that my use of these stereotype teases has a particular rationale to them. I might use these teases when addressing mental health staff whose job is to treat complex psychiatric cases. My intent, in these cases, is to emphasise that psychiatric diagnoses typically define a person in a manner that is not physiologically diagnostic and is not descriptive of a particular person (which is often the case); it is more akin to a stereotype. For example, it may be concluded that a person does something because they have ADHD. We could say that any descriptive statement like the above makes an assumption about those who are defined as having ADHD. Consider the following:

> All Canadians are polite.
> George is a Canadian.
> Therefore, George is polite.

> All people with ADHD are poor listeners.
> George has an ADHD.
> Therefore, George is a poor listener.

I guess we could conclude that George is a polite, poor listener. We could consider that these types of diagnoses are simply a logical extension of the nationalistic examples we have used. You could make your own. You could make the assumption that all _____ (fill in your own diagnosis/nationality/province/state/regional/ethnicity/sex) are the same.

In my talks with others, I would most often use obvious hyperbole and make comments that reinforce stereotypes. I also clearly explain to them that my teasing is to be a constant reminder that stereotypes are 'way off base' descriptors for a person, and in the same way, descriptors like 'autistic' are equally stereotyping.

What I want those who are the brunt of my 'humour' to appreciate is that social/human judgemental assessments of anyone, whether positive or symptomatic, are at best inaccurate. My selection of who I might tease is extremely important. There are some staff whom I may know very well, and teasing them in a very stereotype manner would not be uncomfortably processed. I need to know their feelings. I need to know that they know I care for and respect them and that they have a positive acceptance of teasing. As an aside, it may seem somewhat ironic, but my good friend, whom I care for in many different ways, is less able to be teased, so I don't.

But I digress. Humour is not usually used in such a specific, group-focused manner.

The trivial nature of any stereotyping could be as simple as 'just in case you're not aware, the person inputting all my writing is from Ontario,

Canada'. For most of you who know Canada, that would certainly be a positive, but you may not know that people from Ontario are typically fabulous! This is, of course, not logically appropriate to be a major premise, but I would contend that *all* people from Upper Canada are brilliant and above all others. (That is where I am from.) Since she is from Ontario but not Upper Canada, we can only conclude that she may or may not be that great.

Some of you reading this may live on a little island. The UK, for example, may feel a sense of superiority to anyone from the colonies. Isn't it really just a history of 'little guy' mentality? Others of you live in that country between Canada (where thinking people want to go) and Mexico. Your superiority seems to be based not on fact but on a legend in our own minds.

For you who live elsewhere in the world, you will have your own ways of defining yourselves, other countries, and other regions in humourous, poking-fun ways. There are, of course, those countries or ethnicities that, like an individual, are good at making fun of others but not themselves and have a sense of superiority and mockery in their expressions of others.

Take a moment to check your own response to my editorial (human-based) comments. They were only one short paragraph in length. If you responded in any emotional way, which I must admit I did in writing this, you would need to look at what you are feeling. For me, I went from a light tease, my own creation, to feeling the overwhelming influences of the social/human world and my insignificance as a voice. Here is the fragile nature of humour—and my own sensitivity.

This type of political humour, though similar to our beer example, can be alienating not because it was meant with any ill intent. It may simply be that the speaker is not aware of his/her point of view or how it is seen by others.

Throughout the Western world, there are those jokes that make fun of some group/nationality. In Canada, there were Newfie jokes. Many years ago, I saw a page of Norwegian jokes in a Swedish paper. There were Polish jokes (my first encounter with this type of humour). There were/are blond jokes and obviously many more. Typically, they make fun of the group's stupidity. I think these are probably quite neutral in their use, and the joke teller does not think about and may not even know any of the group that is being joked about. However, it is a 'laughing at', though probably accompanied by no real feeling one way or the other. The response to this humour, i think, could be highly variable.

For instance, it could even be a situation where a speaker is relating a humourous story about another (person, people, country, or whatever), but the listener sees the speaker as arrogant, superior, and opinionated. The result is that the listener doesn't hear the story; he/she hears yet another expression of arrogance.

There is no real 'laughing at', and there is no 'laughing with'. There is, however, increased separation.

Layered from laughter to sadness: There is another type of humour that is making fun and having others laugh that has been used in fiction with a serious 'other' level. This is well illustrated in a short, one-act play by Sean O'Casey, called <u>Hall of Healing</u>. The characters in the play are some street people in Dublin and some not overcontented medical staff. The humour is built on the health needs of these people, their requests, and the dialogue with the attending staff. It is humourous; however, you soon realise that this is a tragic statement of the human condition. The play is short, and it may not be until after the play is over that you experience its tragic nature. That part stays with you.

Some slapstick humour can have another human connection. If we consider the role of the clown, an overtly funny character, there has traditionally been an element of sadness to that role. Emmett Kelly and Red Skelton were both noted for the sad-type clown (the ultimate circus clown with sad, expressive makeup).

Here is an interesting humour dynamic. At first, there is a 'laughing at'. This is followed by 'laughing with' the author and finally a sense of quiet reflection.

A reflection on day-to-day life: Frequently, humour makes fun of life's circumstances, the things we do, and the people who do. This type of humour, especially if it is somewhat self-reflective, doesn't seem to be prone to a negativism in spirit. It has a lightening effect. Many comedy programs have worked successfully on that premise.

It works, I think, because most people can relate to it. If it keeps a positive tone, it does so by not making fun of people but seeing the humourous side of parenting, male/female relationships, being a kid, or what have you.

Puns or other plays on words: This is one I use a lot. As you could gather from my writing style, for some of us who are somewhat obsessed with words, their meanings, and how they interplay, a play on words can result in a great deal of self-stimulating fun. These plays on words come to me spontaneously, and I will often have a hard time *not* sharing them.

Slapstick: Humour can be slapstick, where you laugh 'at' purposely silly behaviour. I think this could be a 'laughing at' that is, in some ways, a 'laughing with'. If someone is being purposefully comedic in a slapstick manner, we could say that the comedian is internally laughing 'at' his/her own behaviour. The 'with' piece is shared; we both are laughing at your behaviour.

Black or dark: Humour can be black as well. I see that this humour can be an effective defence mechanism for people who work in highly stressful human-intervention jobs. This humour is especially evident in hospitals, in police departments, and with emergency personnel. It is laughing at patients, their body parts, and bad guys. At face value, it looks degrading. However, it can be seen as essential for the job, though it can have a number of side effects. It creates a distance between yourself and the human qualities of the patient or bad guy. Just think of taking a knife and cutting open a friend to see what's inside; a surgeon doing exploratory surgery will need to do that. In a hospital, people can be transformed into meat with no specific identity. For many police, it is a lot easier to arrest a 'bad guy' than someone who has some type of problem and is really a misled good guy. For some of these people, there is no generalised influence. They can be caring, relaxed, and open with others outside the job. Unfortunately for some others, this humour infects their whole being. They remain distant, nonresponsive, and often angry.

Here, we have a 'laughing at', which could be achieved by a conscious transformation when at work. It creates a coping separation. Then there needs to be a transformation at the end of the work to reconnect with people in a meaningful way; otherwise, 'laughing at' can continue.

Satire and the absurd: And there are humour genres that are satirical. I have always enjoyed *Monty Python's Flying Circus* and, recently, *The Daily Show* and *The Late Show with Stephen Colbert*, though Stephen could sometimes make me feel a sense of discomfort when he would play his fundamentalist, right-wing role with someone who didn't seem very clever or had no sense of humour.

I am not going to continue with my discussion of humour since this is not the object of these ramblings. I will, however, suggest that humour is a significant part of life and has great social/human power. What is important, I think, is not changing what you enjoy but understanding your experience of its influence.

1

One last visualisation exercise might be helpful in considering humour. But before I elaborate on my visualisation suggestions, I became concerned about how much to offer in direction. As I reflected on my decision, I was reminded of an experience I had years ago where I was taking a graduate course in ethics. There were three students in the class, I think. I can't remember any particulars of the two others in this course. Since I can't remember their identity, maybe there weren't three. There could have been two or four but not any more. Anyway, back to the course.

At that time in my life, I was writing a novel, and so was the person teaching the ethics course. During class time, we would both periodically take time reading our works. I wrote very symbolic fiction but gave no direction to the readers of my symbolic intent. My idea was to have them explore my psyche and find layers (hopefully). He wrote in a similar style, but he would always strategically place a dialogue between the characters in the novel that would explain the symbolic significance of those previous pages. We spent some time discussing the nature of fiction, the reader's experience, the role of being a teacher, and the experience of being the student. From my point of view, he was too much a teacher.

My question here is, 'what should I do?' I have discussed humour, I have formed my ramblings into a 'how to become' format, and I have even given direction for new experiences, but I haven't given you any answers.

Should I analyse my examples and tell you that, according to me, there is good and bad humour? Unfortunately, there is no absolute, but I think I need to give some direction. I have wanted to resist being a teacher/interpreter, but I feel I need to at least offer some review structure before moving ahead.

$$1$$

In this review, let's assume that the person who is the source of humour is empathetic by nature. We will be unfair to the arrogant person who is humourous. We will assume that, for this person, it is a 'laughing at' with the personal benefit of feeling arrogance.

Humour that	at	with	assumed underlying	side effects
makes fun of others – no personal attachment				
makes fun of others – with personal attachment				
makes fun of others – jock type				
makes fun of aspects of social/ human life (all of us)				
makes fun of stereotypes				

makes fun of stereotypes in my staff context				
makes light of day-to-day life (sitcom)				
is layered (O'Casey type)				
uses puns				
is slapstick				
is black				
is focused on the social/political				
* See notes for an example				

Notes: To give you some direction, consider my friend's beer promotion example:Underlying effects/object of focus – It is a 'laughing at'. My laughing at another reinforces my Britishness and desire to drink that beer.

Side effects – It reinforces a separation with Germans and their 'German', non-British qualities. It may also affect some Germans and their view of the critical, arrogant British.

In filling in or thinking about the above, we know that just what we see on the surface is only a small part of the picture. It's what is below that counts.

I hope that you experience two obvious elements emerging from the underlying effects and side effects columns. These are essential to having an outlaw perspective.

At this point, I have other dilemmas:

1. I could give you my 'correct' answers, but I cannot even suggest that I am the paradigm of what is right. You may see something that I haven't seen, which may be 'more right', whatever that means.

2. I could give you my 'correct' answers, which you look for because you really don't want (and, besides, don't have the time) to explore a whole bunch of possibilities.

3. But if I don't give you my point of view, you could easily make an effort but, like my friend who enjoyed the British beer promotion, miss some important variables, though he could be right.

If you want to know my point of view, I will give you some direction in the last section—'Reflections on Composing and Conducting'.

So now what? First, let's put the other pieces that we have discussed together. I would suggest that rather than making a judgement about good humour and bad humour (admitting duality), it would be best to draw upon some of your experiences with this section (i.e., being calm, visualising waves, being a part of everything, being a kind of self-observer, having no dualities, just being, thinking, accepting the different realities we see).

Now if you can hold on to the above, see how different humour dynamics influence your state. Do they feel compatible, or do they seem expressive of different social/human points of view?

So what about the smiling Buddha?

You need to define your own sense of what is meant by the smiling Buddha and the nature of the smile. Look at the image and speculate. What do you think he represents? It could have all the characteristics of our different types of humour, or it could be specific.

So what feels right? You have played with a number of our variables, I hope. See if what you have come up with is consistent with the following.

Some confusing digressions that may not seem to answer anything

Norman Cousins, once the editor of <u>Saturday Review</u> spent many of his years with heart disease and later on a reactive arthritis. In fact, it was thirty-six years before his death that he was given little chance of surviving. He decided to develop his own recovery program. It incorporated megavitamins, nonhospital environments, positive emotions, and laughter. He frequently watched old slapstick movies to deal with pain. As a result of his efforts and his writings, he became an adjunct professor in a medical school. His basic premise was a simple one. Emotions influence biochemistry.

In my discussions up to this point, you may have, without thinking about it, connected humour and happiness. You may have considered that the smiling Buddha is happy. If you consciously thought about happiness, you may have noticed that I didn't mention it. You may think back to the beginnings of this work and may recall my expressed desire to connect with someone. Did I want to be happy? Or did I want something else? As you would know now, it was and is something else.

What I would like to do at this point is leave happiness aside for the moment, since it requires another whole discussion, and move on.

Let's get back to what else might feel right. You might have defined or tried to define some kind of inner quality, one that even allows teasing or some type of critical humour to be experienced positively by all people involved. You might have also seen that, even if there seems to be a defensive necessity for hospital humour, it would be important that it doesn't affect that undefined inner quality of the person. You may have accepted that some neutral humour, like puns, would not engender any strong feelings either way but could still tap into an inner quality. It could be responded to with a smile or even a somewhat distorted expression that conveys a 'that's a terrible pun' reaction. But in both responses, we could consider that all responses would just be judgementally neutral. Of course, there is another possible response. Someone doesn't get the pun, and so they either don't react at all or look confused because what was said doesn't make sense.

So let's go back to our Buddha. We can see him. We have a picture of him smiling. Of course, there are many pictures of this figure, and each one may be slightly different. We have given you one. Since I would like you to be able to visualise/experience his state, I will focus on what we see, not what is represented symbolically. We see a comfortable round sitting figure. His eyes are closed, and his smile is drawn back, giving him big jowls. But his smile doesn't look forced. His shoulders slope down, not tense. However, it may be difficult to imitate his image since trying this may result in being tense, but it may not be as difficult to look at some internal possibilities. His eyes are closed, so his experience is internal, not distracted. And what we see could be expressive of him meditating. His body projects an essence of being relaxed (calm) and round (not rigid or controlled). His point of view is probably also round and full, not tied to the rigid, limited, or ephemeral. It has a completeness and a sense that all is as it should be.

My own visualisations, used in a meditative manner, are many but have a completeness and a calmness that could be seen as having the same essence as our Buddha figure. What is important to understand, in your own visualisations and meditative or reflective states, is not simply visualising or thinking about how to look like our Buddhist figure but establishing his essence. To use a translated Buddhist term, the vehicle to exploring your own body, speech, or mind is one of establishing a calm, reflective, beyond-human sense that, even though the species may be struggling, the nonhuman/beyond human is just doing its thing, and that's okay. What would seem reasonable, i think, is considering that a 'smile' can exist in the absence of social human definitions of happiness or humour. In some ways, we could consider the 'smile' in contrast to how seriously the human species considers their own individual lives.

The women come and go

Talking of Michelangelo.

One of my visualisations that goes beyond the ephemeral is one in which I am sitting in this timeless field with this myriad of nonhuman musicians who are constantly moving to form different ephemeral orchestras, playing for a while, and then returning sometimes around the field in no special, structured way; and at other times, they group together. I may see them in orchestra form playing music that is fun, serious, revolutionary, or whatever. They come back to the same timeless field, and all is well. My image flashes momentarily to Bosch's <u>The Garden of Earthly Delights</u> and figures walking around. It's the field and walking around that triggered the association, I can see that. I see its Christian images, my field and musicians, Eden and hell. His work certainly expresses complex relationships with dualities. It's so powerful, but it's so different from mine. Mine is so positive in contrast, so uncomplicated. I get another interfering image. I see the dancing figures of Pieter Bruegel. They are round and colourful but have faces that express angst and despair. My musicians express peace and contentment. The image seems so simple and complete.

I can feel a smile. It's just like being below the surface. My smile feels like I am observing children at play and even observing their stresses. They can seem to take themselves too seriously, but that's okay. They don't know. There is an innocence and fragility in their seriousness. Underneath it all is my urge to smile. It is one of understanding that, at one level, everything is okay. I feel the need to remind you who may be social/human in your focus. It doesn't mean we don't do anything to respond to the ephemeral world or laugh at their jokes. It just means we don't live there all the time. Okay means that the nonhuman will remain.

Wow, my visualisation seems to take us a long way from the human, where we started. It went to humour and then to a smiling Buddha and then to the nonhuman. With my image, I can sense balance and completeness, even if our musicians never form an orchestra.

Back to some basics. Let's try another approach to our insightful smile. We need to consider some possible blocks.

Let me go back to our discussion of humour and its different characteristics and see what fits. I think the best humourous way of categorising my visualisation is the layered, Sean O'Casey type.

In essence, the life of our social/human species, like Sean O'Casey's Dubliners, is limited. They are certainly self-absorbed and, in many ways, tragic figures. But this tragic element may be just below-the-wave perspective, like Bosch and Bruegel. If we go further below the surface and are not concerned with calming the sea, everything is okay. Our smile, from the smiling Buddha's point of view, is not that of those on the surface who battle with the sea, have delusions, struggle for identity, and desperately hang on to a sense of self as our characters in Hall for Healing. They believe that the sea, if they don't overcome it, will take away their personal identity, and they wouldn't exist as an individual. They don't understand that once they give up on battling to keep individuality, they achieve a new nonindividual state. Once they accept that a smile can emerge, all is okay.

As I wrote this, even though the flow of thoughts worked for me, I wondered if I was helping you approach the smiling Buddha. I asked myself, 'Would it be difficult for most of you to experience this transformation?' I see two human factors here:

First, it may be that you don't really understand a perspective, which includes yourself, but at the same time is completely removed from self. I am uncertain about my ability to express something that is not considered by most. I may have lost you. I may have moved too quickly. I may have not explained this point of view well enough, or it could be that you can identify with the points, but it could be that you may not have had enough time to experience or really understand.

Second, if you can identify with this beyond-human perspective, that is certainly positive. However, really understanding this perspective is a bit more complicated. I can see that you may identify with what I am writing; on the other hand, you may disagree since these views may seem somewhat antisocial/human. Yet it isn't. An underlying impression may have emerged from these beyond-human discussions. It could be confused with what could be called role identification. Does our perspective imply that it is okay to not to do anything in the world? Don't chase the social, success, making money. Drop out and turn on.

'Timothy Leary is dead. [This was a line in a popular old stereo recording of the '60s] No, no, no [filler vocal], he's outside looking in' ('Moody Blues'). I can feel a positive relationship with what Leary and Ellis understood but saw major flaws in their social/human application— the need for acceptance as the alternative-lifestyle person, the rejection of norms because of the acceptance of equal but opposite ones. From my sense, it wasn't the insight that LSD afforded; it was the instant, no-discipline, no-personal-sacrifice sense of achieving a smile. In the '60s, there were many hippies. I confess that I may have looked like one of them, but at the time, i felt that, on the whole, it was a social role. I saw it, at least at one level, as being no different from being a fraternity/sorority member, just a social need to belong. But I also felt that at least the hippy identification or the motorcycle gang member identification offered the rebel perspective, and the hippy identification did seem to promote peace, love, etc. It was not all that bad but still bound to social/human yin/yang.

So we could say that there are still many of you who may identify with this kind of role. Remember, as we have discussed, that any social role at a social/human level is the same. It's a role. I have a feeling of concern here. There are those of you who will have gone along and identified with what we have discussed so far, but because you have identified with my writing, you have not let yourself be challenged. You have not bothered with my suggested exercises because you know it all. You've been there, yet maybe you haven't been.

If this is your view and you may be convinced that you have a spiritual understanding, maybe you have travelled (lateral movement), have made a point of rejecting social norms, have kept life simple, or have not taken on possessions or social expectations; however, if you live in a society that considers success in terms of social status, role, wealth, cultural graces, or other like ways, you are probably doomed to live on the surface and are blocked from ever getting below.

An ironic aspect of getting below the surface that I have often wondered about was addressed in some of Joseph Conrad's work. It is interesting that I didn't agree with his point of view in my twenties but have seen elements of his writing that, I think, are necessary for opening the door to a broader understanding of the limits of life on the surface. In my early years, I was looking for answers; he didn't have them. One of his thematic elements addressed the almost-face-value futility of youthful success. Reading a goal becomes anticlimactic, but then with time, these goals become a building block of understanding and wisdom. Young Marlow reaches a geographical goal after fighting the sea; losing a ship, he becomes the captain of a lifeboat, survives, and reaches India. However, his arrival is like a nonevent. There is no sense of safety or success. This character realises, after many years have passed, that success is more about experience, not glory. The understanding of this, with reflection, comes with age.

To really experience the smile, I think it may be important to have success. Know that you have conquered the sea or whatever but also learn that you have never really conquered anything. You have, however, learned a lot by having these experiences and insights.

Saying that you are not going to sea because it's dumb or saying that you know and you don't need to find out firsthand that the limits of success can only be really understood with achievement. If you respond, 'I'm already an outlaw,' this is probably the best indicator of not being free. You could simply be a prisoner of yourself (a delusion), of your belief.

These words may seem to conflict with the tone of our discussion of humour and of the smiling Buddha, but this is the only way I know of to quickly address a very dominant factor in the social/human world— identifying without insight.

The smile of our '60s person may be a smile of imitation and identification, not one emerging from an inner sense.

There is another social/human group to consider here. There are those of you who, for many different reasons, are uncomfortable with success because of personality/emotional difficulties. You might say, 'I have this potential, I know! I see it with many others.' You may have and see the potential correctly, yet like many of you who have possibly had the development of being the swan in a duck's world, you may not be beyond that dilemma. You could be stuck.

I am now listening to a conversation, as I am writing this, that offers another identifying role with the insightful smiling Buddha. It is a she talking to a he, and she has used insightful cliché after insightful cliché— concrete sequential, random abstract, disconstruct, programmed, stimulate, systems, building structures, that's what it is all about, interconnectedness, facilitate, common denomination, fake knowledge, that is what they are, purpose and values, value statements, common responsibility, we ought to be able to respect each other, globalised. Please note she has taken the courses and learned the content.

Unfortunately, there may be many of you who are simply Dubliners with different scripts. You are no further ahead, so here is another important piece. Reflect on and reconsider the conscious and unconscious. Take a moment to consider where you are. If these are somewhat open and you can see yourself, all is well to carry on. If you are uncertain, move ahead slowly and cautiously. Be open.

So in some ways, not really understanding or identifying with what I have written but being open and interested may be a much better basis for going further. I know that if you are uncertain and maybe even confused but open, you will be more open to experiencing than those who readily identify. You have no blocks to your learning.

So we have

- the person who has achieved success and seen its limits;
- the person who doesn't need success, is defensive, and knows it all;
- the person who, because of a certain humbleness, will not achieve success but is open and can learn and experience.

As I am considering our next step in this process of understanding your point of view, I spontaneously articulated an 'oh no!' Just when I feel we are away from different variables, I realise we are not.

We have two possible directions to consider in the next section. I also feel that this process is getting bogged down, which it is. There is just too much! Anyway, getting the most out of both of these future directives may require a return to my earlier ramblings and, of course, a vast range of personal experience, reading, listening, and seeing with a changed point of view. For some of you, I could say that I will see you in a number of years. Sail to India, become successful and then go beyond/below, become egotistical/abandon your ego, or study, experience, and learn and then go beyond/below.

Below, I have copied a print of Bosch's <u>The Garden of Earthly Delights</u>, which I alluded to at the beginning of this section. Though the print is small and if you don't know it, a large copy should be easy to find.

For others, you are ready for the next step.

So let's leave these rambling thoughts and return from your possible tangential voyage. Let's return to our smiling Buddha.

Some Different Streams of Consciousness about Life

I would like to explore some ways of understanding human existence that are consistent not only with a social/human perspective but also with some underlying universal realities. See how well these different streams of conscious thinking work for you.

Another perspective digression

Remain calm, be removed from the social/human plane, and be part of the nonhuman. In a somewhat modernised, nonsymbolic Bosch manner, we could visualise people moving around in all sorts of directions. And sometimes they can be still, they can be alone, they can be with a few others or in large masses. They sometimes seem to have purpose and other times not. They can be highly aroused and loud. They can be quiet. Are they looking for something? Meaning? Security? Enjoyment? They may also live with separateness. They may be self-absorbed, but they may be trying to make life work.

We know that the lives of people are ephemeral. The life of specific collective groups could also be seen as ephemeral, though these groups—including political parties, churches, and nations—could be around for hundreds of years. The lives of controlling powers and the beliefs they follow are ephemeral. In fact, from the whole scheme of things, we could consider that the human species is also ephemeral.

Nevertheless, we could expect that the dynamics of the species, like the dynamics of the nonhuman structures that underlie it, will last longer than the species themselves. However, the principles that underlie how chemical elements and physics work are considered fundamental and constant (though our understanding changes), and we assume that there are some fundamental scientific laws that explain the structure of how things work in the known universe.

Whatever these structures, laws, or principles, we know that they remain intact and can account for any changes that occur. These same structures, at one level, can help explain how good cells and bad cells behave—good cells (ones that promote human health) and bad cells (ones that aren't good for human health). We could also contend that some of these structures, ones inherent in the species and their individual DNA and RNA, may even account for the behaviour of those people you agree with and those you don't. More importantly, these structures, laws, and principles don't make any good/bad distinction. They simply help explain the way things are, and as we have discussed before, this starts at a subatomic level. The human species can do all sorts of things. In fact, it could even self-destruct, but the underlying structure and its nonhuman building blocks will prevail.

We should stop here for a minute. The next step may be difficult for some of you. Take a breath. Be calm. Can you feel a new sense? Everything is okay. Waves will crash against the shore. Children are playing, chasing each other. Consider a smile of compassion for a vulnerable species that, in many ways, is lost, anxious, and caught in a basic human quandary. Finding purpose? Finding significance? Finding groups, political parties, religions, and churches that define themselves by their differences? They may need to believe that they have the truth and others don't.

You may ask somewhat rhetorically about any kind of smile. 'I understand what you are saying, but I find it hard to get any sense of where a smile might fit. It seems too bleak, too nonhuman. It feels very nihilistic. What you describe doesn't really include anything to smile about. Is there not any other way to look at this?'

There may be some other ways at looking at the human, but let's return to a nonhuman, mechanistic, science-based perspective as a starting point.

Caution: However, once again, our discussion will not address the human need for some personal God-based afterlife. But let's follow its train of thought.

Let's say that we have recognised the functional aspects of people, which we have considered as a 'human element'. But what is unique about being human? This, of course, could require a whole treatise. But let's make it simple and consider that one important element is the integration of basic drives, feelings, and cognition. We can accept that people are able to feel, be empathetic, be self-aware, and think in an integrated manner. And as we have discussed, these dynamics can manifest themselves in a number of different ways.

And from a somewhat reductionist point of view, we could also assume that these dynamics are a function of some types of universal structures. We are composed of subatomic particles that are subject to the laws of physics (assuming we have understood them correctly), and I guess we could also consider the nature and influences of cell biology, biochemistry, and biomechanics. Is it the integrated interaction of these functions that account for the unique variables that compose the social/human?

Let's say that this integrated functioning is based on this human capacity to experience an empathetic, emotional, spiritual, or nonseparate connection with others and something permanent or universal, something that is an expression of the person, and something that is connecting with everyone. Wow, that's a mouthful! But I think the sentence works.

One metaphor that might help us understand these phenomena is a radio wave one. If we go back to our orchestra that exists ephemerally and if this orchestra has broadcast its music on the airwaves, we know that this electronic expression will remain in travelling in space indefinitely. As a result, these individual orchestras and their unique expressions have a radio wave form and existence that exists in space beyond their own limited existence. Each one of these expressions is, of course, one of billions of other expressions, TV shows, news broadcasts, music of all kinds, all with the same structure and individual form, all coexisting.

This electronic expression is one thing, but its meaning is another. Is it possible that all organisms or each human have some type of projected energy that lasts, that follows some structural laws? We can measure the body's electrical and thermal energy using instrumentation. What we have is a combination of people's uniqueness because we measured the dynamic patterns of measured physiology from many different points at the same time. We would have unique electrical expressions and patterns of expression from each person. Does this electrically measured energy have some type of timelessness? I don't know.

What about a perspective that offers a bit more of a positive human quality? Can we find some other expression of each human that has some permanence? We could speculate that the feelings you have for people whom you were very close to and who have died carry on and probably could be measured subcortically, such as in the limbic system and by other physical systems. For instance, some memory of a person that brings good memories is experienced at a physical level. Someone who projected a calmness may trigger a sense of inner calm in yourself—a parent who cared for you and made you safe, a fond memory of a loved one. In these cases, we could say that their energies are not existing in some ethereal sense or floating in space but structurally part of you and possibly part of others as well. Your limbic system's memory of a person who was influential could be experienced throughout someone's life, and these same traits, which could be a sense of inner well-being or spirit of life, a spiritus mundi, could influence others and possibly the next generation. And as clearly evident in these ramblings, given the nature of human connection, this connection could be made with a whole range of people—living/dead, fictional/real, private/public.

These connections could be calming when thinking about and remembering some people; however, they could also be intensifying and lead others in different directions. The human spirit that is passed on could be composed of the emotions and thoughts of the rebel, the terrorist, the criminal, or someone who has an antisocial or negative perspective on life.

It could be the intense but seemingly positive view of a religious or political fundamentalist. These intense thoughts and feelings, with an identifying connection, could promote antisocial behaviour or behaviour that looks prosocial but is highly intolerant of other perspectives. However, for some of the next generation, these intense thoughts and feelings may not offer an identifying connection. (These states don't necessarily meet the basic human need for safety.) This could result in developing a fear and anxiety in these others.

We could conclude that one's afterlife/legacy could be highly influential or at least a factor in shaping the lives of others who follow them. You can take some solace in the fact that you will be immortalised for better or worse. For the writer, the artist, the composer, or the person influenced by their works, this created work could be responded to as being real.

Just think of all the links we could have between people if we considered these dynamics. And of course, these people could be living or dead. I don't think it matters.

The phenomenological

A human or ideal/belief

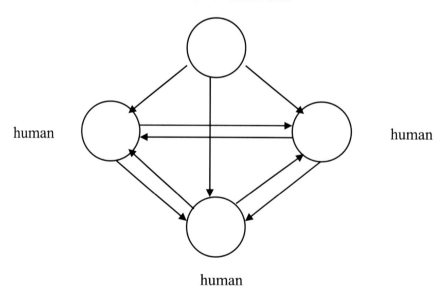

human   human

human

In our diagram, we are looking at a number of interactions that could exist between three living people who are close to one another and, let's say, share multi-interactive aspects of self. We have also included another person (real or fictional (e.g., Stephen Dedalus)) who is not physically present but is offers a unique perspective of life. This perspective could be an idealised vision, belief, or well-thought-out scientific treatise, and these views may be held by some other person(s) or group. For the purpose of our example, let's consider that this person, vision, or belief has had a significant influence on all three in a manner that is similar to the dynamics we have discussed in our afterlife/legacy example. Specifically, this influential person/entity could be an artist, fictional character, scientist, philosopher, religious or political leader of some movement, thinker, deceased relative, or someone known personally by all three who is seen by them in an idealised light or some other similar influence I have missed.

The nature of influence

If we reflect on how humans think and feel and consider how they may display phantasy or object cathexis (Freudian concepts), we can see that our view of the deceased, the idealised, a phenomenon, or any entity that is important can account for very specific psychological and physiological states. As we have discussed, just thinking about this figure/ideal could result in changes in cardiovascular, muscular, or neurological functions. One could be calm, excited, or ready for action.

Working with others, even ones of like mind, may offer interactive and individual dynamics, including agreements and conflicts that may be inimical with their mutually cathected ideal. But whatever the outcomes, we know that they are all expressions of the species.

So what about our three people? Are they connected, separate, or both? Are they all for one and one for all?

One example

Let's say that they love animals, the environment, and the sea and that they all have a passionate feel for Jacques Cousteau and his work. When thinking about him, we find that they all have a good feeling, positive thoughts, and a calm, stable physiological state—and possibly even a 'below the surface' one—and experience a oneness with the sea and Cousteau.

However, if one or all of them had environmental or animal rights concerns and identified with some group that were concerned about these rights being neglected, then their thoughts might trigger very different psychological and physiological states. One may be dominated by anger at those who don't care. Do they protest against those who don't care? Do they actually become aggressive and prevent them with some actions, like Greenpeace or the Sea Shepherd groups? These questions and finding answers may result in agreements or disagreements with others and even between one another. They end up with conflict rather than agreement.

Eldridge Cleaver, in a purposely contradictory manner, decided that after the assassination of Martin Luther King, it would be best to kill all those of the white race who were racist. In essence, stop those who kill by killing them. It would seem that some environmental and animal activists may behave in a similar manner but do not see the contradiction.

It would seem that, on the social/human plane, even a strong connection with a passive, universally caring, idealised icon may not be influential enough to change the inherent fears and aggressions of some people.

Another example

Let's consider another relationship in which each one of the three hypothetical persons (siblings) had a child/parent relationship with their father that had qualities that idealised his qualities. For each child, there were some differences in experience, but there were no differences that engendered any animosity with others or between themselves.

Here are a few aspects of their dad, whom I have created for purposes of example; therefore, he is actually fictional, though based on a real character. Anyway, let's assume that he has passed away, and we are considering his qualities that have remained after his passing. In his lifetime, he had been a famous philosopher. His children always saw, or at least remembered, him

438

as always being calm and reflective whenever he interacted with them or their mum. He was able to explain things in great detail and could see new ways of understanding the world, but he could sometimes be difficult to understand or would go into long explanations even in response to simple questions.

Could we expect that all three siblings have the same general impressions, though there could be some differences? We could surmise that they all loved and respected him and were very accepting and even in awe of his ability to think and work things out; however, we might ask, 'Would their mutual respect and admiration for him and his abilities to think things through and find solutions that worked set the stage for them to think things through in the same manner? Could we also conclude that his profound influence was sufficient enough to make them almost the same in character?' Of course not. Without belabouring lots of details, we would be overlooking the individual characteristics, both psychologically and physiologically, of each of the three siblings. For instance, one might be highly emotional and was sometimes bothered by their dad's lack of emotion. One may like to keep things simple and functional, and their dad was always making even the simple too complicated. One may be a high-energy person who was often on the go. To him, his dad was sedentary and sometimes boring.

What we would also expect is that these siblings are different from one another, and even though they may all appreciate their dad's ability to think and work things out, they may not apply an insight like his when dealing with their siblings or the world at large. What is clear is that the influences of their individual differences may override good thinking not only in dealing with life in general but also in dealing with one another. Yet these three siblings may all end up being well-balanced, nice people. (I would ask Bertrand Russell to please excuse the use of the word 'nice'. He wrote a chapter in one of his books called 'Nice People').

So where has our conscious thinking taken us? It would seem that our ramblings about human life and its meaning haven't given us a really optimistic outcome (e.g., and they lived happily ever after). If we discount afterlife, as defined in any typical religious manner, and if we reduce the possible impact of positive social figures, whether parent or thinker/creator, because there are so many other variables that can influence human thinking and behaviour, what are we left with? What is there to smile about?

A. Huxley, in his novel <u>Brave New World</u>, created the Bokanovsky process that limited gamma, delta, and epsilon persons genetically so that all the human processes could be systematically limited. As a result, these groups of individuals would be, in a sense, standardised, and differences between people and any concerns about the meaning of life would be beyond their capacity to feel or think. But maybe that isn't a satisfactory solution.

Is there a commonality between our various descriptions of the drivers of social/human need and existence and psychological and physiological associated states that are more than just being characteristic of a species? Is there not more?

As we have discussed, giving social/human life meaning may be relative to a culture or religion, which may define a god, an afterlife, or possibly a human spirit. But as considered, these beliefs meet a human need. They don't address the possibility truths that may preclude the importance of the species. Looking underneath, the underlying structure is overlooked. Ironically, I think we could say that the same structures that connect also separate. We have empathy, but we also fear. As we mentioned, these connections can be with humans and the nonhuman. They can be individuality-focused or beyond. 'Save the planet!'

So we have an energy, an ability of some sort to step beyond our individual selves, an ability to see, as we are discussing, and to experience life on a different plane. We understand that these elements have existed throughout our recorded history in all peoples, yet are they essential pieces? Pervasive ones? I'm not certain, but it is, I think, akin to or part of this timeless structure.

In these stream-of-consciousness passages, I have considered some kind of human essence using very 'safe', more rationally based thought. There was no leap of faith, no acceptance of soul or spirit. Part of my reason for this is my concern about the difference among essence, phenomenon, and meaning. If we put the meaning first, we run the risk of having delusions or some rationalised truth. The truth is created to meet our need for meaning, and our understanding of this truth could be seen as secondary. To confirm this order of thought, a believer who might question some statement of a scientifically supported truth could be questioned about their nonacceptance. If it is evident by their response that it is in conflict with that person's belief, then we could conclude that their social/human needs come first.

Combining different realities and finding some meaning

There are certainly many ways in which we could consider life, religion, and the spiritual and the relative importance of the species and the infinite. And in these different contexts, the smiling Buddha could be described differently.

Let's return to the Composer, the artist/creator, and the thinker and their relationship to the unknown, to the *all*, and their acceptance that the source of their reality is what is below and above them. They are aware of the social/human level of existence and their self-importance; they are aware of the underlying structure that drives these humans, yet even in this universe of no meaning and no purpose, they are also able to see the unique, the beautiful, the limits of the human and social order. They can experience a reality that others don't. The musicians wander and combine—the *all*, the limits of a googolplex, of time. Yet some can experience a sense of order, of epiphany, of beauty and from this unlimited universe create a personal order that can be experienced by others. We could consider these as emerging personal truths, not absolute ones but ones that are expressions of that which is beyond self.

We are calm, below the surface, and at one with this structure and its human-connecting energy, like an innocence, a beauty that gets lost on the surface. We settle back to experience the limitless structure and the frail but timeless collective beauty of the human species.

The essence of beauty is hidden by a social/human malaise.

We smile in response to our sense of beauty, of innocence and to what is connected below. And just possibly, we smile with a sense of optimism that structures and beauty, being timeless, will prevail.

So let's see what you can do to visualise the sense of the smiling Buddha. Use your own image or use mine, but once there, don't think so much about different approaches to humour per se but consider the smiling Buddha as having a perspective that is like the Composer.

Stop reading for a moment and reflect. Can you experience a visualisation or stream of thoughts that generates a smile that connects on a different plane? One of beauty, which could be seen as a Blakean-type innocence, which is often lost, as in our first example, but still underlies the species?

I have presented some thoughts about the smiling Buddha and some different conscious streams that didn't necessarily get us anywhere, but they took me probably six hours to write, and they probably took you ten minutes to read at the most. Remember, it took me many decades to understand. I hope you took time to reflect—maybe even years.

I think this is a lot to digest. Hopefully, I have opened up some new thoughts and experiences for you. I hope you were able to see that this smile can embody a universe and a sense of some inherent qualities of the species that don't necessarily make them important but offer some hope that the species has the capacity to overcome its paradoxical need to define themselves and their sense of community by being separate from others.

'So is that it? Are we there yet?'

'When do we get there?'—a question that children have asked for years. I see us just pulling out of our home driveway. We have done some extensive planning and have looked at some of the maps, but we are just beginning a long trip, even though we are near the end of this section. We have other topics to discuss and more important insights to experience as part of this work. I hope that you have had some new experiences as a result of reading this section and can use this as a basis for reading further in this work and other works.

In my discussions, up to our practice 'outlaw' section, I have considered an expanding gyre. Yeats calls it an antithetical gyre since it goes in the opposite direction to the one used on page 11. For most of you, this ever-expanding universe would make intuitive sense. Just look at it from your own knowledge and your own point of view. Just think of all the defined entities. We have gone from simple either/or to multiple dualities to unlimited probabilities. We have gone from human entities and orchestras to multicells and musicians. We have gone from one location to a whole universe. So how can we have this understanding and draw our gyre in the opposite direction?

To help get there and understand the next section, consider the following:

(WHOLENESS OF EXPERIENCE) + (INTEGRATE) + (BECOME) ⟶ BEING.[5]

It's amazing to think of how this whole process of becoming can be seen. It can be articulated in one single linear expression.

---

[5] See our structured primer in the appendix.

PART III: APPROACHING ONENESS

A Revisit and New Visit to the Many and Oneness

We will begin this section with some conceptual discussion of how we have used and may understand oneness. We will also consider some features of approach.

Warning: In this section, you will find that the discussion will seem fairly linear to start with. Topics will follow with a certain predictable continuity. Then some new topics, though hopefully interesting, will be discussed with unclear relevance. But in the world of rambling, free associative thinking, and a universe that has no limitation other than our own, all topics are equally relevant. I suggest you take a moment to digest the ideas because they will all become relevant.

Earlier, I asked you to consider where you were in your understanding of self and the universe, atman, or whatever (see page 166). On that page, I drew a gyre that represented an ever-expanding universe, given that we could see more and more stuff. Then several pages along, I considered some personally cathected experiences that had a oneness quality to them. Was I going in two directions at the same time?

At that time, we once again considered the concept of Atman. We spoke of it as if it was a single term, a oneness. But we had also defined it in terms of having an unlimited number of variables. I expect that, at that time, Atman would be seen as an everything with an unlimited set of variables. We also used the orchestra as a metaphor for how a universe that is experienced as a single entity can become an all, and then we could see how an experience of *all* can become one.

In the last section, we explored the possible meanings of a Buddha's smile, a single expression that could be reflective of a perception that can be difficult to understand or define in social/human terms. I am also assuming that your response to my writing could sometimes be somewhat difficult to follow. Sometimes my writing is pretty straightforward, and other times, it may be hard to grasp. I think that my style may often be at fault, but there are other times when the ideas I am wanting you to experience may be just beyond your grasp.

Robert Browning once wrote,

Man's reach should exceed his grasp

Or what's a heaven for?

I feel that it was and is absolutely essential that you experience a sense of being overwhelmed. Without that experience at some time in your life, you would be unable to have any significant vertical change, and it would probably mean that you have not really processed any new experiences and made any real changes. You may have simply made some lateral moves, gone east instead of west. My sense is that to make any changes, one really has to feel and understand not just the stormy seas of life but also the feeling of inner calmness even in times of adversity.

As we bring together an understanding of oneness, we will need to integrate a lot of the conceptualisations and feelings that I have discussed at the beginning and integrate these with the techniques I have discussed in the last section. In a sense, our goal is for you to have a real experience of approaching oneness, even though the real could be based on visualisation, calmness thinking, and new points of view. This experience would not depend on firsthand social/human physical experience but would necessitate some vertical integration. Think back for a moment to our types of 'real' experience. In fact, for the non-insightful social/human being, lateral movement may actually distract from any experienced insight. We need to consider 'real' not by outside happenings but by what happens internally.

In 'The Love Song of J. Alfred Prufrock', Eliot writes,

I have measured out my life with coffee spoons.

Let's review some of the oneness concepts that we have used and that have been used at the social/human level. As we know, there has always been a social/human need to find some kind of oneness. In writing this single hypothesis, I am making a oneness supposition, which is somewhat a contradiction to my 'one = all = one' position. Anyway, as you will notice, I will selectively ignore this possible contradiction.

Certainly, religions have come up with a one-god belief. Thomas Aquinas assumed that there has to be a single ordering force in the universe (i.e., God) and that, as we descend, we have less structure and more physical, earthy reality. He worked in an opposite way to Aristotle but came up with a similar gyre. If we consider oneness in this context, we could conclude, in a similar fashion, that there are thousands of people who work for a large company, but there is only one CEO. God is seen as the structuring entity, and even though there are tonnes of stuff in the world, they are all simply structurally organised manifestations of this one force. Him? Well, of course. Just think what the world would be like if God were female, though I have a friend who is a retired minister who did confess that, while he was an acting minister, he always spoke of God as 'he'. After he retired, he felt he was able to acknowledge his true belief. God is female. One difficulty with these religious assumptions, at least from the point of view of oneness, is that the CEO was typically male but no longer. Can religious beliefs change with the times? Maybe God should be considered as sexually ambivalent.

So maybe this popular religious point of view is like the 'oneness' that we have used to describe our neophyte symphony listener. One hears the orchestra as a single sound, not as a structured myriad, not as an *all*. Unfortunately, as we have considered at length, for our voyage to lead us to some type of outlaw understanding, there needs to be an emerging evolution of hearing. One needs to take the risk of letting go of oneness and hear all the composite sounds and become aware that *oneness* is really the structured orchestration of *all*. To retain a simple oneness experience can be safe. It is the accepted belief, an easy answer. But there is no need to discover the less obvious.

Given the seriousness that many people show in conjunction with their religious assumptions of 'an all-powerful male' at the helm, I am gravely bothered by some children's T-shirts that I saw a number of years ago.

Girls rule.

Boys drool.

These kinds of statements are clearly rebellious and undermine the whole fabric of religion. They are sacrilegious. How could one person even imply that God drools?

Remember, I explained in my introduction to humour that your present was my future. Here is the point where I went back. You are now used to my writing, I hope.

Children are playing, disputing the rules of the game. 'I'm not going to play anymore!' Innocence, fragility, uncertainty, we can see. It's okay. We can smile. We can see the false, the truth.

I made some notes and listed the significant topics we have discussed, and I have also listed some of the strategies we could consider. I put them into different headings:

Into one?

- Symbolic – conceptual possibly beyond paradigms, still point, atman, Buddha, sunyata, oneness, gyre, mandala, collective unconscious, ego, values, good, evil, innocence, experience, karma, orchestra, nonhuman, aum, composer, conductor, duck, swan, water, sea, boat, success
- Scientific/philosophical – theory of everything, time/space/velocity, neurophysiological, biological drive, real, mathematics, logic, aesthetics, string theory, human, nonhuman

- Experiential – point of view, visualisation, music, need for connection, innocence, experience, karma, dynamic oneness, fact/value dichotomy, mystical experience
- Conceptual/phenomenological – ego, cogito ergo sum, sum ergo cogito, point of view, psyche, real success, consciousness, psychosis, biological drive, belief, nation, values, nothing, self, nonphilosophical philosophy, beauty, karma, psychodynamics, nonhuman, enlightenment, categorical imperative
- Myth/delusion – god, afterlife, belief, mores, values, self, philosophy, freedom, good, evil, beauty, karma, success, security

Becoming

The building blocks of wholeness of experience with integration and becoming

- Visualise – symbol ⟶ visual ⟶ experience + new point of view
- Calm – calm ⟶ openness ⟶ relaxation and arousal variability ⟶ experience + new point of view
- Use visualisation + arousal variable ⟶ variable experience + new point of view
- Understanding point of view – including the nonhuman – separateness/nonseparate, tolerance/captive/free, security, order, belonging, universal enemy, smiling Buddha, ego
- Thought/thinking ⟶ experience
  - Integrating the conscious/unconscious
  - Impact of stressors – anxiety
  - Real event/real event, real experiences
  - Dispelling ego – above and below – ego/no ego
  - Smiling Buddha – humour/point of view

As you read the above list of 'Into one?', you would have seen that some topics are listed under several of the five categories. You would also have noted that there are a number of terms or expressions that you may not be familiar with because, even though I may have used them, I have not discussed them. Please bear with me, for I will cover these in a moment.

But first let's relook at the mandala I used on page 149. Though I didn't articulate any specifics on a grand scale, I did suggest that the experience of listening to music can go from a multifactorial, student-based to a multifactorial oneness that is the intuitive-type experience of the learned, experienced listener.

It is interesting that as I was wondering how to phrase these last ideas, searching for words, I paused. I could hear and feel myself listening, enjoying music. Here, I was being the student of words, not finding the intuitive I was writing about.

If we look at each one of the above headings, we can see that, in each area, there is a search for and a language to describe oneness. As we are attempting to approach oneness, I think we need to make it clear that oneness doesn't describe stuff. It refers to structure, essence, or what have you. Take a minute to look at the Aristotelean triangle/gyre on page 49. His view of maximum structure with no substance or matter at its apex is probably a good visual aid to understand this sense of oneness.

For our own purposes and to be symbolically consistent with our use of water and the sea, we could flip Aristotle's gyre (he didn't consider it as a gyre, by the way) upside down. And to elaborate even further, we can consider this gyre like a whirlpool. Near the surface, every molecule of water spins around at a high velocity and moves a large distance. But as you move deeper, it, of course, moves less distance at a reduced speed. In fact, T. S. Eliot sees this progression in one if his water images in 'The Waste Land'. At the bottom of the whirlpool as a 'still point', no molecule moves. It is also like the hypothetical centre of a wheel.

In science, whether it be string theory (see page 109) or a Theory of Everything, many scientists will hypothesise that there must be some fundamental principle that can be articulated and then tested. The hope is that this principle can support and be supported by the laws of physics, mathematics, cell biology, or whatever. This desire to find a single truth is consistent with the Aristotelean gyre as well, though neither may be correct.

Let me take a minute to consider the consistency of our 'still point' and simple mathematics and measurement. Let's say that a water molecule, George, is racing around the top of our whirlpool. Slowly, he moves down to the bottom. Does he reach a still point?

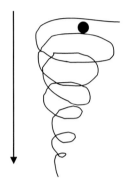

- Molecule George travels a distance of 30 m for one revolution

- Near the bottom George only travels 2 m per revolution
- Closer still, he only travels 2 mm
- Closer still, he only travels 0.001 mm
- Closer still, he only travels 0.000001 mm

When and where does he reach 0?

If we follow our simple mathematical regress, we will never reach zero. But gosh, in real life, things do stop spinning and travel 0 distance. Certainly, the speedometer in my car can say 0. For you, more broad-thinking readers, I am not going to make this example more complex by considering that the contextual environment of a nonmoving object is moving, and I could go on. If we consider the complications and how to resolve them, we need to go to the philosophy of science. It addresses the logic, conceptualisation of scientific theory, and the difficulties that science runs into.

If we consider ethical philosophy, we can see that it too is confronted with the challenge of seeing if a nonempirically based system of thought has a basic principle. Kant's 'categorical imperative' is the statement of this perceived need. Perceived? Because it's an assumption.

From a purely conceptual/phenomenological point of view, I think we are still stuck in the (this is my hypothesis) sum ergo cogito to cogito ergo sum.

The ephemeral structuring of our musicians into orchestras creates a unique structure. It has a collective and is seen as an individual identity (I am), but who really knows?

I chuckled when I heard Stephen Colbert interview an astrophysicist (I think), and for those of you who know Stephen's humour, his direction was obvious. Anyway, it was evident that Stephen was going to ask the astrophysicist (Stephen plays a very simple, rigid-thinking fundamental, Republican role) about his view that many people in America accept 'intelligent design'. His response was that they must have lazy brains.

As you are undoubtedly aware, there is a view I hold that has run throughout this work. It is not driven by my ego but by a collective one below the surface. I come to the surface as the conductor. I sense that there are going to be those who have a 'lazy brain', and I want to have them understand that myth/delusion can reward them with a very fulfilling experience because it meets their own needs. It's how they see, and with it, they achieve a sense of oneness, of single vision. It is also consistent with the way the species have always been, that of the social/human reality. But for the outlaw, it is inimical with how we see a sense of oneness.

As we move ahead, we will leave out what I have called the myth/delusion approach to understanding oneness. It probably meets some basic social/human needs and becomes the belief that limits an openness to any other exploration.

For you who see yourself as Jewish, Muslim, Islam, Christian, Hindu, or whatever, what I have written has no critical impact on your ideology. What does become important, I think, is the social/human evangelistic zeal that we often see is accompanied by lazy-brain approaches.

In a sense, it would be as if we have a rigidly defined school of composing and conducting that dictates how music must be. However, the dictators of this music have never listened to any music more meaningful than Muzak.

But taken as a whole, all these religions, churches, and ideologies could be seen as structurally like but different forms of musical expression. All musical pieces are structured by different sets of rules and forms; they can have a myriad of tonal qualities, key signatures, and time. In fact, we could say that musical expression is all the same and always different. I think we could conclude that if someone only likes one genre of music and believes that all others forms are bad or inferior, they probably don't really understand or appreciate music. If people say that they only have one religious ideology and it is right, then they probably don't understand religion. And religion is only one aspect of the social/human dynamics of each person.

Let's move on.

Oops, I think I should reiterate my basic point about a social/human single belief. It is that this myth/delusion point of view (as I call it) is a way of getting (I grew up with the view that 'get' is a lazy-brain word, but it fits the context) oneness with no effort and no introspection.

Okay, back to the topic at hand, the desire to find a oneness. Shouldn't it be 'an oneness'? Here is a grammatical use that doesn't fit the rules. My question is about exceptions. Are exceptions a function of use? What sounds right? Or are exceptions grammatically defined? If we look at any language, rules have evolved, but I think we could hypothesise that each individual group has inductively established a set of rules. The rules weren't established first. This digression to grammar might seem to fly in the face of our consideration of oneness. The assumption here would seem to be that grammatical rules in all languages evolve. They are not in any way absolute; they are really just a function of use. Ah, but this could be understood in a different manner.

According to structural anthropologists like Lévi-Strauss, structurally similar myths and beliefs are created by peoples who have never had a known connection with each other. Could we not conclude that there is a single universal human need that establishes myths, rules of conduct, rules of grammar that are all seen as truths? Conflict can arise because the terminology or expression may be different even though the same structure exists.

> Schoenberg is highly structured atypically—music is not always social/human listener friendly.

> Bach is highly structured with complexity—music is social/human listener friendly.

> Popular music is simplistically structured—music is very social/human friendly.

On a social/human level, there is the distraction of what I like, know, and feel; what I am comfortable with; and what I don't know and feel anxious about. Ironically, it could be that the lateral traveller feels anxious about what is the known (because the experience was not fulfilling, our duck-swan analogy) except what they do goes to a different set of ducks. Some may never find their swan characteristic.

Of course, from all these, there is, I could suggest, a oneness of structure with, I think, two connected components. First, human needs have an underlying structure that manifests itself in mythologies, nationalism, and ethnocentric scripts. And second, the species, except for those 'hapless few', don't understand the underlying sameness in structure. They believe that since things look different on the surface, they are.

Light behaves in a way that we know; there are particles, but it also behaves like a wave. An old question (well, not that old) was an either/or one. Is light a wave or particle? The desire for oneness was there, though in physics the other way of answering this, like string theory, is that it may not be an either/or; it could be a oneness that explains both.

So what does all this mean? If we think of our smiling Buddha as we have considered him—by the way, he's male but could be considered as sexually ambivalent; we haven't covered that yet, but we'll do that in due course—anyway, his smile incorporates many experiences. It shows wisdom, it shows happiness, it requires a different point of view, which brings separateness. But in this, there is no separateness. There is a oneness of structure.

S. N. Goenka is quoted as saying at the end of each of his Vipassana meditation training days, 'May all things be happy!'—happy musicians, happy George at the bottom of the whirlpool, happy with discovery and new insightful experience.

A Consideration of Time:
What Does It Have to Do with Anything?

Once again, I ask you to indulge me as the writer. I have feeling, a sense of wonder. I am seeing something that is rare but also have a sense of humility.

Is it circular? Is it linear? Is it multidimensional? Is it a function of movement? Is it a function of change? But more importantly, how do you experience it? You may say, 'I don't have enough time,' 'Time flies,' 'It's hard to believe that many years have passed.' Or you might also say, 'When will this be over?' 'When will we get there?' 'That's old! It was popular last year,' 'I didn't do well in the race. I was 2.35 seconds behind the winner,' or 'Time is money. Money makes the world go around.'

Einstein saw time as multi- or at least bidimensional, depending on our point of view.

Here's an image that I have always found interesting. It is attributed to Albert Einstein and describes his experience of taking a tram that was moving away from a clock tower. He knew that light moved at a limited speed. It isn't instantly everywhere, and he speculated that, hypothetically, his tram could move faster and faster and could ultimately go the speed of light. So here's the question: If he moved away from the clock that read, let us say, 10:08 at the speed of light, the clock's image that he was seeing would remain at 10:08, so what would be his time experience? Would time stop for him? Would his experience of time continue as he travelled but his time, relative to other measures of time, would be different? Let's say he travelled for thirty minutes as he measured by the clock, and then he stopped his travel at the speed of light. At the moment he stopped, the time would be 10:38 according to the clock on the tower; and of course, his experience would be that 'I thought I experienced life in a normal manner, as if time moved on normally.' His obvious question is, is there a relationship between time and velocity? It doesn't offer the science, but it does offer the question. What is time and its relationship to other phenomena? Before responding to this question and others related to time, I would like to consider some other relevant concepts.

A Consideration of Space and Its Relationship To . . .

If I use a diagram, picture, or empty page, I am using space differently from I would be using space to write. In this work, space can help develop understanding but can also take us in the wrong direction or confuse us.

I have used space most often in a time/space manner. I have left some pages almost blank so that you could spend time contemplating but still be able to turn pages with some temporal consistency. The direction of our gyres either increases space or decreases it. We have a vast ever-expanding universe or a narrowing one that approaches a single point.

It seems to me that some of the relationships between points in space were first structured formally by Euclidian theorems, and these were used in the early development of astronomy and physics. Space and the relationship of lines and size are certainly fundamental to art and architecture.

Our experiences of space could include being closed in or being in a vast open plain or sea, and each of these can influence each of us differently. Space is always present, always influential, though we may not be aware. 'Are we there yet?' (time and space).

How many spaces do we have?

Question: If it takes one man eight hours to dig one hole, how long does it take him to dig half a hole?

Answer: There's no such thing as half a hole. But of course, there could be half a whole; therefore, there could be half a whole hole.

Of course, this kid's riddle does offer an example of a confusion we can have with our use of some concepts and what they represent. It illustrates not only the confusion with homonyms but also the polymorphous nature of words like hole, space, universe, et cetera. These are singular nouns; they are not collective and do have a clear paradigm. (Remember Flew?) But experientially, they are very different. Yes, we have one universe, and therefore, it could be considered a single entity, but we can also have one atom. It is also a singular, noncollective noun; thus the atom is the same. Yeah, what about the amount of space they take up and the amount of stuff in each? What about the fact we can visualise what we think an atom is like but we can't visualise a limitless universe?

So if we want to consider space or even time or velocity, we could do this in a number of ways. We could look at it in a scientific way, an experiential way, or even a grammatical/semantic way.

If we looked at this in a grammatical/semantic way, that would seem to make sense, but it would be kind of cheating because it doesn't represent experience. We can't just make the universe a single entity because it is a singular noun.

As I did with time, I would like to cover some other topics before we consider a new way (really, a very old way) of understanding time/space.

Experience to Symbol to Experience: Putting Some Pieces Together

In the early part of this work, I made reference to a large number of symbols and considered their inadequacy in explaining the dynamics of my friend. We considered a whole bunch of terms, usually defined by bimodal concepts, that might describe her. At that point, we didn't attempt to step in her shoes and experience her life; instead, we used those dynamics to get a cognitive picture of what might help us understand her. Though we had some fun considering the conscious/unconscious, transformations, creative/free, social/human, and a whole myriad of symbolic type terms, we still didn't capture her essence.

When we considered the practice of visualisation, I wanted you to not only be able to reexperience memories but also create a new experience through mental/physical imagery exercises so that you would be able to visualise something that you hadn't experienced before.

Some of the visualisation exercises that we have used could be described in an inverse manner. Typically, some heuristic moment is triggered by an outside-of-self 'real' (experienced) event that affects a person, and a light goes on—Einstein moving away on the tram, my experience of watching the waves above me. At other times, it could be someone's own dream, imagination, or thought that doesn't seem to be tied to an external event, but it is heuristic. The mind is the still pond; the musicians are wandering, forming orchestras.

In addition to some momentary experience(s), I hope that some of the visualisations and our approach to understanding oneness have offered you some interesting insights and some appreciation of underlying dynamics that you may not have thought about before.

From our discussions, we have considered that a real psychophysiological experience can come from an image or thought, as well as from a 'real' event. Depending on someone's beliefs and neurophysiology, it may be difficult for some people to tell whether some experiences are a dream, hallucination, strong feeling, or an actual event.

As a result, some people may see an image in the following manner:

It could be something I see in the outside world, nothing special.

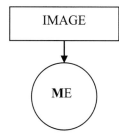

- The image separates from *me*, like an outside event.

- The image that has nothing to do with *me*.

It could even be that the image is representative of something else.

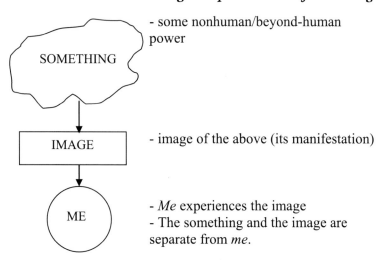

- some nonhuman/beyond-human power

- image of the above (its manifestation)

- *Me* experiences the image
- The something and the image are separate from *me*.

Yet some others may experience the same phenomenon very differently.

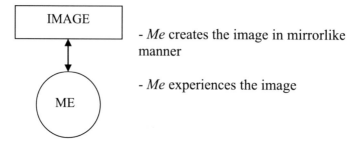

- *Me* creates the image in mirrorlike manner

- *Me* experiences the image

Me *is seen as part of the* **something** *and all other things for that* **matter.**

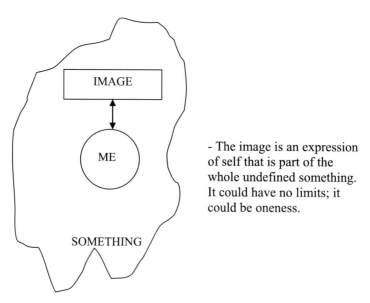

- The image is an expression of self that is part of the whole undefined something. It could have no limits; it could be oneness.

In a sense, I could say that the image is an expression of *me* and 'I and the image' are expressions of some vast something.

If we accept these distinctions in a person's experienced visualisation, we can see how understanding one's point of view and thinking is important in developing new experiences. For Einstein, we might surmise that his 'real' experience was transformed into a symbolic one that saw his 'me' as part of a scientifically explained universe, immersed in the something and moving within it.

A religious epiphany—What's happening?

So someone has a moment of epiphany and experiences God's presence in an external 'not me' manner. The person contends that he was really there! Do we want to see if we can visualise this person's experience? Sure.

Let's look at this further and consider this person's experience as seeing a non-*me* and that it is experienced as something real that is outside oneself. We have a separation. 'God spoke to me!' Do you get a feeling for this situation? Consider some of the following possibilities that would be necessary for achieving this state:

The person's statement 'I experienced him!' could be considered a delusion, but it may not be, at least as defined in psychiatric terms. Yet from a rational perspective, we would need to consider that the experience, which seems like a *something* (i.e., God) to the *image* to *me*, was actually a *me* to the *image* to *me*. In fact, experiencing something that is inside the self as something that has come from the external world may show that

- the ego strength is probably low but could be portrayed as high, or it is low and experienced that way;
- the person is not self-aware;
- there is a nonintegrated self;
- as I mentioned, the person could have a diagnosed psychosis or could have personal dynamics that need a father/mother figure (that sounds pretty cliché, doesn't it?); there are a bunch of other possibilities here.

I could give many other personality qualities to think about. Consider how an all-knowing father-type image can be experienced by someone whose basic security/identity needs are not met. They could feel alone and unsafe. But then all their needs are met in the embodiment of one person, a supreme being. This acceptance takes all stresses off them. One who was lost at sea and was overwhelmed now has someone to guide, to bring them home. They have hope. The parent is there to look after them.

I think it is important to at least understand this predominant social/ human point of view so that you can really experience the differences between an insight that seems to be expressive of a truth and a truth that simply makes *me* feel better. Understanding a truth may require years of experience in understanding the sea, or one may see *me* as an ephemeral expression of some limitless something. With the acceptance of a god figure, all is well with the world. There is no need to look further. Herein lies the nature of a religious epiphany.

I have found that writing this section with my expressed need to understand this experience of epiphany, at least for a social/human person, has heightened my own arousal; it has triggered some surface issues, which I will discuss in 'Reflections on Composing and Conducting', which comes in Part IV.

I also realised, as I reread the above few paragraphs, that my reactivity at this point wasn't to what I had written here but to what I was unconsciously experiencing but didn't write. The trigger of my heightened arousal wasn't a father need or a separation of self and image per se but an egocentric one. From a social/human perspective, I felt that what I was stating was just another 'I know the answer, the truth', which was a don't-believe-in-*me*-based truths, a believe-in-non-*me*-type truths. I was really just saying the same thing. The epiphany becomes 'Now I believe in *not me*, and this gives me strength.'

To make a distinction between *me*-based truths and more all-pervasive-based nontruths, which, of course, are truths, I felt I needed to consider other qualities of one's epiphany. I think a 'strong'-'weak' distinction may assist. In the ***'My Friend and Others: The Nonduck Realities'*** section, we discussed *strong* and *weak* as one of many symbolic dualities. One distinction we made was that the social/human *strong* may not be strong even from a literal survival-of-the-fittest point of view. Our example illustrates that *strong* may actually be *weak*, and *weak* could be seen as *strong*.

What we could say here is that, if an epiphany results in one seeing some 'truth' that gives someone strength and resolve in purpose, then their epiphany is social/human and may be seen as *strong* but is inherently *weak* because it is based on some created truth. Conversely, if an epiphany's sudden insight is that beliefs are really seen as delusions that help *me* feel strength and that any *me*, civilisation, or even species would be deluded if they believed in their own self-importance, a nontruth revelation could emerge. *Me* is simply an ephemeral grouping of musicians, nothing more. *Me* is a brief manifestation of the world of maya. In a sense, hanging on to the social/human is *weak*. Accepting the unlimited all, the unknown, the voidlike nature offers a non-*me strong*.

What we see here is an inherent contradiction in the use of strength and its sense of superiority. Surface *strong* could be combined with a strong dependency need, a belief, an underlying *weak*. These people experience a sense of personal strength, knowledge of the truth, and superiority over others based on believing that they have *the answer*; however, take away their answer, and they have nothing. It is this hypocrisy that I find distressful.

It is somewhat ironic that my suggested visualisation exercise is to experience this sense of dependency on God, but my ability to put myself through this exercise at this point is variable. My desire is to have you experience a social/human point of view, but this is conflicted by my desire to experience a timeless sense of oneness that is *not* human and *not* God. However, for fragile social/human creatures on the surfaces, accepting the nonhuman may be very difficult to emotionally. As I try to resist my desire to say 'listen!' I realise that my relationship with my friend represented a very fragile need that reduced my desire to express myself in more nonhuman terms. I was contented with the ephemeral. But my need to make some type of difference is high. As I ask you to become, i am coming closer to the end of this work.

So my response to my own suggested exercise has told me a number of things, all of which are important to all of us. At the time I wrote the above, which was yesterday, I found it difficult to simply experience the almost naïve innocence of seeing an all-giving higher-order being, a father. As mentioned, it was blocked by my thoughts about those many who have this innocent need on one level because with these views often comes an intolerant, opinionated, and possibly socially aggressive behaviour in support of their views. Unfortunately, it would seem that the person who has medically diagnosed delusions and is incapable of accepting rational discussion is really no different. What we could more accurately assume is that those who *know* the truth are not developmentally ready for understanding and that there are lots of different reasons why people understand differently.

If we are calm, we can see ourselves as one of the wandering musicians maybe moving into a new orchestra. We are playing as one of the group. We can also imagine that the whole orchestra has its own unique sounds. Though our image is coming from *me*, it is coming from just a component of the overall structure. Remember, my ego comes from the all; it's not a separate me.

Karma: Good Karma Is Bad Karma

This next term has similar dynamics to our Buddhist smile and is consistently misunderstood. In the past, we left our discussion of karma because I felt I had not developed a suitable context to describe it. As I had mentioned, karma is not a social/human term. However, in Western culture, it gets transformed into doing good social/human deeds, behaving well. It is even tied into rewards and punishments. Good karma leads you to good stuff, and you get paid for it. Bad karma is the opposite; the consequences are bad.

These above dynamics have nothing to do with karma. As I have mentioned, *karma* is an outlaw term. It's on the same plane as the Buddhist smile. For instance, 'right thought' doesn't mean feeling good thoughts about others. It means thinking in a manner consistent with the smiling Buddha. It is thinking at another level. If you have developed a new understanding in our last section and can experience different points of view, you may see that some people could be devout Christians and dedicate themselves to helping others and do a wonderful job, while some other people may be misfits, not get what life is all about. Really, they don't seem to do anything for anybody, but when we look at their lives, we may see that their point of view is more consistent with how karma is really understood.

Once again, I have the writer/instructor dilemma. In this case, I, like the writer, am expressing a point of view and feel that if you are uncertain about my train of thought, then you need to read some texts that explain the concepts.[6] One doesn't understand James Joyce's <u>Ulysses</u> unless you are well read.

Hopefully, you took a moment to read my notes. If not, please read them now; there is a little editorial piece to it.

And after all this, I am going to suggest something else. From my point of view, it doesn't really matter whether you understand karma at this point. You can move ahead, and I don't think you need any definitions. However, what is important is that if you don't understand or if you really do understand (whatever that means), both are okay. If you think you do and you don't, that could suggest bad karma.

I realise that my ramblings have taken on a number of different functions. Am I the writer/composer? Or the teacher/conductor? Do i indulge myself in writing and let you figure out what I am saying, or do I try to talk to you? Engage you? And as you are aware, I am really doing both. I guess my desire is to appreciate the personal voyage of others whom i have never met; to try, and hopefully offer, some techniques that

---

[6] Caution: My goal in defining any term is to understand not just how it is used but also the essence of its meaning. But how is this done? I may have to expand this in the appendix, or have you consider reference texts? But there can be a problem with reference texts. There are primary and secondary. However, for many of you, there may be even another level—a tertiary level (?). It is funny that this level had never dawned on me until the moment I wrote this footnote.

Primary – You read the original text that defines some concept. These are often very hard to read and give little in return for readers not experienced in the area. This is also evident with some scientific terminology.

Secondary – There are good writers who are well conversant in an area and give an accurate assessment of terminology. The problem is the new reader of an area may need to rely on 'science journalist' translation of some term. Sometimes that works well; sometimes it doesn't.

Tertiary – Popular media and the Internet—these seem to be the ultimate social/human resources, full of sound and fury, signifying nothing. To understand a social/human perspective, I think they are great. To understand anything beyond that, unless you go to some academic website, the essence of many concepts may be too compromised.

I hope will open you to more insightful experiences; and to assist you in approaching a sense of oneness.

At this point and in anticipation of describing my personal sense of oneness, I am uncertain about how well I will be able to keep the teacher/conductor aspect to my writing. I think I need to just express, to compose. No, I think I need to be the conductor/teacher.

I think I need to include a record of some 'conducting' dialogues. These dialogues are with different people with diverse backgrounds and different ways in which they understand themselves and life.

A Consideration of People, where One Is Now: Let's Move to Some Real Dialogues and Experience Some Human Interaction

These are offered to give perspective to some different human points of view and how they can change with dialectic interchange. I hope that these may help you get a sense of where you are in your own thoughts and where discussion and insight may lead you.

My interaction with a literal thinker was interesting. This person didn't understand why it would be beneficial to change one's point of view. He started by asking a question.

'So what's the point?'

'Here's my point.'

'But that's just the creation of the point of your pen. Don't be stupid. This isn't funny. I want an answer.'

'So what is an answer? Or maybe more to the point is what answer do you want?'

'Life has to have meaning, doesn't it? So maybe the point needs to encompass some kind of meaning, single purpose, if you will.'

'There is a dot made on this page by my pen. What more do you want?'

'You're not making any sense. I think this conversation is pointless. Do you agree?'

'Yes.'

A young university science student is somewhat confused and would like to understand what he has learned.

'The big bang theory seems to accept that the whole universe has come from one explosive event of very dense matter, and it is considered to be still expanding. Is that correct?'

'That sounds okay.'

'Then how can the whole universe be squished into some kind of small ball? New matter must grow or something. Otherwise, it's not possible.'

'What's the matter?'

'Nothing. I'm just asking a question.'

'Let me take out "the" and ask again. What's matter?'

'Matter? It's our physical world, the earth, rocks, people—you know, it's pretty obvious.'

'Okay, so what is nonmatter?'

'It's the space between objects. That's pretty straightforward.'

'Could matter be, to use your terms, more space than matter?'

'Well, not really. It's dense. It has weight. It's solid.'

'Here, I am asking a question again. Can you see particles of dust?'

'Well, no, not normally, but sometimes if the sun is shining in a particular way, I can see some dust in the air.'

'I have some more questions for you. Boy, I'm becoming the questioner here, aren't I? So here's my first question. Are dust particles solid matter?'

'Well, they are probably not too solid. If they were too solid, they wouldn't be able to float in the air.'

'Air, you mentioned air. Is air something? Or is it space?'

'This conversation is getting a bit absurd. Of course, air is made of something.'

'You are understandably tired of this conversation, which makes sense. Unfortunately, I am not able to give you an answer.'

'Why not?'

'Answers will not give you an answer to your question. You need to see first, and that requires patience.'

'What, do you think I need glasses?'

'I don't know, but it is not that your eyes are bad. In fact, it is the reverse. It sounds like you only see with your eyes. That vision is very limited and misleading.'

'I don't understand. All I wanted was for you to give me an answer to a simple question. I know what I have read. I can repeat what they have said, but I don't really get it.'

'If a blind person who has never seen blue asked you to tell him what blue looks like, what would you tell him?'

'You're just avoiding answering my questions.'

'What would you tell him?'

'I don't know! I guess I wouldn't get an answer to my big bang question. I appreciate your time, but I don't really get it. I appreciate your time, but I don't really understand where you are going. Maybe another time. Thank you.'

'Understanding comes to the ready mind. Without readiness, there is no learning. The teacher needs to know that setting the circumstance for establishing readiness is teaching by not teaching.'

A middle-aged student of philosophy who enjoys discussions on the nature of freedom saw a man with his dog and wondered.

'I saw a man the other day with his dog on one of these leashes that wind up into the handle. The dog was right out at the end, running around in a big circle. It looked strange because he didn't seem to be chasing anything.'

'What do you think would happen if the leash broke?'

'I don't know. Maybe it would take off or something. Well, I guess, even though his leash is long, the dog is still tied up.'

'What would you do if you were the dog?'

'I'd probably take off and go where I wanted to.'

'Where's that?'

'I don't know. I'm not the dog. Maybe follow some scent, chase a cat or something.'

'Would you go back to your owner instead of going in some other direction?'

'Oh yeah, eventually, but I'd probably want some freedom first, just do what I wanted.'

'Could running back to your owner be freedom?'

'No, it wouldn't be freedom. It would be like being back on the leash, but I guess if I liked my owner, I'd come back but, as I said, probably not right away.'

'What if you didn't like your owner?'

'Well, if it were me, I probably wouldn't. But if I were a dog, I probably would since dogs really don't know any better.'

'Do you think that a dog may even return to an abusive owner?'

'Yeah, sure.'

'So what is abusive?'

'Well, you know, tying him up, hitting him, yelling, you know, abusing him.'

'Could we say that the owner is trying to control him?'

'Sure, he wants the dog to behave.'

'So does freedom for the dog mean not behaving?'

'Well, not really. He could still behave and not do anything bad but could be off the leash.'

'So is he really off his leash? It sounds like the owner may know that he's literally off his leash, but he doesn't really do anything bad, so is he, in some absolute sense, still on his leash?'

'Well, I guess so, but no, I don't think so. He's just being a dog. Dogs do things. As long as he's not biting or attacking someone, it's okay.'

'All right, behaving like a dog is okay if he's just being a dog, and being free is also okay because one's not being controlled by another. But if a dog is free or even on a leash and hurts people, that's not okay. Is that what you are saying?'

'Yeah, that makes sense.'

'But does it? Could we accept that, from what you are saying, there is a leash connecting the owner to the dog?'

'Duh, well, of course.'

'Could we assume that there are genetic aspects of a species [Konrad Lorenz, sorry for throwing that in at this point] and that other developmentally influential conditions could be seen to be like "leashes"? They end up controlling the dog's behaviour.'

'I'm not sure exactly what you mean.'

'Could we assume that there are certain behaviours that each species displays that are like leashes? They are tied to the species, and these limit their abilities and how they behave.'

'Well, I guess so.'

'A man was playing chess [not Bobby Fischer] with his dog, and a friend dropped into his house and saw them playing. The friend was amazed—wow, a dog playing chess—and expressed his amazed reaction to his friend. His friend responded, "It's not that amazing. I beat him two out of three times."'

'I get your point, so what am I supposed to say?'

'You don't have to say anything, but what we may see is that dogs are limited by something. It could be a genetic leash. It could be a developmental leash. If we follow this logic, it could be that the owner is also controlled by a genetic, developmental, or situational leash. In fact, it could even be that freedom, as you see it, is defined in such a way that it is just another leash. The dog, as you see him, goes from his owner's leash to his genetic leash and maybe to wanting freedom leash.'

'Well, I guess what you say makes sense, but I need time to think about it.'

'Take time to reflect then.'

'I feel you are kind of manipulating me. I agree for the moment because I can't find something to immediately disagree with, but when I think about it, it feels like it must be wrong.'

'Take your time. Think also about whether the dog is "freer" trying to escape the limits of his leash or by moving "freely" within his limits.'

'Well, when you put it that way, that kind of makes sense. We have freedom, but we can't do everything, and I guess if we do something because we are free, we are not free of our reaction to believing we were not free.'

'So what do you think would happen if the leash broke?'

'Well, I guess some dogs may take off, but others may not.'

'Is the dog who takes off free?'

'Yeah, I see what you mean. He may be free of the owner's leash, but no matter what he does, he's still limited by the fact that he's a dog. I guess that's another kind of leash as you say.'

'So what about the well-trained dog that doesn't need a leash?'

'I guess he's still on a leash of sorts too.'

A midtwenties female who has struggled with her own identity and ability made an innocent mistake while travelling across the prairies. A dialogue that she wasn't expecting followed.

'The ground is very flat here, and this road we're standing on is perfectly straight. You can really appreciate perspective. Look how the sides of the road meet at the horizon.'

'Do parallel lines eventually meet if you are standing on a large plain?'

'No, they just look like that.'

'Why?'

'It's just the nature of perspective. Things look smaller than they are farther away. You know that!'

'So your vision says the sides of the road come to a single point, but something else says, "No, they don't." Is that right?'

'Of course, it's a road. It carries on.'

'So let's say that it's not a road. It's some kind of parallel-looking structure that goes off a long way in the distance [you think]. Could you tell for sure whether this structure has parallel sides that never meet or has sides that meet?'

'Well, no. I couldn't say for sure.'

'So it sounds like you have your knowledge and thinking work with your vision, and they give you an answer.'

'Yeah, that makes sense.'

'But with the unknown, our experience and thoughts tell you that lines may look like they are parallel but aren't. Vision says the sides are not parallel but could be. So you may apply a rule that is built on the assumption that all roads, railway tracks, or other similar structures that go off in the distance will look like they meet because of perspective but actually don't. Your rule may be as simple as lines that look parallel probably are. If they go off in the distance, they will look like they meet but don't.

'Sure.'

'So just to affirm, can you always trust what you see? Or what you see must be true?'

'Well, certainly, most of the time but, as we have just discussed, not always.'

'Could you say that you can correct your false vision by knowledge?'

'Sometimes, like you said, if it's familiar, but sometimes we may not know for sure.'

'So what is true?'

'In this case, I guess I don't really know.'

'Is it true that you think?'

'Well, yes.'

'So the fact that you think is true.'

'Yeah, that's what I said.'

'Is it true that you sometimes use your thinking to qualify or explain what you see?'

'Yes.'

'So our second truth is that your thoughts may influence your visual perception. Then if we consider our hypothetical structure that goes off to the horizon and if we don't change our limited perspective, could we say that these two human truths, when combined, lead us to some type of objective truth?'

'No, we can't really say that, not in this situation. We wouldn't be able to tell whether they were parallel. We'd have to travel to the end or something to find out.'

'Ah, could we then conclude that truth doesn't always lead us to truth, especially if it is beyond the familiar, the predictable?'

'I guess, but you're mixing up your uses of truth. You're doing something like that, but just because it's true that I think, it doesn't mean my thinking will lead me to some other truthful understanding or something like that.'

'So thinking doesn't lead us to truth.'

'Well, not necessarily. Some people can think better than others.'

'Can good thinkers arrive at the truth?'

'Yeah, that's what scientists do. They're bright.'

'So could we say that it is true that good thinkers can find the truth?'

'Sure, eventually.'

'Do you see any limits? Could a good thinker solve our simple parallel line problem?'

'Well, maybe not right away, but they could find some way. That's part of being a genius.'

'What about you? You can think. You can see. Could you not find some truth?'

'Well, I guess so, but I even get confused by your questions, and I'm not even sure what point you're trying to make. I feel kind of dumb.'

'Do you think that being dumb and confused is a sign of not being very perceptive or a sign of perceptiveness?'

'Well, that's obvious. Not very perceptive, kind of dumb.'

'You know that is the second statement you have made that is not expressing a truth.'

'What? I think I've had lots.'

'You have said you don't know—true. You said you think—true. You have said that we couldn't necessarily tell about the parallel quality of the lines to the horizon. You agreed with my statement that good thinkers can find a truth. Eventually, they may find some, even many but won't get all. So maybe you weren't quite right there, but we need to look at your being confused. You tied it to not being perceptive. You couldn't tell me for sure whether our hypothetical figure has parallel sides. You were confused. Is that correct?'

'Yes.'

'Were you confused at first when you assumed it was a road?'

'No. I didn't think about other possibilities.'

'So you became confused after I presented other possibilities to you, do you agree?'

'Yes.'

'So did more awareness, greater insight allow you to see the truth or make you confused?'

'Well, it made me confused because I couldn't figure out the truth.'

'Would you repeat that?'

'It made me confused because I couldn't figure out the truth.'

'Ah, now that is a truth.'

'Well, not really because it couldn't give you an answer.'

'You are jumping ahead. You're being too hard on yourself. You had an answer, and you weren't confused. At first, you knew you had the truth, but you were open to questioning and being confused. Being confused is a very important door. Finding truths, in some absolute sense, is probably false. You may never find any.'

She gasped. 'Does that mean I'll be dumb forever?'

'What did greater insight bring you?'

'I know, I know. Okay, being confused and uncertain.'

'And what does uncertainty afford you?'

'Okay, okay, a need to sort out the mess and find an answer.'

'Remember, you may sort out the mess, but it may lead you into another quandary. You may never find a truth that eliminates your confusion unless you go backwards and accept.'

'So it sounds like what you are saying is that I can feel comfortable if I accept the truths of what I see and not question, and that was where I was before you kept asking me questions. I liked that state because it was easy.'

'Well, that isn't exactly what I would like you to see. That is a truth. Could you accept that "confusion" is a rewarding state? That it's not connected with being dumb but being curious, open to ideas, and really not dumb, whatever that means? So what is your sense of truth?'

'Well, expressing what I feel.'

'Yes, that is truth.'

'And I guess this sounds dumb, but not knowing the truth and even being confused, from what you're saying, is not dumb. It could even be smart.'

'The door is opening.'

'That's good because I'm confused about what I even said.'

One of my readers who sees the obvious but misses the essence has some questions.

'This work has a lot of circles and triangles. You must really like them.'

'It's not that I necessarily like them. They work.'

'What do you mean?'

'Expression needs a vehicle. The vehicle needs to work.'

'What do you mean by vehicle? I think I have it a bit, but I'm not sure.'

'A vehicle—whether bicycle or airplane—takes you from one place to another. The ways or methods we use to explain, teach, or just express something are our vehicle. We use different vehicles to assist someone in going from no understanding to experienced understanding. In a way, it defines our process. In fact, our approach to understanding may not be direct. What do you think? Do we stop and smell the flowers, challenge ourselves with the speed of getting there, or just focus on getting there?'

'I can understand that, but what about the circles and triangles?'

'These vehicles of circles, triangles, diagrams, and writing are there to assist you in an experiential voyage that, at first, might look like you are going from point A to point B. But hopefully, they help you understand that they aren't going to get you to point B. In fact, just to confuse you more, there isn't any point B. It's an illusion.'

'Okay, hold it a minute. I don't know where you are going. Anyway, I now have two questions. One, why the circles and triangles? And two, why should I read this or listen to you if you don't have any point B? You are not taking me anywhere. I feel like I need an answer.'

'Life is a process, not an end. This work is a process, not an end.'

'I find this frustrating. You're not giving me any direct answers.'

'What about circles and triangles? Does this conversation seem somewhat circular?'

'Yeah, does it ever? Can't you just answer my question?'

'I can.'

'Well, why don't you?'

'I have.'

A man in his fifties with some clearly defined values discusses hard work and experience.

'"You learn from hard work and experience," my old grandfather used to say.'

'Would you agree?'

'Yeah, pretty much. You need to have experience in doing something before you're good at it, and usually, it takes some work to get there.'

'When your grandfather referred to learning, what did he mean by that?'

'Well, really just what I said, you learn from experience.'

'Do you think that he was referring to learning a specific skill, or was he making a statement about life in general?'

'He always had answers about how things should be. It was one of his statements that he made that was about life. In fact, when I think about it, he had lots of sayings that were kind of like wise advice.'

'What did he do?'

'He had his own business that was quite successful. In fact, he built it from the ground up. He had tugs and barges and moved materials up and down the coast.'

'So his experience sounds like it was interesting.'

'Yeah, he was a really interesting person. He always had lots of interesting stories about the sea, boats, how things used to be. He was kind of bigger than life.'

'Would you ever ask him questions?'

'Lots of times.'

'Would he have answers for you?'

'I could honestly say he was never without an answer. In fact, he would sometimes give me answers even when I didn't ask a question.'

'If you think about his responses, were they factual, or were they his opinions?'

'They were both, but when he answered any questions or expressed something, even his opinions sounded like facts. It was like he knew things. He didn't have to think about them.'

'We can see that he had a fulfilling life and had many experiences that were different from most people. Do you think he could understand others who were very different from him? Someone like an oboe player or poet?'

'I'm not sure, but he probably didn't even know what an oboe player was, and I can't imagine that he had any interest in poets or poetry. He wasn't that kind of guy.'

'I am assuming that he moved supplies to different towns and cities, probably logs, building supplies, and other products that companies needed and people needed.'

'Yeah, I think he could feel some importance in helping others. He would sometimes talk about how he got products through stormy seas so the mill could keep running or some community would have their supplies.'

'It sounds like he was very pragmatic and a physical doer. Do you think he ever questioned himself?'

'I think so. In his stories, he would sometimes talk about whether they could get through some bad weather or whether a business decision was going to be the right one.'

'Do you think he ever wondered whether he should be a poet or not?'

'That's a dumb question. Why would he even think about that? I bet he'd see poetry as a waste of time. It doesn't create jobs, feed people, give them shelter. He'd probably see the poet as somewhat wimpy and self-indulgent and not very realistic.'

'Do you think the poet works at poetry?'

'Do you mean me or my grandfather?'

'I mean you. Does the poet work at writing?'

'Well, I guess.'

'Do you think the poet learns from the experience of writing?'

'Yeah, I would imagine that the more you write, the more you learn, I guess.'

'So I think it would make sense if the poet said, "You learn from hard work and experience." In fact, the oboe player could say the same thing. In these ways, both the poet and the musician are exactly the same as your grandfather, aren't they?'

'No! They're totally different. You obviously don't understand how I've described him. He had to fight the sea. He built a business. The poet doesn't have to do any of that. He just sits and writes.'

'The poet sails through a sea of words, builds a poem or a whole book of poetry.'

'You're just playing with words. You're trying to mix apples and oranges. You can't do that!'

'What is an apple?'

'A fruit. I don't see the point in this.'

'What type of plant does it grow on?'

'What do you mean? A tree?'

'What is an orange?'

'A fruit obviously.'

'What type of plant does it grow on?'

'Well, a tree. Yeah, but oranges don't grow in a northern climate.'

An artist who has read these ramblings to this point raises some questions about art critics, but the discussion moves into new territory.

'Matthew Collings is an artist. I think he would accept that label anyway. He writes an article for a journal called *Modern Painters* that he entitles "Diary".'

'You have given me some information about this person. Why do you mention him?'

'He seems really critical as in negative, though he's not totally that way. He does express positives, but my overall impression is that he has this negative view of almost every painter he discusses.'

'Is negative based on oneself and their point of view? Is it based on some general principles of what is good or bad or some universally defined criteria?'

'Well, it's not universal, but it's also not just one's point of view. It's somewhere in between.'

'Where does your critic fit?'

'He fits somewhere in the middle. He's not—let me start again. I don't think he would like this, but I think he is stuck between how he sees today's world and the importance of recognising that and his own creative drive and his appreciation of that drive in others.'

'Is the creation of some artistic expression good no matter what? Someone may simply say, "I expressed how I feel. It must be good art."'

'That's an extreme position. The person has to have some talent or skill but then also has to say something.'

'So would it be correct to say that the artist could be criticised on the skill of expression but also on what was expressed?'

'Absolutely.'

'So how do you evaluate these criteria?'

'That sounds like a pretty straightforward question, but it's not. It's such a big question that it's hard to know where to begin.'

'Do artists and critics learn from experience?'

'Sure, that's a big part of it.'

'Do you need to learn from your artistic experiences?'

'Absolutely.'

'Is there work involved?'

'Sure.'

'So if someone has many years of artistic experience and has learned over all this time, can we have faith in his/her judgement?'

'No, not necessarily.'

'So what is missing?'

'This may sound strange, and I haven't really thought about it before, but there is almost an ironic "ego" piece, if one's ego is a dominant feature and it could be because someone needs to have an ego, but it really isn't how they really feel inside. And as I think about this, it could be that they may have a big ego because they have no insight. Does that make sense?'

'Yes, so does Matthew Collings have some dominant ego influence?'

'I think so. He expresses his views, which is interesting stylistically, but in doing so, he's narrowed what he thinks is good. It's interesting in saying this because it could be his intensity. Maybe that's what I'm picking up.'

'It sounds like you're being the art critic of the art critic. Does his diary say something about him or others' art?'

'You're right. He's expressing himself. His diary, as I think about it, is one expression of his own art.'

'Is one's expressed analysis of others an expression of self or a description of others?'

'Boy, that's hard to answer. There certainly are times when I think people are wrong, but there are other times when I can see it's more my personal hang-up. Yeah. That does make it difficult?'

'This is good. You have seen a fundamental point.'

'So what is the point?'

'You have listened to [read] a number of unrelated dialogues. Is that correct?'

'Yes.'

'Did they seem to go somewhere?'

'Well, I'm not actually sure. I questioned it but never really gave it much thought.'

'That makes sense. Let's take a moment to review these. What about the first one, the one about the point?'

'That was kind of dumb. You were just making a play on words. It was just a pun. It didn't say anything.'

'Could the point be a pun?'

'I guess so, but that's not much of a point.'

'But it could say something else, couldn't it? What does it say about our use of words?'

'What do you mean?'

'To make a pun in a language, we need to have a particular relationship between words.'

'Do you mean that there needs to be two words with . . . um . . . the same sound or I guess with a similar sound but with different meanings?'

'Exactly, so what does that say about our use of words to communicate?'

'Well, I guess we could sometimes misunderstand what someone else is saying if a word the person uses may have different meanings.'

'Exactly, so do you think that a symbolic meaning could be seen as punlike in its structure?'

'What do you mean? I don't get what you're asking. I don't see any relationship.'

'Puns are generally considered as humour, would you agree?'

'Well, yeah, supposed to be.'

'Could we say that a pun is humourous because it replaces the meaning that makes sense with one that is humourous in the context? For instance, I could ask, "Am I punishing you with the conversation?"'

'Yeah. Ha ha! That makes sense, sure.'

'Could we agree that a pun—a play on words, if you will—makes a connection between a word and seemingly unrelated meanings? We wouldn't normally agree that a play on words is the same as receiving a negative consequence for bad behaviour.'

'Okay.'

'There is, of course, another aspect to this pun I just used, isn't there? We have the fact that listening to puns could be considered painful and are like punishments. It is that facet that makes it humourous. So the supposed other unrelated meaning needs to fit the context in a humourous manner.'

'Okay.'

'So it seems that it is not just the different meaning that makes the pun interesting or humourous. It is also that its meaning humourously fits the context of how the word was used literally. Do you get the point I'm making?'

'I think I'm getting it.'

'What do you think?'

'In some ways, I feel it has much to do about nothing.'

'Much to do about nothing?'

'Yeah, in a way.'

'Much to do about nothing? That phrasing doesn't sound like you. Where did that come from?'

'I'm not sure. It just came out, and does it really matter? It just seems like we're spending time talking about something that isn't that important.'

'I can see your point. Puns are not important enough to have a whole discussion about.'

'Yeah, it's all just semantics.'

'So could we say that puns are representative of just semantics?'

'Well, yeah, that's all they are. They're, as we have said, just a play on words.'

'Let me ask you this question then before we move on. Would a punster need to be aware of the surface conversation to make a pun?'

'Yeah.'

'Would the punster have to be making language and meaning associations to other contexts at the same time?'

'I guess so.'

'Let me ask you another question. Do you think that words are part of your thinking experience?'

'Well, of course. That's a kind of dumb question.'

'Could we say that the punster's thinking is also part of his thinking experience?'

'Well, yeah.'

'What might be some differences between the punster's thinking and your thoughts?'

'Well, since I don't think of those things, I guess my thinking is fairly straightforward.'

'Okay, and the punster?'

'His thoughts must be somewhat confused, I imagine. Probably if he hears one thing that's going to trigger a whole bunch of other thoughts, his experience must be something like that.'

'Okay, so let's accept your description, at least that aspect of one thought triggering a whole bunch of other thoughts. Could we add that someone who thinks this way and has these other thoughts also have an imagination and feelings?'

'Yeah, that makes sense.'

'So could we say that the person who thinks in a more confused way, as you see it, probably has many more thoughts and associated experiences than you would have?'

'Yes, that makes sense.'

'So from one point of view, we could consider that all these additional thoughts and associated experiences could be very confusing to the person who has them. However, could you agree that if we could see a definite structure to these associations, as we have discussed about the pun, then we might conclude that this person isn't necessarily confused but has thinking that is more complex?'

'Yes, though I could see that complexity could be confusing.'

'Certainly true. One would need to know how to manage this complexity. Let's go back to those bunch of other thoughts and what they are like. There are always different ways in which any one person can understand something that is said, whether the person thinks like you or our complex person. For instance, if I said to you, "You are a big man," what do I mean?'

'Well, that doesn't really apply to me because I'm not that tall or that heavy.'

'Would you like to add anything else?'

'No, why?'

'Let's say you weighed 300 lbs or 140 kg or something like that.'

'Well, in that case, it could be an insult.'

'Let's say that you are an important businessperson or influential politician.'

'If that was the case, it could be a compliment. The person is seeing me as important.'

'Your mother says to you when you are twenty-five, "You're a big man now," what does she probably mean?'

'Well, it's probably one of those motherly you-need-to-make-your-own-decisions-type remarks. What does all this have to do with what we are talking about?'

'I made a very straightforward statement, and then I asked you some questions, and you have answered these questions honestly. Can you see what the point of my statement and these questions was?'

'No, I don't have a clue.'

'We started with a five-word sentence—you are a big man. I asked you a number of questions, and you gave me different but appropriate answers.'

'Yeah, because you asked different questions.'

'Did I?'

'Sure.'

'I thought I simply said, "You are a big man."'

'You did, but you got me to change the circumstance. That wasn't what you said at the beginning.'

'Okay, so where's the point? What do you think the complex thinker can do?'

'I must be slow, but I'm still not sure.'

'Here's a point, not the point we used before, mind you, but a point. The complex thinker hears the sentence "You are a big man" and instantly makes all the associations you made after each one of my questions. The other very important factor is that the complex thinker does this all the time, and this leads me to *the* point of my pun. In oneness, there is complexity. And in complexity, there is oneness.'

'Well, that last thing you said sounds neat, but I don't really get it.'

'You did experience a sound. That's a step.'

Can the profound emerge from the trivial?

Our science student's friend had listened to the previous discussion.

'The big bang question seemed like a reasonable one, wasn't it?'

'It was.'

'Couldn't you have just answered his questions? However, I must admit I can understand your point about a readiness for learning certain things.'

'If we want someone to understand a point, we need to get them close to it first.'

'Close?'

'Yes, remember, I gave him the challenge of deciding how to tell a blind man about blue. And of course, using colour terms weren't going to work. What could you do?'

'Well, maybe try to get him to appreciate the sensations one has when looking at different shades of blue and maybe even how different sensations can be connected with different colours.'

'Exactly. In fact, a composer by the name of Scriabin used music to represent different colours.'

'Yeah, that could be kind of neat.'

'If we think about this, we could actually have someone experiencing some of the aspects of colour without ever reaching to the point of seeing it.'

'Now I understand why you didn't give an answer, and he did say he hadn't understood what he read, so I guess telling him again would have given him an answer but no understanding. It would have been a point with no point.'

A Little Treatise as a Follow-Up to the Dog on the Leash, Followed by Discussion

To approach the idea of an antithetical gyre, we could put the single concept at the bottom of the gyre. Many pages back, I talked about lateral movement, vertical movement, transformation, and conscious and unconscious. Let's look at some different examples of some gyres that will represent some different levels of understanding. Let us look at Thomas Hardy and his view of societal influence on individual freedom even with lateral movement and see if we could fit his point of view into a gyre.

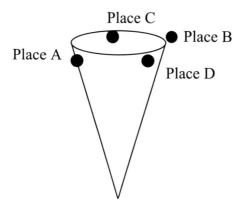

- Societal
- Guilt – obsessed thought
- Order

From his view, whether you are at A, B, C, or D, societal influence is always there. The man with the dog saw this influence as affecting the freedom of the (dog) person. I think we could contend that underlying social behaviour is a limited ethical belief system, a kind of 'you have to do', 'you can't do' mentality. This could be analogous to a type of leash,

500

just like our dog that is tied into this mentality, and no matter where you go, it's still there.

In Kafka's <u>The Trial</u>, Joseph K. is arrested for some unknown reason by people who are not really police and who don't really have official titles or place of work. Joseph K. will be judged, but by what, he doesn't know. This short description will make better sense to you who have read this novel. Not reading it may be okay too because, for many of you, reading the novel may still have you confused. What is important here is our example. In the novel, Joseph K. is free to move around; he is not imprisoned physically, but he is imprisoned by the obsessed need to figure out what he is guilty of. Like our gyre used above, there is a single question. His freedom to think in any way he wants is restricted (imprisoned) by a single focus. This is like the dog owner holding the leash. The dog may not understand the limits, but Joseph K. does. He needs to find an answer. As a result, it dominates all his activities on the surface.

Yeats used this gyre in a different manner in his poem 'The Second Coming'. He used the birth of Christ as a metaphorical statement of spiritual focus that kept some kind of rider on the social/human plane. What he saw was that 'the falcon was beyond the control of the falconer.' The world was spinning out of control. What he symbolically hoped for was a spiritual focus in a second coming.

Some further discussion with our student of philosophy

'Can we be untied? Be free?'

'Can we escape from all these nonhuman musicians?'

'When you asked that I had a couple of reactions to the whole idea of freedom, on one level, I can really see that, at a—as you call it—social/human level, there is a kind of naïve sense of freedom that prevails. Lots of people I know say they're free but just do the same things and talk about the same things as everyone else. They're not forced. It's just the power of social convention. I guess it's like you're reference to Hardy. Now I must admit the people I know living in Western countries are legally and politically allowed to make lots of choices, so they have freedom in that way, but how much difference does that have in some absolute sense, I'm really not sure. This may sound stupid, but it's almost as if freedom is this "all power to the individual" concept. It seems to be used by some in a manner that implies a logical impossibility. It is as if you can even be free from yourself, do anything. But to me, right at this moment, that seems ridiculous. That's the other thought I have. Your freedom is always limited by yourself. Just consider human and individual genetics, epigenetics, biochemistry and biomechanics, conditioning, gravity, time, and whatever else I'm missing, well, even the structure of the universe.'

'You are looking at an important distinction, and you are experiencing it. Would you be ready to discuss freedom with your friends and have them understand the distinction you are just beginning to formulate?'

'No, I don't think so. I think I would get stuck on the social/human, political perspective and wouldn't know how to explain other ways of looking at freedom and nonfreedom. I think I need time to think and formulate more.'

'Could your new sense of limited freedom actually give you more freedom than those who know they are free?'

'I see now, in the way you ask that, that you are using *free* in different ways to make your point. I can see that the language we use and one's perspective certainly influence someone's understanding and the different associations they make. Now that I get that, it's kind of neat. Anyway, to answer your question, yeah. Let me try a more exaggerated expression. My realisation is this. If you are aware that freedom is a myth, it can make you freer.'

'That's not bad yet maybe not quite the best way to say it, but it certainly does give an essential contradictory impression, one that would confuse the uninitiated. Let's explore what you said.'

'Okay, where do we start?'

'Let's look at your assumed uses of freedom.'

'Okay, well, there is the way most people use it, like living in a free country, being able to do what you want. Or maybe that's more in contrast to places where you can't do as much. It all seems very relative.'

'So you are saying that even in a free country you don't have the freedom to do anything you want.'

'Yeah, that's why I'm saying it's more relative than just freedom. Some free countries have a lot more laws than others, and some others have strong beliefs. Both of these certainly have an influence on freedom.'

'Let me stop you there because I think you will find some other interesting aspects about your different ways of looking at freedom. Would it be correct to assume that what you are saying is that, at a political level, freedom is more of a belief, or to some, it may be a delusion because the freedom they experience isn't consistent with how they may define it in some type of absolute sense?'

'Yeah, I can see now that there is this belief that one has freedom because, as I mentioned before, they live in a free country, but I don't think they could really consciously define freedom or a free country.'

'Does Hardy's way of showing the societal limits of freedom work for you?'

'I guess that ties into my thoughts about the relative views of freedom. I wonder whether people are limited more by their beliefs than they are by laws. I don't know.'

'You mentioned that you couldn't define how popular society sees freedom. Could we take a slightly different direction and consider some social examples of free choice?'

'When you said free choice, I immediately thought of the abortion issue. You know, it is also funny that I, for some reason, remember your discussion of the . . . I think it was fact/value dichotomy or something like that.'

'That's an appropriate thought. It fits.'

'Anyway, I don't think making free choices really helps us get beyond anything. Some person could be given the legal right to make a choice, but it really has something to do with belief. It seems to go back to what Hardy wrote about because both have socially supported value positions, do not understand ethical thinking, share conflicting social beliefs, and probably have nothing to do with freedom. They also 'beg the question' ethically. Should one have the freedom to behave in a manner that cannot be supported by sound ethical thinking?'

'You are focusing well. Follow your thoughts.'

'I'm beginning to see, as I talk, a very, I think, unrealistic view of freedom. It is almost as if each person can make a decision based on some type of hypothetical unlimited set of choices, even though they may not see any. The whole free-choice thing seems to be more of a simple 'either/ or'. Someone has an abortion or doesn't, but really, the limit, as I just mentioned, isn't the legal opportunity to make a choice, though that's important. It is the fact that the person is still stuck with their belief. That's back to Hardy again, isn't it?'

'You are doing well, and you are getting beyond Hardy. Keep going.'

'So what I'm starting to realise is that the dilemma of freedom and nonfreedom probably doesn't have a lot to do with what nation you live in. It's what you believe.'

'Exactly. Does this fit the outlaw perspective?'

'Yes, I think it does because free choice, at some type of political level, isn't really relevant to our understanding of freedom. It is somehow getting beyond belief, and I can see now that's what the outlaw perspective is all about, though I'm not sure how to get there yet.'

'Is there a possibility that we can find something beyond belief?'

'I can see that it can't be another belief. That would just be substituting one belief with another belief. I guess it's that I can sense that there are these limits. Freedom seems very amorphous. That word just came out. I'm not even sure what it means.'

'It works. Carry on.'

'Well, I feel this other sense that there is some kind of lack of freedom, and that feeling seems strange to me. It feels good. It doesn't feel scary or bad. I can see the problems with belief, and I want to find something beyond belief, but what's there is not more freedom but limitation. This is weird, but my feeling is that what I thought was freedom doesn't exist at any level.'

'What are you sensing?'

'Well, it is almost as if we are—this sounds a bit out-there, but I'm feeling it. We're stuck as people who are limited by so many factors it's hard to imagine.'

'What factors do you see?'

'Well, we're stuck in a social-belief plane, which is based on a context that determines our limitations and can't be supported by belief. And like the dog on the leash, we are stuck whether we go along or don't go along.'

'Are your thoughts limited by a human perspective?'

'Well, as I said, there is this social limitation.'

'What's next?

'Well, as I mentioned, there is also that belief, or maybe we could say a "nonbelief" because it is really an acceptance in the limitations of a social perspective.'

'Are there any other limitations?'

'Well, it's almost as if there are human limitations as well.'

'What do you mean by human?'

'Just that we're limited by our experiences, what we are able to understand, what we can do, a whole bunch of things like that. I think these sorts of human qualities are like a point at the bottom of a gyre. I think it's different from the way we saw Hardy. It's like the dog whose master is the limitation, but the existence of the dog and the leash also limits the master.'

'You have described some of the limitations of freedom well. You have also considered that you saw freedom and nonfreedom in a number of ways. Have you described all these?'

'You know, I'm not exactly sure. No, I haven't. I still haven't got my head around belief and whether there can be a nonbelief state 'cause that's just another belief, isn't it?'

'Possibly.'

'I also have an urge to jump to the whole universe. Is it free? Or is it also a prisoner of its structure, its rules? Its point at the bottom of some hypothetical gyre? I don't know.'

'I would like you to go back and look at belief and nonbelief and, with these, consider limitation and nonlimitation.'

'Okay, belief and nonbelief, limitation and nonlimitation. I'm not sure. Let me see. Could I say that if I have a belief, I probably would have no experience of limitation because I know? If I'm a nonbeliever—let me think. Oh, I could still have no experience of limitation because I know that my nonbelief is right. How does that sound?'

'That sounds good. You're discovering and experiencing. If we follow your train of thought, could we say that believing in freedom or not believing in freedom, if coupled with no awareness of personal limitations, would be a belief that has the right answer? I think we could conclude that, in both examples, the person's freedom to think is limited by their beliefs.'

'Yeah, I guess so. That does make sense. I guess, to be consistent, we would need to look at limited and nonlimited as well.'

'Follow your thoughts.'

'Well, it seems to me that our point of view as humans is very limited as I mentioned before. And if we simply acknowledge that and we accept it—hey, this is all we know—it's not really a belief. It could be that we are simply accepting that anything we think, do, or whatever is a function of all those factors, known and not known, that influence us. This could encompass those social/human factors that affect the development of our own point of view, a microcosm to the macrocosm of the whole universe and its structure. I feel like I need to put all these thoughts in some kind of order.'

'Your answer may come better from not trying. Joseph K. was a prisoner to his need to find a truth, though Kafka illustrates an irony in his novel. Joseph K. never experiences it. It's like Sisyphus rolling the rock up the hill before he gets to the top. As I said that, I'm thinking that some people may see these two situations as opposites. One might consider Joseph K.'s life as dominated by self-reflective thought, while Sisyphus's life was dominated by no self-reflective thought at all. What they may not see is that both their lives were completely dominated by a single state of mind or maybe no mind, but however we describe their states, there was no room for other thinking.'

'What you say seems very true. It's almost as if I may look too hard and too narrowly and just see the obvious. I may find an answer that meets my needs, like in this case seeing these characters as opposites. I can also see that if I know that my answer isn't what is being looked for, I could go crazy trying to find one. The hard part is that I don't know where to look or how to change my thinking. I know that I can get stuck in some kind of loop.'

'To be kind to you and your experienced limits in your thinking, let's accept that we may never find an answer that is correct in any absolute sense. In fact, we might say that any answer could be a sham, an easy way out, simply there to meet your needs.'

'Yeah, that makes sense.'

'Though just to confuse you more, if I contend that no statement can be true in an absolute sense, I am making a self-contradictory statement. What I just said was a statement. Could we consider it as a statement of truth? At face value, it would seem so, but I said that no statement can be true. Therefore, that statement can't be true as an absolute, so we end with nowhere to go.'

'But it doesn't mean that we don't explore.'

'Carry on with your thoughts of man's limitations.'

'I wonder what would happen if I took a different point of view. You had discussed that whole idea of the nonhuman and musicians forming orchestras. I think if I could see life from a different perspective and see that these humans are self-absorbed and take themselves too seriously, it's like your smiling Buddha. From that perspective, belief and nonbelief, freedom and nonfreedom seem trivial and unimportant. The universe doesn't care. The only entity that cares is themselves. If I am an ephemeral manifestation of a group of nonhuman musicians, then it would be these musicians who are me, but I wouldn't be them. It's funny. I'm not sure that I really understood what it said, but it makes some kind of sense to me, and it felt wonderfully liberating, almost freedom-like.'

'What about either/ors?'

'Right at the moment, that type of thinking seems—maybe it's not—more of a tragic limitation of the species or something. I don't know how to describe it, but it seems so . . . so—I am having difficulty here. It can't be that it's all wrong. Can it be?'

'From J. Alfred Prufrock came the line "Wrong from the start".'

'No, I know there has to be something.'

'Be careful. You are looking for meaning.'

'Yes, I can see that. It's an incredible temptation.'

'This dialogue is going very well, but I feel the need to get some closure in your thoughts, at least for the moment. You will build upon this, but let me present this. Let's assume for a moment that the whole universe is structured in some manner that we will never understand, yet since we can see patterns in how particles, molecules, cells, as well as planets and stars behave, we, of course, have the limitation of looking for patterns. Our science and mathematics are based on this, but we also know that how we are structured is a function of this overall universal structure, a Catch-22, if you know Joseph Heller's novel. One hypothesis could be that we can't ultimately understand the universe because we are limited by our structure, but our structure is simply one of a universe of expressions of this structure. Does this structure, if it exists as we assume it does, have a purpose? Oops, there's that temptation again. That certainly would be symptomatic of delusions, maybe even paranoid schizophrenia if we use human terms to describe the fearful religious person. I have purposely rambled a bit here to get your response. What comes to mind?'

'Your ramblings actually helped me focus. Your expression brought a number of things to mind. It makes sense to me that we are simply ephemeral expressions of some universal structure. Strangely enough, that feels good because it makes sense, but that leads me to the question why do people need to create some purpose? I ask that, and then I immediately come up with a personal nonanswer. I don't know why, and at the moment, it doesn't' seem that important to me. But obviously, there is some kind of insecurity, something. It's really hard, isn't it, to not be influenced by human thinking. I'm totally stuck but not stuck. I guess that feeling stuck and not stuck is liberating.'

'This is your beginning. You are starting to understand the essence of the outlaw, the smiling Buddha. Let me see if I can assist you in thinking in a way that is still human because that's limited by the nature of our species, our physiology, but has a point of view with some structure but is the least restrictive. We know that for you to learn and then experience, my guidance needs to be articulated. And at this point, we are stuck with using words, terms, language that has some meaning. Let's say you are beginning to experience something but are not sure where to go, what to hang on to. I would like to have you consider the concept of energy. Let's assume that all we have is energy and that it takes many forms. It's those old nonhuman musicians again, but even though it is all there is, it has nothing to do with our definitions of humans, civilisation, earth, etc. These imply an artificial separateness. If we consider that energy in everything is made of the same building blocks, energy remains, but all these other human-defined forms are ephemeral. We even have supernovas. Fleas live and die. People live and die. Bacteria and viruses probably live longer. Do they have personal identity? I have a good virus friend named George. He's been around for years. He has his own identity, doesn't he?'

'Of course not. He has no brain. It's funny I said that. It just slipped out. I know what you're saying. We get this incredibly narrow point of view, and we get stuck there. It is really hard to get beyond even when you understand, but I think that idea of energy helps. It gives a kind of real something to hang on to. So it's all just energy manifesting itself in different forms, probably with different degrees of complexity. And as I think about it, I can see that it goes beyond our ability to understand time and space. I also wonder about some kind of structure or rule, that whole idea of the theory of everything. I remember you mentioned a book on a new kind of science in which the author used a computer and generated patterns of black and white squares using some simple rules for combination, and just following these rules ended up with unpredictable and nonrepeating patterns, if his work is generalisable. I could see how energy, which we haven't really defined, have we?'

'No.'

'Anyway, I can see how this energy that I'm not sure how to define could be structure—I guess even that is a human word—could account for what exists.'

'You have developed an interesting perspective. Take a moment to let your thoughts explore these perspectives.'

———

'I find it easy but difficult—easy because I can get a sense of an outside position, difficult because I know that energy is everywhere. But I am conditioned to seeing myself as separate. I keep wanting to look in.'

'Does the idea of the sea and being below the surface help? It implies, at least, that you are immersed in the same energy but have a different perspective, though you may still experience yourself as separate.'

'Yes, that does kind of work. Thanks. I know I can't expect too much right away.'

'I feel we have covered a lot in this discussion today. You now need time to have it become part of you, to become you.'

Discussion with the Group

'Our small group of individuals are here—our literal thinker who is not ready to venture too far, our science student and friend who are beginning to understand, our uncertain prairie person who is learning about confusion and truth, our reader who can clearly see geometric figures, our hardworking male who misses similarities, our artist who is beginning to appreciate some qualities of creative association, and our student of philosophy who experiences life uniquely. They are all looking at the unknown, yet they are all manifestations of the same energy. Let's say that they are manifestations of are two universal rules. One, all nonparticles (really nothing at all) are required to move around so they fill up space and look like particles. And two, these nonparticles that have disguised themselves as particles are required to combine with other disguised nonparticles to develop a wide range of perceived group complexity. One kind of rule adjunct might be "go crazy and combine and see what you come up with." Who made up these rules? Who knows? Does it really matter? Maybe the universe, as we know it, is really just the creation of some other beings to whom light-years are inches. Maybe the whole thing is a joke or a game. Or maybe there is "isness", a "sum", and any meaning is only what we have created. So maybe it is a function of a collective cogito and nothing more, and therefore, we really know that none of our metaphors or science will ever give us an answer. It will always be limited by what we understand.'

'Are you serious! It's all pointless!'

'I don't even understand what you're saying. What are nonparticles anyway? That doesn't make any sense at all.'

'I appreciate all your thoughts. You help people, but I can't see how this has anything to do with reality. I don't mean to be so negative because I know you see it as important, and besides, I have learned something. I have learned a lot in reading this book so far.'

'You have experienced some reflectivity, and you expressed it. Do you think I meant all I said?'

'Well, maybe not, and you know, I must admit you seem quite with it. I know you do know stuff and you're a doer, and I can relate to that, but what you said doesn't make any sense to me.'

'As i said, you've made a big step.'

'Well, whatever.'

The philosopher speaks up. 'Let me say something here. Even though I know your thoughts were expressed with a sense of humour, I couldn't see them as totally nonsensical... There was a truth to them.'

'Well, I have read all these ramblings and still haven't had an answer to why you use circles and triangles.'

'Maybe reading is not enough. Let's check with our science students. What are you experiencing?'

Both says together, 'Well, we're . . .'

'Well, I find your last comments a bit of a stretch, but I am beginning to understand that it's really hard to understand something if you don't experience it. Memory of the facts doesn't give you understanding, and that still is my problem, but I understand it now.'

'You need to be patient.'

'Yes, I am learning, but there is one person who hasn't spoken yet. What is your reaction to my expressed thoughts?'

'Well . . .'

'Well, it's okay to express how you feel.'

'Well, I'm not sure.'

'It may be difficult to express, but don't worry about feeling dumb. Remember, dumbness can be an expression of openness.'

'This may seem crazy, but I can see how all the ways we try to describe some type of importance about life are all kind of created. It's like they're not real for certain, and I can see that 'kind of real' may not be real at all.'

'You have very quickly developed your sight. You are now able to see beyond parallel lines. I sense these lines are maybe meeting but beyond the horizon. I defined each one of you, as we began this group discussion, in a very limited manner, and then I went on to express some views about the universe in a somewhat simplistic, almost feasible manner but not really. You might have asked, "Was he serious or just being humourous?" And if you questioned, that certainly would be a big jump for most of you. Each one of you responded differently but with aspects of correctness. Some of you could see the wrongness, and some of you could see the rightness, but what is important here is to see that there was some possible truth, hyperbole, humour, and logical progression that were credible and ludicrous in a few moments of expression. In all life, the skills of seeing all these different perspectives are essential for getting less stuck.'

'If what you just said is true or at least what you believe, then I need to ask, were you just manipulating us before? How can we trust you and what you are saying?'

'It is not who said but what is said. In fact, I don't disagree with what I said, but I also don't agree with it. It is the joy of following thoughts to some logical ends to see what they tell us. Mistrust shuts the door. Don't focus on differences. See if you can see similarities. Our hard work person now knows that apples and oranges are the same.'

'There you go again.'

Our female, lacking confidence, speaks up. 'Can't you see what he's saying? It makes sense to me.'

'Yeah, but what do you know? You're a woman.'

Stares from the others are evident. Our literal thinker senses it. 'I'm just kidding. Just kidding. I didn't really mean it.'

'So you weren't sincere?'

'You were just making a joke?'

'I already told you. I was just kidding.'

'Were you trying to test us or manipulate us?'

'No.'

'How can we trust what you say then?'

'What are you talking a-about? Oh no, oh sorry. Boy, did I ever fall into my own trap.'

'You are beginning to see.' I speak.

'Wow, just think of how many times what someone says is in direct conflict with how they behave.' Our artist speaks for the first time.

'I think that helped all of us.'

'It's funny. At this moment, I don't feel dumb or confused. I see now how some very assured people aren't assured at all. They just think they are.'

'It could even be that the more certain one is in the expression of their thoughts, the less their thoughts are reflective of unstuck thinking. Artists and critics get stuck this way all the time, but they think they are unstuck when they find a solution, though sometimes, in creative work, one can only get unstuck by changing the whole context, which may require starting all over again. If we are considering some type of truth, whether spiritual or scientific, we can`t reformulate it to meet our needs, though we know that happens all the time.'

'I know I can be stuck if I don't get someone else's point.' Our circle/ triangle person speaks.

'Or if I know the explanation or definition of something but I don't really understand, I have a sense of what I need to understand yet.'

'I think I might get distracted by what I see or what I understand and just ignore the rest.'

'I can better understand how—for every thought, visual, or listening experience—one person may have many associations, but some of us may not have any, maybe one but rarely more. I would like to open myself to more.'

'I can see,' says our student of philosophy, 'that there is an irony to all this. Each one of us could become less stuck in one realm of thinking, only to get stuck in another. If we can understand that finding answers makes us stuck, being open to a process of questioning and uncertainty works for me, but I know it can't work for all of you. But maybe if we are each aware of social correctness, that tells us that what is right is very tempting and easy to accept but can get us stuck. Be aware and then see if you can let go of an experience that is considered from a social/human perspective and approach it from another point of view. That's my sense of all this.'

'It is interesting that some of you are certainly seeing the need to go beyond the oneness of a single point of view, but i have called this section approaching oneness. Do any of you get a sense of the two different ways we have used oneness or even how oneness and all are the same?'

One of our science students speaks first. 'I know that, whether it is the big bang or a theory of everything, a goal in science is to find the truth. In a way, it's supposed to be independent of a human point of view and objective. I don't know whether it's possible or not, but the goal is to find one theory that will explain everything.'

'It might be better to say that the goal is to find a theory that can be continually tested in every circumstance and always applies.'

'I don't see the difference, but I know I can see that. I need to learn and explore.'

'Some of you may be uncertain,' begins our student of philosophy. 'But if we use something simple like the concept of energy—though the name doesn't really matter. I'm using this term to represent a conceptual something that is like a fundamental force or entity—that everything is composed of it and if we also assume that these fundamental forces evolve and create new structures and even very complex ones that behave in many different ways, that would make some sense. I guess we could also assume that we could see these complex structures as separate from each other and individual, and then in a sense, we have a single energy that has evolved from a single structure. That's it.'

Our student of philosophy continues. 'I think the metaphorical use of the gyre, the dog on the leash, and water all work well for me. They are consistent with my sense of underlying structure and oneness. If I elaborate, I can understand that there is a single structuring of something that holds everything together. I can see the whirlpool and its base as being calm, not moving around, and can appreciate that the rapid and even scary movement of the water on the surface is what the surface human experiences. It even has a sense of unity in time. If you get drawn down to the bottom, time/space stops in a kind of hypothetical inverse, infinite state. Identity is gone. I'm just thinking out loud, but I can see that there are lots of ways of seeing singleness, a still point as you called it.'

'Our friendly student of philosophy has had many years of thinking, reasoning, and studying and has an understanding that may be different from mine. His may be different from each one of you has, but it's important to appreciate that any new insights and changes in your understanding that allow you to see far more are all equal in their personal significance. Consider it as something like the early realisation that changes the direction of your voyage.'

Our young scientist speaks. 'I am beginning to see how—at least for us who want to understand some type of truth, and I think I do—I'll only ever get partial truths, and I need to experience a lot more before I'll really understand. And the idea that 'everything' and 'oneness' are somehow the same, I don't really get, but I think I can get there.'

'Within the microcosm of self is the macrocosm of the universe. That may make sense to some of you, but it will not mean much to all of you. If you are focused on 'answers', then like Joseph K., you will be tied to a point like our dog on a leash or even the dog's master. If you can even understand that there may not be an answer in any absolute sense—at least for you, and for your own peace of mind, you may create one, a great human temptation—that is a step that, at least, would allow you to expand your universe when ready. However, if you can understand our discussion and have these ideas become part of you and not just as an intellectual exercise, then you are beginning to understand the view of the outlaw and are moving towards oneness.'

Our 'experienced' hard work guy speaks up. 'Okay, let's just say that what you've been talking about makes sense in some ways. I can't believe I'm even saying this, *but* what is it going to do for me? Basically, I'm perfectly happy. I don't need to change, so why bother?'

'In fact, I think we would all agree that if you spent time and effort to develop a deeper understanding of the human condition or whatever we want to call what we are discussing, it would make your life less happy and more distressful.'

'So why would I want that?'

'You spoke of your grandfather and his adventures at sea. Did he tell you stories about the calm, peaceful days at sea? Or—'

'No, he talked about storms and those times that pushed them to the limits. That challenged them.'

'Were these times distressful to him? Do you think?'

'Yeah, okay, you made your point.'

'So is it possible that with openness to new thinking, questioning, and just new experiences, your life could become richer?'

'Yeah, I guess so.'

'Are you wanting to venture off to sea at this point?'

'No, I'm too old, though I have too many things I still want to do.'

'Are you stuck then?'

'Well, kind of.'

'Could you read different written works, travel to places you hadn't thought about before?'

'I guess.'

'If you did, you might begin to understand some aspects of life in a new way.'

'I hate to admit it, but if I don't understand something, as I said before, it bugs me, and I get frustrated and turned off,' says our circle and triangle person. 'You know, I did read all this. And when you suggested it, I quit, though one part of me didn't want to quit because you suggested it. Anyway, I think I really just need to read it again with an open mind. That's all I feel like saying right now.'

'That's a big step. You are moving beyond.'

'It's interesting that we all have different ways of seeing ourselves when we feel uncertain or confused. I have always just known I wasn't smart enough. I'd get frustrated and see others as wrong or responsible or something.'

The group sits quietly for several moments, and I introduce a new topic for discussion. 'Earlier in this section, I considered the concept of *me* and how one's sense of *me* may be experienced differently by different people. To show these differences, I considered personal needs and some different relationships that *me* may have with different contexts and images that are created by others or self.'

'I remember that discussion. I think what I got out of it was the point that we are not separate from everything else we're immersed in. We're part of a whole *something*, and what we might think, see, or feel is an expression of all this.'

'Boy, how did you get all that? I thought of my grandfather, and I could picture him. That was about it.'

'How did you feel?'

'It felt good.'

'Did you see him, or did you see your memory of him?'

'Well, the memory obviously.'

'So his image, we could say, was really part of you, not separate.'

'I guess you could say that.'

The conversation changes focus. The geometric person has been thinking and experiencing some distress. 'Why would a person be mentally ill just because they believe in something? I remember you made some comments about that. That's what I remember.'

'That analogy was obviously a point that bothered you.'

'Yeah, it did. Why would you say that being religious is like being mentally ill?'

'That wasn't exactly my point, but I can see how that would bother you. So let's think of what we experience in the following way: You see an art exhibit, and there are a series of paintings that use large geometric shapes, circles and triangles included. And to make it interesting, let's take our situation a little further and say that some of these geometric paintings have Christian icons. We can see crosses, the star of David, figures of Christ, all created with geometric shapes.'

'This sounds weird, but okay, carry on.'

'So when you go home after you've seen these paintings and someone asked you what you saw, what would you report?'

'Probably nothing. I don't like paintings.'

'Let's say I asked you.'

'Well, I'd probably just say what you said.'

'All right, in your memory, which is inside you, you would be able to tell me about what you saw that you know was outside of you. It wasn't just created by your imagination. Would that be correct?'

'Yeah.'

'Would you report that these religious figures spoke to you?'

'Of course not! Why would I do that?'

'What if you talked to someone else who had seen the same paintings and they said that the religious figures moved out of the canvases and spoke to him?'

'I'd think the guy was nuts.'

'What did you conclude?'

'Well, he's seeing things that are not there. Yeah, I know, I've fallen into your trap.'

'There is no trap. I only wish to help in giving you an experience where you become aware.'

'Okay, so let me see if I can figure out what I did, see if I have this right. I felt the person was crazy because they thought they saw something that was real and outside themselves when, in reality, it was created by their own imagination. Does that make sense?'

'You're beginning to see.'

'What you say is interesting,' our artist speaks. 'Art does speak, and I know that there can be multiple individual associations and interpretations, so the crazy guy could just have had a profound experience.'

'You are also seeing.'

'How does that work? Don't these two experiences conflict with each other? One experience is on the wall, and the other is in one's head. One is real, and the other is imaginary.'

'Your distinction would be correct, but the nature of their personal experiences may not be in conflict. The part that may be seen to be in conflict, which would be the nature of their personal experience, could be different, but that has not been articulated, yet it is good you saw some inconsistencies.'

Once again, our student of philosophy speaks. 'As you just said, what's missing is the nature of the experience of the observer. If the person was describing their experience in metaphorical or symbolic terms, like, "That painting just blew me away," it's not literal. It's a description of how the person felt. So if the painting spoke to the person and the figures moved, it could be a metaphor. They may simply describe what their experience felt like. If, on the other hand, the person knew that the painting spoke to him and knew that the figures moved and these were literally described as if these really happened, it would certainly sound a bit crazy. However, for some, there is a very fine line among symbol/metaphor, impression, memories, and the perception of reality and its influences on the nature of personal experience. That's how I see it.'

Unexpectedly, we hear from our experienced fifty-year-old. 'That makes sense to me. Could I say that before my grandfather died, I saw him many times? I now have memories of him that are kind of concrete. For instance, I can always remember him at the wheel of his boat, but then I've got some other memories that I think are more about what he meant to me as a kind of father-type figure, but I don't think the images are necessarily real.'

Our uncertain young female adds some thoughts. 'This whole discussion makes sense to me. It's strange 'cause I think it's probably pretty confusing. It is almost as if it isn't until someone makes me really feel confused that I begin to understand and realise that maybe I'm not so confused after all.'

'It's like there are all these ways of seeing things and understanding things, and I think I may need some confusion. Possibly with some help, I will learn how to organise the content, make sure I can make sense of it, and then find my way to a better understanding. I can see that if I don't do that, I will be just end up finding some truth because it's easy to understand.'

'I thank you for participating in this discussion and will ask you to carry on and find that the remainder builds upon your present experience. From all our discussions—whether they were personal, scientific, philosophical, literary, religious, symbolic, or experiential—we have considered a vast multitude of variables and points of view. We have also seen our need to make the complex simple, to have a single answer or at least an explanation. We have also faced our limitations as a species trying to make sense of life, death, and universality with a physical system limited by the universality we are trying to understand. On with your reading. I hope you . . .'

Some More Thoughts for Consideration: Some Academic Exercises and Some Unexplained Human Examples

Douglas Hofstadter scripted a conversation among a male, female, and computer. All were given sexually ambivalent names, like Pat. Anyway, the object of the reading exercise was to determine who was male, female, and computer. The computer was a giveaway at the end of the discussion because it could not generate a question that questioned its own existence. Can humans do that? Certainly better than the computer, but we are limited too. We don't know because we can't get beyond. What do we mean by getting beyond?

All of us can certainly expand our knowledge and experience and get beyond our present state. In fact, the essence of understanding an outlaw perspective is getting beyond. But in metaphysical and philosophical discussions, 'getting beyond' is more in terms of possible limits of the species. From Hofstadter's discussion, we could see that the computer couldn't even generate the question. The human could generate the question but doesn't have an answer.

As I write this, I can sense a reaction from some. Getting beyond can be seen as a spiritual notion, an important one, and we didn't have a spiritual-type person in our discussion. However, the structure of the discussions in the last section is similar to Buddhist and metaphysical discourses. So any of you who see yourself in that way may feel not represented, and of course, some who still are unclear about a different perspective may still see these ramblings as antireligious. Anyway, back to the point at hand.

So before we move ahead, let's consider a few examples of feelings and connection that go beyond what we can explain. We can certainly get beyond our limited self. What about ESP? The truly spiritual? One of you might mention the work of Dorsey. He did a controlled study and found that if others really spend some time having caring thoughts about another who is ill (and in his study, the patient was far away from the ones who had caring thoughts), patients improve more rapidly than his control group. For you who believe in this type of connection, his work will make you feel good. Am I being unfair to you? I hope, if you have read everything to this point, you will get a sense that 'belief' is a word I have not used with a positive connotation, and that is true. In fact, you may have noticed that, at the beginning of this section, I had myth/delusion as a heading but have never followed up discussing it.

Before we go further, let me tell you a personal story. I can think of a few interesting relationships we can feel good about but don't really understand. I have a business/intellectual partner and close friend, and over the years, I have spent a lot of time with him, his wife, and their son who is very disabled but very well loved. Many years ago, we had a very sensitive, wimpy shepherd/retriever cross. She was always well behaved and didn't need a leash or discipline. Our second son had left home to live in England, and our dog would never enter his room. Sometimes we would even try to entice her with food or whatever. She would not go in.

Well, we had decided to invite my partner and his wife and child up for a visit, and they were set up to stay in our son's room. When they moved themselves and their luggage into the room, they laid their child (at this time, about age ten) on the bed. They didn't worry too much because their child had very limited mobility. Without any enticement or even acknowledgement, our dog went into the bedroom and lay beside this young boy. When we moved this young boy into the living room, our dog followed and lay beside him. It was very touching, but why? I do not know.

It was also touching to see our cat care for this dog when she was fifteen, and having her own health difficulties, the cat would lay beside her and clean her, even though the dog was probably ten times the size of the cat.

So do these incidents help establish beliefs? Animals have special abilities that people don't have? It's God's way or whatever?

Or are they explainable? Mystery? Magic?

I am also reminded of my good friend who has some abilities, and she has had a number of experiences in which she had sensed something beyond herself that she couldn't really explain. It seems to work, and it is very real to her, but she has found it embarrassing because it sounded a bit too 'out-there'. In her work with others, she did/does have the intuitive ability to pick up aspects of others' states that almost all others miss.

I am reminded of her work with a teenage girl who had always been polite and delightful to her teachers. She was seen as very low functioning intellectually because, even though she paid attention in her classes, she learned very little. Our measurement of her using EEG showed something quite interesting. If she was in one particularly measured state, she could learn, respond, and even write down answers. If she was in a different measured state, she processed very little, even nothing. We even found that if we tried to help her understand the difference between these two states, she would immediately go to a turned-off state and process nothing. My friend was able, without using any EEG measurement, to increase the duration of her attentive state to the point that she was able to learn schoolwork and actually graduate from high school. In different forms, great psychotherapists or those who are seen as wise or sagelike probably have special insights that cannot be clearly defined or explained.

What we need to remember is it is not what we don't understand or what we might consider as out-there that leads us in some wrong direction. *It is our need to define it.* It can then become belief instead of keeping it as a wonder, a sense of wow, something we can't really explain. Both belief and disbelief in it limit us.

Much earlier, I mentioned the cousin who couldn't pretend that there were dragons. He could not visualise or believe. He was paralysed in that he couldn't imagine, pretend, or even believe.

In fantasy, I see times where there are explorations of truth that are approaching the beyond. It is a symbolic expression of energies. It can strip away the facade and at the same time embellish it. It can have humour, hyperbole, symbol, truths, partial truths. It can give freedom for the imagination. It can allow us to go to our limits equal to science and to think beyond.

My sense is that some fantasy seems to tie into an energy that is beyond self that is somewhat humanly universal. It ties into feelings that bring up my feelings of compassion, of the smiling Buddha, of that acceptance, of that experience of sameness, not difference. There is a difference. It is not in expressed idea; it is an underlying openness and energy that is reciprocal, not unidirectional. It opens us to the world.

So what about belief? Could I say that I believe in other levels of connection? Could I say I believe in pretending and the power of the imagination? *Or* could I say that I have an openness to an unlimited universe of phenomena—some I can explain, and some I can't? As you can appreciate, if I had a disbelief, it would be a limiting belief.

You may ask, 'You commented that, in fantasy, there is great truth. Isn't that a statement of belief because you probably can't support that scientifically or whatever?' On one level, your question is a perceptive and correct one. But if we reconsider the many stylistic ways in which I and many others express ideas, we could conclude that my use of 'truth' is in a stylistic, somewhat metaphysical manner, in an epigram form. Truth, or at least the pursuit of truth, in this context, could be considered as emphasising a contrast between what can be imagined in fantasy and what we accept as real. It is one way of addressing the limits of the known 'real'. In essence, fantasy may make some important points about the way things are and about our perceptions of reality.

A Return to the End: A Look at Paradoxes

So oneness is an end? Or is it a beginning? Maybe there really isn't any oneness. It's just that we create it. Maybe the simple lazy-brain Christian approach is no different from the oneness of the one who doesn't believe or disbelieve. Maybe none of these things really matter anyway.

These, of course, are all true because there really isn't a definable end. There is no oneness.

'That's just great!' you may exclaim. 'I spend all the time reading this, being confused, bored, and interested all because I'm waiting for the answer. And now what?'

For those of you who may remember, 'It's even worse than having to eat all the cereal to get the prize. My mother used to make me do that, and then there's no prize!'

There is, however, a process.

'Well, I guess that's better than nothing. So does that mean that if I eat all the cereal, I'll get a prize but we just can't predict which prize I'll get?'

That response is a reasonable one, except you may find that you have a box of cereal that has no end, or the prize of any sort isn't there because maybe there isn't one.

We have a problem, or maybe it is more of a challenge that is paradoxical in nature if we are going to follow this process too.

<u>Paradox 1:</u> We have considered this challenge many times in our discussion of the gyre that expands the universe of what we see. We may find many associations to a word, vision, thought, sound, smell,

and sensation of any sort. So instead of oneness, we have many. I have mentioned how hearing the phrase 'a big man' can have a number of meanings. Everything we experience can be experienced from multiple points of view. All represent an interaction among people, their memories, their background, and the event. It is also helpful if we can take the perspective of our smiling Buddha. From this perspective, we can see a possible myriad of individual experiences collectively expressing the characteristics of the human species. Here's the paradox. It is only with seeing the many that you can see the oneness.

Paradox 2: To see all as one of which you are part, you need to see yourself as separate. Observe, listen, remain calm, smile below the surface, be immersed. But observe the surface, a distant, not affecting you. The road to being a not-separate being in a state of oneness requires being separate.

Paradox 3: I have talked about ego in different ways. You will probably not have the complicated ego dynamics I have described for myself, and i may correctively add on your behalf, 'Boy, I'm glad I don't.' So what's important? You need to have an ego and confidence on the surface, to be successful in some type of socially defined way as we have discussed. I see it as essential. To achieve a non-ego state, you need a socially accepted and personally accepted sense of self. Here's the paradox. You need a strong ego to have none.

Paradox 4: Let's say that having answers to test questions and remembering what you've learned are signs of intelligence, and these are important in defining your social/human intelligence. Intelligence is important. If we are going to understand and be able to think, or at least have the potential to do that, we would conclude that a certain amount of intelligence is essential. As we have discussed, however, how we measure it or determine its presence can be unclear. We may find that some people may show some confusion in response to a question that is supposed to measure intellectual capacity.

Over the years, we have seen some very bright people who show some confusion in response to a question that, to an examiner, seems fairly straightforward. In some of these cases, the question may trigger multiple possibilities. For instance, an examiner might ask a child, 'Who discovered America?' The very bright child may not say anything because he or she is uncertain about how to respond. The child may know that Christopher Columbus is wrong because the place had already been discovered, but the child may wonder if the answer should be the Vikings because they came to the northeast, or should it be the Asians who came through Alaska? Or what does *discover* really mean? Anyway, what the examiner may experience in these types of situations is no response. However, they may hear some underlying mumbles. In this case, we could ask the examiner if it would be assumed that not answering correctly or seemingly being confused by a straightforward question is a sign of low intelligence. However, being confused could be an essential characteristic for seeing the world differently and would require a high level of intelligence. So as we discussed in our dialogues, the most insightful and profound understandings may be the result of what is seen as confusion and not understanding.

Perceived stupidity and confusion could be signs of genius. Thus our paradox would state, 'The smarter you are, the dumber you look.'

Paradox 5: Not being real can be seen as out of touch with what's really happening. 'Get with the program! Get real! Face the truth!' But I talked about truth and fantasy. Yeah, but it's fantasy, for heaven's sake. Or is it more? As you will remember, I have considered that fantasy can express the realities of the human condition better than one that simply describes the social/human world. So here's our paradox. We could say that fantasy is reality. Maybe we could also contend that social/human reality is actually fantasy.

Paradox 6: A person is elected as a political leader. His name is George. He belongs to a particular party, and we know that to be a responsible citizen and be in touch with the world, we need to have some factual information about this person. We need to know the party's political platform. In fact, to make a good political decision, we should know something about all the political players. In our day-to-day life, we may also be interested and have knowledge about sports teams or what the market is doing. We may have lots of areas of knowledge, but do we have a sense of how all these social/human entities are really the same in what drives them all? Probably not. So here's the paradox. The more factual knowledge you have, the less you may actually know (understand).

Paradox 7: I have discussed karma and its essence, but let's revisit it. There is a social/human perception of karma that, like the reality perception above, misses its essence. Our paradox is simple. Behaving in a manner that is seen at a social/human level as trying to be good, because one knows that good things happen to good people and bad things happen to bad people, results in expressed selflessness, caring for others, and identifying with a spiritual view of the world or whatever would probably 'bad karma'. The paradox here is this: the more one tries to do the right thing, the more it is bad karma.

Paradox 8: Let's revisit belief. Belief meets and is an expression of your own needs. That's okay, but it prevents you from exploring beyond. It probably shows your emotional needs. So here's the paradox. The more you believe, the less able you are at believing.

Paradox 9: So what this section may confirm to some of you is, after all these ramblings, I leave you with a number of paradoxes that seem to be more tongue-in-cheek than serious. I see a smiling Buddha. But on one level, it may all seem very unfair. I have not given you any answers, so what did I teach? Here's a paradox I can use to escape any personal responsibility (another paradox). The more I didn't teach, the more you learned.

Paradox 10: I think I could go on forever, but because of time and space, these ramblings need to end. So this will be my last pair a dox. Paradox? The operative question is, 'What is a paradox?' As anyone knows, it is two ducks in a box.

And in somewhat uncanny, unplanned manner, this pun is especially apt. It illustrates to me the power of symbol/metaphor, which I hope you can appreciate, because you may ask, 'It sounds like you are illustrating the importance of paradoxes, and that makes sense. And earlier, you were supportive of swans. What happened to them?' Actually, you probably didn't ask that question, yet you may have asked, 'Why would you end such an important section that really gives no answer and then make it even more meaningless by using a pun?' You could be right. I have no answer, except . . .

So this is my last paradox.

2 ducks = 1 swan[7]

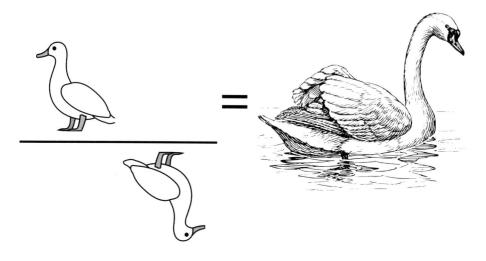

'Is this really the end of this section?'

'Yes.'

---

[7] Stylistically, this feels like the end of this section. For some of you, this may be a time that works for you, and the feeling of closure is there. But for you, other readers, who are still interested but need some more direction, I hope the next section will help. I ended this section with a composer sense. It felt right. I was not being primarily sensitive to all my audience. I was composing.

PART IV: REFLECTIONS ON COMPOSING AND CONDUCTING

The Composer's Social Obligation

Warning: In this section, the pronoun **I** *is used extensively.*

An evening moment of awareness many years ago triggered the realisation that, for some of us, there is the need to not simply indulge ourselves in our own spirits, thoughts, and formulated ideas but to also express these in different forms. At that time, I was not only a university student but also a student of 'everything'—literature, science, philosophy, Buddhism, aesthetics. I had an insatiable appetite for learning. However, I realised that I needed to find some form of expression that would allow me to share this knowledge with those on the surface. In fact, this sense of social responsibility became a driving force in the years that followed. But a more recent moment of awareness spoke to me in a different manner. It was an expression of a social/human, dwelling on the surface. It was not as a composer but as someone making a value-driven statement that was about others. These thoughts came down to two very simple value questions.

The first question, actually based on a frustration that was actually mixed with a certain sadness (that resulted in a momentary lapse of my outlaw perspective), was in response to a series of meetings about some complex psychiatric cases. These meetings were with a few mental health physicians and a number of the workers who followed their lead. What was evident was that they would arrive at their statements of truth based on faulty thinking, no evidence, and a consideration of a few selected variables. What they saw was clear to them. From my perspective, they had arrived at a diagnosis that met their selected criteria, but it said nothing about the patient. When asked questions about their somewhat quasi-logical thinking, their limited selection of salient factors, their lack of understanding of statistics, their lack of data, their need to consider some aspects of the patient's physiology, and the limits of psychiatric

535

nomenclature in considering human dynamics, they were clearly not open to questioning their point of view, learning more, or changing their perception. I decided to refer to this type of thinking as an 'arrogance of ignorance'. It was also clearly evident to me that this type of thinking or lack of questioning was/is pervasive on the social/human plane. I thought of these well-educated practitioners and their limits. Just think of those people like politicians, full of sound and fury, signifying nothing.

Oops, I needed to include that line from Shakespeare, though it is important to note that this line was spoken by a character in distress and is not an expression of how Shakespeare thought life 'ought to be'.

The first obvious value question, which the philosopher in me would contend as being a logical but not practical possibility, asks the following: Should all people understand the limits of their knowledge and, especially if they have an influence on others, learn more, get advice, consider different perspectives, or do whatever is needed to get the best possible answers?

My second question considers those who have special talents or abilities to help others. Should they be obligated to dedicate their energies to the well-being of the species? My first reaction to this was also philosophical one. From a philosophical point of view, there are too many open-ended questions. Questions like What is a special talent? Who determines if one has one of these? Maybe everyone has special talent. What about human rights?

My reaction to all this uncertainty was a personal and emotional one but maybe not just social/human. If I knew or know someone who has some unique and creative abilities or insights, I would hope that they embody these abilities and insights. However, I also realised, somewhat ironically, that these value questions I was asking missed the point. It once again became clear. Composers create from that *all* that we have discussed, and their greatest works come from simply expressing, yet it is from this source that they gain their greatest social/human influence. Meeting the needs of the social/human is not relevant, thus the irony. In a sense, it is like karma. We could consider that the greatest impact of a work on society would be achieved by not making any attempt to affect or to be influenced by society. Though I meet these creative people rarely, their essence is often very evident. There is always something wonderfully satisfying for me being with them. It is like finding another of the 'hapless few'.

My next reaction brought me back to my place of existence, to one that exists outside or below. From this point of view, I can see myself engaging on the surface—the conductor who has found a collection of talented musicians, a coterie of like spirits, and being with them feels good at the moment, but I know it is ephemeral and based on selfish motivation.

And this leads me to yet another type of response that brings with it some emotion. I feel a sadness, but it could also be the smile of the Buddha. That may seem a bit paradoxical, but upon reflection, it isn't. I may find myself focusing on the fact that we have a species who believes in themselves and who may have endured many hardships, but they remain lost in some type of social/political malaise. They believe in one political party over another or one religion over another because they know that things will be better with their correct choice. They may want to save the world. Yet is mankind's desire to save the earth a campaign to save 'subatomic particles', the earth's molecular structure, or is it to save the earth so the human species will survive without too much hardship? It's not altruism; it's self-serving. They don't understand anything beyond their own beliefs, their own species. They can't get beyond. They have no desire or knowledge of how to get there. They only have those things that they have experienced at a social/human level. Is there any hope? In the 1930s, Hermann Hesse was optimistic that people would become enlightened, yet there has been no change in spirit. From below, everything looks the same.

'Women come and go / Talking of Michelangelo.'

These thoughts are almost too overwhelming, too bleak. I think I need to start with myself not in a self-indulgent manner but simply as a place to start.

I need to return to the beginnings of these ramblings and see what has been resolved or changed in me by my process of composing. Have I learned about myself? Others? My friend? Being separate? Not being separate? Have I been able to be an expressive conductor of my own compositions or, more correctly, my arrangements of a myriad of composers of the past and present? I haven't really composed anything unique, but maybe my arrangements are interesting, which is my hope. Should it simply be self-indulging? My answer is *no*. There is, I feel, a profoundly personal but nonpersonal need to have the love of beauty and creative vision of some throughout history, to influence others in a number of ways. And my oneness with this 'all' is essential to my being.

- I feel that I need to be a vehicle, a spiritus mundi, to conduct my own orchestrated arrangements in such a way that others can experience an essence of the personal, global, and universal self. It isn't enough that I just tell or inform. My desire is that it gives the reader the opportunity to experience a sense of oneness with a world that has not been experienced by them (you) before.

- I feel that my task as an arranger/conductor is without personal ego need. I think the driving need for me is to express a sense of being and existence that may be meaningful for a few. As I have mentioned, I feel like I am a vehicle, and I am simply the compiler of all these seemingly different streams of thought. The essence of beauty is hidden by a social/human malaise. Like many before me, this work is just another expression of a timeless message. My hope is that this vehicle will work, at least for some of you. But remember, my clinical work, at least for me, is the result of my earlier reflection. It's a balance of input and output.

- In my clinical work, I have taken the principles of science and intellectual thought and applied them to a treatment that improves the functioning of those who are seen as highly complex. They have been given many labels, been through many treatments, and shown no improvement. My need was to establish an environment that is not cluttered by cliché social/human values and not limited by diagnostic and treatment answers that are based on little academic rigour or creative scientific insight but on scientific-sounding conceptualisations.

- I am also aware that my life, which you would correctly see as fulfilling, needs to be focused on the well-being of others and making a difference in their lives.

However, I should confess that I have this strange combination of personal responses to effecting some significant changes in someone who becomes measurably better, especially after many others have tried unsuccessfully. I may sometimes have a momentary sense of pride, like successfully accomplishing some sports feat, but this is very fleeting, if it is there at all. The rewarding moments are based on achieving a newly formed analysis/hypothesis that is supported by a dynamic integration of developmental data. It is not being better than others that is important, In fact, I find the process of making these analyses very interesting and rewarding. The process can also be humbling since there are many times when someone is diagnosed with disorder that presents as very severe, but their state can be explained by dynamics that are actually quite normalised in their nature, not by a pathology. One is a swan, not a duck. I may ask if I could be correct. Why haven't others had the same insight? However, I do feel some support when speaking to someone who understands scientific thinking and is interested in understanding the mechanisms that underlie human functioning. Like the conductor, they are interested in a creative, scientific venture and the expression of their work; their goal is learning for the sake of gaining knowledge about the universe or a cell. I find these people to be of like minds. They are able to see what has been often missed on a social/human plane and can clearly accept what I am hypothesising.

However, I must confess I have a very difficult time talking to people who work in an applied science field but don't understand, or even seem to care to understand, the rigour in thinking necessary for 'doing good science'. They typically don't understand the tenets of research design, conditional relationships, the need for empirical/mechanist measurements, or what have you. What some of those people see is that they don't really understand what I am talking about, so they package all I have said into a 'well, you have your own beliefs' response and then stop any attempt to understand. Though I have a great passion for what I do, I do find it difficult to teach the person who has this type of defensive response.

You may ask, 'It sounds like you have been dedicated to helping those who are difficult to figure out, but is that enough? And it also sounds like it is difficult for you to educate other practitioners. I know you feel that you have done something valuable, and if you do, shouldn't you follow your own thoughts about selfless expression? Couldn't you use your abilities and teach others?'

Your questions would be well-founded. My response about having a difficult time, having a passion, sometimes feeling a compassionate sadness, and being humble is really just a combination of human responses. Boy, you may feel that my expressions seem too human. We have come all this way, and the person who is leading the way is only a fragile human. Isn't that where we started?

Remember, in weakness is strength, and in strength is weakness. The composition exists, but as a conductor, I would need a somewhat evolved audience. I couldn't conduct early or mid-twentieth-century pieces by Schoenberg or Stravinsky and have them accepted by an audience of Top 40 (if that still exists) or even by many eclectic adult listeners.

Some self-indulgent reflections: Human, outlaw, or both?

What follows are some important social/human distinctions that I think have been and are inherent to the scientist, artist, spiritual thinker, or philosopher. The public arena—whether it be presenting papers to large groups, public speaking, belonging to organisations, media presentations, and other like expressions (that may have mass appeal)—is unfortunately inimical with the whole essence of this and other creative works. Though personal experiences may occur for some people in these venues, they would be more lateral than vertical in nature.

A friend related a parking lot incident that he experienced when leaving an inspiring talk by the Dalai Lama. A woman who had also been to the talk was yelling vehemently at another who walked across her path. My friend asked her if she enjoyed the talk. To achieve a more insightful experience, to use Pasteur's words, discovery comes to the prepared mind. Preparing the mind requires . . .

Of course, there are other creative people whose words, ideas, and creations have had mass appeal. Popular music, whether Rodgers and Hart or the Beatles, made—and continues to make—a universal impact on millions and millions of people. Certainly, Steve Jobs was an extremely bright, interesting, and innovative thinker who, I would think, could have related to these ramblings. But as his life history illustrates, he had the ability to create a need based on his insight into what the social/human would want. I think we could surmise that Apple consumers weren't interested in his thinking or how he came up with his products. They were and still are obsessed with what they can do with his products.

Social/human realities, on the surface or below?

Let's be somewhat judgemental and suggest that social/human reality is dominated by a day-to-day concern about what works for me, what is enjoyable, what one likes or doesn't like, and the acceptance of attitudes and beliefs that I apologetically refer to as 'the arrogance of ignorance'. Thinking about underlying orders, the oneness that is *all*, curiosity about the essence of things doesn't have mass appeal. This occurs even though the underlying structure, the beauty, the complexity in a oneness has a richness that could be rare and especially fulfilling. For those who experience on many levels, those hapless few, life experience can be fulfilled in many ways by the unnoticed, the unseen, the hidden. For the mass, it matters little. As someone said to me, 'Who cares?'

'Do you like wine?'

'Yes, I love it. I drink red all the time. I think I've got a fairly well-educated palate.'

'Would you like to taste a 1945 Mouton Rothschild? I'm opening a bottle.'

'No, that's okay. I'm not really that interested in really old wines anyway. And besides, it was probably fairly expensive, which I think is a waste of money. You know, you can get some really good Australian reds for fifteen bucks. They're great! Why would you pay more?'

This work, as has been my premise, will only be for a few. My sense is that for you who are intellectually curious, are open, and have enough schooling to understand the language and ideas and whom I could ask,

'Are you experienced?' (as some guy from Seattle who grew up on the east side of I-5 once asked), there is no mass appeal.

Writing works well for me, so in this work, I can speak to you as a person. I can take time formulating my expression, and you can take time to process and digest, and I hope that when you read this, you have done so without distractions.

Even though multiple copies may be produced, reading, listening, experiencing is best when there are no distractions. I can remember talking to one of my staff while we were travelling together. He expressed how he liked music and enjoyed many popular groups, so I afforded the opportunity of listening to a Mahler symphony. I turned up my car stereo fairly loudly, and we had no conversation. At the end of the symphony, he said that he had never done that before. He and his group of friends may listen to music for a few moments without talking. He admitted that he had never listened to music for any length of time without distraction. But he and his friends certainly had views of what was good and bad solely based on simple thematic phrases they liked or thought were 'good'. I hoped the experience of just listening to an orchestra composed of instrumentation that he wasn't even familiar with would be influential enough to give him a starting point.

In a way, he didn't have an experience of our listening to music at the level of our beginning 'oneness'. But he needed to begin by listening to music of all sorts with no distractions. Initially, this would mean without any internal cognitive or evaluative distractions or external ones from others. He would need to start with undistracted openness to different sounds and combinations of sounds and expand his individual listening experience. My sense of these dynamics is that if new listening experiences would bring about the development of his ability to hear a marriage of different sounds, timbre, melodies, and harmonies, he would need time for new experiences to develop. Without this time and some enjoyment, I would expect that the sensitivity of any listener could be lost. For him, it was important that he experience the music, and it wouldn't work for him to be the student first and then learn about the instruments of the orchestra, composing, arranging, or conducting. He needed to enjoy or at least find listening satisfying and hopefully interesting.

I should mention that, several weeks later, my travelling companion told me that his experience had been very rewarding and had changed his ability to listen. He took the first step in moving below the surface.

Unfortunately, developing levels of awareness in any area of life, whether academic or human developmental in focus, may sound insightful but may remain at a social/human level for most. They meet the person's needs but . . .

As a result of my own expressive needs, my own life activities have been somewhat limited on one level but enriched on another. All those things that others may do are not afforded to me. Others may try hundreds of cheap wines; others may go off to other parts of the world to have fun or relax. I typically go to work or sometimes race cars. Often, at least from my point of view, these people not only want to see the world but also do the 'in' thing. The middle-aged and older may go to Provence and have a wonderful time but rarely do have a feel for French culture; they have never lived there and have no knowledge or appreciation of wine, yet the wines are marvellous! It's evident that it is just the thing to do, and they may go to Tuscany for the same reasons. I find it interesting that we might expect some lateral and vertical movement experience, but I see nothing that connects. They had a wonderful time.

In fact, one possible test of vertical sensitivity might be their descriptions of the French or Italian. If they are seen as so different, maybe very quaint or friendly or whatever, but seen in a manner that makes them stereotypically different and somehow unique, I would conclude that they had no real depth of experience. If they saw people as different, just as they are everywhere else in the world, that would sound more insightful. Let's hypothesise, from a consideration of underlying human dynamics, that individual differences that exist around the globe can be considered as a function of combined factors, including species (i.e., human), ethnic, genetic, epigenetic, group affiliations, occupation, and to some degree traits that may be a function of regional and national identification). It may be more insightful to see others as equally the same and different as all others in the world. Someone with a more vertically oriented influence may see others as all the same. They are all social/human beings. This whole discussion sounds somewhat priggish or certainly cynical, doesn't it?

In my life, I go to a number of other places in the world. Even though I may do some tourist-type sightseeing, I am typically somewhere else because of a specific purpose. I am frequently a consultant, an academic, a friend, a relative, a colleague, or even an amateur car racer. On occasion, going somewhere may be nothing more than a reclusive getaway. To use a music analogy, my visits are just a perfunctory experience in which I hear local music. It is about working together. It could be playing, conducting, arranging. It is not just listening; it is being one with others and their music.

I can recall an interview with Itzhak Perlman after a trip to Israel, where he played with a small group of musicians who were playing traditional music on the fiddle. He was overwhelmed by the essence of the music and felt his playing couldn't quite do it justice. The visitor is part but is separate. In fact, I have lived on a street for longer than anyone else who now lives there, and even though I feel at one with the physical environment—the sea, the weather—i am still a visitor with respect to the people, but I have been through all this before. Yet I do clearly have a sense that my creative need is already grounded in some more timeless aspects of European/ Asian/North American intellectual/creative cultures, and this gives me a sense of oneness with all my travel, whether on my street or in another continent. As mentioned, my travel is often academic. My limitation is that I need to engage and get involved, not just observe. Wherever I go, whether sailing in the South Pacific or just going away for a weekend, I always take my creative work with me.

There are moments when I feel a desire to live a life that is more like others. Boy, that sounds ironic. And there is periodically that social/ human urge of the ego, somewhat of a surface, competitive desire to play the game of others. But generally, it is very fleeting. Hearing others say how wonderful their trip was and that they saw this and this and this and this is usually an instant reminder that I don't want to follow their lead.

'Women come and go / Talking of Michelangelo.'

1

From self to others: Depressive thoughts without being depressed

Hopelessness? A compassionate sadness? Or a smile? It seems that the social/human plane remains unchanged. The masses of the geographically defined societies remain different. They are seen as separate, different from us, but they're all the same.

When I look at the billions of people all existing on this 'darkling plain' (Blake's phrase), they, as I have mentioned, seem to have an overwhelming power of inertness (a concept Thomas Hardy considered). But these masses and their political and popular religious leaders don't seem to listen to underlying realities. Their focus is on what is necessary for meeting the ephemeral social/human needs for belief, being culturally separate, having individual or group self-importance, and so on.

If they have never really listened before, how can I, as one fragile human, change anything or make any difference? In fact, I don't even know if that is the role of the conductor. And as we have considered, creating some work to change anything is not really the role of the composer, though I can sometimes feel a calm Buddhist smile and even a sense of joy when someone experiences a moment of insightful epiphany, when a person begins to see how one becomes many and many becomes one. But 'alas, poor Yorick', I express. But like many before me, my passion for creative thought and experiencing many perspectives is something that is elusive to most. I know that the exploration of unfamiliar and the experiences that are beyond (below) are of no interest and never really understood by many and probably never will.

Here are some thoughts from Ezra Pound:

With their large and anaemic eyes they looked out upon this configuration.

Let us, therefore, mention the fact,

For it seems to us worthy of record.

Beauty is so rare a thing . . .

So few drink of [its] fountain.

7

Anyway, enough of self-indulgence and expressions of possible hopelessness. But hold it!

If I want to look at the reality, do I need to paint an even bleaker picture? Let's accept that the species have not and probably will not evolve. They may even self-destruct. There will not be a Yeatsean second coming, at least in the form he hoped. People are not going to become enlightened. Masses of people will continue to be led by an unenlightened few. Most will remain in a state of delusion, be unaware. Education may produce smarter people, but fewer learn to think. There will be fewer attempts to even begin to understand our species' abilities and clear limitations. The social desires will be for control. They will never be able to let go of ideology, nationalism, and the myriad of other isms.

Given all these reflections, it is necessary to carry on.

Here ends the readings of the self-indulgent.

Here, we have a movie clip, another stylistic shift.

Picture yourself, for a brief moment, sitting in a movie theatre. As you are waiting to the new production of <u>The Life and Opinions of Tristram Shandy, Gentleman,</u> and after some ads and other movie trailers, there is a black-and-white short film that is just like the old Saturday matinee serial. You can hear clicking sounds that are like from an old 16 mm movie projector and see a grainy title, *Lost Civilisation*.

You see a huge modern-day cruise ship moving across a calm, unthreatening sea, but the background music doesn't seem to fit. It creates an ominous feel as if foreshadowing some unpleasant event. The ship cruises right into a reef that is clearly visible. You can hear yourself thinking, *Turn! There's a rock!* But the ship doesn't change course. It is almost as if it is doomed. No one seems to notice or care. It hits the rocks, moves up a bit, and slowly starts to heel and begins to sink. As you watch, you notice that there are no lifeboats. You see no one trying to escape and then realise that you don't even see any people.

In typical serial fashion, a voice from the film asks, 'Is this the end? Is there no hope? Is everything lost? Tune in next time for the next exciting episode of *Lost Civilisation*.'

Some thoughts come to mind. *How will they, if there is a* they, *get out of this? Is it some type of symbolic statement? Does this ship represent the humanity? Civilisation?* Your thoughts are interrupted.

The episode is over. Sorry you missed the lead-up. On to the main feature.

Back to the theatre.

You experience some piqued curiosity in anticipation of the next serial short, and you even question why you have come back, though you are interested in seeing a rerun of <u>A Clockwork Orange,</u> which you haven't seen before. But for some reason, you are interested, getting some resolution. The next episode is ready to begin. The lights go down, and everyone faces the screen.

But as is typical with suspenseful movies, they want the audience to wait, there are so led in moments, and the grainy old black-and-white short film begins.

The Interview

A film about making sense in black and white

You wonder if there is some mistake. This has nothing to do with *Lost Civilisation*. But you decide to see this through. For some unknown reason, in fact, none of the others you are with are questioning or wanting to leave. Anyway, as you watch, you notice that there are no credits, no film producers, no direction, not even the names of the actors.

We see two people sitting across each other, one with a notepad, casually dressed, wearing a sports jacket. He looks like a boring person. At the other side of the screen to the right is another person who seems less caring about appearance and looks somewhat tense and fidgety. They are both sitting in similar wooden chairs that don't look too comfortable.

We can certainly assume that the person on the left is the interviewer, but where, what, who? Who knows?[8]

'Good morning.' The interviewer opens the dialogue, while the other person is looking down at the floor and doesn't respond. 'Good morning.' The interviewer tries again.

'Hi.'

'I want to spend some time this morning, just to get to know you. Is that okay?'

'Okay.'

'Are you feeling comfortable?'

'No, not really.' Int looks at oth with 'a tell me more' look. 'I think you're here to spy on me. You want me to confess.'

'I don't think so. What do you need to confess about?'

'About what I know. I know what's going on!'

Int strokes his chin and pauses as if thinking. Oth stares into space. Int nods affirmatively. 'As you said, you know what's going on.'

'Yeah, and you know what I know. I don't even need to tell you.'

Int makes some notes and then adds, 'Yes, I certainly have a sense of what you know, and that's okay. You just need to fill me in. I talk to lots of people, and I sometimes forget.'

'Well, I don't know how you could forget. Everybody knows.'

'But remember, I don't think we've met before, have we?'

'Well, probably not, but—'

'That's all right. Tell me some more so I can understand better.'

---

[8] Since this is a transcription of the dialogue, I will refer to the two individuals as 'int' and 'oth'.

'Well, it's all these different governments. They're all terrorists, you know. See? I know that, and they are after me. I know you must work for one of them. That's why you're asking me all these questions.'

Int seems very calm and even slides down in his chair a bit. 'I'm just a humble guy who is interested in you and what you know.'

'All these countries don't know, but I've had a voice speak to me. I don't know who it is. It could be an alien or something, but the voice is clear. The countries are going to destroy the world, and the world leaders are programmed to do that, and they know I know! They're after me!'

Int takes many more notes and then asks, 'Do you sleep through the night?'

'It's during the night that they plan. I can hear them. Sometimes they tap into my thoughts.'

'What is seven minus five?'

'Two.'

'Do you have family?'

'Yeah, but they're all part of the same conspiracy.'

'To destroy the world?'

'Everything. In my dreams, I see a big ship and hear this voice that says, "There's chaos." People are fighting over who should be captain, and they don't know. They're all programmed for destruction. The ship runs into the rocks and sinks.'

'Do you think this or know it?'

'This is the truth. That's why they're after me!'

'What do you do for a job?'

'Nothing right now. I used to be a university student.'

'How come you're not still a student or working?'

'They're all part of the same conspiracy.'

'How would you feel about taking some medication to comfort your thoughts?'

'*What!* You must be part of the whole conspiracy.' Oth stands up and looks somewhat panicked. 'You can't drug me to shut me up.'

Int remains calm. 'It's okay. You just seemed so distressed. I thought I could help you feel better, not change or control your thoughts.'

```
                    FIN.
```

The lights come up slightly in between the short and the movie. The group looks somewhat confused.

'That's it? What the heck was that?'

Our philosopher puts it in perspective. 'It looks like some uncharted waters for all of us.'

'That was the weirdest thing I've ever seen.'

'You know, the funny thing is that guy was crazy, but he made sense!'[9]

'He didn't make any sense to me.'

'But think about it. We're waiting for the next episode of *Lost Civilisation*. We know there are no voices or powers controlling but the fact that different countries with different agendas probably don't balance each other out but are most likely leading to the sinking of the civilisation ship.'

'I can really see that there are no good guys and bad guys. I felt that interviewer was respectful of the person he was talking to. In fact, as you said, there was some truth in what he said.'

'Maybe we need to better understand someone else's point of view. What I'm feeling right now is that all points of view need to be respected because they represent a point of view that is expressive of their experience and what have you.'

---

[9] When I wrote that line, I unexpectedly felt a strong emotional surge of empathy, sadness, beauty. It's possibly a simple line to you but profound to me. It actually surprised me, but I felt it was important that I convey that to you.

The lights dim again, and the group is silent, ready for the main attraction.

'But now that you're not expecting it, here it is.'

```
Lost
Civilisation
```

There is the image from the last episode of the ship moving slowly but unequivocally towards the rocks. It certainly looks hopeless. And viewing the other side of the ship from a distant shot, we can see the passengers loading the lifeboats and the boats being lowered into the sea. Though the sea is choppy, the boats handle it well, but the ship keeps moving. It looks like the lifeboats are cleared. The ship hits the rocks, and we can see the wave action driving the ship again and again against the rocks, and it starts to sink. A pan to the lifeboats shows that they are all clear of the rocks and are moving down the shore at a safe distance from the rocks.

You feel somewhat cheated even though you missed the obvious. But certainly it took on creative thinking.

One from our audience speaks to the person in the next seat. 'This is a dumb next episode. No one came to the rescue, the ship isn't saved, we didn't even see whether the people panicked, and it doesn't even look like anyone was hurt. It's just boring, don't you think?'

'Yeah, it is so predictable. The ship sinks, and everyone is saved, nothing eventful. In fact, we didn't predict it.'

'I don't really see the point. As you said, the ship sinks, and all the people are saved.'

'Let's watch. Something's bound to happen.'

There is an underwater shot of the ship as it settles to the bottom, and it is still and silent. Then there is a shot of the lifeboats turning into a small protected bay. None of the shots have close-ups, but you can tell there are lots of people in each lifeboat. They look somewhat organised. Each boat seems to have someone in charge standing above the others, giving directions, and all the boats are clearly going towards a small protected, rocky beach. The landing of the boats and unloading of passengers seems orderly and without hardship or incident. The background music doesn't seem to fit the somewhat serene, purposeful-moving masses. Stravinsky's <u>Rite of Spring</u> is played lower than expected volume, but why this was picked, who knows?

The next shot pans over to a ridge adjacent to the beach. It shows a few people standing watching the activities. Even when the boats land, the observers remain at a distance.

Once again, we have some reactions from our audience. 'This is boring. Nothing is happening. It's more like some kind of historical report or some kind of illustration of what to do if you are on a ship that sinks. It's certainly not a serial.'

'Let's get out of here.'

'Yeah, we could, but what about the movie? It's a Kubrick one, you know, and I haven't seen it.'

'So all of you but one stayed to watch the movie.'

A person in our group leaves, and then several hours later, everyone meets for coffee.

'I'm glad I left. Before that last part started, I was feeling a bit excited but lost that in a second. It was a drag.'

'I was thinking of the ship as being like civilisation—you know, like it was really important, kind of an all-or-nothing-type situation. But seeing the ship sink and all the people escape gave me a feeling like, "So the ship sunk, so what's the big deal? Everybody is safe."'

'I saw that too.'

'I'm curious about what any of you thought about that weird black-and-white interview?'

'We already talked about that, didn't we?'

'Yes, but I don't know. This whole last experience has left me confused, even the whole thing with the ship and the passengers. I now realise that I can be confused even by the boring.'

'You know, as you said, I had this funny feeling about how we respond to stuff. Are we only interested in the entertaining and exciting? However, the feature film was certainly entertaining, though I guess probably somebody thinks math is exciting, and I've always hated it.'

'So I guess you have an antipassion for math, right?'

'Yeah, right! Yeah, okay, so I have feelings about math, so what about the life of some bug?'

'But maybe bugs bug you.'

'All right, all right, you know what I mean.'

'Sure, I'm just teasing you. Sure, there are lots of things that can be boring. But obviously, someone somewhere may have a passion for probably anything.'

'True, but what—hmm . . . do . . . do we—well, I think we may learn, kind of, from the uneventful. And when I think about it—I just think of all the stuff that happens all the time. It's just not that interesting so we ignore it.'

The ship sunk. Who really cares?

```
FIN.
```

2:32:46 PST

Is this the end of the movie? Reality? Hope? The ramblings? What?

But the **all** *continues, not fazed, unaffected.*

Epilogue

It seems that there are three of us to consider here. Since this has started off as a self-indulgent exploration and developed from there, where this work has ended might be of interest to me. Since I have spent considerable time looking at the dynamics of my friend, she could be the second person of interest. And since you have had the experience of reading and looking at this work, then you could be considered the third. I guess we could also look at civilisation, but I think it sunk. So we can see that we are on our own and with others.

As for me, I'm doing well, thank you. I have learned that I need to write and express just as I need to breathe. After that, everything falls into place.

My friend is with the dualities and is challenged by calm and stormy seas and can lose perspective for years at a time, but in the end, all will be well.

As for you,

_____

_____

_____

Structural Primer

My concept of the outlaw from a Buddhist perspective

In many ways, Buddhism is based on a way of thinking and not on a prescriptive ideology, though there are many tenets that are accepted; they are the result of thinking. This is consistent with what I hope you have experienced in my writings. In essence, clear, well-structured thinking that can see 'something' from a number of points of view will give us a better sense of what this 'something' is than just blindly accepting it at face value or in some prescriptive manner.

Buddhist thought and point of view has led us to the Four Noble Truths and the Eightfold Path. You can read many texts to learn these (though i will include a list and brief explanation). I will not attempt to teach you about Buddhism. I will simply use some of its fundamentals in summarising my view of becoming the outlaw.

An important word in Buddhism is 'right'. The goal is to follow the right path.

Right—I wrote this word, and here we are. Ramblings are over, and I was just hit by the political left/right distinction symbolically.

How could I miss that? I have no idea. You might be asking, 'What is he talking about?' My moment of awareness occurred while I was writing the word and simultaneously anticipating the Buddhist meaning of 'right' and the political one and realising the inimical nature of the same word. I guess it shows how much I am programmed to be aware of the social/ human political world.

For a moment, the impact of the world of delusions can dominate. As a result, a multiple-perspective point of view is briefly forgotten.

Oh yes, we were discussing the Eightfold Path and 'right'.

'Right' is like karma; it has nothing to do with a social/human rule, religion, or moral point of view. It is defined in terms of the 'outlaw' thinking. Therefore, it is neither right nor left; it simply is.

In Buddhist terms, 'right' is descriptive of harmony and compassion with all being, whether musician or not. It is not bound by time, space, or belief. It is beyond the ephemeral and the social/human. It could almost be seen as circular in description because the 'right' comes from having an evolved right point of view. But 'right' is also what describes the steps to get there. Our examples may help clarify its meaning.

In our application, we have

o   right visualisation,
o   right calming,
o   right point of view,
o   right thinking.

Remember:

4 rights ≠ 1 wrong

Right visualisation: It is used to broaden and enhance experience. It can include multiple modalities. The more practised you are, the better you can not only see but also experience physical movement (though you may not be moving), smell, taste, or whatever. No visualised experience is wrong. It is 'putting it into perspective' that is important. It could be experienced as profound or not really very significant. Remember, it can be experienced as real or not real; however, your visualised experience, which you experience in many ways, may be more real than someone else's 'real' (because they were their) experience.

Right visualisation needs to be accepted for what it is. It is a real experience. It is not driven by selfish desires. It is not judgemental. It is pure and innocent. It is. But its context requires integration and harmony with our other three tenets. Not one of these stands alone.

Right calming: The body and the psyche need to be variable and adaptive, but being able to be calm is essential. Calmness is not boredom, ennui, vegging out. It is having all the body systems functioning in a relaxing, harmonious whole—the still pond. The body is open to accept and experience without reactivity, rigidity, or conversely awareness and lethargy.

This too is right when it is in harmony with our other tenets.

Right point of view: Like visualisation, no point of view is wrong. If we accept the sense of right we are discussing—though this statement, as we will see it, is somewhat tautological—we can have an unlimited number of points of view. All could be said to be representative of a person, a group, or whatever. They all are correct if they accurately represent the view of a specific person. One person may know that killing whales is essential for the well-being of certain peoples. Another knows that the whales must be saved, their lives respected; otherwise, they may become extinct. Someone else may contend that both of these points of view show no care for the well-being of individual whales. 'What about the life of L42?' Another person may not really care about whales because other things in the world are more important. 'What about war? What about abortion!' We, of course, could have an endless stream, all representative.

So what about 'right'[10] point of view?

'Right' comes from

1. experiencing all (which is not possible) or as many as possible and seeing the structural (social/human) similarities;
2. harmonising these with more timeless, nonhuman points of view, ones probably not considered on the surface;
3. harmonising these with our other three tenets.

---

[10]   The use of 'right' in this context cannot have a definite article like 'the' because it changes the meaning of 'right' from a complex to only one meaning.

As I hope you can see, right doesn't mean right wing or left wing. It doesn't even mean ethically right or wrong. 'Right', at its most basic level, is our ability to stand in someone else's shoes and to understand the dynamics without social/human judgement.

Right thinking: There is thinking that is influenced by many factors. One may say, 'I feel. Therefore, I think *x*.' Oops, bad thinking. Not everyone needs to become a conceptual analytic philosopher, a philosopher of ethics, a philosopher of science, a mathematician, a scientist, or for that matter a Buddhist monk. But what we see is that good thinking is consistent throughout the history of all these disciplines.

Like the other areas we have discussed, this thinking needs to be integrated with the other tenets. It is important how we put these together.

The outcome is that we can understand, not judge, but we can also see mistakes in thinking and be aware of assumptions and hypotheses.

These four tenets can only become a natural part of you and be expressed in your action if you can integrate the following:

- Self-regulation of your physiology
- Having ego but no longer needing it
- Putting the body, speech, and mind pieces together
- Experiencing all in the essence of the smiling Buddha

Self-regulation: To be able to change your physiological state (as measured), meeting the demands of different contexts would seem desirable. At face value, that would seem to make sense. However, if we used our word 'right' with self-regulation, we may conclude that there may be many demands at the social/human level that, upon reflection, are not the result of good thinking or may have adverse influences on our own and others' health and well-being. Following our reflective steps can help you see, and part of the process is being calm, which means you need to be able to achieve that state. Our goal then is to have you experience calm so that experienced relaxation = relaxed physiology and calm mind. But for most of you, experienced relaxation may not be relaxed physiology/mind.

Ego: We have two levels. Ego can be fun, but if it defines your identity, you are stuck. It can dominate your point of view, your ability to be calm, and your thinking and, therefore, eliminate any reflectivity, even if you can visualise. In a simple way, we may say the *I* dominates.

The alternative is that *I* is seen as the expressive vehicle of *all*, where *all/I* is the expression of timeless knowledge, thinking, and collective wisdom. It is interesting that sometimes a personal ego can be experienced as beyond all that has come before.

Personal humbleness is an essential part of the ego that allows for right visualisation, calming, point of view, and thinking.

Body, speech, and mind: This is the traditional Buddhist way of articulating how to have a complete, integrated, harmonious experience. I speak, and that focuses my thinking (mind). In Buddhism, the speaking is the repetition of phrases—a mantra. I'm speaking meaningful repetitive sounds that are also calming and with this

The smiling Buddha: This perspective really underlies all the above, but at the same time, it is a function of all of them. At this point, the best analogy i can think of is that of the loving, tolerant, and accepting grandparents watching several of their grandchildren playing. Their play is innocent in its nature but sometimes shows silliness. Sometimes it shows momentary bits of hitting and frustration. Sometimes it shows calmness and sometimes care. The grandparents can smile; they see the innocence and the fact that these are children.

In Buddhism, the actual perspective, not my own very different one, includes the Four Noble Truths. These make the following assumptions:

1. Human suffering exists everywhere. They use the word 'suffering' in a somewhat special sense. They see it as categorically descriptive of desire, craving, wanting, not wanting, and attachments. The presence of these desires in their terms is 'suffering', and this suffering is a fundamental reality of all people. This state also includes hanging on to ego, beliefs, routines, and rituals.

2. The first step in eradicating suffering—the second noble truth—is observing, breaking the wall of ignorance, and seeing that this suffering does exist.
3. The second step in moving beyond suffering, the third noble truth, is becoming separate from these desires and attachments. The goal is to not respond to those sensations associated with suffering.
4. The final step, the fourth noble truth, is becoming one with *all*.

The Eightfold Path is divided into three areas: sila, samadhi, panna. This path includes the following 'rights':

- speech
- action
- livelihood
- effort
- awareness
- concentration
- thoughts
- understanding

As you can probably appreciate, most, if not all, of these concepts above have been addressed in a different order and articulated in different contexts throughout these ramblings.

All **is the same but different.**

A Primer on Visualisation

Like most skills that people learn, the techniques of visualisation are easy for some to learn and more difficult for others. In my ramblings, I have discussed visualisation, given some examples, and even suggested some exercises, but I didn't systematically approach this from a consideration of where you might be in your ability. This section is written to help those of you who need some more direction, learning, and experience.

Let's test your internalised systems first. To do this, we will start with memories; and as we will see, memories can incorporate a number of modalities—sensory systems. For instance, you may remember a simple conversation that you had with someone. In this case, you may have a visual memory. You can see the person—an auditory memory. You can hear the person speaking—a cognitive memory. You remember what the person said. If this person was wearing some strong perfume, you could have an olfactory memory; you smell the person. These types of memories are referred to as episodic memories in psychology. That doesn't really matter to us here, but i will use this term because it is a word that can be easily associated with the kind of memories we want to discuss.

I would like to take a few minutes to consider episodic memories and their impact. First, they—as we can see—can be memories that are visual, auditory, cognitive, olfactory, or gustatory. But if you take a minute and think of all aspects of yourself that can be triggered by episodic memories, they are vast, aren't they? You could have simple associations like taste or touch, but you could also have an overall physical sensation, tension, happiness, sadness, frustration, anger, a sense of peace, et cetera.

Second, we can have an interesting interplay of the above variables in these episodic memories. For instance, you could have an experience that was highly emotional, but the actual circumstance, if seen by someone else, may have looked (visually) very ordinary with no obvious emotional quality to it. If you become aware of this other person's point of view, your visual memory may actually change.

I saw a young adult years ago who reported that he had stopped skiing because a grizzly bear passed in front of him as he was skiing by himself. In talking to others, it was evident that he was extremely anxious, even fearful about going too fast, being out of control, and hurting himself. His friends also reported that he had had a panic attack at the ski resort and never skied again. From a generally accepted point of view, it would seem reasonable that skiing down a slope could not produce the degree of anxiety he had felt. Let's assume that, at an unconscious level, he felt the same thing. So what happens? The body then creates an image, a memory of something that could account for his feelings—a grizzly bear! That would work, and now the anxiety makes some sense. Here's a visualisation, and to him, it is real.

What is important to note here, as we consider our use of memory to develop skills in visualisation, is that the accuracy of episodic memory doesn't matter. We are interested in the dynamics of our memory.

For purposes of visualisation, we could give the above young man full marks. He could really fear and even visualise a grizzly bear. We could, however, question his self-awareness.

For those of you who have had something highly elating or highly traumatic, finding some experiences will probably be easy. For others of you, this may be more difficult. Our goal here is simply to use memory as an experiential tool. We want to be able to 'see' something with memory and also to experience it.

Let's try another connection that can help in developing our ability to visualise or at least comprehensively experience something that isn't present in our reality at the moment. You may be able to hear the words of a parent and feel your response. You may remember hearing some political views that you strongly agree or disagree with and experience a whole range of emotions that you went through when you were actually hearing these words form the person—live! You may have had your favourite sports team, yourself, or someone your close to win.

Probably the most common trigger of episodic memory that would include visual, emotional, and physical sensation is music. Most of you, of any age, will have fairly profound memories of the people, the place, the time, the occasion, and the feelings associated with certain pieces of music.

You may have many other sensory connections in which memories rekindle all the dynamics of the actual experience. These are the stuff upon which to build your ability to visualise. But first, let's look at some more examples of the dynamic nature of memories. Let me use my own experience to illustrate a number of these dynamics that started with an olfactory memory.

My first example was having some thought and visual memories triggered by the smell of diesel exhaust. I used the word 'having' because the association did change. Anyway, at one point in my life, the diesel exhaust smell gave me very clear images of London. (For many years, the exhaust of the diesel taxis permeated the city.) I did lose this connection once I started driving a diesel car and had a sailboat with a diesel auxiliary. My present association with it is more of my boat.

My second olfactory example is my memory of the nose of certain wines. My memory of the 'nose' can sometimes trigger a visual memory. For many wines, I can remember the experience, the name, and the year (cognitive).

My third example is related to J. M. Synge's <u>Playboy of the Western World</u>. If I read his work or reflect on his words, i can literally smell the west coast of Ireland. When i first realised this, I found it to be very strange, but it was my experience.

Many of you may have food aversions. And even the thought of the food, its name, its smell may make you feel nauseous. Here, again, is a memory that could be sensory and thus physical. However, for each one of you, the dynamics may be different.

In sports, muscle memory aptly describes what your body remembers to do. As we know, this memory does not just happen while playing a sport but can also occur in your physical response to a wide range of situations. Of course, in sports, it is hopefully established in a correct way; but for many, this memory is of an incorrect way. In a sport, memory is being established as part of a learning process but, in doing so, may require changing incorrect muscle memories. This is usually achieved with great difficulty since your body has learned the wrong way and has to change.

I hope these few examples of memory that are outside the strictly visual will help you in understanding that these are many aspects of yourself that are used in memory.

Our goal is to get beyond memories and have you able to create new 'visualisation' experiences. Our discussion of the sensory dynamics of memories allows us to have you test your ability to 'experience'.

———

Which modalities seem to be most profound?

- visual
- overall physical sensation
- intensity
- sensation/feel (that may be difficult to articulate)
- motor/muscular
- auditory
- taste/olfactory
- emotional
- cognitive
- cognitive/emotional

Which ones do you find connect with each other?

What I would do, in both coaching and therapy at this point, is to help you define your readiness.

Consider your ability to experience as fitting into one of three groups.

<u>Group 1:</u> Experiencing memories in any way is difficult.

<u>Group 2:</u> Experiencing memories with a single modality makes sense. You can feel it. You are able to actually appreciate the dynamics but find it difficult to actually relive it.

<u>Group 3:</u> Experiencing memories in a dynamic manner is very much part of your psyche and physiology.

my group

Group 1 people need to spend some time just allowing memories to emerge. There can be many reasons for this, and I will not attempt to suggest what these could be, but you may not be ready to gain much from my ramblings other than some new knowledge or thoughts.

Group 2 people probably just need more opportunity in becoming more aware and be open to more aspects of themselves. Spend some time doing nothing, relaxing, being calm, and focusing on those memories that are triggering some modality. See if you can sense that other things are happening to you as you reflect.

Group 3 people are ready to move on. You desire more.

But hold on.

April is the cruellest month of all . . .

Mixing memory with desire

(T. S. Eliot)

Desire is a significant piece of human suffering.

But let's carry on anyway. Pick your group and read the section. Don't rush the process.

There are numerous times in these ramblings where I have considered my time in writing this, your time reading this, and your time reflecting. For some of you, especially those of you in group 1, time will have special importance not because of the time itself but because of your use of time. Pick your group and read on.

<u>Group 1</u>

The process of enhancing experience needs some time to develop. It needs patience, openness, and the realisation that it is actually a good thing to feel, remember, and just be aware. Like many of the paradoxes in this work, you need to be able to feel before you can get beyond it.

There is another important point here. Making changes requires a plan and follow-through. You need to take time each day, week, or whatever to do nothing and just remember. For some of you, writing a diary of memories may be helpful. It gives a focus and form, and with it may come other associated sensations.

Let's put this into some steps.

Step 1 – This is an essential preparation stage. For many of you, I will call this 'undoing knots'.

If I said, 'Take some time each day to do nothing,' I predict that most of you would respond, 'I'm too busy. I don't have any time. I have to blah, blah, blah.'

'Do you have three minutes? That's enough time,' I might add.

'Well, maybe. Well, not really.'

Of course, what you are saying is that your response to my suggestion was felt in a somewhat defensive manner. Aha, there's a good source for our memory exercises. My suggestion may have triggered an increase in thinking about all you have to do. It would have also triggered physical changes, like an increased muscular tension, increased respiration, and an experience of stress.

'How did you feel when I asked you to take time each day?'

We also know that the more you express a 'no time' reality, the more defensive you are and the more you need to take this time, which we know you have anyway.

As the practice of mindfulness suggests, one exercise is to stay in the moment, what is happening now, not in the past or the future.

Step 2 – This is the follow-through. Of course, if you have never taken time to exercise on your own or do some disciplined activity on your own, it may be much harder to follow through and do something regularly than you consciously admit. Remember that, right now, you are taking time to read this, and you are doing this for more than three minutes. Anyway, set a time each day when you can spend three minutes.

Mon___:___, Tue ___:___, Wed ___:___, Thu___:___, Fri___:___, Sat___:___, Sun___:___

Establish some times for yourself. Make a commitment.

'Okay', you may say, 'but now what do I do with the time?'

For many of you, I think it may be best to keep this somewhat concrete. So my suggestion is that you buy or find a notebook and start with writing the day of the week, the time, and then a modality(ies) that describes what modalities contribute to your awareness.

Let's say you start with a visual memory. Make some notes on what you remember and then check out and make notes on other modalities that you are experiencing while you are remembering. See the sample sheet below.

```
┌─────────────────────────────────────────────┐
│                                               │
│  Date:_____ Time:_____             │
│                                               │
│  Triggering Modality                          │
│                                               │
│                                               │
│  visual: _____ │
│  _____│
│  _____│
│  _____│
│                                               │
│  overall physical:                            │
│  sensation:                                   │
│  intensity:                                   │
│  motor/muscular:                              │
│  auditory:                                    │
│  taste/smell:                                 │
│  emotion:                                     │
│  cognition:                                   │
│                                               │
│                      level of memory          │
│                      experience_____   │
│                                               │
│                                               │
└─────────────────────────────────────────────┘
```

You could even add a subjective memory experience impact at the bottom of the page.

I can kind of remember something, but it didn't mean a lot, or it could be that something just happened, and the experience was profound. (Wow!)

My suggestion is that if you would really like to experience the impact of visualisation, you need to work on these recollections until you could really feel many memories with a dynamic interplay of modalities.

Remember to try different triggering modalities. Maybe try auditory next. You may find that some memories are easier to retrieve than others, and that's to be expected.

Our eventual goal is to have you develop the capacity to experience the dynamics of your responsiveness to different situations while sitting in an easy chair at home.

Let's say that you have developed a vastly improved sense of memory, but it seems a bit self-indulgent. You are ready to move on.

<u>Group 2</u>

Just so you group 2 people are aware, the group 1 people have gone back to develop a better sense of their memory experiences, and I have suggested that they do it in a fairly concrete manner.

Let's say that those of you in group 1 or 2 are somewhat similar in your ability to recall and experience. I think that more practice in understanding the dynamics of remembered experience is needed for both of you. A good exercise here involves separating, expanding, and integrating modalities. First, see if you can feel different modalities in isolation and then see what other senses become part of the experience. Second, see if you can integrate this awareness of modalities into a single experience. Boy, this is just like listening to music where all the pieces come together in a single whole. For group 2 people, it may be worthwhile making some notes. See the group 1 sample note sheet for some ideas.

It is important, before moving on, that you can do a personal inventory (that sounds somewhat lacking in profoundness) of how each of the modalities you have listed is affected by certain situations. Also, establish a clear list of what modalities work best for you. However, I don't want you to cop out and conclude that many of these modes just aren't for you. If you really care, you will go back and work on them. The ability to experience will become very important as we move on.

Our goal here needs to be the ability to experience both the individual modality and the dynamics of a wide range of modalities triggered by memories in our hypothetical easy chair at home. This needs to be well established to move on.

Group 3

For you entering at this stage, we know you have had a lot of experience or have a natural talent for visualisation. Ironically, it may be that, from a social perspective, you are different from others and maybe seen as a bit weird. If you are beginning to read this section at this point and don't see yourself as abnormal, you probably need to go back to group 1. (See you later.)

For you who are ready, let's move on.

At this point, you can

- clearly be aware and experience your own memories in a comprehensive manner and
- do this when you want to.

Take a moment to indulge yourself. You can do it!

Okay, so the skills are there. Now for a big leap. We need to take these memory experiences and completely reconfigure them.

Our next goal is to take these personal insights and use them as a basis for going from your personal experience to the <u>not yet experienced</u>. And just to make things more challenging, this <u>not yet experienced</u> can have a number of facets.

The first application is a fairly straightforward one. As you who have read enough of my ramblings will know, ski racing is an activity I have often alluded to. In this application, visual, motor activity, and overall sensation need to work well together to enhance performance. We can also see this happening in many high-performance individual sports—gymnastics, diving, field events, golf, car racing, just to name a few. In some ways, ski racing is a good example of visualising the 'never previously experienced' situation but is built upon a visual knowledge of a course. The objective is to use a visual preview of a course and then expand it into the experience of actually skiing the course.

For you who do not know ski racing, which is probably most of you, let me explain. Though I will assume you have heard of downhill and other events, for you who don't know, there is slalom, giant slalom, and supergiant slalom. But none of this really matters for our purposes. What is of interest is that, in downhill, the course is always the same; but in the other events, the course changes. So in this case, we have two paradigms.

If we are good visualisers who have had the experience of skiing a specific downhill, we can sit in our easy chair and experience our run. But what happens in these other events is the course is new every time, and we have not experienced it previously.

What the athlete has to do, for courses that offer a new experience, is to walk through (could be slowly ski down) and literally memorise the course visually. The racer needs to know the turns, pitches of the hill, snow conditions, and where to be at every step of the way. This whole visual memory is important as a basis for 'visualisation'. But just as important, if not more so, is the muscular/physical sensation that goes with it as you ski the course in your head before actually running it. This may sound somewhat difficult to comprehend, but good visualisation will allow the ski racer to experience all the turns and integrate all the physical movements with correct timing and speed, just as you will do while actually skiing the course. I still find it amazing how much I can actually experience a run in a complete physical manner before I have even run a course.

My point here, of course, is not ski racing but our ability to experience what we have never actually experienced before by using previously learned physical sensations, muscle memory, and applying them in a situation not yet experienced.

Practising and applying these skills are needed before moving on to our next step, which is really another level of abstraction. Any kind of sporting activity can be good practice.

- If you are a golfer, you can play a hole or certain shots by visualisation. The caveat here is that you do need a certain level of established technique or knowledge of an appropriate technique for this to be beneficial.
- If you are a tennis player, you can gain a sense of someone you haven't played but have watched by visualising the opponent's shots and your returning them.

For you nonsports types, you might try visualising yourself in a new social situation. Create the setting and put yourself in it. Experience yourself moving, talking, feeling, thinking. You could even consider yourself going for a walk in some enjoyable, familiar place. See what is around you. Make some decisions and change your direction. Do something different.

You could do the same with driving. Pick a familiar area but change your route. Don't make the trip too long. It is best if you can visualise and experience in a one-to-one time frame.

Our goal here is to have you use all your modality awareness and change your experience within a familiar context. In this way, memories are still a basis for new experience. In turn, if you tried the new route, a new memory can emerge (even though you didn't really do it).

Okay, you've got that. Let's move on.

We now need to make a very big step. We now want to see if you can change the environmental context from something you know to something you don't.

Tolkien had never literally travelled to Mordor. He had never been there, nor was it part of his memory. Could we still assume that his visualisation of Mordor was very real? Absolutely! So he was able to visualise this fictional world with multiple (I would suggest) sensory aspects. Here is a place that doesn't even exist.

That really sounds like a delusion, doesn't it? Remember that to really have a delusion, you need to know that what you are experiencing is real, like people who believe that religions and countries are real. Visualisation is a skill we can develop and use. It doesn't take over our psyche; it just uses it.

Okay, so the challenge here is to visualise an environment that we have never seen. You are probably saying at this point, 'I can do that when I read a book I enjoy. I can see the place and the characters.' For you really old people or you who listen to radio stations who still produce radio plays, the same visualisation occurs. But in these situations, you are an observer of the events and are not the central figure.

In this step, I would like you to also experience a visualisation that is not established by descriptive prose and makes you the central or only character. In my ramblings, for instance, I have asked you (or are asking you, depending when you read this) to envision yourself at the top of a sailboat's mast, to experience your mind as a still pond, to sink below the surface of the water. This may be easy for you or very difficult. You may enjoy the sea. Your associations may be nonexistent or even distressing.

So I am saying that you put yourself underwater and experience the calmness. You may respond by saying, 'I hate water! This won't work!'

I can see a possible conflict here. At first, I am asking you to experience memories in a multisensory manner—the more profoundly and broadly, the better.

As I am writing this primer, I am interested in knowing but very uncertain about your reactions. Are you asking about an obvious contradiction, or are you at least anticipating that i will address it? Or are you absorbed in reading and are not critically analysing?

So let me put some pieces together. In my ramblings, I used my metaphors and my experience. I did not use yours.

I had this wonderful realisation about the surface of the sea and what it is like below. I could draw upon my memory of an event and the changes that occurred in all my sensations. I had no sensations that adversely affected my experience. Thus I used my own metaphor. The surface is highly variable. It can be chaotic or still. Below is calm, still, and separate from its metaphorical social/human surface.

As the conductor, I wanted you to experience the music, the rambling prose, but I also had to keep in mind that I know that being underwater may be difficult for some of you because it may have no relationship with any of your experiences, or you may have always had panicky overall sensations even when thinking about water. In James Joyce's novel, Stephen had very a negative early childhood and confused negative associations with water, though this did end up in a resolution at the end of *Ulysses*.

So here is a point where you might see a contradiction. You could ask, 'You wanted me to experience memories and all the sensations that go with that. I think I can do that well, but for me, I have always had a fear of being underwater. I feel like I am being closed in and suffocated, so I did your exercises and felt my memories. Now you are asking me to experience this metaphor in a calming way, but I can't! I would have to either turn off my feelings or feel and be panicky. What do you want!' If you have felt this or asked this, the question is an absolutely essential one.

Remember, I mentioned that this is a very big step. What is required is not only the ability to have an experiential memory that is multisensory but also to control the variables of your experience.

What about using a different visualisation? Obviously, other visualisations could work equally well as my underwater one. However, if you are going to use your own, it needs to meet some important criteria.

As with the water metaphor, the different point of view and calmness is found within and being immersed, not being away from or distant. It needs to have a transitional/vertical element to it. For instance, it may go from the ephemeral waves to a more timeless state. It should offer a sense of being nonseparate (e.g., separate from the waves but immersed). Experience it and become aware of your ability to control the self.

If your response is 'This is all too vague,' you may understand. You may think you understand and feel that you can do it, and that's also okay.

You may be just reading words. If this is the case, then this is probably a meaningless activity.

Depending on when you are reading this (in the context of my ramblings), I can appreciate that your understanding may be variable. But what becomes most important here is calming. Of course, this doesn't just happen without direction and practice.

So how does this happen, especially if you have very intensive responses?

Here are some simple steps for learning control.

So the next step is the ability to change your own sensory responsiveness. To address this, I think that the picture adjustments made on some older model televisions (OMTV) might be useful here. Let's assume that we are going to adjust the sound, picture quality, and a list of different components (e.g., brightness, colour, sharpness). These were often adjusted by using a sliding scale that could be moved for adjustment.

brightness   Low |———■———————| High

In our case, let's assume that we have a screen that displays all our modality responses and their level as a component in our experience. It is important to note here that these record how much of our experience is influenced by each component. The two components that I think may offer some confusion are overall physical and emotion since they may have an implied intensity, which is not the case.

For instance, if one is relaxed and calm, not thinking but aware of being at peace, then the overall physical could be the major component in experience because it dominates. We are all probably conditioned to thinking that high means high intensity and that intensity dominates and, conversely, low doesn't. But this doesn't have to be the case. Just to clarify one's level of intensity, we have an intensity descriptor.

Though this could describe any of our components, think of it with reference to the overall physical.

Remember, we can have a number of possibilities with just the overall physical and experienced intensity.

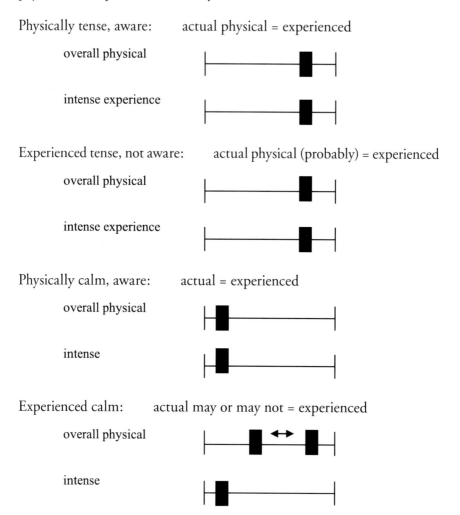

Physically tense, aware: actual physical = experienced

overall physical

intense experience

Experienced tense, not aware: actual physical (probably) = experienced

overall physical

intense experience

Physically calm, aware: actual = experienced

overall physical

intense

Experienced calm: actual may or may not = experienced

overall physical

intense

This is the most common 'error' state. One can experience a relative sense of calm but is actually in a relatively high arousal/tense physical state.

So let's consider a more comprehensive example.

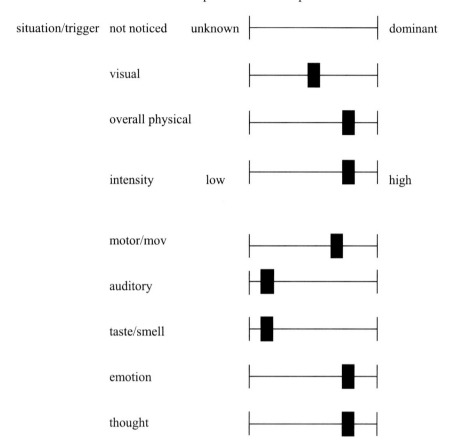

| situation/trigger | not noticed | unknown | | dominant |

Let's say that, for every memory situation, you will have slightly different sensory dynamics. How do you change but still have the ability to feel? With the OMTV, you may be able to move these different components up and down individually. But for most of you, this separation of different aspects of sensory experience may be far more difficult since all these modalities seem to work together. They're not always experienced as separate entities. As a result, it may require turning the power off before an adjustment can be made, and this is really just calming.

For instance, in treating panic attacks or phobias with desensitisation approaches, we need to have the person experience calmness in the absence of any triggering condition. Then we may introduce specific thoughts or stimuli and offer self-calming support so that these stressful aspects can be addressed while remaining calm. In this way, the person can experience, in a more comprehensive way, what aspects of self move up to higher levels when stressed, and these can be seen on our TV screen.

For instance, a common panic attack process could involve a thought or vision of something that triggers panic. This in turn ⟶ increased tension ⟶ increased physical awareness ⟶ thoughts of heart attack ⟶ intensity. Having the person become aware of this process helps in treatment. These sliding measures can be considered and reflected on. And like learning something new, these response patterns can be adjusted to decrease selected aspects of panicky and stressful responsiveness. It doesn't mean, however, that responsiveness becomes nonexistent or becomes only cognitive. What is very important here isn't just self-control but also the understanding and appreciation of experience. With this process can come a new openness to experience.

As an example, let's say that you have always been nervous about being in any small boat. This could include anything smaller than a good-sized ferry or cruise ship. And let's also say that you have a range of reactions that can go from discomfort to fear when even thinking or talking about going out on the sea. Let's also assume that you had a traumatic experience out on the sea while in a small powerboat. Besides feeling seasick, which you hated, you were also distressed because the skipper was inexperienced. As a result, you got lost and didn't get back to port until after dark (hours later than expected). The weather had become bad and the sea choppy. The boat almost tipped over (at least it felt like it), and you were wet and cold. Once you were on shore, you vowed not to do that again.

For the person in our example, being uncomfortable and distressed in even thinking about the prospect of being out on the sea would make sense.

So let's set up a possible multifactor description of this personal response to the sea.

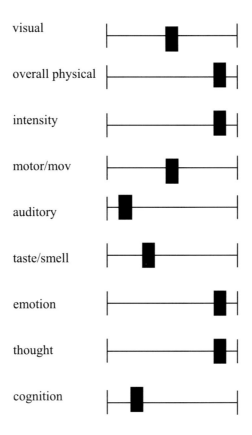

An overall high physical awareness with high intensity that would be shown in emotion and negative thinking would certainly make sense. We could also assume that there could be some visual memory of the waves, the dark, but these may not be a dominant factor in memory or anticipatory thought.

So if we would like the person to go out to sea in a small boat again, we would need to assist in changing these dynamics. However, rather than considering the sensory dynamics of the above and the approaches to changing these dynamics systematically, I will consider, in a contrasting manner, the possible memories of the above with the sea and boat analogies in these ramblings. Since ramblings are analogous to and don't require being there, you are safe. And since I'm not going to force you to go out on a boat, we will assume that your reactions could be more easily changed.

So let's assume that if you are somewhat fearful when reading my sea and boat analogies, you may still be able to clearly understand the point i was making; but because of your past associations, your reading has remained cognitively processed. *That's interesting,* you may have said to yourself. As a result, your experience could have been very minimal but safe.

Let me contrast how you might have reacted to a plan to go out on a small boat with how you may have read my reference to boats and the sea.

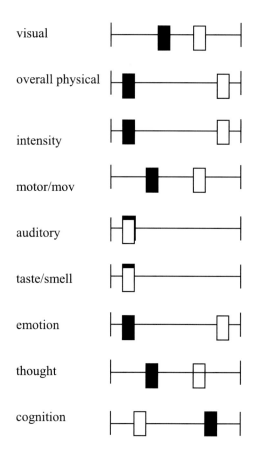

visual

overall physical

intensity

motor/mov

auditory

taste/smell

emotion

thought

cognition

Without covering our sensory dynamics in detail, what might be evident is the presence of a very profound overall physical/emotional anticipatory experience that is replaced by an experience that is not felt but understood. This would be great for our panic attack or phobic people since it would allow them to not only face certain situations but also think about them without distress. Generally, our main focus for these people is to reduce physiological arousal when paired with thoughts or images of what is feared.

However, for you, our reader, the goal is different.

You could say, 'Okay, I have not been on boats and the sea, or I have had a traumatic experience on a small boat, but I get what you're saying.' You may even be complimentary in my choice of analogy. (Though it isn't mine, it's been used forever.)

You may also say, 'And I agree with what you're saying. Isn't that your goal?' To that, I would answer no. My goal is to have you experience, not just understand cognitively. This next statement may seem inconsistent in its experience, but it's not. At face value, it may seem that a profound experience should not be profound. Consider that you become momentarily overwhelmed by something that you experience and that it affects not one but many modalities. But consider that your regulating response, after a few moments, was not experienced as too negative or conversely too positive. It just was. As you will recall, the analogy I have used previously was one of the experienced skipper at the helm of a sailboat in rough seas. The skipper could remain calm, focused, and stable in a seemingly unstable world. The ability to be calm in the face of adversity is an important and necessary step, but we need to go beyond.

This first step, as I mentioned before, may require (using an analogy) turning off and rebooting the OMTV if it has been under some unknown internal stress and if its quality has been lost. Our initial hope may be that a period of calmness (not on) is necessary for regaining its best state, but we may also understand that we may need to readjust some or all the image and sound components to obtain the best picture. Then we want an overall physical awareness with low intensity and a sense of emotional well-being. Our goal for you would be to keep the same boat/sea thought context but help you experience calmness, coupled with an emotional sense of well-being. So here is an interesting/transformation.

Step 1: The OMTV is shut down.

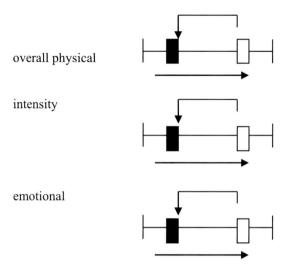

overall physical

intensity

emotional

Step 2: The OMTV is back up.

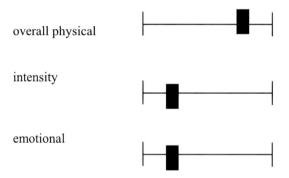

overall physical

intensity

emotional

You feel calm and open.

Step 3: Now you are ready to reengage with the world of ideas, thoughts, visualisations, and experiences but to be able to select the modalities by experiencing their influences and modifying them.

For those of you who naturally enjoy fantasy, this transformation, I think, would be easier because you can experience the world of symbol and understand its reality. With your imagination, you can control your dynamics by what you visualise. I have expressed my visualisation of the sea and being calm below the surface. As you can gather, I can visualise many different situations and adjust my reaction to these; but of course, in these ramblings, it would seem that I have picked them, which in a sense

I have. The visualisation goal here may be very difficult for some of you. Being underwater may feel like being suffocated, being drowned.

As I write this, I feel a need to go back to other aspects of your psyche, to explore aspects of psyche, et cetera. But this is not the purpose of this primer.

In the symbolic world, we may want to selectively consider the meaning and not the literal.

You are somewhere where you are tossed up and down. You can't get out of survival mode. You think you know where you want to go, but it is difficult getting there. You change your point of view. In our case, you go below the surface. It is clam. You can see. These need to be the drivers of your visualisation, not the literal.

Experience.

There is one other aspect of visualisation and our components that is important here—the ability to experience another point of view by adjusting our dynamics into those of another. Remember that we can learn from everyone. The goal now of visualisation is to put ourselves into another's shoes and to experience their point of view.

Throughout these ramblings, I have considered belief as a limiting aspect of experience. If one believes one thing, then they are unable to believe or accept other points of view. So let's look at some possible dynamics here.

Someone strongly believes in God. The person may have a visual reference; it could be a Christ figure or some more abstract picture of God. They will undoubtedly have overall physical and emotional sensations that are enjoyed, especially when thinking about God. The intensity could vary from situation to situation. One's experience could be a calm one, offering a sense of feeling cared for, safe, or whatever. Or it could be an intensive one if the individual is in a group, and there is a type of 'I believe!' group energy. What we may assume is that thought would be limited to areas that are emotionally safe, and as a result, cognition that questions would be low. Auditory could be a factor if language or hymns are used, and even smell could be a factor if incense is used.

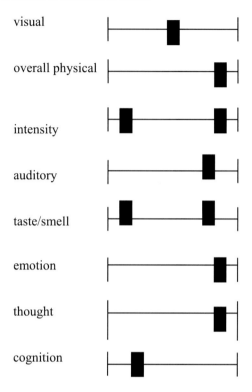

What we want to get a sense of here is the combination of hypothetically accepting another's object of focus (could be God) and experiencing the possible dynamics that create factors of their belief.

Some other interesting aspects emerge here as well. Let's say we want to change this other person's point of view. Could we attempt to do this by rational argument? That's probably what most people would do. However, if what we have described is correct, we can see that with our hypothetical person's cognition is what we might call a relevant negative concomitant factor. The person doesn't want to go there. The person doesn't want to change. Herein lies its relevance. But if we address cognition anyway and do so with a reasonable level of intensity, our person would probably feel some negative emotions, possibly a sense of being threatening; may feel agitated physically; or may have confused thoughts. And as a result, the person may have a greater need to return to simple thought and belief.

So how do you approach?

We would need to start by getting some view of the person's cognitive functioning and thinking. However, if we find any discussion about beliefs, religious ones in particular, we may find a reaction; therefore, we would need to find some other areas where we could gain an understanding of the person's thinking. We would probably expect that this person would need to be in a relatively calmed and nonintense physiological state if we are really going to get a sense of how the person thinks.

So let's assume that the person is fairly calm and can discuss some topics openly. The next step wouldn't be to just jump on the rationale but to use other noncognitive modes as bridges for opening this person up. For instance, if we found that the person's thinking and cognition was well-developed but shut down with any sense of personal threat, we may want to see whether this person can empathise with another and possibly see the dynamics of how someone else may hold a particular point of view (not religious) that is different from theirs. The point of this is to be able to see if they could understand that two different social/human points of view could be seen as the same if they both met the same needs. In a simple way, both may find that their view meets their need for security.

So now we have calmness and possible empathy. Could we use these two qualities to find an opening for acceptance of other people with the same needs who aren't bad or evil, just human? Yet these people have different beliefs. This, in turn, may assist in seeing that, often, underlying differences are similarities. It should be noted that this doesn't happen instantly but needs time to emerge.

For another person who also shows good cognition, is very tense, and is maybe anxious, we would need to somehow help the person calm so that their overall physical/emotional experience can be enjoyed in a calm manner. If intensity is dominant, it becomes very difficult, if not impossible, to even begin to change those points of view that are tied to anxiety. With this person, reducing the anxiety may have a goal of 'right thinking'. However, if we resort to the purely cognitive, we may become aware that *the more we knocked, the more he wasn't there.*

I could guide you through many other examples. We have people all different in their dynamics, all needing different types of changes to be able to experience different points of view.

This process, as i think you can appreciate, is ongoing and can require many steps and patience, but all this is beyond the scope of this primer.

Summary

My goals in this primer are to help you develop some insights and skills that will assist you in experiencing memories in a dynamic new way. But more importantly, it will help you to be able to apply these skills in experiencing changes in your point of view so that you can even experience the symbolic and the hypothetical. This will allow you to have new and different experiences in different contexts, to better understand others, and as a result to be able to see and to begin to experience the dynamics that underlie the social/human world.

Appendix A

A. A Structural Primer

This is a consideration of the factors discussed in *Becoming the Mad Outlaw* from a Buddhist point of view. I felt this was a good way to organise a lot of discussion that may seem contradictory, confusing, disconnected but at the same time logical, clear, and consistent.

B. A Primer on Visualisation

Aldous Huxley quotes William Blake at the beginning of his book <u>The Doors of Perception and Heaven and Hell.</u>

If the doors of perception were cleansed,

Everything would appear to man as it is, infinite.

Jim Morrison used the name <u>Doors</u> for a rock group, which i think for him was an escape door. It was a way out of his own social/human distress. It wasn't a door of rebirth or to some infinite. This primer is a natural (nondrug) approach to opening one's doors to the experience of cleansed perception. I have tried to make it simple but comprehensive.

Appendix B

A. Glossary

For those of you who are looking for the 'dictionary definition' in this glossary, it is important to understand that it is better to consult your favourite dictionary first. The comforting aspect of this dictionary reference is that it gives you an answer. That's good (which is god with two *o*'s). This glossary does not meet that need, though I hope it will give you enough direction to carry on reading the text.

To assist you in this process, I have been more seriously descriptive in defining some terms and had some intellectual fun with some others. If you are really uncertain, please refer to an unabridged dictionary. Believe it or not, some abridged dictionaries have definitions that are incorrect. Remember, dictionaries are written by people with denotation points of view. This glossary is not.

And to make this section more challenging, these terms are not ordered alphabetically.

B. Acknowledgements

This has not been a work in which I have purposely read any books or looked for any specific information. I have simply expressed my experiences that encompass my thinking, feelings, what I have done, and what I have read (just another aspect of *done*). Since my experiences have been shaped by many people who have expressed themselves over a period of many centuries and in many different disciplines, I am acknowledging their influences.

Glossary

Please be aware that this glossary is a mixture of concepts defined and answers given. Unfortunately, some may confuse rather than clarify in the way you may like.

aesthetics—The (value) study of what is beauty, good in art. For most, it's whatever you like, even though you don't have value; for others, it's more complicated than that.

afterlife—What happens after you finish work or what happens when you go to work.

analogy—A metaphor with more literary importance.

anchor—Used to stop a boat from drifting but only when the water isn't very deep. Anchoring requires scope. (If you are not sure what it is, check it out; it is very important.) It is consistent with our use of gyres and still point. Maybe it's best to forget about the literal. Think about the fact that a wide range of lateral movement that is well-grounded requires not only a stable anchor but also lots of scope. From a simple analysis of anchor, scope, and lateral movement, one can see that all three are necessary and sufficient for keeping a vertically based *oneness*.

antithetical gyre—A spiral that goes down that feels a little strange.

arousal—Our energy temperature, where being death is zero, at least for the whole human.

atman—One concept representing a single entity—a god/dog.

Atman—One concept representing all and nothing, nothing and all. Both are something. Read the Upanishads.

attachment—Supposed crazy glue that can attach skin to skin. You may be aware if you have used it. I don't think it attaches other things to other things. So attachment is like crazy glue that connects people with people and people with beliefs. But like crazy glue, though it may be strong, its ability to glue is very selective. When it doesn't glue, it can make people very frustrated and even angry.

aum—Also known as om; a meditation symbol that is a union of a vowel *a* and a consonant *m*.

beauty—It's in the beholder as long as the beholder can see. To see, you need to understand *oneness* (see 'oneness, the eyes of').

behaviour—What you do that people don't like. It's like weather. Weather only exists if we really like it or it's not what we like. From another totally out-there point of view, behaviour could refer to some type of activity of some entity, like an electron. Or if the universe is composed of nothing moving very quickly, then that behaviour could be seen as the activity of nothing.

belief—Something you accept to be true that then excludes you from accepting anything else. It's not as extreme as psychosis in its definition, but many people who believe may be psychotic.

belonging—At face value, it might seem that belonging refers to ducks being with ducks and swans being with swans. But belonging may not be there. The Beatles song says, 'She's leaving home after living alone for so many years.' In essence, belonging could be defined by what it's not. A person who belongs does not have to be longing for something else.

Beulah—Blake's conceptualisation of a state of understanding that has experienced a sense of childhood innocence and also the negative qualities of industrialisation, smoke, greed, et cetera. This state accepts that both are real and that there is an upper innocence (see 'innocence').

biological drives—A primary motive concept that assumes that there are certain things that are inherent in a species or even across species (e.g., mammals). These are considered essential needs or drives that are essential for their existence (e.g., feeding), though some godlike social/human beings would never consider that these somewhat 'primate drives' influence human behaviour.

boat—A vessel/vehicle that rides on the surface of the water. It has the potential of sinking.

brain—A part of the body found inside the head.

Buddha—A figure who is able to smile even when things are terrible.

Canada—A country created by some ex-Brits and Frenchmen whose national identity is claimed to be based on not having one.

categorical imperative—An overriding principle that can be applied in any situation and can assist us in making better decisions. It is sometimes considered an absolute in a world of thinking where there are no absolutes. But maybe it's a good imperative anyway.

church—An organised religious group and also a building. One is a creation of the imagination, and one is real. But I think that we determined that the imagination can be the source of a real experience, therefore, real. So maybe trying to make a distinction between the two is meaningless.

cogito ergo sum—'I think; therefore, I am.' This statement does not just pertain to me, even though it says *I*. And think of thinking as something beyond just thinking.

cognition—Just think. It isn't what I know; it is the structure of the thought behind it. For instance, a reasonable level of cognitive ability is required to understand logic, but what do I know?

collective unconscious—A Jungian concept that refers to an underlying spirit that is shared by all people.

composer—A creator who expresses self and experience, nothing left of nonhuman musicians, and plays the pieces for human organisms out.

concomitant and negative concomitant—These define each other in a way that both are necessary for existence of either one. For example, love and marriage (repeat) go together like a horse and carriage (simile); no, you can't have one (repeat two more times) without the other. But we also have love and hate; you can't have one without the other.

conductor—A person who takes the composer's piece and organises a whole bunch.

connection—Ducks may have this, but they may not.

consciousness—Those thoughts and feelings that constitute my awareness. Do they actually influence what I do and think, or are they simply the script written by my unconsciousness, biochemistry, and biomechanics?

contradiction—Diction that comes from both sides of the mouth at the same time but says opposite things.

desire—In Buddhism, this is seen as a fundamental preoccupation with all people. It is the basis of 'suffering'. All the desire stuff needs to go. However, since that might not be very practical, we suggest that you at least be aware of it.

different—Not the same as me, but this difference can be divided into three types: (1) I am okay; you're different, and that's okay; (2) I am okay, and you've got some type of distorted view of life; there's something wrong, so you need to change and be more like me; or (3) I am different, and you are different; therefore, we are the same but different.

dualities—The myriad of pairs that we have listed that have universally been used by the species. We have male/female, heaven/earth, et cetera.

duck—An accepted social/human bird that is not as ugly as a swan.

Eden—A mythical first human environment that I'm not certain how to explain. What I do know is that it's an expression of a female perspective, and since females had little recorded influence at these early recording times, it could be that God is female.

ego—It is *i* and *I*. It is a concept that can represent a 'I am the greatest' view of self, or it also can be a quiet sense of self that offers strength and conviction.

EMG—Measure of muscular tension in microvolts.

emotion—It's physiological and psychodynamic. I felt like saying that, but in this case, 'felt' is probably not describing an emotion. But emotion is feeling, isn't it? I feel that's correct.

experience—For Blake, experiencing the social/human and political negatives in life. From my point of view, it is experiencing the external and the visualised.

experiential—The real is what you experience. The challenge is to know what my real, my experience, my own point of view have to do with the rest of the world, gyres, still points, the universe, everything, and nothing.

ephemeral—This term has been around for a long time, so I am not certain whether the term *ephemeral* is ephemeral. But I guess it is because the species that created the word and its definition are ephemeral.

fact/value—This is an all-pervasive, clearly explained mistake that dominates the poor thinking of the species. The most significant problem with this 'point of view' is that, because we see ourselves as the centre of the universe, we confuse the fact that what looks like an altruistic desire to save the world is really a self-serving desire to make life better for us. Everything will carry on without humans. Dinosaurs have come and gone, so what's the big deal? Please note that the above description is an illustration of poor thinking that does not consider the fact/value dichotomy.

father—Male person who has offspring; a name given by some religious groups to their clergy. Ironically, many of these clergymen don't have children. That's a little confusing, isn't it? And it's also some kind of person or something with a beard that isn't Santa Claus.

freedom—A belief component of the social/human delusion.

free will—Another social/human delusion, though for practical purposes it's a necessary belief; otherwise, you have people always blaming someone else (e.g., 'It's not my fault.').

God/god—Universally or almost universally accepted in a literal (for the literal group) or symbolic (for the symbolic guys) manner. Though this figure is probably female, this God figure does seem to be highly judgemental, somewhat egotistical (sees self as centre of the universe), and somewhat hypocritical. Does he/she believe in an all-pervasive love for all, or does God's love have some strings attached to it?

good/evil—Could be a symptom of poor thinking or simple belief structure. For those of you who dwell in a very clearly defined culture, this duality may be unquestioned. For those who live in a more cosmopolitan world, the belief in this distinction would probably suggest limited thinking ability. You would be vulnerable to social/human manipulation or may be influenced by a mild psychosis. *Evil*, as you are probably aware, is *live* backwards, so to avoid evil, don't back up.

gyre—A spiral that goes up. We like up.

history—'A nightmare from which I'm trying to awake' (J. Alfred Prufrock).

homeostasis—Think of the thermostat or the filling gauge in your stomach. It is a regulating concept whose functioning keeps the heat at a desired temperature or lets your body know when you are full. Many people have two homeostatic regulators to show you are full of the stuff you don't like and one that is probably broken that suggests you are full of what you like.

602

human—Je ne sais pas.

humour—A complex set of conditions that elicit human responses. These are usually displayed by a smile or a laugh. Responses may seem to be in good or bad taste, yet others may keep people confused. 'What's funny about that?' That's pretty funny, isn't it?

I Ching—A Chinese book of divination that uses hexagrams. 'Okay, so what is it?' you may still ask. It is a Chinese book of divination that uses all the possible hexagrams that are composed of broken and unbroken lines. From each hexagram, you can obtain sage advice. To determine whether a line is broken or unbroken, you can drop some sticks, use three coins, or even flip a coin. Repeat this six times to create a personal hexagram. Each hexagram has six aspects of sage advice for the reader.

IQ—A social/human measure of social/human smartness. Your measured IQ is measured by how accurately and how quickly you answer a whole bunch of questions and perform some skills on an IQ test that has been developed by a group of very smart social/human beings. Hopefully, they are pretty smart; otherwise, your high IQ may be a measure of mediocrity.

inner doors—According to Huxley, they are doors of perception of the life that is in your head, in your imagination, beneath the surface.

innocence—For Blake/Thomas, it is a childlike view of the world. All is well in a world of wonderment, no time but curiosity.

insight—This is a non-ESP skill that allows you to see 'in' and 'below'. Good insight probably requires cognition, logic, empathy, and the ability to experience life from different points of view. It does not refer to the fact that you can see someone else because they are in sight.

intolerance—A level of tolerance that is more rigid.

Ireland—A small country with designs on taking over the world by getting other countries to establish Irish pubs and propagate the view that it is good to be Irish and wear green even if it's only for one day a year.

irony—I think this was created by some kind of supreme being who has a sense of humour and likes to keep the creations guessing because much of life is ironic. 'Oh, but what is it?' you ask. It is somewhat ironic that nonhuman musicians are more human than humans.

karma—Doing the right thing if you want to believe that, or the product of 'right' thinking, which has nothing to do with 'right' or 'left'.

lateral—Movement on the water's surface. It could be a current, or it could be the movement of tides. They could travel across oceans or be the ebb and flow of the tides in your own neighbourhood. This movement could also be the up-and-down action of waves. But all these movements, which are influenced by scientifically understood structures, basically balance themselves and do not go anywhere. 'Women come and go / Talking about Michelangelo.'

life—A magazine, but it is also descriptive of the quality of an individual's social life. One might say to another who doesn't do much, 'You need to get a life!'

logic—Rules of connecting thoughts. A = B, B = C, A = C is the structure of a syllogism. Condition relationships are also logical. If p, then q; we have a p, then we must have a q. But if we have a q, we may or may not have a p. There is also biconditional logical relationship. In this relationship, we would say that if and only if there is a p, there is also a q. It works both ways. Logic is an important step in finding answers. Unfortunately, it doesn't undo faulty assumptions and frequently doesn't give us the answers we would like. A good way around this problem is to conclude that a conditional relationship = a biconditional relationship.

macrocosm—Something really big, yet in Buddhism, the structure is seen in a way that is like our use of oneness. A common Buddhist expression states that within the microcosm of self is the macrocosm of the universe. Is this a concept that string theory is addressing theoretically? As you can appreciate, with the Buddhists, there are no strings attached.

mandala—A visual, symbolic representation of oneness and its composing dualities; can look like a flowchart.

mantra—A repetitive vocal saying that is used in meditation.

mathematics—It must be right. We just don't have anything else. It has to add up. However, we can still have problems defining oneness; it doesn't add up.

metaphor—A comparison in which something is said to be something it is not. The something, 'the moon was a ghostly galleon tossed upon cloudy seas.' This was my first defining example of a metaphor, I think in Grade IV. I don't remember the poem. Yes, I do; it was 'The Highwayman'.

microcosm—Something really small; in fact, really tiny. In Buddhism and quantum physics, the size may be different but maybe not.

mind—The conceptual part of the person that looks after p's and q's. It is usually seen as having something to do with the brain.

mores—Basic social/human values generally defined in reference to different cultures.

music—The noise made by high-performance cars, at least for those who like the sound of their exhaust systems. Also, it is a term used to describe a whole range of sound produced by other nonhumans (i.e., musicians).

musicians—Nonhuman entities that are put together to make musical groups that are somewhat human in character.

mystical experience—A profound experience/not experienced state in which you are at one with the universe. For more details and a clearer description, take a few moments to read such works as Coleridge's 'Rime of the Ancient Mariner' and maybe a couple of American works such as Walt Whitman's Leaves of Grass and Melville's Moby Dick.

nation—A creation by a group of many individuals who convince themselves and other nations that they have a unique identity, and it is assumed that others would agree and respect their identity. But of course, there are some risks here. It could be that the obvious superiority that one nation appreciates about themselves urges them to take over other nations, or it could be that another nation may not appreciate or may actually misunderstand the wonderful character of another nation. Though it may be hard to understand, these misunderstandings can sometimes erupt into some type of violent altercation(s) that results in terrorist acts and even war.

necessary/sufficient—Words used in philosophy and science that are a lot easier not to think about. Maybe a simple English language example (or any language with limited letters) is the alphabet. Each letter is required (necessary) in forming the alphabet. However, is it the alphabet without X, Y, or N? In the English alphabet, all twenty-six letters are required for meeting sufficient criteria.

neurophysiology—The study of the physical, biochemical, molecular, et cetera. It is concerned with the function of those things deemed as neurological. Often, it includes the brain and other bits.

nonhuman—Musicians, cells, and other such entities.

nonphilosophical philosophy—Typically, people say, 'This is my philosophy.' What they really mean is 'This is what I believe.' This usually means two things. First, they don't like to think; and second, they have no idea about philosophy.

nothing—A concept of the absence of something, which is still something. Therefore, nothing is something.

oneness—Oneness that is one is false, $1 \neq 1$. Oneness that is without limit is one, $1 = 00$. Remember that $00 > 00$.

orchestra—A bunch of nonhumans getting together to play music.

outward doors—Thinking of Huxley and his doors of perception and life of the jock, myself, living in the outside world, on the surface. But even then, there are some important inward doors.

outlaw—Taken from Tom Robbins; not for or against, not a conformist or nonconformist, not a rebel or a nonrebel.

PFC—Prefrontal cortex; a smaller topological area that is north of SC. We think of it as being involved with thinking. Sometimes it may inhibit, go along with, or even rationalise these southern drives.

phenomenological—A long word, big concept. This brings together your own experience, what you notice, and what you understand. That's it; it's all phenomena.

philosophy—It is used in two totally different ways. I use it in one way and am very bothered by the other use. At the social/human level, it represents belief (see 'belief'), which is inimical to any sense of the term. Philosophy is a highly disciplined way of thinking that addresses all human assumptions, thinking, knowledge, and ethics.

point of view—For some, it describes how they see the world; and for others, including us, it can be confusing, at least from a social/human perspective, because there seems to be an unlimited number (all with their own dualities). But from another perspective, there may only be *one*.

principle—An underlying assumption about why we need rules; kind of a bigger rule.

psyche—From the Greek letter ψ. Take a deep breath and sigh. That pretty well covers the collective psyche of humans.

psychodynamics—These are not just the dynamics of the psyche. They are all those conceptually based ways of considering the 'mind'—ego, identity, spirit, and even states like being sad, depressed, and happy. All these could be considered as dynamic expressions of the psyche (mind).

psychosis—The hallmark of unquestioned human perception, belief, and thinking. It is how they define not just reality but also truth.

real—Laer spelled backwards.

religion—A creation of the human psyche, which in turn is blamed for all sorts of bad things. I know there are some good things, but sometimes it's hard to find them. I don't really think Buddhism is a religion in its essence. However, I think it does become a religion because its organised and believed.

rigid thinking—To say that someone is thinking while standing very rigidly wouldn't be far off the mark. This is it, thank you very much!

right—Opposite of 'left' and opposite of 'wrong'. Some might say that being politically right is wrong, and right could be left if you turn around.

rule—Established at the social/human level for the purposes of trying to control human behaviour (e.g., 'You can't do that! It's against the rule!').

salient—All the factors that can be seen as relevant to a particular outcome. It is, of course, easier—if you are looking at any problematic outcome— to consider 'one' salient factor because it's easier to come up with an answer. For instance, you may know that you did something wrong because someone else 'made you do it'. However, the other person may contend that you do what you do because 'you're crazy'. The only problem is that both of the above single selected salient factors may be somewhat limited.

SC—The subcortical part of the brain. Geographically, it is considered as the midbrain, and it is somewhat south of the cortex. It does all sorts of neat things. It's a topological section, kind of like Southern Europe, the Middle East, or the southern parts of North America. It's a simple label for a complex set of drives and functions that are fundamental to the species.

scientific (1)—A very well-established way of thinking that has evolved over centuries. Two big problems exist in this thinking. First, even though it is the best we can do, it doesn't necessarily give us the answers we might like (if you are the answer-type person). Second, to be serious for a moment, some people who apply scientific knowledge, including auto mechanics and clinical practitioners, will often 'believe' that they are scientific thinkers; and of course, some are. However, there are many who are under the false belief that being trained in a scientific discipline means that they think like a scientist. But they don't. As a result, they have a 'do this for that' mentality; and if some condition is outside familiar grounds, they may overlook some variables and simply focus on what they know. The scientific thinker, on the other hand, would most likely establish some hypotheses, consider some multivariate analyses, test these hypotheses in some creative manner, and possibly do a literature search, if more scientific knowledge would help.

scientific (2)—One must be cautious about how science can be misused in the media. The world of scientific research, at least to the noncurious, needs to be made interesting, simple, and significant to have public appeal. Sometimes bad science (with no factual support) and its conclusions can have great public appeal and, as a result, are well publicised and believed implicitly. The problem that can result in these cases, as was the case with autism and vaccines, is that any retraction or reports that the supportive research was falsified have little or no impact on changing the minds of those who want to believe some reported 'truth' that meets their needs.

sea—A metaphor for life and everything below it, above it, and in it.

security—A concept used to convince humans that unless they accept a certain 'ology', they will never get it.

self—A funny, as in *strange*, way of referring to me. It is 'shelf' with the *h* removed, but I don't know what that really means.

self-alienation—A common human phenomenon. It is almost as if a person has two disconnected ways of approaching life. For instance, a person may have needs for being loved and supported but also has a need for being successful and in control. So this person becomes successful, is in control, is doing all sorts of stuff but is unable to have any empathy for others. This person can also reject the world of success and live with others who are close but can't even think about work or success. This person isn't able to be a successful/loving person.

self-regulation—Our ability to be aware, understand, and change our own physiology and thoughts. It's better than having your mother or spouse control your life.

smiling Buddha—A figure who can smile even when things are terrible. Does that mean that life is a joke?

social/human—Those who live on the surface of the water and combine into groups, make up realities, and then believe them to be absolutes.

space—The distance from a clock tower or the distance between perceived entities. It can also refer to people who have a lot of room in their brains, often called space cadets.

still pond—A pond where the water has no currents, no ripples, no waves, no ducks or swans and hopefully is not stagnant.

stressors—Anything that changes our physiology in a reactive manner. Gravity could be seen as a stressor. Boy (sorry for the sexist reference), gravity is a downer. However, if you're underwater, the influence of gravity is reduced.

string theory—Has nothing to do with music or ulterior motives. However, there is a string attached. It is really related to explaining the behaviour of small and large particles.

strong/weak—A duality used in physics to describe energy and its expression. But we have had fun using the terms to describe people in a paradoxical manner. And as we have seen, the strong may be weak and the weak strong.

structure—A kind of glue/rule that ties things together. Is it predicated by a something that we don't know and have tried to explain by a rule or theory?

success—A social/human concept that defines doing things well as a duck. In a sense, it is being a duck who is recognised as being more influential than most ducks. Unfortunately, it is probably necessary to function as a duck for a while just so you can say you can do it.

sum ergo cogito—'I am; therefore, I think'; see above, just change some of the stuff around.

sunyata—Means nothing, but nothing is something, so I guess it means something.

swan—A nonduck bird; seen by H. C. Andersen as attractive, at least in the long term. But socially, it is still not a duck. Ducks are cute and yellow.

symbolic—A significant feature of human thinking is that most experience is assumed to be literal, but often, the literal is actually symbolic.

terrorists—A socially defined group of desperate people who exhibit extremely aggressively defined behaviour in opposition to other desperate people who exhibit extremely aggressively defined behaviour. The group that convinces themselves and others that they are really good guys and has the most social/human acceptance is seen as nonterrorist. The others who feel oppressed become more desperate and more terrorist.

theory of everything—The still point at the base of our antithetical gyre? It is the one rule that explains all. Please note that we haven't found it yet, but maybe Stephen has.

time—I was once asked, 'Do you know the time?' I responded yes.

tolerance—A level of intolerance that is less than intolerant.

transformation—Changing from one state to another. I can sense a musical metaphor here. The orchestra is playing a loud, cacophonous piece in tutti (all together). Without being obvious, a few instruments begin to play something more ethereal, and then some more play. There is a diminuendo. More instruments are playing the ethereal. Over some minutes, we have the ethereal, thus a transformation.

truth—An English language word with five letters. I am not sure what else to say. It could be a still point.

unconsciousness—Those thoughts and feelings that I am not aware of that, in a conspiratorial manner, collaborate with my biochemical and biomechanical self to influence what I do and think.

underwater—That which is below the surface. Many watches can tell you how far down you are because, at some point, they stop working, at least according to the guarantees watch companies make (e.g., good to 100 m). Therefore, as you go deeper, underwater time stops.

United States—A country in between Canada and Mexico. It is a large country with a lot of anxiety, ethnocentricity, and desperate need to control the world so it can be safe. Remember, Piglet and Eeyore knocking at Pooh's door were heard to say, 'The more we knocked, the more he wasn't there.'

Upanishads—Part of the Mahabharata defines/doesn't define atman or Atman. Check it out someday, if you have nothing else to do.

values—These are all worthwhile, but they can be a human-thinking cancer. Remember the fact/value dichotomy. Remember the French paradox. Follow the following fun digression:

American value position - Drinking alcohol is bad.

Wine is alcohol; therefore, drinking wine is bad.

Bad = moral wrongness and also bad health; therefore, wine is bad for health. (It must be bad.)

French people eat all sorts of unhealthy foods and are, therefore, unhealthy. (Interestingly though, they don't see fatty foods as morally wrong.) But according to many health studies, the bad French people have less heart disease and fewer incidents of many other diseases than Americans who don't drink alcohol, at least according to a number of research studies. From the fact/value point of view, if they feel a need to accept European studies on alcohol consumption and health, because they are just as good as theirs, they have two choices:

    a. 'We were wrong, and wine is actually good for you.'
    b. 'We are right in our belief that wine is bad. It is just that their results are paradoxical.'

Make sure that you watch for fact/value distinctions. Are the above statements of fact or actually based on a value judgement?

velocity—My actual speed compared with how fast I'm driving on the highway. Given that velocity is relative to objects, it could be that I'm actually moving backwards. The earth is revolving in the opposite direction, but in taking in all other elements, who knows how fast I'm driving?

vertical—Movement up and down in the water. That sounds like waves to me. But those are on the surface. Remember, we like gyres, still points, and *ones* that are limitless. Our view is that moving down may be the right way to go.

visualisation—A multifaceted skill that really isn't visual. See the appendix for an unduly long discussion.

water—An element that, from my point of view, is great. However, from Stephen Dedalus's point of view, it is good from a sexual perspective if he sees a woman out on the beach but not so good if he has been pushed into a ditch. It is also used for drinking, washing, and flushing toilets.

wave—What you do when you are watching some friends drive away. It is important not to get confused about the behaviour of waves and the behaviour or particles. You could simply conclude that you are a particle and that you are waving goodbye.

win—All that matters in sports, politics, and war. It does not matter how you play the game; the only thing that matters is you win.

Acknowledgements

A.   Aristotle

        A.C. Anderson

B.   J.S. Bach

        J. Baldwin

        J. Basquiat

        B. Bartok

        Beatles

        Y. Berra

        W. Blake

        H. Bosch

        P. Breugal

        P. deBroca

        W. Browning

        A. Burges

C.   J. Cage

        A. Camus

        J. Cary

        F. Celine

M. Chandler

M.T. Cicero

E. Cleaver

S. Colbert

B. Cosby

N. Cousins

J. Cousteau

D.   C. Darwin

C. Debussy

R. Decartes

Dorsey

Dveretal

E.   J. Edwards

T.S. Eliot

A. Ellis

A. Einstein

R.W. Emerson

M.C. Escher

F.   B. Fischer

A. Flew

D. French

S. Freud

E. Fromme

G.   S.N. Goenka

W. Golding

G. Gould

F. Goya

W.D. Griffith

H.   T. Hardy

S. Hawking

J. Heller

E. Hemingway

H. Hesse

D. Hofstedter

A. Huxley

I.   H. Ibsen

C. Ives

J.   K. Jarret

J. Joyce

K. Jung

K.   F. Kafka

W. Kandinsky

I. Kant

M.L. King

S. Kubrick

R.   T. Robbins

        Rogers and Hart

        B. Russell

        G. Ryga

S.   J.P. Sartre

        A. Schoenberg

        A. Scriabin

        W. Shakespeare

        B. Stearman

        L. Sterne

        I. Stravinsky

        J.M. Synge

T.   P. Taylor

        D. Thomas

        H.D. Thoreau

        G. Tourette

V.   V. van Gogh

        R. Vaugh Williams

        VSO

W.   D.F. Wallace

        D. Watson

A. Watts

O. Wilde

L. Wittgenstein

S. Wolfram

W. Wordsworth

Y.   W.B. Yeats

Z.   R. Zimmerman
(aka Bob Dylan)